ITALY AND HER INVADERS

PART FIVE

FRANKISH INVASIONS. THE FRANKISH EMPIRE

A.D. 745-814

THOMAS HODGKIN

BOOK VIII.
FRANKISH INVASIONS.

I. INTRODUCTION. THE MEROVINGIAN KINGS. EARLY FRANKISH HISTORY.
II. THE EARLY ARNULFINGS
III. PIPPIN OF HERISTAL AND CHARLES MARTEL
IV. DUKES OF BAVARIA
V. THE GREAT RENUNCIATION
VI. THE ANOINTING OF PIPPIN
VII. THE DONATION OF CONSTANTINE
VIII. THE STRUGGLE FOR THE EXARCHATE
IX. THE PONTIFICATE OP PAUL I (757-767).
X. A PAPAL CHAOS.
XI. THE PONTIFICATE OF STEPHEN III.
XII. RAVENNA AND ROME.
XIII. THE ACCESSION OF POPE HADRIAN.
XIV. END OF THE LOMBARD MONARCHY.

BOOK IX
THE FRANKISH EMPIRE
774-814

I. THE PONTIFICATE OF HADRIAN I.
Frankish and Byzantine Affairs,
II. THE PONTIFICATE OF HADRIAN I.
Italian Affairs.
III. TASSILO OF BAVARIA.
IV. TWO COURTS : CONSTANTINOPLE AND AACHEN
V. POPE AND EMPEROR.
VI. CHARLES AND IRENE.
VII. VENICE.
VIII. THE FINAL RECOGNITION.
IX. CAROLUS MORTUUS.
X. THE LIFE OF THE PEOPLE

BOOK VIII
THE FRANKISH INVASIONS
A.D. 744-774

CHAPTER I.
INTRODUCTION. THE MEROVINGIAN KINGS.

EARLY FRANKISH HISTORY.

We have reached a decisive point in the history of Italy and its relations to the rest of Europe. The Visigoth dealt a mortal blow to the Roman State: the Hun and the Vandal mocked its dying agonies; the Ostrogoth tried, but tried in vain, to resuscitate its life, breathing his Teutonic energy into its outworn frame; then the Lombard came, at first a ruthless barbarian, pillaging and destroying, but gradually won over to Christianity and civilization by the unquenchable influence of the beautiful land. For nearly two centuries three powers were engaged in a struggle for supremacy in Italy: the Lombard king, the Byzantine Emperor, and the Pope of Rome. Between the last two, the relations were nominally relations of friendship and alliance, the Pope being in theory the submissive subject of the Emperor; but there had none the less been real opposition between them, sometimes breaking out into actual strife, and since the publication of the Iconoclastic decrees (726), there had been complete estrangement, though not as yet any formal renunciation of the Imperial sovereignty on the part of the Pope.

We are now about to see the balance of power which had been thus far maintained between these three opposing interests, roughly destroyed. Under the impact of the Lombard kings the Empire will lose Ravenna and all but disappear from the Peninsula. The Popes, thus left alone face to face with their hereditary enemies, the Lombards, will in their despair look beyond the Alps for help. The Frankish kings will answer to their call, and by blow upon blow, will lay the Lombard monarchy in the dust. Italy will thus be drawn into close political union with France and Germany, and those relations will be established with the latter country, which will subsist in one shape or another down to the beginning of the nineteenth century.

Finally, after the conquest of Italy by the Franks, the Roman Empire will be revived in the person of the Frankish King, and Medieval Europe will come into being.

The struggles which I have thus briefly described, and which will form the subject of the present volume, must have contained many elements of the highest human interest. The fall of Ravenna, the last fight of the Lombard nation for dominion in Italy, might each have furnished material for a noble epic poem: but unfortunately not only the 'sacred poet', but even the humbler historian is almost entirely wanting. We hear absolutely nothing from the Byzantines as to the details of the capture of Ravenna. Owing to the silence of Paulus Diaconus—a silence which was no doubt politic, but which his readers must always regret —we hear nothing from Lombard sources as to any of the events after the death of Liutprand. The gallant Lombard nation 'dies and makes no sign'. We have to discover the course of events as best we can from the meagre notices of Frankish chroniclers, from the verbose and never graphic letters sent forth from the Papal Chancery, from the lives of the Popes included in the *Liber Pontificalis*. This last source does give us some interesting facts, and it is that from which we shall have mainly to draw; but it is very incomplete, leaving sometimes large spaces of time wholly without record, and its passionate unfairness to all who came into collision with the Papacy greatly lessens its historical value.

In accordance with the plan pursued in the previous volumes, a detailed history of the new Invaders, the Franks, should here precede the story of their conquest. So much, however, has already been said about them in several preceding volumes, that a slight retrospective sketch of their deeds will here be sufficient.

The fierce tribes of the lower Rhine and Meuse, Sicambri and Chatti, and probably some of their neighbours, Bructeri, Chamavi and Chasuarii, appear in the third century after Christ to have coalesced into one great confederacy, which took to itself the proud name of Franks or Free-men. This confederacy however became divided, how or why we know not, into two smaller federations, the Salians and the Ripuarians. The Salian Franks probably derived their name from the river Yssel, the most northerly of the branches by which the Rhine flows westward into the German Ocean. In the middle of the fifth century they held the districts which now bear the names of Belgium, Artois, and part of Picardy. The Ripuarian Franks settled on the left bank (*ripa*) of the Rhine, and occupied the pleasant vine-clad hills on the west of it between Mayence and Cologne, as well as the valley of the Moselle, from its confluence with the Rhine to its source in the mountains of the Vosges. The chief seat of their power seems to have been the Roman city, which under its modern name of Cologne still preserves the memory of Colonia Agrippina. There appears to have been a certain feeling of a common nationality, connecting, though loosely, these two great divisions of the Frankish nation; and each tribe, the Salians and the Ripuarians, was split up into many smaller fragments, obeying the sway of their own petty kings.

One of these petty kings, or rather chieftains, Hlodwig, Ludovicus, Louis, or Clovis, in 481 began to bear rule over the Salian Franks at Tournai. He was then fifteen years of age, and he succeeded his father Childeric, hero of some strange Frankish sagas, who twenty-four years previously had succeeded his father Merovech. Merovech, from whom the line of Clovis took its well-known name of Merovings, was himself fabled to be the son of a Frankish queen, begotten by a sea-monster or demi-god. So near still to the age of mythology was the heathen nation of the Franks when the young Clovis, himself heathen, began to lead forth its armies to battle.

We may mark five stages in the career of this extraordinary man, who beginning life as *regulus* of a fragment of the Salian Franks, ended it as unquestioned lord of two-thirds of France and of no small part of Germany.

I. First came his victory over Syagrius, the Roman king (so called) of Soissons, the correspondent of Apollinaris Sidonius, the eager student of the language of his German neighbours; Syagrius, whom all his state-craft and all his linguistic accomplishments availed not to save from the conquering battle-axe of the young Merovingian. This conquest took place in 486 and gave to Clovis the remainder of Picardy, the greater part of the Isle of France including Paris itself, Champagne and a considerable portion of

Lorraine. A glance at the map will show what a mighty stride towards dominion over Gaul was thus made by the son of Childeric, who was still only twenty years of age. After history proved that his people felt the immense importance of this conquest. In the division of his realm among his sons and grandsons the kingdom of Syagrius was evidently always regarded as the head of the Frankish dominion.

II. Secondly, came the great victories won by Clovis over the Thuringians and the Alamanni, victories which apparently were won in the years 491 and. 496. The Thuringians, here mentioned, are probably a detachment of the nation settled on the left bank of the Rhine. The Alamanni occupied and gave their name to the region which is otherwise known as Swabia (Alsace, Baden, and Würtemberg).

This victory over the Alamanni, however important in itself (since it opened up to Clovis the whole country of the Upper Rhine and carried him to the sources of the Danube), was yet more important for its indirect results. The Frankish king, who had long resisted the entreaties of his wife, the Burgundian princess Clotilda, that he would embrace Christianity, when he saw himself in danger of being overwhelmed by the dense masses of the Alamanni, lifted up to heaven his tear-streaming eyes and said, "0 Jesus Christ, whom Clotilda affirms to be Son of the living God, and who are said to give victory to them that trust in You; if You will grant me the victory over these mine enemies, I will believe and be baptized in Your name. For I have called on my own gods and had no help from them, wherefore I believe that they have no power".

It was probably at the Christmas of 496 that Clovis stood in the white robes of a Catechumen in the Basilica of Rheims, and heard from bishop Remigius the often-quoted words, "'Meekly bow thy neck, O Sicambrian, adore what thou hast heretofore burned, and burn what thou hast adored".

III. The baptism of Clovis by bishop Remigius proclaimed him a champion of the Catholic faith against the Arian form of Christianity, which was at this time dominant among the Teutonic invaders of the Roman Empire. The Vandal in Africa, the Ostrogoth in Italy, the Burgundian in the valley of the Rhine, the Visigoth in Spain and Aquitaine were all upholders of that which the orthodox denounced as 'the Arian pravity'. Now that the fierce heathen, whose example was at once followed by three thousand of his followers, had become not merely Christian but a professed believer in the doctrine of the *Homoousion*, every Catholic priest, at any rate in Gaul, felt that here was one who by throwing his sword into the scale of orthodoxy might ensure its early triumph.

It seemed as though the Burgundian kingdom would be the first to fall under the blows of the Frankish convert. In 500, Gundobad, the Burgundian king who reigned at Lyons, fled before the army of Clovis which came to the assistance of his traitorous brother Godegisel of Geneva. But by a sudden change in the fortune of war, Godegisel was defeated and slain, and Gundobad regained his throne. The end of Burgundian independence was not yet.

Seven years later, however, came the most important conquest effected by Clovis in the name of Catholic orthodoxy. Having announced to his assembled warriors that "he took it ill that those Arians should hold so large a part of Gaul", he crossed the Loire, met the Visigoths in battle near Poitiers, defeated them and slew their king Alaric II, and after two years of warfare succeeded in adding to his dominions the whole of the fair region of Aquitaine, while Gallia Narbonensis and Provence remained under the rule of Alaric's Ostrogothic kinsman, Theodoric of Italy.

IV. The chieftain who had thus carried far and wide over Gaul the terror of the Frankish arms, was not likely to remain a mere member of a partnership of kings in his own nation. At some time or other in his career, probably towards the beginning of his reign, he succeeded in sweeping off the board the other petty kings of the Salian Franks. Ragnachar, who reigned at Cambrai, had helped Clovis in his war against Syagrius, but when the time came for removing him he was forced into war, conquered in fight and then killed for disgracing his royal house by permitting himself to be beaten. Chararic, another Salian king, was craftily captured, shorn of his long Merovingian locks and turned into a priest. His son, who was at the same time shorn of his hair and ordained deacon, was overheard comforting his weeping lather by the reflection that leaves might yet sprout forth from their lopped branches, and thereupon both father and son were put to death.

V. Lastly, Sigibert, king of the Ripuarians, who had been the ally of Clovis in his war against Alaric the Visigoth, had to be put out of the way. His son was incited to murder him and then was himself assassinated by one of the henchmen of Clovis. It is strange after reading the plain unsoftened story of the crimes by which this 'baptized Pagan' hewed his way to solitary dominion over all Frankish men, to read the following sentence in the pages of Gregory, bishop of Tours, "Thus did God daily humble his enemies under his hand and increase his kingdom, because he walked before Him with righteous heart and did those things which were pleasing in His sight". Fascinated, apparently, by the very wickedness of his hero, Gregory, after describing some more royal murders, goes on to say, "Having slain these and many other kings and their noble relations, of whom he was jealous, lest they should rob him of the kingdom, Clovis extended his sway over the whole of Gaul. However, having on a certain occasion collected his followers together, he spoke concerning his relations whom he had himself destroyed, "Woe is me, that I remain as a stranger in a strange land and have none of mine own kindred who could help me if adversity came upon me", But he said this not in real sorrow for their death, but in guile, and in order that, if he could by chance find any such surviving him, he might kill him".

Thus, then ere he had passed middle life, the petty chieftain of the Salian Franks whose principality had been once almost bounded by the horizon of Tournai, had become ruler of the larger part of the lands between the Atlantic and the Rhine. In 508, after Clovis had overthrown the Visigothic kingdom in Gaul, he received from the Emperor Anastasius a letter conferring upon him the dignity of Consul; and donning in the basilica of St. Martin the purple tunic and the *chlamys* of a Roman senator, rode through the streets of Tours, scattering largesse among the crowd. This letter from Anastasius was the first of a series of courtesies—ending in something quite other than courtesies—which passed between the Roman Emperors and the orthodox kings of the Franks.

Clovis died at Paris in 511, having only attained the age of forty-five years. He was certainly a scoundrel, but he was a successful scoundrel and he had some of the qualities of a statesman. Moreover, he was the first of the long line of 'the most Christian kings of *Francia*'.

The only conceivable palliation for any of the crimes which Clovis committed would have been the advantage of securing the unity of the Frankish state. Yet that unity was immediately impaired by the division of his dominions between his four sons. By one means or another, partly by events which happened in the course of nature and partly by fratricidal crimes, the monarchy thus divided became one again under Chlotochar I, the last survivor of the sons of Clovis; but it remained united for only three years, and was then again divided among his four sons, not to be reunited till the year 613, under Chlotochar II, great grandson of Clovis. Thus, throughout the whole of the sixth century we may think of 'Francia' as generally divided into four parts, which corresponded in the main with the four great natural divisions of the realm, Austrasia, Neustria, Aquitaine, and Burgundy.

Austrasia (otherwise called Auster, or Austria) seems to have included all the lands which had belonged to the Ripuarian Franks, together with those conquered from the Thuringians, and with those wherein the Bavarians and Alamanni had been made subject to Frankish rule. But it must also have included at least the Eastern half of the old 'kingdom' of Syagrius, since the countries which were afterwards called Champagne and Lorraine formed part of the Austrasian kingdom.

As Austrasia was the land of the Ripuarians, so *Neustria* seems to have been specially identified with the territory of the Salian Franks, and hence it had what appears on the map as a curious prolongation north-eastward to the river Scheldt, and in fact must have included at least half of the modern kingdom of Belgium. All western France, north of the Loire, belonged theoretically to the Neustrian kingdom, though the sovereignty which its rulers were able to assert over the restless Bretons of Armorica was a perpetually changing quantity.

Aquitaine was the former kingdom of the Visigoths in Gaul, and it had its well-marked boundaries in the great river Loire and the mountains of the Cevennes. The Roman influence, strong in Neustria, was yet stronger here, and it may be doubted how far it was ever bound except by bonds of fear and compulsion to the Frankish monarchy.

Burgundy, which included the valleys of the Rhine and the Saone, and which reached up to the western slopes of the Alps, was, as we have seen, still unconquered at the death of Clovis. Its annexation to the Frankish state was the work of his sons, one of whom fell in battle in the second campaign. The story of the conquest (523—534) has been told with some detail in a previous volume, on account of its connection with the family history of Theodoric whose daughter was married to Sigismund, king of Burgundy.

The connection of the Franks with the history of Italy, during the period of this first partition of the Frankish kingdom, brought little glory to the descendants of Clovis, but much disaster to the Italian peninsula. When Belisarius began his brilliant enterprise for the recovery of Italy, the Frankish kings seized the opportunity to threaten the Ostrogothic possessions in Gaul. They were quieted for the time by the surrender of those possessions (consisting of Provence and part of Dauphiné), which were ceded to them by Witigis in 536. But three years later, Theudebert, king of Austrasia, a grandson of Clovis, crossed the Alps, and his savage warriors poured like a torrent over Northern Italy. They made war alike upon the Goths and the soldiers of the Empire: they sacked cities and ravaged vineyards, till at last disease, the result of their own brutal excesses, and a threatening message from the indignant Belisarius, caused them to return to their own land.

When Totila raised again the standard of Gothic independence, the Franks, whose manifest policy it was to fish in troubled waters, again intervened in Italy; and owing to the reluctance of both parties to engage with another antagonist, succeeded in making the greater part of the three northern provinces (Liguria, Alpes Cottiae, and Venetia), subject to tribute. All Italy north of the Po, and both slopes of the Maritime Alps, except some seaport towns which were held by the Empire, and a few scattered fortresses still garrisoned by the Goths, were thus added to the Frankish dominion.

This state of things probably lasted for about ten years. When the powerful and aspiring Theudebert was succeeded by his son, the sickly Theudebald (A.D. 548), the reins of sovereignty were relaxed, and hence it came to pass that the Alamannic brethren, Leuthar and Butilin, were allowed to make their objectless and ill-managed raid into Italy. The utter failure of this expedition (554) doubtless weakened the hold of the Franks on the valley of the Po, and three years afterwards we learn that under the rule of Narses the Empire recovered all that portion of Italy which Theudebert had once held.

It was, however, probably in consequence of this temporary possession of Northern Italy, that the Franks held so much of the northern half of Raetia as we find them to have possessed a few years later on, when they came into collision with the Lombards.

In 558, a year after the Empire had reconquered the territory north of the Po, Chlotochar I (as has been already said) became, by the death of his last surviving brother, sole monarch of the Franks. Three years afterwards he died, and his kingdom was divided between his four sons, whose number was reduced to three in the year 567 by the death of Charibert, king of Paris. And now we are upon the threshold of the Lombard invasion of Italy which, as the reader may remember, occurred in the year 568. Thenceforward, for nearly two hundred years, the Frankish kings had a Lombard state touching them as their south-eastern frontier, and the intervening Alps did not prevent the two powers from meeting, sometimes in friendship but more often with the clash of battle. In the first eight years of their sojourn in Italy (568575), the Lombards made five invasions of Frankish territory. These invasions, which harried the districts of Dauphiné and Provence, were conducted without military skill or generalship, and were without much difficulty repelled by the soldiers of Guntram, the Frankish king of Burgundy. This senseless and wanton warfare had one permanent effect, which proved eventually disastrous for the Lombard state, since it left the valleys of Aosta and Susa, on the Italian side of the Alps, in the possession of the Franks.

The return visits of the Franks to Italy under Chramnichis, about 576, and under Childebert between 584 and 590, were like those of the Lombards, ravaging and plundering expeditions, effectual doubtless for the devastation of the country, but powerless for its conquest. A noticeable fact about the later invasions of Childebert is that they were undertaken at the suggestion of the Byzantine Court and to some extent in cooperation with the Byzantine armies, the lever which the Imperial Court used with the king of Austrasia being the presence at Constantinople of the unfortunate child Athanagild, the son of Childebert's sister, Ingunthis. This conjunction of Imperial and Frankish power might, had it been often repeated, have proved disastrous for the Lombard state : but, partly owing to ill-planned combinations, it effected nothing of importance in 590 (when Maurice was Emperor and Childebert Frankish king), nor was it repeated at any later time. At the close of the sixth century, Agilulf, king of the Lombards, concluded 'a perpetual peace' with the Franks, both Italy and Germany being then menaced by the invasions of the barbarous Avars; and this peace, probably owing to the increasing impotence of the Merovingian kings, actually endured for a century and a half. We must however except one trifling interruption soon after the accession of Grimwald (662), when a Frankish army (perhaps espousing the cause of the banished Perctarit) entered Italy from Provence, but was easily defeated by the Lombard king near Asti in Piedmont.

The peace thus long maintained between the once hostile nations was not only peace but sometimes alliance. Thus in the year 630, when Dagobert the Frank, through the insolence of his ambassadors, had become involved in a war with Samo, a Frankish merchant who had cunningly raised himself to the position of king of the Wends or Sclaves on Dagobert's eastern frontier, the Lombards sent soldiers to the assistance of the Franks. These auxiliaries together with the Alamanni, were victorious, and carried off a multitude of captives, while Dagobert himself appears to have suffered a disastrous defeat.

And again, when Charles Martel (about 737) was somewhat hardly pressed by a Saracen invasion of Provence, he called on his brother-in-law, Liutprand, for help, and called not in vain. Liutprand led a great army across the Maritime Alps, and at his approach the Saracens fled in terror.

During this century and a half of peace between the Franks and Italy, Merovingian royalty had been sinking ever lower and lower into mere fatuity and impotence, while the power of one great Austrasian house, which furnished a succession of hereditary Prime Ministers to the State, had been almost as steadily rising.

As to the Merovingians, the lifelong duel between the two queens, Fredegundis and Brunichildis, the vices of Chilperic of Neustria, 'the Nero and Herod of his time' (the husband of Fredegundis), and the fierce energy of Theodoric II, king of Burgundy (grandson of Brunichildis), shed a sort of lurid light over the royalty of the descendants of Clovis at the close of the sixth century. Chlotochar II, king of Neustria, son of Fredegundis, succeeded in uniting all the Frankish kingdoms under his own sceptre (613), and annihilated the rival Austrasian line. He and his son, Dagobert I, showed some energy and power of rule, but after Dagobert's death (638) the royal line became utterly effete, and for a hundred years, kings rightly named Do-nothings (*Fainéants*) nominally reigned over Gaul and Germany. The short lives of these kings sufficiently indicate the decay of their vital powers, caused by their vicious habits. The following are the ages at which the kings died who reigned between Dagobert I and the last of his line, Childeric III: twenty-six, twenty-four, twenty-seven, eighteen, twenty, thirty-eight, seventeen, fifty (but this king only reigned five years, and had the advantage of spending most of his life in exile), thirty-six, twenty-four, and twenty-one.

The manner of life of these hapless inheritors of dignity divorced from duty is described for us by Einhard, the biographer of Charlemagne, in a passage which has been often quoted, and which, though modern criticism finds in it somewhat to object to on the score of strict accuracy, may be quoted once again.

"The Merovingian race, from which the Franks were wont to choose their kings, is considered to have lasted down to king Childeric, who by order of Stephen the Roman pontiff was deposed and tonsured and thrust into a monastery. But though it may seem to have ended in him, it had for a long while possessed no real vigour, nor had had anything to show for itself except the empty title of king: for all the wealth and power of the kingdom were centred in the Prefects of the Palace, who were called *Majores Domus*, and to whom supremacy in the State belonged. For nothing else was left to the king except this, that satisfied with the mere royal name, with his long locks and flowing beard, he sat upon the throne and played at sovereignty, receiving the ambassadors who came to him from all quarters, and repeating to them on their departure the replies which he had been taught or ordered to deliver, as though they came from his own decision. Thus, except the useless name of king and a precarious allowance which the Prefect of the Palace afforded him as he thought fit, he possessed nothing else of his own, save one estate (*villa*) with a very poor revenue, on which he had his house, and out of which he kept the slender train of servants who performed the necessary services for him and gave him a show of obedience. When he must needs go on a journey, he went in a wagon, which was drawn by yoked oxen with a rustic cowherd driving them. Thus he went to his palace, thus to the public assembly of the people, which was held once a year to deliberate on the affairs of the realm, and thus was he wont to return to his home. As for the administration of the kingdom and all those things which had to be done or arranged for at home or abroad, they were all provided for by the Prefect of the Palace".

This picture may be slightly over-coloured. It is possible that some of the details, such as the oxen drawing the rude royal chariot, may really be due only to the inherent conservatism of the Teutonic race, which preserved in the king's household at Soissons or Paris archaic usages derived from bygone centuries when the king dwelt in a rustic hut on a forest-clearing in the heart of Germany. But the broad outline of the picture is undoubtedly correct. The Merovingian kings in the fifth generation from Clovis had sunk into mere ciphers. Intent on drinking their cup of muddy pleasure to the dregs, they left all the hard work of life, and all the duties of royalty, in war, in judgment, in finance, to the servants who clustered about the Court; and of these servants one, foremost in rank and position, gathered up the reins of government as they fell from the nerveless hands of the Merovingians, and became king in fact, while they for a hundred years remained kings in name. This allpowerful servant was the Mayor of the Palace, and when his power was once firmly established, it was too late for the descendants of Clovis, even had a man of energy and virtue arisen among them, to recover the lost dominion.

The institution of Mayor of the Palace was not peculiar to the Frankish nation. Traces of it may be found among the Ostrogoths, Burgundians, Lombards, perhaps even among the Vandals but nowhere else had it the same great development which it attained in the Frankish people. That some such official should emerge out of chaos, that many of the powers of the State should crystallize round him, was however inherent in the nature of things. Clovis and his sons, men of ruthless will and barbarous energy, had formed a State whose corner-stone was military conquest. Apparently the old liberties, the ancient germs of self-government, which had existed among the Franks as in nearly all the Teutonic peoples, had been crushed out under the centralizing sway of these barbarian kings, flattered and caressed as they had been by the Catholic ecclesiastics of Gaul. The old tribal nobility of the Salians and Ripuarians had probably also disappeared, and had been replaced by a new order of nobility who drew all their splendour from the royal majesty in whose rays they basked. The Palace had become the State, and he who was great in the king's household was great in the Frankish realm.

The inevitable limitation of autocracy comes from the love of ease. After all, government means work, and though for a few generations men may be found so lustful of power that they will 'spurn delights and live laborious days', in order to rule with power over a mighty empire, in the course of this tremendous energy wears itself out.

Some member of the royal family comes to the throne who finds that 'slumber is more sweet than toil', and that power is not worth having at the price of an utter sacrifice of all the restful pleasures of life. He hands over the reins of government to some obsequious servant who is only too glad to take them from him and to govern in the king's name. The Merovingian has found his Mayor of the Palace, the Bourbon king his Richelieu or his Alberoni, the Mikado of Japan his Taicoon.

It is possible that at first the duties of the Mayor of the Palace were strictly those of a master of the household. Merovingian royalty owned vast domains, cultivated for the most part by slave labour. The king and his great train of courtiers went in progress from one villa, or big estate, to another, consuming the produce of each villa in succession, and then moving on to that which was nearest. The mere superintendence of the receipts and expenditure of one of these great domains was in itself a considerable business, and may at first have been the chief concernment of the Mayor of the Palace, for in his humbler days it is possible that there may have been one *Major Domus* to every residence of a Frankish king. In the course of time, however—and by this I mean within a century from the death of Clovis—the Mayor had become such an important person that there was only one of his class in each of the four kingdoms, into which the Frankish monarchy generally fell apart, one for Austrasia, one for Neustria, one for Burgundy, one (perhaps) for Aquitaine.

And what were the duties of the Mayor of the Palace when he had thus emerged from the condition of a head-servant into that of a great official of the State? Perhaps we may say that still his chief functions were financial. Like the *Comes Rerum Privatarum* of the later empire, it was his business to administer the revenues, not now of one villa or palace, but of all the royal domains within the limits of his master's kingdom. A most important part of his functions in this capacity was that of confirming alienations of the royal domain. Throughout the seventh century, as we have reason to believe, the new landed aristocracy which was forming itself was getting grants of *beneficia* either from the Church or the Crown; and a weak Merovingian king was under great temptation to strengthen his party by lavish grants of the Crown lands to importunate and blustering petitioners. Just at this point, therefore, the control exercised by the Mayor of the Palace would have an important effect on the fortunes of the aristocracy, since it was in his power to forbid all grants of *beneficia* to his foes and to encourage similar grants to his friends.

He had, moreover, such power over the collection of the taxes (however rude and undeveloped the Merovingian system of taxation may have been) as gave him great opportunities for enriching himself while professing to serve the royal exchequer. Thus it was matter of bitter complaint against Protadius, Mayor of the Palace of Burgundy under Theodoric (grandson of Brunichildis), that though a man of great ability and energy, he committed grievous injustice against individuals, straining the rights of the royal fisc, ingeniously striving to fill the royal treasury at the expense of private persons and at the same time to enrich himself. The general attitude which the Mayor of the Palace at first assumed, especially in Neustria, was that of championship of the rights of the Crown against the aristocracy, though in the end he became strong enough to set Crown and aristocracy alike at defiance.

Lastly, in addition to the powers of administration and finance which the Mayor of the Palace exercised, he must have eventually gathered into his hands the supreme command of the nation-army of the Franks, though apparently we have but little information of the steps by which a Grand Chamberlain was thus transformed into a Commander-in-Chief.

After this brief sketch of the general character of the office of *Major Domus*, let us trace the fortunes of that Austrasian family which more than all others made it illustrious.

CHAPTER II.

THE EARLY ARNULFINGS.

The first appearance of the ancestors of Charles the Great on the stage of history is in the year 613, when the long duel between the houses of Sigibert and Chilperic, kings respectively of Austrasia and Neustria, and husbands of Brunichildis and Fredegundis, was brought to a close. As has been said, Chlotochar II, son of Chilperic and Fredegundis, invaded Austrasia, then under the nominal rule of the infant Sigibert, really governed by his great grandmother, the once beautiful, always ambitious, and now vindictive Brunichildis. We are told that it was at the instigation of Arnulf and Pippin and the other nobles of Austrasia that this invasion was made. Partly by the help of those men, and partly by the devices of the *Major domus* Warnachar (who discovered that Brunichildis was plotting against him and turned conspirator to save his life), Chlotochar's invasion was crowned with complete success. The whole Frankish realm was reunited under the sceptre of the Neustrian king, and the son of Fredegundis doomed his mother's rival to a cruel and shameful death.

Who, then, were these two men who at a critical moment led the Austrasian aristocracy to victory in their lifelong struggle against the domineering but statesmanlike Brunichildis?

Arnulf, Archbishop of Metz, was sprung from a noble family among the Ripuarian Franks. More than this cannot be stated concerning his ancestry, though the imaginative zeal of later genealogists invented for him a pedigree adorned with the names of kings, saints, and senators. He seems to have been born about 582, and to have come as a young and clever lad to the Austrasian Court when Theudebert was reigning there after the expulsion of his grandmother Brunichildis (599). He rose into high favour with Gundulf, the Austrasian Mayor of the Palace, showed himself an efficient servant of the Crown, both in peace and war, and was promoted, we are told, to the presidency over six 'provinces' which were usually assigned to as many governors. He married a noble lady, who bore him two sons, Anschisus and Chlodulf, and he formed what proved to be a lifelong friendship with another officer of the Court named Romaric. The talk of the two friends turned often on religious subjects, and they not unfrequently discussed a plan for renouncing the world, retiring to some convent, and there continuing their friendly dialogues till death should sever them.

It was during this period of immersion in worldly affairs, while his heart longed for the cloister, that the following incident is said to have happened. He was walking one day over the bridge at Metz, penitent for his sins and doubtful whether his repentance was accepted in the sight of God. Looking down into the deep currents of the Moselle, the bottom of which his eye failed to reach, be drew off the ring from his finger and cast it into the depths of the river. "Then", said he to himself, "when I shall receive again this ring which I now cast away, shall I feel sure that I am loosed from the bonds of mine iniquities". Years after, when he was sitting on the episcopal throne of Metz, a fish was brought to the palace and prepared for the evening meal. In the fish's intestines the cook found the well-known ring and brought it to his master, who received with joy this token of the Divine forgiveness, but felt himself bound thereby to a life of even greater austerity than aforetime.

This anecdote was related by the great Emperor Charles, Arnulf's descendant in the fifth generation, to his friend and secretary Einhard. It of course recalls to our mind the well-known story of Polycrates, tyrant of Samos, but the moral of the two stories is quite dissimilar, and it may be doubted whether Einhard, and much more whether his master, had ever scanned the pages of Herodotus.

The holy conversations with Romaric continued, and the two friends were about to execute their purpose of retiring from the world. Arnulf's pious eagerness to divide his property among the poor was acquiesced in by his elder son Anschisus, but opposed by Chlodulf. Divine Providence, so it was held by later generations, rewarded each brother according to his works. Chlodulf, with his heart set on wealth, reached no higher dignity than that of Archbishop of Metz, and dying left no seed, while Anschisus became virtually chief ruler of Austrasia and was the progenitor of kings and emperors.

When the two friends were at last on the point of retiring into the wilderness, the Archbishop of Metz died, and the citizens with one voice demanded that Arnulf, 'domestic and counsellor of the king', should be ordained in his stead. There was the usual resistance on Arnulf's part, followed by his compulsory assumption of the dignity: and this elevation appears to have taken place about Christmas, 611, very shortly before the overthrow of Theudebert.

Though practising the usual austerities of a medieval saint, fasting for three days at a time, living on barley-bread and water, wearing a hair-shirt and working miracles, Arnulf did not lay down the office, whatever it was, which he held in the Austrasian Court. And in his guidance of the affairs of the kingdom he was powerfully aided by his friend Pippin, who is usually known as Pippin of Landen, and who was an Austrasian nobleman with large possessions between the Meuse and the Moselle.

Between them these two statesmen succeeded in foiling the designs of Brunichildis to become regent of Austrasia after the death of her two grandsons Theudebert and Theodoric, and as we have seen, by their timely defection, they won a bloodless victory for Chlotochar II, who thus became sole monarch of the Frankish kingdom (613).

But the Austrasian spirit of independence required a separate ruler, and accordingly in 622 Chlotochar delegated the sovereignty of Austrasia to his son Dagobert, a young man of about twenty years of age. Arnulf and Pippin were recognized as the chief advisers of the young king, and the latter nobleman probably held the office of Mayor of the Palace. On the testimony of historians who were their contemporaries, and who had therefore no especial reason for flattering the ancestors of Charlemagne, Dagobert's Austrasian sovereignty under the guidance of these two men was a time of wise and firm government. A certain Chrodoald, descended from the dukes of Bavaria, who like some turbulent baron of the Middle Ages was trampling on the rights of the lowly and setting himself against the administrators of the law, was by their advice condemned to death, and this sentence was carried into effect, notwithstanding the attempted mediation of Chlotochar on his behalf. This execution of

Chrodoald perhaps brought to a head the discord between father and son. Dagobert had not received the kingdom of Austrasia in its fullness, but had been limited to the regions eastward of the Ardennes and the Vosges mountains. This limitation rankled in his mind and in that of his subjects and would perhaps have led to civil war, but the matter was referred to the arbitration of twelve Franks, Bishop Arnulf among them, by whom it was amicably arranged, Dagobert receiving all the Austrasian kingdom properly so-called, but renouncing all claim to the outlying portions in Aquitaine and Provence, which had been hitherto held by his predecessors at Metz.

After Dagobert had been five years on the Austrasian throne, he lost the more eminent of his two counsellors. Arnulf's desire for solitude and seclusion could be no longer repressed, and in the year 627 he announced to the king that he was about to lay down his episcopal dignity and depart to the wilderness. Enraged at this threatened desertion, Dagobert said, "Unless thou stayest with me, I cut off the heads of thy two sons". "My sons' lives", said the bishop, "are in the hands of God, nor will thy life be long if thou takest away the life of the innocent". Dagobert in his anger began to pluck at the dagger which hung from his belt; but the saint, not heeding his wrath, said, "What are you doing, most miserable of men? Would you repay evil for good? If you will stain that dagger with my blood. I do not fear to die in obedience to the commands of Him who died for me". A courtier intervened: the queen came upon the scene, and soon the royal pair were kneeling at the bishop's feet, beseeching him with tears to go to the wilderness, to do what he would, if only he would grant them forgiveness for Dagobert's wicked words.

Emerging from the palace, Arnulf met a sight which doubtless shook his resolution more than all the threats of his master. The lame and blind, the widows and orphans, of the city, who had heard of his intended abdication of the see, crowded round the palace gates, crying with doleful voices, "O good shepherd! who will give us food and clothing when thou art gone? We pray thee, in Christ's name, do not leave us". Arnulf gently assured them that some good and merciful man would be found, to be his successor, and comforted them with the story of Lazarus, as miserable as any of them, yet carried by angels into Abraham's bosom. So he passed through the weeping throng, and gained the haven of his oratory.

A successor named Goeric or Abbo, a man somewhat of his own type of character, was found to fill his place. The faithful Romaric, who had long before retired from the world, came to escort his friend to the place which he had prepared for his reception in the wilderness. But a miracle was to be wrought ere the late bishop could leave his cathedral city. A fire broke out in Metz the night before the day fixed for his departure. The royal store-house was already consumed: the house in which Arnulf was dwelling was threatened. Romaric and his friends burst into the house, found the saint singing psalms, told him that the horses were at the door, and adjured him to fly.

"Not so", said Arnulf. "Take me hence, and set me where I can see this impious conflagration. If it be God's will that I be burned, I am in His hand". They went together to the burning house; they knelt in prayer: the saint raised the banner of the Cross against the raging flames, which at once began to die down. Arnulf and his friends having sung matins, returned to their beds and passed the rest of the night in sleep.

Having disposed of all his worldly goods—now it must be supposed, with the consent of both his sons—Arnulf retired into the wilderness, apparently somewhere among the solitudes of the Vosges Mountains, and there with his friend Romaric passed the last fourteen years of his life. He had a few monks with him, as well as certain lepers, upon whom he waited, performing the most repulsive and menial offices for them with alacrity. He died in July or August, 641; and his body, at first buried by his friend Romaric at the place which, called after that friend, still bears the name Remiremont, was carried with great solemnity by his successor Goeric, to the city of Metz, where the great cathedral of St. Arnoulf preserves his memory to this day.

The veneration for the canonized bishop of Metz soon spread over Gaul, and he was accounted in an especial manner the patron of the Frankish nation. We who read his life with colder sympathies, can yet see that here was a man who deserved to be held in reverence, a statesman and one acquainted with courts, who nevertheless held the joys and the rewards of the life eternal more precious than worldly rank and station. In reading his life, one cannot but feel that in some way the Frankish nation, or at least the Austrasian portion of it, has groped its way upwards since the fifth century. Bishop Arnulf s is an utterly different type of character from the greedy, turbulent, licentious prelates who deface the pages of Gregory of Tours. And when we study the deeds of the great race of statesmen and of kings who sprang from the loins of Arnulf, we shall be often reminded how different was their original from that of the Merovingian race. The half-heathen and wholly vicious Clovis, descendant of the sea-monster, was a fitting ancestor of the Chilperics and Childerics, who slew their kinsfolk when they were strong and their own manhood when they were weak. The saintly and yet wise-hearted Arnulf was a worthy progenitor of the Pippins and Charleses, who were for two centuries among the foremost men in Europe, and whose lives, whatever might be their faults, were one long battle on behalf of Christianity and civilization.

Of the other great ancestor of Charlemagne, Pippin 'of Landen', there is less to tell than of Arnulf.

In the year 628, very shortly after Arnulf's retirement from the Court, Chlotochar II, king of Neustria and Burgundy, died, and his son Dagobert went from the Rhine-land to Paris to wield the sceptre over the whole Frankish realm. His advent was hailed with acclamation, for all Neustria had heard of the young king's wise and just rule over the Austrasian kingdom.

But it was soon and sadly seen how much of that reputation was really due to his counsellors Arnulf and Pippin. The air of Neustria, the influence of the corrupt Gallo-Roman civilization, awoke the slumbering vices of the Merovingian. Three queens at once, and more concubines than the chronicler cares to enumerate, flaunted it in the Court of Paris, and to supply their extravagances and his own craving for luxury, Dagobert laid greedy hands on the property both of his *leudes* and of the Church. This latter charge (as the story of his life is written by churchmen) perhaps requires us not to give too implicit faith to the harsh judgment which they have pronounced on his character.

The relation borne by Pippin of Landen to Dagobert after the death of his father is not very clear. He seems to have followed his young sovereign to Paris, and to have sought to continue to guide him in the administration of his kingdom. But doubtless there was jealousy in Neustria of the influence of the Austrasian counsellor, and strangely enough from Austrasia also came a growl of rage against the too powerful minister. Probably the turbulent nobles against whom he had asserted the royal prerogatives, now saw their opportunity of revenge. The chronicler tells us "The fury of the Austrasians against him grew so vehement that they even sought to render him odious to Dagobert in order that he might be slain". These evil designs were foiled, but

Pippin seems to have lost all power at Court, and to have passed the next eight years (630-638) in retirement, possibly at Orleans, where he was perhaps charged with the education of Dagobert's young son, Sigibert.

It was during this time of obscurity, probably near its commencement, that the fortunes of the two retired ministers were linked together by the marriage of their children. Somewhere about the year 630, Ansegisel (or Anschisus), the younger son of St. Arnulf, married Becga, daughter of Pippin and sister of the sainted Gertrude, who was the first abbess of the convent of Nivelles in Brabant, founded by her mother.

On the death of Dagobert in 638, we are told that Pippin and the other leaders of the Austrasians, who up to the king's death had been kept in control, unanimously asked for Sigibert as their king. Pippin renewed his former strong friendship with Cunibert, bishop of Cologne, drew to his side all the Austrasian *leudes*, and by his prudent and gentle rule obtained their friendship, and kept it to the end. Apparently we have here the story of something like a counterrevolution after the death of Dagobert, by which Pippin, now a man of about fifty years of age, was recalled amid the acclamations of his countrymen to undertake the duties of *Major Domus* for the young king. In this capacity he accomplished the important task of dividing the treasures unjustly accumulated by Dagobert. Along with Bishop Cunibert and other Austrasian nobles, he met at the 'villa' of Compendium the widowed queen Nantildis and the magnates of Neustria. One-third of the treasure was assigned to Clovis, the boy-king of Neustria, one-third to the queen dowager, and the remaining third, allotted to Sigibert, was carried by Cunibert and Pippin to the palace at Metz. Shortly after this transaction, in the year 639 or 640, Pippin died, 'and by his death caused great sorrow to all the people of Auster (Austrasia), because he had been loved by them for his goodness and his zeal on behalf of justice'. His friend St. Arnulf, who doubtless heard of his death in his wilderness abode, followed him to the tomb in little more than a year.

For sixteen years after the death of Pippin of Landen, the foremost figure in Austrasian history was his son Grimwald. His name and some points in his history remind us of his more famous contemporary, Grimwald the Lombard, duke of Benevento, and, by a successful stroke of treason, king of the Lombards. There was, as we have seen, some friendly intercourse between Franks and Lombards in the early part of the sixth century, but apparently there is nothing to justify us in considering the Austrasian duke as namesake of the Lombard king.

Not immediately on the death of the elder Pippin did Grimwald obtain the position of *Major Domus* in the Austrasian kingdom. That position seems to have been at first held by a certain Otto, who had been tutor to the new king Sigibert in his childhood, but after two or three years of struggle, Otto was slain by Leuthar, duke of the Alamanni, who was 'of the faction of Grimwald', and the son of Pippin was recognized by all as *Major Domus* in his father's place. As to Grimwald's government during the thirteen or fourteen years that followed (643 or 642 to 656), we know very little. We are told that he was loved like his father, and it is conjectured that he fostered the pious inclinations of his young king, and was, like him, a liberal friend to the Church: but it is by his premature attempt to turn Major-domat into sovereignty that he is alone famous in history. When Sigibert, king of Austrasia, died in 656, at the age (for a Merovingian king, the advanced age) of twenty-six, Grimwald had the long locks of his son Dagobert shorn off, and sent him to lead a holy life in an Irish monastery, proclaiming his own son, to whom he had given the Merovingian name Childebert, king of the Franks.

But the time was not yet ripe for such a revolution; neither had the family of Pippin, though wealthy, powerful, and perhaps popular, yet done any such deeds as justified them in claiming, as of hereditary right, the allegiance even of Austrasia, much less of all the Frankish kingdoms. "The Franks", we are told by a chronicler, "being moved with great indignation, laid snares for Grimwald, and taking him prisoner carried him to Clovis [the Second, brother of Sigibert] for condemnation. Being confined in prison in the city of Paris, and afflicted with the agony of chains, he, who was worthy of death for his practices against his lord, ended his life in mighty torments".

The result of this premature attempt at revolution was for a time to obscure the fortunes of the two great Austrasian houses. Anschisus, or Ansegisel, Grimwald's brother-in-law, who is the least noticeable figure among the Arnulfings, after holding the office of *Major Domus* for a few years (632-638), before the return of the elder Pippin, subsides into obscurity, and we hear no more concerning him save for a late and doubtful statement that he was treacherously slain in 685 by a certain Gunduin, and that his death was gloriously avenged by his son. To the deeds of that son, Pippin 'of Heristal,' grandson of St. Arnulf on his father's side, grandson of Pippin 'of Landen' on his mother's side, we now turn : for now, at last, the shadows are beginning to disperse, and we begin to see something of the well-known

'shapes that must undergo mortality.'

CHAPTER III.

PIPPIN OF HERISTAL AND CHARLES MARTEL.

In the year 656, the same year which saw the death of Sigibert of Austrasia and the premature attempt of Grimwald to fill the vacant throne, Clovis II of Neustria died also. His sons, (Chlotochar III, 656-670; Childeric II, 660-673; Theodoric HI, 673-691; their cousin Dagobert II, son of Sigibert II, king of Austrasia, 674-678), Merovingians of the usual imbecile type, were for the next thirty years the nominal rulers of the three Frankish kingdoms, at first under the regency of their mother, the sainted Balthildis, an Anglo-Saxon, originally the slave of a Mayor of the Palace, afterwards wife of Clovis II. But the one figure which dominates the obscure and bloody history of the quarter of a century following the fall of Grimwald, is that of Ebroin, who was during the greater part of that time Mayor of the Palace in Neustria and Burgundy. He had more than one sharp struggle for power, especially with the turbulent Leodegarius, bishop of Autun, who figures in the ecclesiastical calendar as St. Leger; but from all these struggles, from the prison and the convent-cell, he emerged triumphant. A hard, cruel, and unscrupulous man he was, yet perhaps as good a ruler as the putrescent western Frankish kingdoms of that day deserved, and he did something to arrest the rapid process of disintegration which had set in.

Meanwhile in Austrasia a position somewhat similar to that of Ebroin had been held by a certain Mayor of the Palace named Wulfwald, who for eighteen years seems to have striven to uphold the royal power and the authority of the central government against the usurpations of the nobles. In 674, in order to avoid union with Neustria, the half-forgotten son of Sigibert was fetched from the Irish monastery to which, seventeen years before, Grimwald had banished him, and was raised to the Austrasian throne under the title of Dagobert II. In five years, however, his troubled reign was at an end, and then it seemed inevitable that the Neustrian king, whose rule, as all men knew, meant simply the rule of the terrible Ebroin, must reign in Austrasia. To avert this danger, the nobles put an army in the field (678), and the leaders of that army were Pippin of Heristal and a confederate, possibly a kinsman named Martin. Battle was joined, probably in the neighbourhood of Laon, and the Austrasians were routed with terrible slaughter. Pippin escaped: Martin shut himself up in Laon, and was besieged there by Ebroin. He was summoned to surrender, and the messengers of Ebroin swore to him on certain boxes, which were believed to contain very holy relics of saints, that his life should be spared. Unfortunately for Martin the boxes when opened were found to be empty, and the tremendous oath could therefore be violated with impunity. He and his comrades were put to death, and Austrasia, like her sister kingdoms, came under the harsh rule of Ebroin.

Three years after this defeat of the Austrasians, Ebroin perished, a victim to private revenge. He was assassinated by a certain Frankish nobleman named Hermenfrid, whose property he had confiscated, and who, waiting by the door of his house in the grey of the morning, slew him as he was setting out for mass. The thought that he had thus been sent out of life 'unhousel'd, unanneaied', gave a keener edge to the joy of the avenger.

The murderer of Ebroin fled to Pippin for refuge, and the successor of Ebroin in the Mayoralty of the Palace, who was named Waratto, made a treaty of peace, exchanging hostages with the same Austrasian chief, whose fortunes were evidently now beginning to recover from the effects of the great disaster of Laon. Moreover, there were dissensions in the family of Waratto. These Neustrian mayors lacked that instinct of family cohesion which was so strong in the early generations of the Arnulfings. Waratto's son Ghislemar, apparently an able but shifty person, intrigued against his father and thrust him out of the Major-domat (683). He carried on the perpetual feud of Neustria against Austrasia, fighting a hard battle against Pippin at Namur, and probably defeating him, for we are told that 'after swearing a false oath, he slew very many of the noble followers of Pippin'. Returning to his home, however, 'he was struck by the hand of God, and, as he deserved, yielded up his most wicked spirit' (684). Waratto hereupon recovered his dignity of Mayor of the Palace, which he held for two years, years of peace between him and the Austrasian chief.

On the death of Waratto in 686, he was succeeded in the office of Major Domus by his son-in-law Berchar, a man whose small stature and pitiable self-earned for him the contempt of the Neustrian nobles. In the war which almost as a matter of course was waged between Neustria and Austrasia, the disaffection of the Neustrian nobility led to a momentous result. The armies met at Textri in Picardy (687). The puppet king Theodoric III was there as well as his insignificant *Major Domus*, but the best men in Neustria seem to have been in the opposite camp, and Pippin won a decisive victory. Berchar escaped from the field of battle, but only to die at home by the weapon of an assassin, instigated, it was said, by his mother-in-law Ausfled. Pippin obtained possession of the person of the Merovingian king and of the royal hoard, arranged all things in the palace according to his good will and pleasure, and returned into Austrasia, now practically the unquestioned lord of all the three kingdoms.

The year 687, the date of the battle of Textri, is one of three, which are the most noteworthy steps in the ascent of the Arnulfing house to the headship of Western Europe. The dreary and chaotic period of miscellaneous mayoralties is over. From henceforward, with one very slight break, the supremacy of the great Austrasian family is unquestioned and incontestable.

Of the twenty-seven years (687-714) during which Pippin of Heristal was the virtual sovereign of France, we have very meagre accounts in the chronicles. *Fainéant* Merovingian kings, Theodoric III and his sons, come and go, but history refuses to take account of them save to notice that though they still receive the flattering titles 'renowned' and 'glorious', they are actually spoken of as subject to their nominal servant the Mayor of the Palace. The principal figure of this period, after Pippin's, seems to be that of Ratbod, chief or king of the Frisians, who remained obdurate in his Paganism, and with whom Pippin had more than one sharp encounter, and whom he at last decisively defeated at Durestede near Utrecht. We are somewhat surprised to find a daughter of this 'Gentile' chief given in marriage to Pippin's son Grimwald, but we may conjecture that she was received into the Christian Church before the espousals, and that the marriage was a pledge of the alliance and consequent peace which seems to have prevailed between Pippin and the Frisians for the last twenty years of his Major-domat.

We hear of Pippin also as invading the country of the Alamanni, that is to say, the region afterwards known as Swabia. From this and other slight indications, we may infer that while ruling Neustria and Burgundy by the means either of a faithful adherent or of a son holding the office of *Major Domus* in those kingdoms, his own work was chiefly Austrasian, and consisted in re-establishing the Frankish power in those lands east of the Rhine which, under the rule of the effete Merovingians, had been gradually dropping off from the monarchy.

The last years of Pippin of Heristal were clouded by family bereavement. By his wife Plectrude, who is spoken of as a 'noble and very prudent woman', but who seems to have been ambitious and perhaps somewhat intriguing, he had two sons, Drogo and Grimwald. In the year 708, Drogo died of fever and was laid in the basilica of his sainted ancestor Arnulf at Metz. In 714 the second son Grimwald, whom we have just met with as son-in-law of the Frisian chief, and who was already *Major Domus* of Neustria, was on his way to visit his father who was lying sick at Jupille on the Meuse in the neighbourhood of Liège. Turning to pray at the basilica of St. Lambert in Liège, he was waylaid and slain by 'a certain most cruel man, a son of Belial, the heathen Rantgar'. The mention of the heathenism of Rantgar suggests the conjecture that he was a Frisian, and that the cause of quarrel may have been connected with Grimwald's marriage with the daughter of Ratbod.

Grimwald left one son, Theudwald, the offspring not of his marriage with the Frisian princess, but of a connection unblessed by the Church. This boy appears to have been at once promoted to his father's Neustrian mayoralty, and on the death of his grand-father Pippin, which happened soon after (hastened very probably by the tragedy of Grimwald's murder), he was recognized as the heir to all his greatness. Of course the nominal rule of such a child implied a regency, and that regency was also of course wielded by the ambitious widow of Pippin. As the chronicler, who is somewhat of an admirer of the new regent, tells us, "Plectrude with her grandsons and the king governed all things with discreet rule". The use of the word 'grandsons' in the plural probably points to the association in the government of a son of the deceased Drogo, named Hugo, who was at this time about eighteen years of age, but who had already entered the Church, and afterwards rose to be abbot of St. Wandril and archbishop of Rouen.

The position of affairs, as indicated by the chronicler, was certainly a sufficiently absurd one. Here was this nominal king Dagobert III, now fifteen years of age. His Mayor of the Palace, that is, his confidential adviser and practical man of affairs, was a little child of perhaps six years old: but that child again was advised, and of course absolutely governed, by his grandmother, a 'very prudent' but not very popular person, and a young clerical cousin who was mounting the ladder of ecclesiastical preferment.

What made the situation more preposterous was that there was already in the Arnulfing house a man of full age, a son of the just deceased statesman, one in every way admirably qualified to hold the reins of power, and kept in the background only by a beldame's jealousy. This was Charles, ever after to be known as Charles Martel, son of Pippin of Heristal and Alpaida. Whether Alpaida were wife or concubine cannot be safely said, but as she was living at the same time as Plectrude, and as her son was younger than the sons of her rival, the legitimacy of Charles can only be maintained by resorting to an elaborate theory of divorces and remarriages for which there does not seem to be any warrant in the authorities. The Arnulfings, though not as outrageously profligate as the Merovingians, were notoriously lax in their marriage relations, which with them tended to assume the character of polygamy, and legitimacy or illegitimacy was not a matter of supreme importance.

The origin of the name Charles, which has since figured so prominently in the royal houses, not of France and Germany alone, but also of Spain, England, Sweden, and Naples, is thus told by an old Saga. At the time of his birth a messenger was sent to inform the child's father. Bursting into the presence of the great Austrasian, he found him sitting with Plectrude by his side; and, perhaps overawed by the presence of the rival princess, the messenger stammered out, "Long live the king! It is a Karl", using a colloquial term for a boy. "And a good name too", laughed the delighted if somewhat embarrassed father. "Let him be called Karl".

Fearing the obvious danger to her rule which existed in the person of this hated step-son, Plectrude immediately on her husband's death shut up Charles in prison. Then burst forth a storm which very nearly shattered the Frankish monarchy. The Neustrians, who had no mind to accept the rule of a baby Mayor of the Palace from the hated Austrasians, proclaimed one of their own countrymen, Raginfrid, Mayor, and declared war upon Plectrude and her grandson. In a battle which was fought in the Cotian forest (near Compiègne), the Austrasians were utterly defeated, the boy-mayor. Theudwald fled from the field, and apparently the Merovingian king Dagobert III fell into the hands of Raginfrid (715). On Dagobert's death shortly after, a certain priest of Merovingian extraction named Daniel was fetched out of the church and proclaimed king under the title of Chilperic II. Here at last was a Merovingian king of full age, for this Daniel was a man of between forty and fifty; and when the long locks began to grow where the clerical tonsure had been, he was probably able to play the part with more dignity than the boy-kings his predecessors. He even seems to have entered with some energy into the struggle with the Austrasian house, but in that struggle, however necessary it may have seemed for the preservation of Merovingian kingship, the far more important interests of the great Frankish monarchy which Pippin of Heristal had so assiduously promoted were like to have been utterly ruined. The Neustrian king and his Mayor joined hands with the old heathen Ratbod king of the Frisians, pressed on to the Meuse, besieged Plectrude in Cologne, and at last having received from the dismayed dowager a large part of the treasure accumulated by her husband, marched back into their own land (716).

The one favourable symptom in this perilous conjuncture of affairs was, that in the confusion caused by the civil war, Charles Martel had escaped from his step-mother's keeping. Gradually the loyal followers, the *leudes* of his father, gathered round him. Defeated at first with great loss by Frisian Ratbod, and unsuccessful in his war against the Neustrians, he still held on his way, and now, falling on the triumphant invaders at a place called Amblaya, he inflicted upon them a severe defeat and carried back the paternal treasure to Cologne. A still more crushing defeat which Chilperic and Raginfrid sustained next year (717) at Vincy near Cambrai was the crisis of Charles's fortunes. He visited Paris as a conqueror, and when he returned to Cologne Plectrude handed over to him the remaining treasures of his father and retired into obscurity. His nephew Theudwald appears to have taken orders as an ecclesiastic and to have died not many years after. Charles was now the admitted head of the Arnulfing house, the acknowledged Mayor of the Palace for Austrasia: and though the civil war with Neustria still lingered, chiefly owing to the powerful aid which Raginfrid received from Eudo, the virtually independent duke of Aquitaine, it was ended in 720 by a convenient compromise. Along with the Neustrian treasure Chilperic II was handed over to Charles, whose own puppet-king had just died, and who could therefore easily admit him to the vacant dignity. Raginfrid, whose opposition was obstinate and protracted, does not seem to have been finally subdued till 725, when he was allowed to retain the position of Count of Angers.

Thus after our review of two centuries of Frankish history we have come down to the accession to power of the hero whose period of rule, as before stated, almost exactly coincided with that of the last great Lombard king, Liutprand.

The one event of world-historical importance in Charles Martel's leadership of the Franks was his victory over the Mussulman invaders of Gaul in the year 732. In 711 the Moors (as the Saracen conquerors were called owing to their having entered Europe from Mauretania) had crossed the Straits of Gibraltar and had in one battle overthrown the effete, priest-ridden monarchy of the Visigoths. Five years afterwards they entered Gaul: four years after that (720) they took Narbonne and made the old Gothic province of Septimania their own. Eudo of Aquitaine, who had just made his peace with Charles Martel, compelled them in that year to retreat from the unconquered city of Toulouse, and that ineffectual siege may be considered as the first sign of the reflux of the wave of Saracen invasion. But five years later (725) the Moors had actually penetrated as far as Autun in Burgundy. How little most students of modern history grasp the fact that the standard of the Crescent once floated within a hundred miles of the Lake of Geneva! During these years the opposition of Eudo to the Moorish advance was intermitted, and from the champion of Christianity he seemed in danger of becoming its betrayer. They were on his part years of revolt against Frankish supremacy, and of alliance, even matrimonial alliance, with the Mussulman, for Eudo's daughter Lampegia was given in marriage to a Berber chief named Munuza. In 731 there was war in earnest between Charles Martel and Eudo of Aquitaine. The Austrasian twice crossed the Loire, defeated Eudo, and returned home each time with great booty.

But in 732 these relations were suddenly changed. Eudo's son-in-law the Berber chief had been put to death by the lawful Moorish governor of Spain, and now that governor, Abderrahman, crossed the Pyrenees with a mighty army, intent on punishing Eudo, but doubtless also intent on adding Gaul as well as Spain to the countries which professed the faith of Mohammed. Laying waste the land and burning the churches, the Saracens reached the Garonne and laid siege to Bordeaux. Eudo, striving to deliver the city, was defeated with terrible loss and fled to his late enemy Charles, imploring his succour. The invaders pressed on by the great Roman road which led northward from the Garonne to the Loire. They reached Poictiers, where they burned the church of St. Hilary: they were threatening the yet more venerated sanctuary of St. Martin at Tours. But Count Eudo had not reckoned in vain on the statesmanlike generosity of Charles Martel, who, forgetful of all the recent causes of quarrel between Austrasia and Aquitaine, determined at any cost to repel the onslaught of the Islamites. Having collected a large army, in which probably Frisians, Saxons and Alamanni served as well as Franks, he moved rapidly across the Loire and took up a strong position near the town of Old Poitiers between the rivers Elain and Vienne, barring the road to Tours.

A terrible battle followed. The fervour of the sons of desert, who perchance like the first warriors of Islam deemed that they already saw the flashing eyes of the houris waiting to receive them into Paradise, was met, was chilled, was broken by the stolid courage of the soldiers from Rhineland, who stood, says the historian, rigid and immovable as a wall of ice. Yet from that icy wall flashed forth countless swords wielded by strong arms and held as in the grasp of iron hands; and under their strokes Abderrahman himself and thousands of his bravest warriors fell prostrate. Grievous however were also the losses of the Frankish army, but with stout hearts they nerved themselves for the expected contest of the morrow. But when the morrow dawned the long rows of the tents of the Saracens were seen to be strangely solitary and unpeopled. The Franks feared a snare and an ambuscade, but gradually their scouts venturing into the hostile lines brought back word that the camp was indeed deserted, that there was an abundance of spoil in the tents, that the enemy, disheartened by the terrible slaughter of the previous day, had fled under cover of the night. The scene which followed must have been like that described by the Jewish historian after the flight of the Syrian host. The Austrasian soldiers peaceably divided among themselves the immense spoil of the Saracens, and returned with joy to their own land, where doubtless many barbarian fingers handled and barbarian eyes appraised with wonder the tissues woven in the looms of Damascus and the cunning work of the goldsmiths of Seville.

Thus was the great blow struck, and Europe, at least Europe north of the Pyrenees, was freed from the nightmare of Mussulman invasion. Charles Martel was hailed as the great deliverer of Christendom, and popular report, which 'lied like a bulletin', so magnified his victory that barely half a century after the event an honest and sober historian like Paulus Diaconus could write, and could expect his readers to believe, that the Franks slew 375,000 Saracens, with a loss of only 1,500 of their own countrymen.

Three years after this great victory Count Eudo Later died (735), and a Frankish invasion of Aquitaine seems to have been necessary in order to reduce his son Hunold to the same degree of dependence on the central monarchy in which Eudo had acquiesced since the day of his great deliverance. Two years later (737) there was again war between the Saracens and Charles, but not apparently on the vast scale of the earlier campaign. The invaders were aided by disunion or treachery among the Christians. A certain duke Maurontus, in league with other rebel nobles of Provence who probably resented the pretensions of the Austrasian Mayor to rule their southern land, conspired with the Saracens of Septimania and enabled them to possess themselves of the strong city of Avignon as well as of the more exposed city of Arles. Charles, who was now growing old, and who was besides always more or less engaged in hostile operations against the Frisians and Saxons on his northern border, sent his brother, or halfbrother, 'an industrious man, Childebrand', with a large army and many dukes and counts under him to recover the lost territory. Our interest in this industrious kinsman or offshoot of the great Austrasian house is increased when we find that it is to him and his son Nibelung that we owe the order for the composition of those chronicles (the Continuation of Fredegarius) from which almost all our slender knowledge of the history of this period is derived. Avignon was blockaded: Charles himself appeared upon the scene : there were the sounding of trumpets and the shouting of warriors 'as at Jericho', but there were also engines of war and ropes and cords before which ere long the defence fell powerless. The Franks streamed in at the breach, slaying and burning, and Avignon was recovered from the infidels.

From Avignon Charles pressed on across the Rhone, defeated the Saracens in a great battle near the sea-coast south of Narbonne, and slew their leader Omar, but failed to take Narbonne itself, though he took Nimes and Agde and demolished their walls. Through the meagre sentences of the chronicler we seem dimly to discern that, as already hinted, there was something more in this campaign than the opposition between Christian and Moslem, that the Romanised and meridional children of Provence resented the domination of the rough Teutonic warriors from Rhineland, and were even willing to join hands with the Saracens in order to break the Austrasian yoke from off their necks.

It was apparently at the time of this Saracen invasion that Charles Martel asked for and obtained that help from his brother-in-law Liutprand king of the Lombards which has been described in a previous volume.

Next year Charles again sent Childebrand to Provence to complete the work of subjugation, and again followed in his kinsman's footsteps. Though Narbonne was not taken and Septimania remained Saracen, all Provence was apparently won back and firmly united to the Frankish monarchy. The traitor Maurontus escaped 'by safest ways over inaccessible rocks', doubtless, that is to say, by the narrow gorges and snow-blocked passes of the Maritime Alps.

Charles Martel was now sole ruler of the great Frankish monarchy, for on the death of the *fainéant* king Theodoric IV in 737 he had not thought it necessary to put another puppet in his place. On his return from this last expedition to Provence (in 738) to his villa at Verimbria near Compiegne he began to sicken, and for the remaining three years of his life he was in feeble health. While he was in this condition came those two embassies which have been already described, from Pope Gregory III beseeching his assistance against the Lombard kings Liutprand and Hildeprand. They returned ineffectual, though they brought to the great Mayor, besides many other precious gifts, the chains of St. Peter, the keys of his sepulchre, and the honour (which it was not for the Pope to bestow) of a Roman consulship. But Charles, besides the natural dissuasions of enfeebled health and approaching old age, had no inclination to engage for the Pope's sake in a war with a kinsman, an ally, and the knightly godfather of his son Pippin. Any warlike deeds that had to be done in the few remaining years of his supremacy were done by his sons. He tarried peaceably at home, gave great gifts to the church of St. Denis at Paris in which his bones were to be laid, and then departing to his favourite villa of Cariciacum (now Quierzy-sur-Oise) he was there seized with a fever of which he died on the 22nd of October, 741.

In his reign (for such we may truly call his mayoralty) of nearly twenty-five years, Charles had accomplished great things. With many a warlike blow, corresponding to his surname the Hammer, he had welded the once-discordant kingdoms, Neustria, Austrasia, and Burgundy, into unity. He had done something towards the more difficult work of forcing Aquitaine to renounce its semi-independence and become a loyal member of the Frankish monarchy. In the north and in the south he had shown himself a valorous champion of the Christian Church militant, since not only had he repelled the Mussulman invasions of Gaul, but by his perpetual and in the main successful wars with the Frisians he had made possible those missionary expeditions by which our countryman Wynfrith, better known as Boniface, chastised the heathen, destroyed their idols, and with energy of arm as well as of tongue made Christianity triumphant along the whole course of the Rhine.

But all these valiant deeds on behalf of the Church availed not to save the memory of Charles Martel from the ecclesiastical ban to which he alone of all the early descendants of St. Arnulf is obnoxious. The ancestors of Charles in their upward struggle towards the supreme power had uniformly leant upon the arm of the Church: but that Church in the disorganization of the later Merovingian monarchy had grown so rich and so headstrong that probably any wise and statesmanlike ruler was bound to come into collision with its hierarchs. That Charles's acts in derogation of its power were all wise and statesmanlike it would be rash to assert. He was a great military chieftain, with a number of hungry followers to provide for. Not only the consolidation of his own power in Neustria and Austrasia, but his border wars with Frisians and Saxons, his tremendous struggle with the Saracens, all had to be carried on by the help of generals and officers versed in the arts of war, who assuredly were not backward in urging their claims to tangible rewards. But the great Crown lands, out of which in earlier days a Merovingian king might have appeased his hungry followers, were, there is reason to think, in large measure by this time alienated to ecclesiastical purposes. It is probable that a large part of the land of Gaul was now held of the Church under the name of *beneficia* by tenants who were bound to make a certain yearly payment to their ecclesiastical lords. What Charles Martel appears to have done in the difficult circumstances in which he found himself, was not indeed to order a general confiscation of Church property—of that he seems to be unjustly accused—but in many cases to use the right of resumption of grants which at least theoretically resided in the Crown, in order to take away lands from a bishopric here or a monastery there, and bestow them on some stout warrior whom he was sending as Count to rule a distant province or to fight the Frisian or the Saracen. In many such cases the actual occupation of the soil would not be changed, but the holder of the *beneficium* would be ordered to pay his rent (as we should call it) not to the Churchman but to the Count.

Of course these acts of spoliation, however necessary they may have been for the salvation of the state, were resented by the ecclesiastics at whose expense they were performed. A proceeding which looked less violent but which was really far more perilous to the best life of the Church, was the bestowal on Charles's own henchmen—mere warriors without any pretence to the religious character—of the prelacies and abbacies which were endowed for a very different purpose. Nor did he confine himself to bestowing one only at a time upon his favourites. The pluralist abuse now also crept into the Church. His follower Milo ('who was a clergyman only by his tonsure') received the headship of the convents of Trier and Rheims; and his nephew Hugo was actually crowned with the three mitres of Paris, Rouen, and Bayeux, and was at the same time abbot of Fontenelle and Jumièges.

Such a high-handed policy towards the Church was certain to excite the anger of the ecclesiastics who had it in their power to bless or to curse, in this world at any rate, if not in the next. Possibly also Charles's refusal to aid the Pope against the Lombards may have added an article to the indictment against him. In the next century, Archbishop Hincmar, writing the life of St. Eucherius, bishop of Orleans, related that the saint, being one day engaged in prayer, was allowed to have a beatific vision of the other world, in the course of which by the gift of the Lord he was permitted to see Charles tormented in the lowest hell. Enquiring the cause of this punishment, Eucherius was told by an angel that in Charles's case the judgment of the last day was anticipated, and that he had to suffer the punishment not only of his own sins but of the sins of all those who had devised lands and houses for the support of the servants of Christ and for lighting candles in the churches, but whose pious intentions had been frustrated by his confiscations. On recovering consciousness the saint called to him St. Boniface and Fulrad abbot of St. Denis and bade them go to the church and open Charles's tomb. If they found that empty they would surely then believe that he had seen a true vision. They went; they opened the vault; a dragon issued forth, and all the interior of the vault was black and charred with fire. "This is written", says the chronicler, "that all who read it may take note of the righteous damnation of him by whom the property of the Church has been unjustly taken away".

So wrote Hincmar about the middle of the ninth century. The story is hard to believe, since the bishop Eucherius died three years before Charles Martel.

CHAPTER IV.

DUKES OF BAVARIA.

There is a neighbour land of Italy to whose history we must give some little attention if we would understand the events which preceded and followed the downfall of the Lombard state.

We have seen how closely for more than a century the dynasty which reigned over the Lombards was connected with the rulers of Bavaria. The two countries touched most closely in that region which we now know as the Tyrol, where the valley of the Adige from a little above Trent downwards was ruled by a Lombard duke, while the upper waters of the Adige and the Eisach, with the Vintschgau, Meran, Botzen and Brixen were all as a rule subject to the Bavarians. With the addition of this Alpine territory and of Upper Austria and Salzburg and with the subtraction of a strip of land west of the river Lech, and of the valley of the Main in the north-west, the duchy of Bavaria corresponded pretty closely with the modern kingdom of that name. A large square block of fruitful land watered by the Danube and the Inn, this duchy, bordering on Alamannia on the west and Italy on the south, was sure to play an important part in the politics of central Europe. The Bavarians themselves appear to have been a Suevic tribe who wandered into the old Roman province of Vindelicia, then lying desolate and unoccupied, a sort of No-man's-land between the Danube and the Alps, and to have settled there in the early part of the sixth century. Almost from the very beginning of their Danubian settlement they seem to have been subject to the overlordship of the Frankish kings, but the yoke was lightly imposed, perhaps as the result of peaceful arrangement rather than of war, and does not appear to have involved, as in many other cases, the payment of a tribute.

Almost at the outset of their history as settlers in Vindelicia we find the Bavarians under the leadership of a great ducal house, the Agilolfings. Of the origin of this family we have no certain information, but there are many indications which point to the conclusion that they were themselves of Frankish descent, possibly allied to the Merovingian kings.

The first of these Agilolfing rulers of whom history makes mention is Garibald, husband of the Lombard princess Walderada, who was the divorced wife of the Frankish king Chlotochar. His daughter Theudelinda was the celebrated and saintly queen of the Lombards. The reader may remember the romantic stories of her wooing by the disguised Authari and of the cup of wine which she handed to the favoured Agilulf. From some cause which is unknown to us Garibald incurred the displeasure of his Frankish lords and probably had to submit to a Frankish invasion. There is no proof however that he lost his ducal crown, and about the year 596 he seems to have been succeeded by a son named Tassilo I (596-611). It is indeed nowhere distinctly stated that this was the relationship between the two princes, but the fact that Tassilo's son and successor was named Garibald II renders it probable.

Of the reigns of these early dukes of Bavaria we know very little, nor can we with any certainty fix the date of the second Garibald's possession of power. It seems clear, however, that through the greater part of the seventh century the bond of allegiance to the Frankish monarchy was growing looser and looser; *fainéant* Merovingian kings and warring Mayors of the Palace having little power to enforce its obligations. The duke seems to have surrounded himself with seneschal and marischal and all the other satellites of a sovereign prince, and his capital, Ratisbon on the Danube, doubtless outshone Paris and Metz in the eyes of his Bavarian subjects.

With the accession to the ducal throne of Theodo I (660-722) we gain a clearer vision of Bavarian affairs from the lives of the saints, Rupert, Emmeran, and Corbinian, who came from Gaul and from Ireland to effect the conversion of the people. It is indeed surprising to us who have witnessed the earnest zeal of the Bavarian Theudelinda, not merely for Christianity but for orthodoxy among her Italian subjects, to find that, two generations later, her own Bavarian countrymen still needed conversion. But apparently the Christianity of Garibald's court was not much more than a court fashion (the result very possibly of his own Frankish origin), and had not deeply leavened the mass of his subjects. Probably we are in the habit of under-estimating the stubbornness of the resistance of Teutonic heathenism to the new faith. When a tribe like the Franks or the Burgundians settled in the midst of a people already imbued with Christian ideas through their subjection to the Empire, it was comparatively easy to persuade them to renounce idolatry or to change the Arian form of Christianity for the Athanasian. But when the messengers of the Church had to deal with nations all Teutonic and all heathen, like the Frisians, the Saxons, or the Bavarians, the process of conversion (as we know from the history of our own forefathers) was much slower and more laborious. Thus it came to pass that in the middle of the seventh century the mass of the Bavarian folk were apparently still heathen, worshipping the mysterious goddess Nerthus, and venerating a statue of Irmin in the sacred wood, feasting on horse-flesh in the half-ruined temple which had perhaps once been dedicated to Jupiter or Isis, and offering, with drunken orgies, sacrifices of rams and goats beside the bier of their dead comrades, to commemorate their entrance into Walhalla.

Into this rude, more than half-Pagan world came towards the end of the seventh century bishop Rupert or Hroudbert of Worms. His ancestry and birthplace are doubtful. Some have described him as sprung from Ireland, while others make him a Frank, of kin to the royal house of the Merovingians. He came into Bavaria, we are told, at the invitation of the duke, but probably also with the full consent if not at the actual suggestion of the great Frankish Mayor, Pippin of Heristal, who at this time not only by warlike expeditions but also by wise and politic counsels was tightening once more the loosened bonds which bound the Bavarians as well as the other nations east of the Rhine to the Frankish kingdom.

At the outset of his operations Rupert baptized duke Theodo and then proceeded with the conversion of the heathen remnant of his people to Christianity, reconsecrating old temples which still bore the names we are told of Juno and Cybele, and dedicating them to the Virgin, and ever on the quest for some one place where he might found a monastery which he might make the centre of his missionary work. Not desirous apparently of too near neighbourhood to the ducal court at Ratisbon, he decided at last upon the little Waller See about seven miles from Salzburg, where he founded the monastery of the Church-by-the-Lake (See-Kirche). But not long had he dwelt here when the desolate ruins of the once stately Roman city of Juvavia attracted his notice. Still desolate, two centuries after that destruction which St. Severinus had foretold of them and the other cities of Noricum, they attracted and fascinated him by their mouldering greatness. He obtained from duke Theodo a grant of the old city and of the fort above, with twenty farms and twenty salt-pans at Reichenhall, eighty 'Romans' with their slaves, all the unoccupied lands in the district of Salzburg, and other rights and royalties. High up on that noble hill which still bears the name of the Monk's Mountain Rupert reared his church, which he dedicated to St. Peter, and founded there his monastery, which he put under the guidance of twelve young Franks, his disciples and fellow-countrymen. Such was the beginning of the great and rich bishopric of Salzburg.

It was probably about the time of Rupert's first missionary operations in Bavaria that duke Theodo, now past the middle of life, divided his duchy between himself and three of his sons. Of these sons the only one of whom we hear anything important is Grimwald, whose capital was Freising, about twenty miles north-east of Munich, and who probably ruled over that part of Bavaria which lies between the Danube and the Alps.

Soon after this division of the duchy and about the time of the death of Pippin of Heristal, we may conjecturally place the appearance of the second great Frankish missionary in Bavaria, *Emmeran* of Poitiers: a meteoric appearance which heralded storm and was strangely quenched in darkness. Emmeran came, we are told, into Bavaria, intending only to traverse the country on his way to the barbarous Avars, of whom he desired to make proselytes. He came to the strongly fortified city of Ratisbon and stood before duke Theodo, but an interpreter was needed to mediate between the speech of Aquitaine and the speech of Bavaria. He explained to the duke the object of his mission, and Theodo replied, "That land to which thou wouldest fain go, on the banks of the Ens, is lying all waste and desolate, through the incursions of the Avars. Stay rather here and I will make thee bishop in this province, or give thee the oversight of some abbey". And Emmeran, learning that the conversion of the Bavarians was yet but half-accomplished and that they still blended their heathen sacrifices with the Supper of the Lord, was persuaded to stay in that fruitful land, whose inhabitants pleased him well, and he preached there during three years.

Now Emmeran was a man of noble stature and comely face, generous both of speech and of money, and 'extraordinarily affable to women as well as to men': evidently a courtly bishop rather than an austere recluse. Unfortunately at the end of the three years the princess Ota, duke Theodo's daughter who had fallen into sin, accused the Frankish missionary as her seducer, and either through consciousness of guilt, or through unworldly carelessness as to his good name, he took no steps to clear himself of the charge. He left Bavaria indeed, but it was not to prosecute his journey to Avar-land, but to cross the Alps to Rome. A son of duke Theodo named Lantpert pursued after him, and having overtaken him ere he had reached the mountains, inflicted upon him the punishment of an incontinent slave, mutilation of the tongue, the hands and the feet. He died of his wounds, and the Church (which was persuaded of his innocence of the charge against him) reverenced him as a martyr.

In the year 716, soon probably after the death of Emmeran, Theodo with a long train of dependants visited Rome to pray at the tomb of St. Peter. As has been already suggested, the visit was probably connected in some way with the terrible event which had preceded it, and it is possible that the reconciliation of the ducal family to the Pope may have been accomplished at the price of some concessions which made the Bavarian Church more dependent on the see of Rome.

The third great Frankish missionary, *Corbinian*, was a man of hot and choleric temper, and he, like Emmeran, had his quarrels with the ducal house of Bavaria, though they did not for him end in such dire disaster. Born at a place called Castrus near Melun about the year 680, he was the son of a mother already widowed who probably fostered her child's domineering and impetuous disposition. He seems also to have been a man of wealth and some social importance, and accordingly, when his genius took the direction of miracle-working and monastic austerity, the fame of his young saintliness easily penetrated the court and reached the ears of the aged Pippin of Heristal, who probably encouraged him to turn his energies to the building up of a Frankish-Christian Church in barbarous Bavaria. After fourteen years of retirement in his cell, he journeyed to Rome, 'in order to ask of the Pope permission to spend his life in solitude',' says his admiring biographer Aribo. But the Pope, we are told, perceiving his fitness for active work in the Church, and determined that he should not hide his light under a bushel, utterly refused to grant him the required permission to lead an anchorite's life, pushed him rapidly through all the lower grades of the hierarchy and consecrated him bishop, without however assigning him any definite see, so that he must have been looked upon as a bishop *in partibus*. After this consecration we are surprised to hear of his spending the next seven years in the cell of St. Germanus in his native place. This and some other suspicious circumstances of the story incline some scholars to believe that the whole tale of this earlier episcopate is a figment of the biographer.

After this interval of seven years Corbinian appears in Bavaria, intent, we are told, on undertaking a second journey to Rome. He chose, says Aribo, 'the more secret way through Alamannia, Germany, and Noricum' [Bavaria], instead of taking 'the public road' from the regions of Gaul. Arrived in Bavaria he found there the devout Theodo, who had lately accomplished the partition of his duchy with his sons. The eldest survivor of these sons, Grimwald, eagerly welcomed the saint, and offered if he would remain to make him co-heir with his own children, doubtless only of his personal property. Corbinian however rejected this offer, and insisted on continuing his journey to Rome. Finding it impossible to change his purpose, Grimwald dismissed him with large presents and gave him an honourable escort, but at the same time gave secret orders to the dwellers in the Vintschgau that on his return he should be arrested at the moment of his crossing the Bavarian frontier. We see at once that there is something more here than the biographer chooses to communicate. The Bavarian prince looks on the expected return of the great ecclesiastic from beyond the Alps with the same sort of feelings which induced Plantagenet princes to decree the penalties of *praemunire* against any one who should import into England bulls from Rome.

Corbinian accomplished his journey into Italy. He was ill-treated by Husingus, duke of Trent, who stole from him a beautiful stallion which he refused to sell, but was kindly received by king Liutprand at Pavia. He remained here seven days, chiefly occupied in preaching to the king, who listened with gladness to his copious eloquence. When he was leaving the capital he again had one of his horses stolen, by a Lombard courtier, whose dishonesty he detected and whose punishment he foretold. At last after divers adventures he reached Rome, and here, in spite of his entreaties and his tears, the Pope (probably Gregory II) ordered him once more to abjure a life of solitude and to undertake active ecclesiastical work. On his return he again visited Pavia, and on his arrival at that place the first object that met his gaze was the body of the Lombard nobleman who had stolen his horse laid upon a bier and carried forth to burial. The horse was restored, and the widow of the culprit, grovelling at the saint's feet, besought him to accept 200 solidi (£120), which her husband on his death-bed had ordered her to pay as the penalty of his crime

With a long train of horses and servants Corbinian now took his journey up the valley of the Adige in order to return into Bavaria by the pass of the Brenner. Scarcely, however, had he entered the Bavarian territory when by Grimwald's orders he was arrested at Castrum Magense.

And now we hear something more of the cause of Grimwald's fear of the holy man. The Bavarian duke had married a young Frankish lady of noble birth named Piltrudis, who was the widow of his brother Theudebald. Against this kind of union, as we know, Rome uttered strong though not always irrevocable protests, and it was possibly from fear of Corbinian's bringing across the Alps a bull of excommunication of the guilty pair that Grimwald had given orders for his arrest on entering the duchy. However, after a struggle, the details of which are very obscurely given, Corbinian obtained a temporary victory. Grimwald obeyed the order of the saint, backed as he probably was by the Frankish *Major-Domus*, and within the specified time of forty days put away Piltrudis.

It is needless to say that the divorced wife, who is looked upon by the ecclesiastical historians as another Herodias, was full of resentment against the author of her disgrace and vowed to compass his downfall. If we read the story rightly, the saint's own choleric temper—even his biographer confesses that he was easily roused to anger by vice, though ready to forgive—aided her designs.

One day when Corbinian was reclining at the table with the duke he made the sign of the cross over the food set before him, at the same time giving praise to God. But the prince took a piece of bread and thoughtlessly threw it to a favourite hound. Thereat the man of God was so enraged that he kicked over the three-legged table on which the meal was spread and scattered all the silver dishes on the floor. Then starting up from his seat he said, "The man is unworthy of so great a blessing who is not ashamed to cast it to dogs". Then he stalked out of the house, declaring that he would never again eat or drink with the prince nor visit his court.

Some time after this there was another and more violent outbreak of the saint's ill-temper. Riding forth one day from the royal palace he met a woman who, as he was told, had effected the cure of one of the young princes by art-magic. At this he trembled with fury, and leaping from his horse he assaulted the woman with his fists, took from her the rich rewards for the cure which she was carrying away from the palace, and ordered them to be distributed among the poor. The beaten and plundered sorceress, who was perhaps only a skillful female physician, presented herself in Grimwald's hall of audience with face still bleeding from the saintly fists, and clamoured for redress. Piltrudis, who seems to have returned to her old position, seconded her prayer, and Corbinian was banished from the ducal presence. He had already received from his patron a grant of the place upon which he had set his heart, Camina, about five miles north of Meran in the Tyrol, with its arable land, its vineyards, its meadows, and a large tract of the Rhaetian Alps behind it, and thither he retired to watch for the fulfillment of the prophecies which he had uttered against the new Ahab and Jezebel.

The longed-for vindication came partly from foreign arms, partly from domestic treachery. It is possible that Grimwald had to meet a combined invasion both from the north and from the south, for, as Paulus Diaconus informs us, Liutprand, king of the Lombards, 'in the beginning of his reign took many places from the Bavarians'. This may be the record of some warlike operations undertaken in the troublous years which followed the death of old duke Theodo (722), and may point to some attempt on the part of the Lombard king, who had married the niece of Grimwald, to vindicate the claims of her brother Hucpert, whom Grimwald seems to have excluded from the inheritance of his father's share in the duchy. This however is only conjecture, and as Liutprand came to the throne in 712 it is not perhaps a very probable one. But it is certain that in 725 the great Frankish Mayor, Charles Martel, entered the Bavarian duchy, possibly to support the claims of Hucpert, but doubtless also in order to rivet anew the chain of allegiance which bound Bavaria to the Frankish monarchy. In 728 he again invaded the country, and this invasion was speedily followed by the death of Grimwald (729). He was slain by conspirators says the biographer of Corbinian, who adds, with pious satisfaction, that all his sons, 'deprived of the royal dignity, with much tribulation gave up the breath of life', but it is probable that all these events were connected with the blow to Grimwald's semi-regal state which had been dealt by Charles the Hammer.

After one of his invasions of Bavaria, perhaps the first of the two, Charles Martel carried back with him into Frankland two Bavarian princesses, Piltrudis, the 'Herodias' of Corbinian's denunciations, and her niece Swanahild, sister of Hucpert. The latter lady became, after the fashion adopted by these lax moralists of the Carolingian line, first the mistress and afterwards the wife of her captor, and she with the son Grifo whom she bare to Charles caused in after years no small trouble to the Frankish state.

The result of this overthrow of Grimwald was the establishment on the Bavarian throne of his nephew Hucpert, son of Theudebert, brother-in-law of Liutprand the Lombard and Charles the Frank, who ruled for eight uneventful years, at peace apparently with his nominal overlord the Merovingian king and his mighty deputy. On his death in 737 the vacant dignity was given to his cousin Otilo who ruled for eleven years (737-748), and to whom Charles Martel gave his daughter Hiltrudis in marriage.

The reign of Otilo (737-748) was chiefly memorable for the reorganisation of the Bavarian Church by the labours of an Anglo-Saxon missionary, the great archbishop Boniface. The offshoot of Roman Christianity planted in Britain by direction of Gregory the Great had now at last, after much battling with the opposition both of heathenism and of Celtic Christianity, taken deep root and was overspreading the land. It is not too much to say that in the eighth century the most learned and the most exemplary ecclesiastics in the whole of Western Christendom were to be found among those Anglian and Saxon islanders whose not remote ancestors had been the fiercest of Pagan idolaters. But precisely because they were such recent converts and because the question between the Celtic Christianity of Iona and the Roman Christianity of Canterbury had long hung doubtful in the scale, were these learned, well-trained ecclesiastics among the most enthusiastic champions of the supremacy of the Roman see. To us who know what changes the years have brought, it seems a strange inversion of their parts to find the Celtic populations of Ireland and the Hebrides long resisting, and at last only with sullenness accepting, the Papal mandates, while a sturdy Englishman such as Boniface almost anticipates Loyola in his devotion to the Pope, or Xavier in his eagerness to convert new nations to the Papal obedience.

Born at Crediton in Devonshire about 775, and the son of noble parents, the young Wynfrith (for that was his baptismal name), after spending some years in a Hampshire monastery and receiving priest's orders, determined to set forth as a missionary to the lands beyond the Rhine, in order to complete the work which had been began by his fellow-countryman Willibrord. With his work in Frisia and Thuringia we have here no concern. We hasten on to a visit, apparently a second visit, which he paid to Rome about the year 722 when he had already reached middle life. It was on this occasion probably that he assumed the name of Bonifatius; and at the same time he took an oath of unqualified obedience to the see of Rome, the same which was taken by the little suburbicarian bishops of the Campagna, save that they bound themselves to loyal obedience to 'the most pious Prince and the Republic' ,an obligation which Boniface in his contemplated wanderings over central Europe, free from all connection with Imperial Constantinople or with the civic community of Rome, refused to take upon himself. His eager obedience was rewarded by a circular letter from the Pope calling on all Christian men to aid the missionary efforts of 'our most reverend brother Boniface', now consecrated bishop *in partibus infidelium*, and setting forth to convert those nations in Germany and on the eastern bank of the Rhine who were still worshipping idols and living in the shadow of death. At the same time a letter of commendation addressed to the Pope's 'glorious son duke Charles' obtained from Charles Martel a letter under his hand and seal addressed to 'all bishops, dukes, counts, vicars, lesser officers, agents and friends' warning them that bishop Boniface was now under the *mundeburdium* of the great Mayor, and that if any had cause of complaint against him it must be argued before Charles in person.

As has been already observed, the protection thus granted by the mighty Austrasian to the Anglo-Saxon missionary powerfully aided his efforts for the Christianization of Germany. The terror of the Frankish arms, as well as a certain vague desire to watch the issue of the conflict between Christ and Odin, may have kept the Hessian idolaters tranquil while the elderly Boniface struck his strong and smashing blows at the holy oak of Geismar. At any rate, true-hearted and courageous preachers of the faith as were Boniface and the multitude of his fellow-countrymen and fellow-countrywomen who crossed the seas to aid his great campaign, it is clear that the fortunes of that spiritual campaign did in some measure ebb and flow with the varying fortunes of the Frankish arms east of the Rhine.

Some time after the death of Gregory II Boniface again visited Rome (about 737) and received, apparently at this time, from Gregory III the dignity of Archbishop and a commission to set in order the affairs of the Church in Bavaria. In fulfilling this commission he must have had the entire support of the then reigning duke Otilo; but it is not so certain that he was still acting in entire harmony with the Frankish Mayor. We have seen that after his death the memory of Charles Martel was subjected to a process the very opposite of canonization, and there are some indications that at this time the obedient Otilo of Bavaria was looked upon at Borne with more favour than the too independent Mayor of the Palace who refused to help the Pope against his brother-in-law the king of the Lombards. However this may be, it is clear that Boniface accomplished in Bavaria something not far short of a spiritual revolution. He had been instructed by the Pope to root out the erroneous teaching of false and heretical priests and of intruding Britons. The latter clause must be intended for the yet unreconciled missionaries of the Celtic Church. Is it possible that the Frankish emissaries were also looked upon with somewhat of suspicion, that the work of the Emmerans and Corbinians was only half approved at Rome, even as the life of Boniface certainly shines out in favourable contrast with the ill-regulated lives of those strange preachers of the Gospel?

"Therefore",'says the Pope to the Archbishop, "since you have informed us that you have gone to the Bavarian nation and have found them living outside the order of the Church, since they had no bishops in the Church save one named Vivilo [bishop of Passau], whom we ordained long ago, and since with the assent of Otilo, duke of the same Bavaria, and of the nobles of the province you have ordained three more bishops and have divided that province into four *parrochiae*, of which each bishop is to keep one, you have done well and wisely, my brother, since you have fulfilled the apostolic precept in our stead. Therefore cease not, most reverend brother, to teach them the holy Catholic and Apostolic tradition of the Roman see, that those rough men may be enlightened and may hold the way of salvation whereby they may arrive at eternal rewards".

Here then at the end of the fourth decade of the eighth century we leave the great Anglo-Saxon archbishop uprooting the last remnants of heathenism which his predecessors had allowed to grow up alongside of the rites of Christianity ; forbidding the eating of horseflesh, the sacrifices for the dead, and the more ghastly sacrifices of the living for which even so-called Christian men had dared to sell their slaves; everywhere working for civilization and Christianity, but doubtless at the same time working to bring all things into more absolute dependence on the see of Rome. In him we see the founder, perhaps the unconscious founder, of that militant and lavishly endowed Churchmanship which found its expression later on in the great Elector-Bishoprics of the Rhine. We shall meet again in future chapters both with Boniface and with the Dukes of Bavaria.

CHAPTER V.

THE GREAT RENUNCIATION.

The five years from 740 to 744 may be said to mark the close of a generation, for during that short period the thrones of Constantinople and of Pavia, the Frankish mayoralty and the Roman papacy, were all vacated by death.

On the 18th of June, 740, died the great Iconoclast Emperor, Leo the Third, after a reign of twenty-four years, marked by many great calamities, by earthquake, pestilence and civil war, but also by legal reforms, by 7a fresh bracing up of the energies of the state both for administration and for war, by the repulse of a menacing attack of the Saracens on Constantinople, and by a great victory over their army gained by the Emperor in person in the uplands of Phrygia. Leo III was Emperor succeeded by his son Constantine V, to whom the ecclesiastical writers of the image-worshipping party have affixed a foul nickname, and whose memory they have assailed with even fiercer invective than that of his father. He was undoubtedly a harsh and overbearing man, who carried through his father's image-breaking policy with as little regard for the consciences of those who differed from him as was shown by a Theodosius or a Justinian, but he was also a brave soldier and an able ruler, one of the men who by their rough vigour restored the fainting energies of the Byzantine state. While he was absent in Asia Minor continuing his father's campaigns against the Saracens, his brother-in-law, the Armenian Artavasdus, grasped at the diadem, and by the help of the image-worshipping party succeeded in maintaining himself in power for nearly three years; but Constantine, who had been at first obliged to fly for his life, received steadfast and loyal support from the troops quartered in the Anatolic theme, and by their aid won two decisive victories over his rival. After a short siege of Constantinople he was again installed in the imperial palace, and celebrated his triumph by chariot races in the Hippodrome, at which Artavasdus and his two sons, bound with chains, were exposed to the derision of the populace. With this short interruption the reign of Constantine V lasted for thirty-five years (740-775), a period during which memorable events were taking place in Western Europe.

On the 10th of December, 741, Pope Gregory II died and was succeeded (as has been already stated) by Zacharias, whose pontificate lasted for more than ten years. The new Pope, like so many of his predecessors, was a Greek : in fact, for some reason which it is not easy to discern, it was a rare thing at this time for the bishop of Rome to be of Roman birth. Among the more important events of his pontificate were those interviews with Liutprand at Terni (742) and at Pavia (29 June, 743) which resulted in the surrender of the Lombard conquests in Etruria, the Sabine territory, and the district round Ravenna, and which have been fully described in an earlier volume. But far the most important act of the papacy of Zacharias was that consent which near the close of his life he gave to the change of the royal dynasty of the Franks, a transaction which will form the subject of the following chapter.

Two months before this change in the wearer of the papal tiara had come that vacancy in the office of the Frankish mayoralty which, as before stated was caused by the death of Charles Martel at Carisiacum (October 21, 741).

Two sons, Carloman and Pippin, the issue of his first marriage, inherited the greater part of the vast states which were now practically recognized as the dominions of the great *Major Domus*, who for the last four years had been ruling without even the pretence of a Merovingian shadow-king above him. Of these two young men, Carloman, the eldest, was probably about thirty, Pippin about twenty-seven when they became possessed of supreme power by the death of their father. As far as we can discern anything of their respective characters from the scanty indications in the chronicles, Carloman seems to have been the more impulsive and passionate, but perhaps also the more generous, and, in the deeper sense of the word, the more religious of the two brothers. Pippin seems to have been of calmer mood, clement and placable, a good friend to the Church, but also a man who from beginning to end had a pretty keen sense of that which would make for his own advantage in this world or the next.

In the division of the inheritance, Carloman, as the elder son, received all the Austrasian lands, the stronghold of the Arnulfing family, together with Swabia and Thuringia. To Pippin fell as his share Neustria, Burgundy, and the reconquered land of Provence. That Bavaria in the east and Aquitaine in the west are omitted in the recital of this division is a striking proof of the still half-independent condition of those broad territories.

But besides several confessedly illegitimate sons of the late Major Domus, there was one who both by his mother's almost royal birth and by the fact of her marriage (possibly after his birth) to Charles Martel had some claim, not altogether shadowy, to share in the inheritance. This was Grifo, son of the Bavarian princess Swanahild, at the time of his father's death a lad of about fifteen. Already during Charles Martel's lifetime Swanahild appears to have played the part of a turbulent wife, and in league with Gairefrid, count of Paris, to have actually barred her husband out of his Neustrian capital and appropriated some part of the revenues of the great abbey of S. Denis. Either the turbulence of the rebellious or the blandishments of the reconciled wife appear to have so far prevailed with the dying Mayor of the Palace that he left to the young Grifo a principality in the centre of his dominions carved out of the three contiguous states, Austrasia, Neustria, and Burgundy. But almost immediately on Charles's death the discord between Swanahild's son and his brothers burst into a flame. Whether Grifo took the initiative, occupied Laon by a *coup de main*, and declared war on his brothers aiming at the exclusive possession of the whole realm, or whether the Franks, hating Swanahild and her son, rose in armed protest against this division of the realm and blockaded Grifo in his own city of Laon, we cannot determine. In either case the result was the same: Laon surrendered, Grifo was taken captive, and handed over to the custody of Carloman, who for six years kept him a close prisoner at 'the New Castle' near the Ardennes. Swanahild was sent to the convent of Chelles, where she probably ended her days.

A little more than two years after the death of Charles Martel, in January, 744, his brother-in-law Liutprand, king of the Lombards, also departed this life. The papal biographer who records the death of a wise and patriotic king with unholy joy attributes it to the prayers of Pope Zacharias, calumniating, as we may surely believe, that eminent pontiff, who had received many favours from Liutprand, and who seems also to have been a man of kindlier temper than many Popes, and still more than the Papal biographers.

On the death of Liutprand, his nephew and the partner of his throne, Hildeprand, succeeded of course to the undivided sovereignty. That unhelpful prince, however, whose whole career corresponded too closely with the ill omen which marked his accession, was after little more than half a year dethroned by his discontented subjects. In his stead Ratchis, the brave duke of Friuli, son of Pemmo victor of the Sclovenic invaders and hero of the fight at the bridge over the Metaurus, was chosen king of the Lombards. His accession appears to have taken place in the latter part of September, 744. What became of his dethroned rival we know not, but the silence of historians is ominous as to his fate.

Immediately on his accession Ratchis concluded a truce with Pope Zacharias, or rather perhaps with the civil governor of the *Ducatus Romae*, which was to last for twenty years: and in fact the relations between Roman and Lombard were peaceable ones during almost the whole of his short reign. But now that we have lost the guidance of Paulus Diaconus—an irreparable loss for this period—it is practically impossible to continue the narrative in the court of the Lombard kings. History will insist in concerning herself chiefly with the actions of four men—Zacharias the Greek, Boniface the man of Devonshire, and the two Frankish Mayors of the Palace. When she is not listening to the discussions in the Lateran patriarchate, she overpasses the Alps and waits upon the march of the Frankish armies, or follows the archbishop of Germany in his holy war against paganism and heresy.

The troubles of Carloman and Pippin did not end with the suppression of Grifo's rebellion. All round the borders of the realm the clouds hung menacing. In Aquitaine, Hunold son of Eudo was again raising his head and endeavouring to assert his independence. Otilo of Bavaria had probably abetted the revolt of his nephew Grifo, and certainly chafed like Hunold under the Frankish yoke. The Alamanni in the south, the Saxons in the north, were all arming against the Franks. It was probably in part at least as the result of these troubles that the two brothers determined to 'regularise their position', if we may borrow a word from the dialect of modern diplomacy, by seating another shadow on the spectral throne of the Merovingians. Since the death of Theodoric IV in 737 there had been no *fainéant* king sitting in a royal villa or nominally presiding over the national assembly of the *Campus Martius*. A certain Childeric, third king of that name and last of all the Childerics and Chilperics and Theodorics who for the previous century had been playing at kingship, was drawn forth from the seclusion probably of some monastery, was set on the archaic chariot to which the white oxen were yoked, was drawn to the place of meeting, and solemnly saluted as king. This Childeric's very place in the royal pedigree is a matter of debate. In the documents which bear his name he meekly alludes to 'the famous man Carloman, Mayor of the Palace, who hath installed us in the throne of this realm'. That he was enthroned in 743 and dethroned in 751 is practically all that is known of this melancholy figure, *ignavissimus Hildericus.*

Having thus guarded themselves against the danger of an attack from behind in the name of Merovingian legitimacy, Carloman and Pippin, who always wrought with wonderful unanimity for the defence of their joint dominion, entered upon a campaign against Otilo, duke of Bavaria. Otilo, as has been said, had probably aided his young nephew Grifo in his attempt at revolution. He had also formed a league with Hunold, duke of Aquitaine, and with Theobald, duke of the Alamanni, and openly aimed at getting rid of the overlordship of the Frankish rulers. Further to embitter the relations between the two states, he had married Hiltrudis, daughter of Charles Martel, contrary to the wish of her two brothers. To avenge all these wrongs and to repress all these attempts at independence 'the glorious brothers' led their army into the Danubian plains and encamped on the left bank of the Lech, the river which flows past Augsburg and was then the western boundary of the Bavarian duchy. On the opposite bank was the Bavarian army, with a large number of Alamannic, Saxon, and Sclavic auxiliaries. So the two armies lay for fifteen days. The river was deemed unfordable, yet Otilo as a matter of extraordinary precaution had drawn a strong rampart round his camp.

The fortnight passed amid the jeers of the threatened Bavarians. Possibly too there may have been some heart-searching in the tent of the Frankish Mayors, for near the close of that period there appeared in the camp the presbyter Sergius, a messenger from Pope Zacharias, professing to bring the papal interdict on the war and a command to leave the land of the Bavarians uninvaded. However, at the end of the fifteen days the Franks, who had found out a ford by which waggons were wont to pass, crossed the Lech by night, and with forces divided into two bands fell upon the camp of the Bavarians. The unexpected attack was completely victorious; the rampart apparently was not defended; the Bavarian host was cut to pieces, and Otilo himself with a few followers escaped with difficulty from the field and placed the river Inn between himself and his triumphant foe. Theobald the Alamannic duke, who must have been also present in the Bavarian camp, saved himself by flight. But the priest Sergius was taken, and with Gauzebald, bishop of Ratisbon, was brought into the presence of the two princes. Thereupon Pippin with calm soul addressed the trembling legate. "Now we know, master Sergius, that you are not the holy apostle Peter, nor do you truly bear a commission from him. For you said to us yesterday that the Apostolic Lord, by St. Peter's authority and his own, forbade our enterprise against the Bavarians. And we then said to you that neither St. Peter nor the Apostolic Lord had given you any such commission. Now then you may observe that if St. Peter had not been aware of the justice of our claim he would not this day have given us his help in this battle. And be very sure that it is by the intercession of the blessed Peter the Prince of Apostles and by the just judgment of God that it is decreed that Bavaria and the Bavarians shall form part of the Empire of the Franks".

The invading army remained for fifty-two days in the conquered province. Otilo seems to have visited the Frankish court as a suppliant, and obtained at length (perhaps not till after the lapse of a year) the restoration of his ducal dignity, but with his dependence on the Frankish overlords more stringently asserted than before, and with a considerably diminished territory, almost all the land north of the Danube being shorn away from Bavaria and annexed to Austrasia. Otilo appears to have lived about five years after his restoration to his duchy, and to have died in 748, leaving an infant son Tassilo III, of whose fortunes much will have to be said in the following pages.

For the time, however, we are more concerned with the relation of Carloman and Pippin to Pope Zacharias; and this indeed is that which has made it necessary to tell with some detail the story of the Bavarian campaign. Priest Sergius said that he brought a message from the Pope forbidding the Frankish princes to make war on Bavaria. Is it certain that he had not in truth such a commission? He is spoken of by the annalist as the envoy of the Pope, and though after the battle of the Lech it might be convenient for the Pope and all belonging to him to acquiesce in the decision of St. Peter as manifested by the disaster to the Bavarian arms, it is by no means clear that Zacharias, both as a lover of peace desirous to stay the effusion of Christian blood and also as a special ally and patron of the lately Christianized Bavarian state, did not endeavour by spiritual weapons to repel the entrance of the Franks into that land. Late and doubtful as is the source from which the story of the mission of Sergius is drawn, it has a certain value as coinciding with other indications to make us believe that the Papacy still looked coldly on the Frankish power, that the remembrance of Charles Martel and his high-handed dealings with Church property was still bitter, and that we are yet in 743 a long way from that entire accord between Pope and Frankish sovereign which is the characteristic feature of the second half of the eighth century.

To the influence of one man, a countryman of our own, more than to any other cause was this momentous change in the relation of the two powers to be attributed. The amalgam between these most dissimilar metals, the mediator between these two once discordant rulers, was Boniface of Crediton, the virtual Metropolitan of North Germany. We have already seen how he consolidated the ecclesiastical organization of Bavaria, reducing it, as an old Proconsul of the Republic might have done, into the form of a province abjectly submissive to Rome. Thuringia and Hesse felt his forming hand. From Carloman, who was becoming more and more fascinated by his religious fervour, he obtained a grant of sixteen square miles of sylvan solitude in the modern territory of Hesse Cassel, where he founded the renowned monastery of Fulda, which he destined for the retreat of his old age. But not yet did he dream of retiring from his church-moulding labours. His influence was felt even in Neustria, and he might almost have been called at this time the Metropolitan of the whole Frankish realm.

Devoted as Boniface was to the cause of the Papacy, he shrank not from speaking unpalatable truths even to the Pope when he deemed that the cause of the good government of the Church required him to do so. In the collection of his letters there are some which remarkably illustrate this freedom of speech on the part of the English missionary. In one, Boniface calls upon Zacharias to put down the 'auguries, phylacteries and incantations' detestable to all Christians, which were practised on New Year's Day by the citizens of Rome, probably in order to obtain a knowledge of the events which should happen in the newly-opened year. Then again, after Boniface had prayed the Pope to grant the archiepiscopal *pallium* to the bishops of Rouen, Rheims and Sens, and Zacharias had agreed to the proposal and sent the coveted garments, Boniface seems to have changed his mind and limited his request to one only, on discovering or suspecting that the Papal curia was asking an exorbitant sum for each of the *pallia*. Even the gentle Zacharias was roused to wrath by what seemed to him the inconstancy and suspiciousness of his correspondent. "We have fallen", he said, "into a certain maze and wonderment on the receipt of your letters, so discordant from those which you addressed to us last August. For in those you informed us that by the help of God and with the consent and attestation of Carloman you had held a council, had suspended from their sacred office the false priests who were not worthy to minister about holy things, and had ordained three archbishops, giving to each his own metropolis, namely to Grimo the city which is called Rodoma (Rouen), to Abel the city which is called Remi (Rheims), and to Hartbert the city which is called Sennis (Sens). All which was at the same time conveyed to us by the letters of Carloman and Pippin in which you [all three] suggested to us that we ought to send three *pallia* to the before-mentioned prelates, and these we granted to them accordingly for the sake of the unity and reformation of the Churches of Christ. But now on receiving this last letter of yours we are, as we have said, greatly surprised to hear that you in conjunction with the aforesaid princes of Gaul have suggested one *pallium* instead of three, and that for Grimo alone. Pray let your Brotherhood inform us why you first asked for three and then for one, that we may be sure that we understand your meaning and that there may be no ambiguity in this matter. We find also in this letter of yours what has greatly disturbed our mind, that you hint such things concerning us as if we were corrupters of the canons, abrogators of the traditions of the fathers, and thus—perish the thought— were falling along with our clergy into the sin of simony, by compelling those to whom we grant the pallium to pay us money for the same. Now, dearest brother, we exhort your Holiness that your Brotherhood do not write anything of this kind to us again; since we find it both annoying and insulting that you should attribute to us an action which we detest with all our heart. Be it far from us and from our clergy that we should sell for a price the gift which we have received from the favour of the Holy Ghost. For as regards those three *pallia* which as we have said we granted at your request, no one has sought for any advantage from them. Moreover, the charters of confirmation, which according to custom are issued from our chancery, were granted of our mere good will, without our taking anything from the receivers. Never let such a crime as simony be imputed to us by your Brotherhood, for we anathematize all who dare to sell for a price the gift of the Holy Spirit".

It would be of course a hopeless attempt to endeavour to ascertain the cause of this strange misunderstanding between two men who seem to have been both in earnest in their desire for the good government of the Church. Certainly the impression which we derive from the correspondence is that the Papal Curia was charging a fee for the bestowal of the pallium, and such an exorbitant fee that Boniface felt that he must limit his application to one, when in the interests of the Gaulish Church he would have desired to appoint three archbishops. It may perhaps be conjectured that the officials of the Curia were in this matter obeying only their own rapacious instincts and were acting without the knowledge of their chief, whose character, if we read it aright, was too gentle and unworldly to make him a strenuous master of such subordinates. It speaks well for the earnestness and magnanimity of both Pope and Bishop that the friendly relations between them do not appear to have been permanently disturbed. Even the letter just quoted concludes with these words: "You have asked if you were to have the same right of free preaching in the province of Bavaria which was granted you by our predecessor. Yes, God helping us, we do not diminish but increase whatever was bestowed upon you by him. And not only as to Bavaria, but as to the whole province of the Gauls, so long as the Divine Majesty ordains that you shall live, do you by that office of preaching which we have laid upon you study in our stead to reform whatsoever you shall find to be done contrary to the canons and to the Christian religion, and bring the people into conformity with the law of righteousness".

It will be seen how wide was the commission thus given to Boniface, covering in fact the whole Frankish realm. In conformity therewith we find him holding synods, not only in Austrasia under the presidency of Carloman, but also in Neustria under that of his brother; the object of both synods and of others held at Boniface's instigation being the reform of the morals of the clergy, the eradication of the last offshoots of idolatry, the tightening of the reins of Church discipline. Churchmen were forbidden to bear arms or to accompany the army except in the capacity of chaplains. They were not to keep hawks or falcons, to hunt, or to roam about in the forests with their dogs. Severe punishments were ordained for clerical incontinence, especially for the not uncommon case of the seduction of a nun. A list of survivals of heathenism, rich in interest for the antiquary and the philologer, was appended to the proceedings of one of the synods, as well as a short catechism in the German tongue, containing the catechumen's promise to renounce the devil and all his works, with Thunar, Woden and Saxnote and all the fiends of their company.

By all this reforming zeal Boniface made himself many enemies. Nothing but the powerful support of the Pope and the two Frankish Mayors probably saved him and his Anglo-Saxon companions ('the strangers' as they were invidiously called) from being hustled out of the realm by the Gaulish bishops, who for centuries had scarcely seen a synod assembled. However, with that support and strong in the goodness of his cause Boniface triumphed. At the synod of 745 Cologne was fixed upon as the metropolitan see of 'the Pagan border-lands and the regions inhabited by the German nations', and over this great archbishopric Boniface was chosen to preside. Two years later the metropolitan dignity was transferred to the more central and safer position of Mainz, Boniface still holding the supreme ecclesiastical dignity. In frequent correspondence with Zacharias and steadily supported by him, he deposed a predecessor in the see of Mainz who had in true old German fashion obeyed the law of the blood-feud by slaying the slayer of his father. He procured the condemnation of two bishops whom he accused of wild, but doubtless much exaggerated heresies. We read with regret that Boniface was not content with deposing these men from their offices in the Church, but insisted on invoking the help of the secular arm to ensure their life-long imprisonment.

While these events were taking place in the Church, other events in camps and battlefields were preparing the way for a change in the occupants of the palace, which took all the world by surprise. The two brothers Carloman and Pippin fought as before against the Saxons (745) and against the duke of Aquitaine (746), punishing the latter for his confederacy with Otilo of Bavaria. But against the restless and faith-breaking Alamanni Carloman fought alone, and here his impulsive nature, lacking the counterpoise of Pippin's calmer temperament, urged him into a dreadful deed, and one which darkened the rest of his days. Something, we are not precisely told what, but apparently some fresh instance of treachery and instability on the part of the Alamanni, aroused his resentment, and he entered the Swabian territory with an army. He summoned a *placitum*, a meeting of the nation under arms, at Cannstadt on the Neckar. It is suggested that the avowed object of the *placitum* was a joint campaign against the Saxons, but this is only a conjecture. Apparently however the Alamanni came, suspecting nothing, to the place of meeting appointed by the Frankish ruler. Carloman adroitly stationed his army (doubtless much the more numerous of the two) so as to surround the Alamannic host, and the latter thus found themselves helpless when some sort of signal was given for their capture. Some were taken prisoners, but many thousands, it is said, were slain. Theobald their chief and the nobles who had joined with him in making a league with Otilo were taken, and 'compassionately dealt with according to their several deservings'. Probably this means that there was a kind of judicial enquiry into their cases, and some may have escaped from the general massacre.

When he came to himself and reflected on what he had done, when he saw, it may be, how this unknightly deed, more worthy of the chamberlain of a Byzantine emperor than of a brave duke of the Franks, struck the minds of his brother warriors, Carloman was filled with remorse. This then was the end of all those conversations with Boniface, of all those aspirations after a better and holier life, which had upward drawn his soul. He, the friend of saints, the reformer of Churches, had done a deed which his rude barbarian forefathers, the worshippers of Thunor and Woden, would have blushed to sanction. There was then no possibility of salvation for him in this world of strife and turmoil. If he would win a heavenly crown he must lay down the Frankish mayoralty. "In this year Carloman laid open to his brother Pippin a thing upon which he had long been meditating, namely his desire to relinquish his secular conversation and to serve God in the habit of a monk. Wherefore postponing any expedition for that year in order that he might accomplish Carloman's wishes and arrange for his intended journey to Rome, Pippin gave his whole attention to this, that his brother should arrive honourably and with befitting retinue at the goal of his pilgrimage".

It was near the end of the year 747 when Carloman, with a long train of noble followers, set out for Italy. He visited on his road the celebrated monastery of St. Gall, the friend of Columbanus, which he enriched with valuable gifts. Having therefore probably descended into Italy by the pass of the Splügen, he proceeded at once to Rome, where he worshipped at the tomb of St. Peter, and again gave innumerable gifts to the sacred shrine, among them a silver bow weighing seventy pounds. The fair locks of the Frankish duke were clipped away; he assumed the tonsure and received the monastic habit from the hands of Pope Zacharias. From Rome he withdrew to the solitude of Mount Soracte, and there founded a monastery in honour of Pope Silvester, who was fabled to have sought this refuge from the persecution of the Emperor Constantine.

What visitor to Rome has not looked forth towards the north-western horizon to behold the shape, if once seen never to be forgotten, of Soracte? In winter sometimes, as Horace saw it, 'white with deep snow', in summer purple against the sunset sky, but always, (according to the well-known words of Byron), Soracte

> 'from out the plain
> Heaves like a long-swept wave about to break
> And on the curl hangs pausing.'

But though most travellers are content to behold it from afar, he who would visit Soraete will find himself well rewarded for the few hours spent on his pilgrimage. Leaving Rome by the railway to Florence, the modern equivalent of the Via Flaminia, after a journey of about forty miles he reaches a station from which a drive of five miles up towards the hills and out of the valley of the Tiber brings him to Civita Castellana, the representative of that ancient Etruscan city of Falerii which according to Livy's story was voluntarily surrendered to Camillus by the grateful parents whose sons had flogged their treacherous schoolmaster back from the camp to the city.

Aptly is this place called 'the castle-city', for it looks indeed like a natural fortress, standing on a high hill with the land round it intersected by deep rocky gorges, and these gorges lined with caves, the tombs of the vanished Etruscans. Soracte soars above in the near foreground, and thither the traveller repairs, driving for some time through the ilex-woods which border its base, and then mounting upwards to the little town of St. Oreste—a corruption probably of Soracte—which nestles on a shoulder of the mountain. Here the carriage-road ends, but a good bridle-path leads to the convent of S. Silvestro on the highest point of the mountain. Ever as the traveller works his way upwards through the grateful shade of the ilex-woods, he is reminded of Byron's beautiful simile, and feels that he is indeed walking along the crest of a mighty earth-wave, spell-bound in the act of breaking. Here on the rocky summit of the mountain,

2,270 feet above the sea-level, stands the desolate edifice which, though for the most part less than four centuries old, still contains some of the building reared by Carloman in honour of Pope Silvester. Unhappily all the local traditions are concerned with this utterly mythical figure of the papal hermit. The rock on which Silvester lay down every night to sleep, the altar at which he said mass, the little garden in which his turnips grew miraculously in one night from seed to full-fed root, all these are shown, but there is no tradition connecting the little oratory with the far more interesting and historical figure of the Carolingian prince. But the landscape at least, which we see from this mountain solitude, must be the same that he gazed upon: immediately below us Civita Castellana with its towers and its ravines; eastward, on the other side of the valley of the Tiber, the grand forms of the Sabine mountains; on the west the Ciminian forest, the Lago Bracciano, and the faintly discerned rim of the sea; southward the wide plains of the Campagna and the Hollow Mountain which broods over Alba Longa.

 Here, for some years apparently, Carloman abode in the monastery which he had founded. But even lonely Soracte was too near to the clamour and the flatteries of the world. The Frankish pilgrims visiting Rome would doubtless often turn aside and climb the mountain on which dwelt the son of the warrior Charles, himself so lately their ruler. Longing to be undisturbed in his monastic seclusion and fearing to be enticed back again into the world of courtly men, Carloman withdrew to the less accessible sanctuary of Monte Cassino. Of his life there we have only one description, and it reaches us from a somewhat questionable source, the Chronicle of Regino, who lived a hundred years after the death of Carloman; but as the chronicler tells us that he made up his history partly from the narration of old men his contemporaries, we may suffer him to paint for us at least a not impossible picture of the Benedictine life of the Frankish prince. According to this writer, Carloman fled at night from Soracte with one faithful follower, taking with him only a few necessary provisions, and reaching the sacred mountain knocked at the door of the convent and asked for an interview with its head. As soon as the abbot appeared he fell on the ground before him and said, "Father abbot! a homicide, a man guilty of all manner of crimes, seeks your compassion and would fain find here a place of repentance". Perceiving that he was a foreigner, the abbot asked him of his nation and his fatherland, to which he replied, "I am a Frank, and I have quitted my country on account of my crimes, but I heed not exile if only I may not miss of the heavenly father-land". Thereupon the abbot granted his prayer and received him and his comrade as novices into the convent, but mindful of the precept, "Try the spirits whether they are of God", laid upon them a specially severe discipline, inasmuch as they came from far and belonged to a barbarous race. All this Carloman bore with patience, and at the end of a year he was allowed to profess the rule of St. Benedict and to receive the habit of the order. Though beginning to be renowned among the brethren for his practice of every monastic virtue, he was not of course exempted from the usual drudgery of the convent, and once a week it fell to his lot to serve in the kitchen. Here, notwithstanding his willingness to help, his ignorance caused him to commit many blunders, and one day the head-cook, who was heated with wine, gave him a slap in the face, saying, "Is that the way in which you serve the brethren?". To which with meek face he only answered, "God pardon thee, my brother"; adding half-audibly, "and Carloman also". Twice this thing happened, and each time the drunken cook's blows were met by the same gentle answer. But the third time, the faithful henchman, indignant at seeing his master thus insulted, snatched up the pestle with which they pounded the bread that had to be mixed with vegetables for the convent dinner, and with it struck the cook with all his force, saying, "Neither may God spare thee, caitiff slave, nor may Carloman pardon thee".

At this act of violence on the part of a stranger received out of compassion into the convent, the brethren were at once up in arms. The henchman was placed in custody, and next day was brought up for severe punishment. When asked why he had dared to lift up his hand against a serving-brother he replied, "Because I saw that vile slave not only taunt but even strike a man who is the best and noblest of all that I have ever known in this world". Such an answer only increased the wrath of the monks. "Who is this unknown stranger, whom you place before all other men, not even excepting the father abbot himself?". Then he, unable longer to keep the secret which God had determined to reveal, said, "That man is Carloman, formerly ruler of the Franks, who for the love of Christ has left the kingdoms of this world and the glory of them, and who from such magnificence has stooped so low that he is now not only upbraided but beaten by the vilest of men". At these words the monks all arose in terror from their seats, threw themselves at Carloman's feet and implored his pardon, professing their ignorance of his rank. He, not to be outdone in humility, cast himself on the ground before them, declared with tears that he was not Carloman, but a miserable sinner and homicide, and insisted that his henchman's statement was an idle tale trumped up to save himself from punishment. But it was all in vain. The truth would make itself manifest. He was recognized as the Frankish nobleman, and for all the rest of his sojourn in the convent he was treated with the utmost deference by the brethren.

It was in 747 that Carloman entered the convent. Two years later his example was followed by the Lombard king, but there is reason to think that in his case the abdication was not so voluntary an act as it was with Carloman. King Ratchis, we are told, 'with vehement indignation' marched against Perugia and the cities of the Pentapolis. Apparently these cities were not included in the strictly local truce which he had concluded for twenty years with the rulers of the *Ducatus Romae*. But Pope Zacharias, mindful of his previous successes in dealing with these impetuous Lombards, went as speedily as possible northwards with some of the chief men of his clergy. He found Ratchis besieging Perugia, but exhorted him so earnestly to abandon the siege that Ratchis retired from the untaken city. Nay, more, says the papal biographer (for it is his narrative that we are here following), Zacharias awakened in the king's mind such earnest care about the state of his soul, that after some days he laid aside his royal dignity, came with his wife and daughters to kneel at the tombs of the Apostles, received the tonsure from the Pope, and retired to the monastery of Cassino, where he ended his days.

This is the papal story of king Ratchis' abdication, but a study of the laws of his successor seems to confirm the statement (made it is true on no very good authority) that it was really the result of a revolution. This authority, the Chronicon Benedictanum , tells us that the queen of Ratchis, Tassia, was a Roman lady, and that under her influence Ratchis had broken down the old Lombard customs of *morgincap* and *met-fiu* (the money payments made on the betrothal and marriage of a Lombard damsel), and had given grants of land to Romans according to Roman law. All this may have made him unpopular with the stern old-world patriots among his Lombard subjects. But it is conjectured with some improbability that it was their king's retreat from the walls of untaken Perugia and his too easy compliance with the entreaties of Zacharias which at last snapped the straining bond of his subjects' loyalty.

Whatever the cause may have been, the fact is certain. The Lombard throne was declared to be empty, and Aistulf, brother of the displaced king, was invited to ascend it (July, 7491). There may not have been bloodshed, but there was almost certainly resistance on the part of the dethroned monarch, for the first section of the new king's laws, published soon after his accession, provides that, 'As for those grants which were made by king Ratchis and his wife Tassia, all of these which bear date after the accession of Aistulf shall be of no validity unless confirmed by Aistulf himself.'

Thus these two men, lately powerful sovereigns, Carloman and Ratchis, are meeting in church and refectory in the high-built sanctuary of St. Benedict on Monte Cassino. We shall hereafter have to note the emergence of both from that seclusion, on two different occasions and with widely different motives.

CHAPTER VI

THE ANOINTING OF PIPPIN.

On the abdication of Carloman the stream of events in the Frankish state flowed on for a few years with little change. If there was any thought of Carloman's sons succeeding to their father's inheritance, such thought was soon abandoned. Pippin is seen both in Austrasia and Neustria ruling with unquestioned power, nor do we hear any hint of his being a regent on behalf of his nephews. The first act of his sole mayoralty was to release his half-brother Grifo from the captivity in which Carloman had kept him for six years. It proved to be an ill-judged act of mercy, for Grifo, embittered no doubt by his long imprisonment, still refused to acquiesce in his exclusion from sovereign power. It was true that Pippin gave him an honourable seat in his palace, with countships and large revenues. These failed however to soothe his angry spirit. He gathered many of the nobles to his banner, but, unable apparently to conquer any strongholds within the Frankish realm, he fled from the land, and accompanied by a band of young noblemen bent on adventure, he sought the country of the Saxons and the tribe of the Nordo-Squavi. These men were possibly descendants of those Swabians whose settlement in the country of the Saxons and wars with their predecessors returning from the conquest of Italy have been described in a previous volume. Pippin with his army pursued his brother into the Saxon territory. The two hosts encamped not far from the river Ocher in the duchy of Brunswick, but parted without a battle, the Saxons having apparently feared to trust the fortune of war against an adversary of superior strength. Grifo fled to Bavaria, the country of his mother Swanahild, where the opportune death of his cousin and brother-in-law, duke Otilo, seemed to open a convenient field for his ambitious designs. He was at first successful. His sister Hiltrudis and her child, the little duke Tassilo, fell into his hands. For a short time Grifo, who received help both from Bavaria and from Alamannic rebels against the Frankish supremacy, succeeded in establishing himself at Ratisbon, but soon had to meet the irresistible Frankish army. The Bavarian rebels retreated to the further bank of the Inn; Pippin prepared to cross it with his ships, and the Bavarians, affrighted, renounced the combat. Grifo was taken prisoner and was carried back into Frank-land. His long-suffering brother gave him the lordship of twelve Neustrian counties, with Le Mans for his capital; but all was in vain to win back that rebellious soul. In Aquitaine, in Italy, wherever there was an enemy of Pippin, there was Grifo's friend. We will anticipate the course of events by five years in order to end the story of this often-pardoned Pretender. In 753, when a storm was already brewing between Pippin and the Lombard king, Grifo essayed to pass over Mont Cenis into Italy to join his brother's foes. He was stopped at S. Jean de Maurienne by two noblemen loyal to Pippin, Theudo, count of Vienne, and Frederic, count of Transjurane Burgundy. The skirmish which followed seems to have been a desperate one; for all three leaders, both Grifo and the Burgundian counts, were slain. 'Whose death, though he was a traitor to his country, was a cause of grief to Pippin'.

In these central years of the eighth century, where the annals give us such scanty historical details, our fullest source of information as to the thoughts which were passing through the minds of the leaders of the people is furnished by the copious correspondence of the Saxon apostle Boniface. His letters to Pope Zacharias and that Pope's answers are especially interesting, and give us on the whole a favourable impression of the character of both men. They are no doubt, as we have already seen in the case of Aldebert and Clemens, too anxious to use the power of the state for the suppression of what they deem to be heresy, and they may have been too confident in the correctness of their own faculty of distinguishing between divinely inspired truth and dangerous error. For instance, the theory advanced by Virgil, bishop of Salzburg, that there is another world beneath our feet, with inhabitants of its own and lighted by its own sun and moon, does not appear to us such a wicked, atheistic and soul-destroying doctrine as it appeared to Zacharias and Boniface. But in the main, the energies of Pope and Archbishop were directed in the right channel. They laboured together for the eradication of the superstitious, sometimes impure or cruel practices of Teutonic heathendom, for the maintenance of the sanctity of the Christian family, for the restoration of discipline and the elevation of the standard of morals among the nominally Christian Franks of Western Gaul. Throughout this period we are impressed by the moral superiority of both the Saxons and the Germans to the Gallo-Roman inhabitants of Neustria and Burgundy. The 'transmarine Saxons' (as our countrymen are called) and the dwellers by the Rhine and in Thuringia remained much longer stiff and stubborn in their idolatry than the Burgundians or the Salian Franks, but when they did embrace Christianity they submitted to its moral restraints more loyally and aspired after holiness of life more ardently than the inhabitants of those western regions into whose life there had entered not only the softness but something also of the corruptness of the old Roman civilization. It is true that this very same quality of whole-heartedness, as has been already pointed out, made the newly-converted nations much more enthusiastic champions than their Neustrian neighbours of the spiritual autocracy of Rome. The Anglo-Saxon missionary and his German disciples are the Ultramontanes of the eighth century, while even in the indiscipline of the Neustrian ecclesiastics we seem to perceive the germ of the famous Gallican liberties of a later age.

One of the perplexities which pressed most heavily on the conscience of Boniface, and on which he sought the advice both of the Pope and of his brother bishops in England, was the doubt how far he could without sacrifice of his principles exchange the ordinary courtesies of social life with the demoralized and (as he deemed them) heretical prelates of the Frankish court. 'I swore,' he says, 'on the body of St. Peter to the venerable Pope Gregory II, when he sent me forth to preach the word of faith to the German nations, that I would help all true and regularly ordained bishops and presbyters in word and deed, and would abstain from the communion of false priests, hypocrites, and seducers of the people if I could not bring them back into the way of salvation. Now such men as these last do I find, when on account of the Church's necessities I visit the court of the prince of the Franks. I cannot avoid such visits, for without the patronage of that prince I can neither govern the Church itself, nor defend the presbyters and clergy, the monks and the handmaidens of God; nor can I without his mandate and the terror of his name prohibit the rites of the pagans and the sacrilegious worship of idols which prevail in Germany. This being so, though I do not join with these men in the Holy Communion, and though I feel that I have in spirit fulfilled my vow, since my soul has not entered into their counsel, yet I have not been able to abstain from bodily contact with them. Thus on the one side I am pressed by the obligations of my oath, and on the other by the thought of the loss which will be sustained by my people if I should not visit the prince of the Franks.'

In answer to this case of conscience the bishop of Winchester reminded Boniface of the words of St. Paul, 'for then must we needs go out of the world'; and Zacharias assured him that for his conversations with these men, if he was not a sharer in their iniquity, he incurred no blame in the sight of God. If they hearkened to his voice and obeyed his preaching they would be saved, but if they continued in their sin they would perish, while he himself, according to the words of the prophet Ezekiel, would have delivered his own soul.

We obtain a glimpse of the kind of men, ecclesiastical courtiers of Pippin, with whom the zealous Boniface shrank from holding communion, when we read the story of Milo, archbishop of Rheims and of Trier. Son and nephew of bishops, but of bishops who had held also the dignities of duke and of count, and himself brother of a count, this man was an eminent example of that tendency to make the high places of the Church hereditary and to bestow them on members of the nobility, which was also noticeable in the Gaul of Sidonius and of Gregory of Tours. As a soldier he had shared the campaigns of Charles Martel, who, in jovial mood probably, tossed to his battle-comrade the mitre of Rheims. 'An ecclesiastic only in the tonsure' as the scandalized chronicler described him, he soon laid violent hands on the adjacent diocese of Trier. Both provinces seem to have groaned under his yoke, but we are specially told of the diocese of Rheims that he left many of the suffragan bishoprics vacant, handed over the episcopal residences to laymen, and turned the regions under his sway into a sort of ecclesiastical No-man's-land into which flocked all the 'criminous clerks' who fled from the jurisdiction of their own bishops, and there with disorderly monks and nuns lived a life of licence and utter defiance of the Church's discipline. In order to remedy these disorders, Boniface procured the consecration of his countryman Abel as Archbishop of Rheims, and, as we have already seen, obtained for him from the Pope the grant of the coveted pallium. But Pope and apostle alike seem to have been powerless against the stout soldier and court-favourite Milo. The meek stranger Abel soon vanishes from the scene. Milo retains possession not only of one but of both metropolitan sees, and at last, 'after forty years' tyrannical invasion of the Church' (says the chronicler), he meets his death in the forest, not like his great namesake Milo of Crotona in a vain display of his mighty strength, but from the tusks of a wild boar which he has been chasing. The contrast of the lives of the two men, Milo and Boniface, brings forcibly before us the nature of the work which had to be done in demoralized Neustria, and which was at length accomplished by the united exertions of Austrasia and of Rome.

In one of Boniface's letters to the Pope he alludes to 'certain secrets of my own which Lul the bearer of this letter' (the friend and eventually the successor of Boniface) 'will communicate *viva voce* to your Piety.' In this mysterious sentence some commentators have seen an allusion to the approaching revolution in the Frankish kingdom. The conjecture is plausible; the time fits, for the letter must have been written in the autumn of 751, but it is after all nothing but a conjecture. It is, however, probable enough that during the years 749 to 751, of which little is heard in the chronicles, Pippin was preparing the minds of his subjects, and especially of the great churchmen of his court, for the momentous change which was approaching.

That change will be best told in the simple words of the monkish chronicler who wrote the Annales Laurissenses Minores.

'In the year 750 of the Lord's incarnation Pippin sent ambassadors to Rome to Pope Zacharias, to ask concerning the kings of the Franks who were of the royal line and were called kings, but had no power in the kingdom, save only that charters and privileges were drawn up in their names, but they had absolutely no kingly power, but did whatever the *Major Domus* of the Franks desired. But on the [first] day of March in the Campus [Martius], according to ancient custom gifts were offered to these kings by the people, and the king himself sat in the royal seat with the army standing round him and the *Major Domus* in his presence, and he commanded on that day whatever was decreed by the Franks, but on all other days thenceforward he sat [quietly] at home. Pope Zacharias therefore in the exercise of his apostolical authority replied to their question that it seemed to him better and more expedient that the man who held power in the kingdom should be called king and be king, rather than he who falsely bore that name. Therefore the aforesaid Pope commanded the king and people of the Franks that Pippin who was using royal power should be called king, and should be settled in the royal seat. Which was therefore done by the anointing of the holy archbishop Boniface in the city of Soissons : Pippin is proclaimed king, and Childeric, who was falsely called king, is tonsured and sent into a monastery'.

The kindred chronicle, which is called simply Annales Laurissenses, with fewer words gives us some more particulars:—

'Burchard, bishop of Wurzburg, and Folrad the chaplain were sent to Pope Zacharias to ask concerning the kings in Frank-land who at that time had no royal power, whether this were good or no. And Pope Zacharias commanded Pippin that it would be better that he should be called king who had the power, rather than he who was remaining without any royal power. That order might not be disturbed, by his apostolic authority he ordered that Pippin should be made king.'

'Pippin, according to the manner of the Franks, was elected king, and anointed by the hand of archbishop Boniface of holy memory, and he was raised to the kingdom by the Franks in the city of Soissons. But Hilderic, who was falsely called king, was tonsured and sent into a monastery.'

One more entry, this time from the Continuer of Fredegarius, completes the contemporary or nearly contemporary accounts of the great transaction:—

'At which time, by the advice and with the consent of all the Franks, a report was sent to the Apostolic See, and on the receipt of authority [from thence] the lofty Pippin, by the election of the whole Frankish nation into the seat of royalty, with consecration of the bishops and submission of the nobles, together with his queen Bertrada (as the order from of old requires), is raised on high in the kingdom.'

Thus then was the revolution, towards which the whole course of Frankish history had been tending for more than a century, at last consummated. The phantasm disappeared and the reality was hailed by its true name. The unfortunate Childeric, upon whom came the punishment for all the wasted lives of so many licentious Merovingian ancestors, had to end his days in the dreary solitude of his cell. But yesterday the deeds and charters which counted the years from his accession styled him 'gloriosus dominus noster Hildericus'; now he is simply known by some monastic name, brother Martin it may be or brother Felix, in the monastery of St. Medard at Soissons. His wife, according to some accounts, and in the following year his son, were each compelled into the same monastic seclusion. The race of Clovis and Meroveus, the descendants of the sea-monster, disappear from history. Yet who knows? The Merovingian blood may have filtered down into the lowest strata of society. Among the fishwives who dragged Louis XVI in triumph back to Paris from Versailles, among the unwashed rabble who haunted the galleries of the Convention and shouted for the death of that innocent victim, there may have been some men and women who, if they had known the names of their progenitors, might have claimed descent from Dagobert and Chlotochar.

Turning away then from the grave of the Merovingian monarchy, let us contemplate the new monarchy which is installed in the person of the descendant of the sainted Arnulf. We observe that Pippin is 'exalted into the kingdom, according to the ancient manner of the Franks'. We also observe that there is a distinct statement that he was 'elected' to his new dignity. We may therefore assert that on this occasion, in the utter failure and decay of the hereditary principle, there was a reversion to the old Teutonic principle of elective royalty, and we may probably infer that, as the outward and visible sign of that election, Pippin was raised on a buckler amid the acclamations of the assembled warriors of his people, even as Alaric and Clovis had been raised in earlier centuries. It is to be noticed also that the ceremony took place at Soissons, a place which was not a royal residence, and which had not been frequently heard of in the later Merovingian time, but which, on account of its memories of Clovis and Syagrius, was evidently looked upon as one of the holy places of the Frankish monarchy.

Far more important, however, for practical purposes than these sentimental reversions to the old Teutonic usages and associations was the emphatic sanction given by the Roman Church to the new order of things. It may be that the thought of a mission to Rome to enquire of Pope Zacharias was in the first place only an expedient for the quieting of troubled consciences, whether of Pippin himself or of some of his subjects, as to this step, which looked like a breach of trust on the part of the legitimate king's Prime Minister. Thus looked at, the embassy of one Austrasian and one Neustrian ecclesiastic to Rome—Burchardt, bishop of Wurzburg, and Folrad, abbot of S. Denis and private chaplain to the king—may have been somewhat like those embassies which used to be sent to the oracle of Apollo at Delphi when one of the Grecian states was about to enter upon a course of action which strained the obligations of political morality. But with whatever notions undertaken, there can be no doubt that the appeal to Rome on such a subject and at such a crisis of the nation's history enormously increased the authority of St. Peter's representative with the Frankish nation. We have only to look at the language of the chroniclers to see for how much the papal sanction counted in the establishment of the new dynasty. 'The Pope commanded the king and people of the Franks that Pippin should be called king'; 'Pope Zacharias, . . that order should not be disturbed by his apostolic authority, commanded that Pippin should become king '; 'According to the sanction of the Roman pontiff, Pippin was called king of the Franks'; and so on. The tone of the chroniclers seems to be that of men who are describing an event as to the moral colour of which they are not themselves fully satisfied, but they quiet their consciences with the reflection that it must after all have been right because it was sanctioned by the authority of the head of Western Christendom.

To emphasise this fact of the papal consent to the great revolution the chief actor in the religious part of the ceremony was Boniface, of whose untiring devotion to the Roman see so many examples have been given in the preceding pages. True, the other bishops were present, possibly some of them, especially some of the Neustrian bishops, scowling at this officious Saxon who dared to oust the successor of Remigius from his rights and to take the foremost place in their own historical sanctuary of Soissons. But of any such growlings of discontent we have no historic evidence. The fact emphasized by chroniclers and most needlessly questioned by some modern historical sceptics was that Boniface, archbishop and soon to be martyr, performed the solemn ceremony of anointing, probably also the ceremony of crowning, for the new king of the Franks.

By long habit we are so accustomed to the sound of the words 'an anointed king' that we hardly realize its full significance in the case before us. Speaking broadly, it may be said that to pour oil upon the head of the ruler and to anoint therewith his hands and his feet is not a Teutonic, nor even an Aryan, but essentially a Semitic rite. No German *thiudans*, no Greek or Roman *basileus* or *rex*, as far as we know, was ever anointed. The rite comes from the burning East, from that Hebrew people who named 'corn and wine and oil' as the three great voices with which the earth praised Jehovah. 'I have found David My servant, with My holy oil have I anointed him,' was the verse of the Psalms which was doubtless present to the mind of Boniface when he poured the consecrated oil upon the bowed head of the Frankish king. The Eastern emperors, though Christian, had not taken over this ceremony from Judaism. Late in the day, probably about the middle of the seventh century, it had been adopted by the Visigothic kings of Spain. In our own country it seems probable that the petty kings of Wales were anointed, before their Saxon rivals submitted to the rite. However this may be, it is clear that in imitation of Samuel and Zadok the Christian ecclesiastics of the eighth century were now magnifying their office by pouring the oil of consecration on the head that was about to receive a kingly crown. Possibly, as a German scholar suggests, the religious sanction which the Christian Church thus gave to the new dynasty was meant to compensate for the lost glamour of a descent from the gods of Walhalla to which the posterity of St. Arnulf could with no consistency lay claim.

Thus then the elevation of Pippin to the Frankish throne, dictated as it was by the inexorable logic of fact, and heartily acquiesced in by the nation, received the solemn sanction of the great Patriarch of Western Christendom. Such favours are not usually given by ecclesiastics gratuitously. The immediate result of the ceremony at Soissons was undoubtedly the consolidation of the power of Boniface as representing the Pope in Neustria and Burgundy. We may be sure that 'the Gallican liberties' (which in this century meant the Gallican anarchy) suffered a new constraint from the day when Pippin felt the anointing hand of the Apostle of Germany. But the king himself also, by invoking the aid of the bishop of Rome, had incurred an obligation which brought him, and that right speedily, into the troubled zone of Italian politics.

CHAPTER VII

THE DONATION OF CONSTANTINE.

It is one of the commonplaces of history, that in considering the causes which have produced any given event, we have often to deal not only with that which is True and can be proved, but also with that which though False is yet believed. The undoubted fable of the descent of the founders of Rome from the defenders of Troy distinctly influenced the policy of the Republic both in Greece and Asia. Some effect on Jewish history was produced by the story of Judas Maccabeus' treaty with Rome engraved on a tablet of brass. The shadowy and almost fabulous claim of the Saxon kings to lordship over Scotland suggested the wars of Edward the First with the northern kingdom. The so-called 'Will of Peter the Great'—almost certainly spurious—has been a mighty rallying-cry both to friends and foes of the extension of the dominion of the Tsars in Europe and Asia. But there is no need to multiply instances, when the one eminent instance of the fable of the greased cartridges as a plot against the religion of the Sepoy, a fable which so nearly lost us India, is present to the memory of us all.

Just such a fable was working powerfully on the minds of men, at any rate of Roman citizens and ecclesiastics, in the middle of the eighth century; a fable which dealt with the acts and deeds of the great Emperor Constantine and of his contemporary Pope Silvester. Though the body of the Caesar had been for more than four centuries mouldering in its vault in the great church of the Holy Apostles at Constantinople, and though sixty pontiffs had sat in the patriarchal chair of the Lateran since Silvester was carried to his grave, it may be safely said that these two men, or rather not these two men but a mythical Constantine and a mythical Silvester, were then exerting as great an influence as any living Emperor or Pope on the politics of Europe.

In fewest possible words let us recall the events in the life of the historic Emperor *Constantine the Great*. Born about the year 274, the son of an emperor who though a heathen was conspicuously favourable to the Christians, he was acclaimed as Caesar by the soldiers of his deceased father at Eburacum in the year 306. For eighteen years he was engaged more or less continuously in struggles with other wearers of the Imperial diadem. Maximian, Maxentius, Licinius fell before him, until at last, in 324, he emerged from a series of deadly civil wars, sole ruler of the Roman world. At each step of his upward progress some burden was taken off the Christian Church, which from the beginning of his career recognized in him its patron and protector. In the year 313, in concert with his partner in the empire, Licinius, he issued the celebrated Edict of Milan which secured full toleration to the Christians. His own personal relation to the new faith, at least during the middle years of his life, is somewhat obscure. In spite of the story of the miraculous Labarum affixed to his standards in his campaign against Maxentius (312) he appears for some years to have professed, or at all events practised, a kind of eclectic theism, seeking to combine a reverence for Christ with some remains of the paganism which had been hitherto the official religion of the Roman state. But always even during this transition period he took a kindly and intelligent interest in the affairs of the Christian Church, labouring especially for the preservation of its internal harmony. Thus his famous presidency at the council of Nicaea (325) was entirely in keeping with his previous attitude towards the Church ever since he had assumed the diadem. Within three or four years after that celebrated event he wrought his other even more world-famous work, the foundation of the city of Constantinople. Still, though more and more showing himself as the patron of Christianity and making it now not only a permitted but a dominant, almost a persecuting form of faith, he himself postponed for a long while his formal reception into the Christian Church. This took place at last at his villa of Ancyrona in Bithynia, where in the spring of 337 Eusebius the Arian bishop of Nicaea administered to him the rite of Christian baptism, which in a few days was followed by his death.

Contemporary with Constantine during the greater part of his reign was Silvester, who held the office of bishop of Rome from 314 to 335. He was a man apparently of no great force of character, who probably ruled his diocese well (since we hear of no complaints or disputes during his long episcopate), and who was excused on the score of age from attending at the council of Nicaea, at which he was represented by two presbyters. It seems probable that Silvester was the Pope who received from Constantine the gift of the Lateran Palace in the south-east of Rome, with a large and doubtless valuable plot of ground adjoining it, on which the Emperor may have built the great basilica which bears the proud title, 'Omnium ecclesiarum in orbe sedes et caput'. It is quite possible that other estates in the city and in the Italian provinces may have been bestowed upon the Roman see during the papacy of Silvester by the first Christian emperor, who was undoubtedly a generous giver to the Churches throughout his empire.

Such in outline are the figures of the historic Constantine and the historic Silvester. Now let us see how they are drawn and coloured by the legends of later and barbarous centuries.

The Vita Silvestri, a book written probably about the year 500, that is to say nearly two centuries after Silvester's pontificate, describes in the usual style of religious biography the youthful virtues of its hero, his hospitality, his courageously manifested sympathy with Timotheus, a martyr during the persecution of Diocletian, his ordination as deacon and as priest, and his involuntary elevation to the papacy on the death of Miltiades (314). It then goes on to relate some of the marvellous works performed by the new Pope, chief among them the chaining up of a certain noisome dragon which by its baleful breath poisoned the whole city, dwelling as it did in a subterranean cave under the Tarpeian rock, reached by a staircase of three hundred and sixty-five steps. After this event a cruel persecution of the Christians is said to have been set on foot by the Emperor Constantine. Silvester, bowing his head to the storm, departed from Rome and took refuge in a cave on Mount 'Syraption', which later transmitters of the story have identified with Soracte. While he was still in hiding, the Emperor Constantine, as a punishment for his cruelties towards the Christians, was afflicted with a grievous leprosy. The physicians were unable to cure him, and he sought the aid of the priest of the Capitol, who assured him that he could only be healed by bathing in a laver filled with the blood of newly-born infants. A multitude of sucklings from all parts of the empire were collected for the ghastly purification, but with the babes came of course then mothers, who rent the air with such piteous cries that Constantine, moved with pity, countermanded the massacre, declaring that he would rather continue to suffer from his disease than purchase health at the cost of so great sorrow. That night in a dream two venerable figures appeared to him, and as a reward for his forbearance told him that if he would send for Silvester he should by his means be healed of his malady. Messengers were accordingly sent to Soracte, who brought Silvester into the presence of the Emperor. Two pictures were exhibited by the Pope, and Constantine at once recognized in them the likenesses of the personages who appeared to him in his dream.

'What are the names of these gods,' says the Emperor, that I may worship them?'

' They are no gods,' replies the Pope, 'but the holy Apostles Peter and Paul, servants of the living God and of His Son Jesus Christ ' : and thereupon he expounds to him the rudiments of Christianity. Constantine expresses his willingness to receive baptism; they journey to Rome, and the rite is administered in a porphyry vase in the Lateran. At the moment of immersion a bright light dazzles his eyes and the eyes of the beholders. He rises from the lustral waters cured of the plague of leprosy. Constantine then proceeds to issue various edicts on behalf of his new faith. Christ is to be adored throughout his Empire; the blasphemers of His name are to be severely punished; the churches are to be inviolable places of refuge; new churches are to be built out of the proceeds of tithes levied on the imperial domains; the bishops of the whole Empire are to be subject to the Pope, even as the civil magistrates are subject to the Emperor. Constantine himself repairs to the Vatican hill and begins to dig the foundations of the new church of St. Peter. Next day he commences a similar work at the Lateran. He convenes a great assembly of the senate and people of Rome in the *Basilica Ulpiana*, announces his own conversion in the presence of the senators (who for the most part adhere absolutely to their old idolatry), but declares that faith shall be free and that no one shall be forced to become Christian against his will. At this point, however, he receives a letter from his mother, the widowed Empress Helena, residing in Bithynia, who while congratulating him on having renounced the worship of idols, implores him to adopt, not Christianity, but the only true religion, Judaism. Hereupon a disputation is held as to the merits of the two religions, between the Pope on one side and twelve Rabbis on the other. After argument is exhausted, recourse is had to the test of miracles. A bull is brought in, and the Rabbi who champions the faith of Moses whispers in its ear the mysterious Name revealed on Sinai. The bull falls dead, and all the bystanders feel that the Jew has triumphed; but then Silvester draws near and whispers in the creature's ear the name of Christ, whereupon the bull comes to life again and stands upright on its feet. Then the Christian cause is admitted to have triumphed. Constantine sets off for the East to found Constantinople, and Helena repairs to Jerusalem where she discovers the Holy Cross.

Such is the *farrago* of nonsensical romance which, at the period that we have now reached, passed generally current as the true history of the baptism of the first Christian emperor. There is no need to point out how utterly at every turn the story contradicts the undoubted facts of history. The marvellous thing is that these facts had been fully and correctly stated by authors of high repute in the Church, such as Eusebius and Jerome, and the slightest acquaintance with their works must have shown any Roman ecclesiastic that it was impossible that the story told in the *Gesta Silvestri* could be true. When and where it originated can only be a matter of conjecture. Abbé Duchesne, the learned and impartial editor of the *Liber Pontificalis* (into which, strange as it may appear, this extravagant fiction has made its way), thinks that it probably had its origin in the Church of Armenia. Dollinger, without expressing a decided opinion on this point, agrees with Duchesne in the conclusion which has been already stated that the fable obtained credence in Rome about the end of the fifth century, at which time it is alluded to in some of the treatises called forth by the trial of Pope Symmachus From the decision of such experts as these there can be no appeal; but it is certainly difficult to understand how such a wild travesty of the facts could have been believed little more than a century after the death of the son of Constantine; and it is also hard to reconcile the existence of the story in the year 500 with the entire silence respecting it which we find in all the writings of Gregory the Great, yet a hundred years later. Remembering how large a part of his papal life was occupied in controversy with the Patriarch of Constantinople or respectful opposition to his master the Emperor, we find it difficult to understand why there should never be an allusion to a story which, if it had been true, would have so greatly enhanced the glory of the see of Rome at the expense of the see of Constantinople. Possibly the difficulty may be explained by Abbé Duchesne's suggestion that the currency of the story and even the authority of the Liber Pontificalis were at this time confined to the less educated portion of the Roman clergy and laity, and that scholars and statesmen, such as Gregory I, did not confute, because they too utterly despised them

However, preposterous as this story of the conversion of Constantine might be, by frequent repetition through barbarous and ignorant ages it succeeded in getting itself accepted as truth. Even at this day not only the unlettered peasant from the Campagna, but many of the better educated foreign visitors to Rome, who enter the interesting fortress-church of the *Quattro Incoronati*, between the Colosseum and the Lateran, little know what an audacious travesty of history is represented in the quaint frescoes on its walls. They see the unhappy Emperor covered with the spots of leprosy, the glad mothers with their babes restored, the two Apostles appearing to the dreaming sovereign, the gay horsemen seeking Pope Silvester in his cave, the recognition of St. Peter and St. Paul, Constantine standing in the regenerating waters, Constantine kneeling before the Pope and offering him a diadem, Constantine leading Silvester's horse into Rome and walking groomlike by his stirrup : they see all this, and imagine that they are looking on a representation, quaint indeed but not impossible, of events that actually occurred, nor do they grasp the fact that they are looking on a great pictured falsehood, the memory of which and the consequences of which, perturbing all the relations of the Christian Church and the civil ruler, dividing Guelf from Ghibelin and Swabian from Angevin, prolonged for centuries the agony of Italy.

A fiction like that of the Roman baptism of Constantine once taken home into the minds of the people soon gathers round it other fictions. Thus it came to pass that at some uncertain time in the eighth century there was brought to birth the yet more monstrous fiction of *The Donation of Constantine*. The document which purports to contain this donation is of portentous length, containing about five thousand words, and there are in it many repetitions which suggest the idea that its fabricator has added one or two codicils to his original draft, as points occurred to him on which a fuller explanation might be expedient. I extract a few of the more important sentences.

'In the name of the holy and undivided Trinity, Father, Son and Holy Ghost, the Emperor Caesar Flavius Constantinus, ... faithful, gentle, mightiest, beneficent, conqueror of the Goths, of the Sarmatians, of the Germans, of the Britons and of the Huns (!), pious, fortunate, conqueror and triumpher, ever Augustus, to the most holy and blessed Father of Fathers, Silvester, bishop of Rome and Pope, and to all his successors in the seat of St. Peter to the end of the world... and to all the most reverend...Catholic bishops in the whole world who are by this our imperial decree made subject to the same Holy Roman Church,... Grace, peace, charity, joy, long-suffering and compassion from God the Father Almighty, and from Jesus Christ His Son, and the Holy Ghost, be with all of you.'

After a long exposition of his new creed and a repetition of the story of the leprosy, the vision, the baptism and miraculous cure, the Emperor continues:—

'Therefore we, along with all our Satraps (!) and the whole Senate, Nobles and People subject to the Roman Church, have thought it desirable that even as St. Peter is on earth the appointed Vicar of God, so also the Pontiffs his vicegerents should receive from us and from our empire power and principality greater than belongs to our earthly empire. For we choose the same Prince of the Apostles and his vicars to be our patrons before God, and we decree that even like unto our own earthly imperial power so shall the sacro-sanct Church of Rome be honoured and venerated, and that higher than our terrestrial throne shall the most sacred seat of St. Peter be gloriously exalted.

'Let him who for the time presides over the holy Church of Rome have supremacy over the four sees of Alexandria, of Antioch, of Jerusalem, and of Constantinople, and let him be sovereign of all the priests in the whole world, and by his judgment let all things which pertain to the worship of God or the faith of Christians be regulated.

'We wish all nations in the whole world to be informed that we have within our Lateran palace reared from its foundations a church to our Saviour and Lord God, Jesus Christ; and know ye that we have from the foundations thereof borne on our own shoulders twelve baskets-full of earth according to the number of the twelve Apostles. Which most holy church we decree shall be called the head and summit of all churches in the whole world, and shall be venerated and proclaimed as such, even as we have ordained in other our imperial decrees. We have also built churches for the blessed Peter and Paul, chiefs of the Apostles, enriching them with gold and silver, and have laid their most sacred bodies therein with great reverence, making for them coffins of amber (which is surpassed in strength by none of the elements), and on each of these coffins we have placed a cross of purest gold and most precious gems, fastening them thereto with golden nails.

'On these churches, for the maintenance of the lights burned in them, we have bestowed sundry farm- properties, and have enriched them with divers estates both in the East and the West, in the North and the South, namely in Judaea, Greece, Asia, Thrace, Africa and Italy, as well as in divers islands. All these are to be administered by the hands of our most blessed father Silvester, *Summus Pontifex*, and his successors. -----

'We grant to the said Silvester and his successors the imperial palace of the Lateran, and also the diadem or crown, and the *Phrygium* : moreover the *superhumerale* or necklace which is wont to surround our imperial neck : the purple mantle also and scarlet tunic and all the imperial trappings, as well as the dignity of the imperial mounted guards. We bestow upon him also the imperial sceptre, with all standards and banners and similar imperial ornaments, and in short the whole array of our imperial dignity and the glory of our power.

'To the men of a different rank, namely the most reverend clergy of the Roman Church, we grant the same height of dignity wherewith our most illustrious Senate is adorned, namely that they be made patricians and consuls, and we announce that they shall be adorned with other imperial dignities.

'And as our own civil service hath its special decorations, so we decree that the clergy of the holy Roman Church shall be adorned: and that the said Church be ministered unto by janitors and chamberlains, such as those who wait upon us, the Emperor. And that the pontifical splendour may shine forth as brilliantly as possible, we decree that the clergy of the Roman Church ride on horses adorned with saddle-cloths and trappings of the purest white : and like our senators, let them wear udones or white shoes : and thus let the heavenly ranks, like the earthly ranks, be adorned for the greater glory of God.

'The blessed Silvester and his successors shall have the power of enrolling whom they will in the number of the clergy, none presuming to say that they have acted arrogantly herein.

'We have already decreed that he and his successors should wear a diadem such as ours of purest gold and precious stones. But the most blessed Pope would not consent to use a golden crown besides the crown of clerisy which he wears to the glory of the most blessed Peter. We have however with our own hands placed on his most holy head a tiara of dazzling whiteness, symbolizing the resurrection of our Lord; and holding the bridle of his horse we have performed for him the duties of a groom out of our reverence for the blessed Peter; ordaining that his successors shall use the same tiara in processions, in imitation of our imperial style.'

The reader who has had the patience to proceed thus far may very likely think that though the document is tedious, sometimes inconsistent with itself, and instinct with all an ecclesiastic's love for goodly raiment, there is nothing which need have made the Donation of Constantine, whether true or false, a landmark in the history of Italy. The important paragraph is that which follows, and which, as every word is here of weight, shall be translated literally:—

'Wherefore, that the pontifical crown may not grow too cheap, but may be adorned with glory and influence even beyond the dignity of the earthly empire, lo! we hand over and relinquish our palace, the city of Rome, and all the provinces, places and cities of Italy and [or] the western regions, to the most blessed Pontiff and universal Pope, Silvester; and we ordain by our pragmatic constitution that they shall be governed by him and his successors, and we grant that they shall remain under the authority of the holy Roman Church.

'Wherefore we have thought it fitting that our empire and our royal power be transferred to the Eastern regions, and that a city bearing our name be built in an excellent place in the province of Byzantia, and that there our empire be founded, since where the sovereign of priests and the head of the Christian religion has been placed by the Heavenly Emperor, it is not fitting that there the earthly emperor should also bear sway.'

The document ends with solemn injunctions to all future Emperors, to all nobles, 'satraps', and senators, to keep this grant for ever inviolate. Anathemas are uttered on any one who shall dare to infringe it; and hell-fire is invoked for his destruction. As the fabricator of the document must have known that he was, on the most favourable construction of his conduct, writing a mere ecclesiastical romance, these references to eternal punishment should not have been included. The document is laid on the body of the blessed Peter as a pledge to the Apostle that Constantine on his part will keep it ever inviolable.

It bears date on the third day before the Kalends of April (30th of March), Constantine being for the fourth time consul, with Gallicanus for his colleague. No such consulship exists in the Fasti. The Emperor was for the fourth time consul in 315, with his brother-in-law and co-Emperor Licinius for his colleague. The consulship of Gallicanus was in 330, five years after the council of Nicaea, and the Emperor Constantine was not his colleague.

A few words must be said as to the place and time wherein this extraordinary fiction had its birth. An attempt has been made to cast off upon some Greek ecclesiastic the responsibility for its authorship, but this attempt is now generally admitted to have failed. It undoubtedly springs from Rome, probably from the papal chancery in Rome. The earnestness with which the writer exerts himself to secure for the Roman clergy the use of *mappulae et linteamina* makes it probable that he was one of the favoured persons who had the right to perambulate the streets of ruined Rome on a steed covered with a horsecloth of dazzling whiteness. The general similarity of style to some of the eighth-century lives in the *Liber Pontificalis* suggests the thought that the author of the Donation may have been one of the scribes who in the pages of that compilation denounced the 'most unutterable' Aistulf or celebrated the mildness of the 'quasi-angelic' Stephen.

For, to come to the question of date, there is not its date, much doubt that this document belongs to the middle or possibly the later half of the eighth century. It is already included in the so-called Decretals of Isidore, published about 840, and in the collection of Formulae of S. Denis of about the same period. But we may probably trace it to an earlier date than this; for it is almost certain that Pope Hadrian alludes to this document in a letter which he wrote to Charles the Great in 7772, and there is some force in Dollinger's argument that a document of this kind would not have been fabricated after 774, when the Frankish king showed his determination to found a kingdom for himself on the ruins of the Lombard monarchy. There is therefore much to be said for the view that the Donation was fabricated shortly before the year 754. But on this subject there may probably for some time be considerable variation of opinion, as one theory after another is advanced by scholars to account for the original concoction of a document so wildly at variance with historical fact.

With any more detailed discussion on this point I do not think it necessary to trouble my readers. Nor do I feel myself bound even to speak of it as a forgery, much less to impute complicity with the forgery to any one of the Popes who cross the stage of my history. In an absolutely ignorant and uncritical age many a fiction passes for fact without deliberate and conscious imposture on the part of any single individual. There were doubtless romancers and story-tellers after their dull fashion in that eighth century as in our own, for the human imagination has never been lulled into absolute torpor. What if some clerk in the papal chancery amused his leisure by composing, in a style not always unskilfully imitated from that of Justinian or Theodosius, an edict which the first Christian Emperor might have published on the morrow of that Roman baptism which, though itself imaginary, was then firmly believed to be real? What if this paper, recognized at the time by all who knew its author as a mere romance, was left in the papal archives and (it may be years after the death of its author) was found by some zealous *exceptor* eager for material wherewith to confute the Lombard or convince the Frank? In some such way as this it is surely possible that, without any deliberate act of fraud on any one's part, the lie may have got itself recognized as truth.

Into the after-history of this fabrication I must not now enter minutely, though there is something almost fascinating in the subject, and indeed the story of the Donation of Constantine fully told would almost be the history of the Middle Ages. It was hidden, as it were, for a time under a bushel, and was not made so much use of by the Popes of the ninth and tenth centuries as we should have expected. But towards the end of the eleventh century we find it put in the forefront of the battle by the advocates of Hildebrand's world-ruling papal theocracy. Under Innocent III, Gregory IX, Boniface

VIII, it is constantly appealed to in support of their pretensions to rule as feudal suzerains over Italy, over the Holy Roman Empire, over the world. For three centuries after this, the canonists take the Donation as the basis of their airy edifices, some expanding, some restricting its purport, but none of them apparently entertaining any suspicion of the genuineness of the document itself.

So long-lived and so mighty is Falsehood. Like the Genie in the Arabian Nights, this story of an imperial abdication in favour of the Pope, which had crept out of that dark *scriptorium* in the Lateran palace grew and swelled and overshadowed all Europe. Then came a scholar of the Renaissance and uttered a few words of caustic doubt, and the Genie shrank back into the bottle and was hurled into the depths of the sea, whence it can no more emerge to trouble the nations.

The 'Declamatio' of Laurentius Valla, too declamatory as it is and not always attacking from the right quarter (for he seems to accept the Roman baptism of the Emperor as an undoubted fact), still had the effect of piercing the bubble which had so long befooled the world. Some feeble attempts were made to restore the credit of the Constantinian Donation, but they were judged hopeless by the rapidly growing scholarship of the fifteenth and sixteenth centuries; and when at last even Cardinal Baronius, that staunch supporter of papal claims, who fought even for the baptism of the Emperor by Silvester, abandoned the edict which was said to have followed it, all Europe knew that this question at least was laid to rest, and that it would hear no more of any claims seriously urged in right of the Donation of Constantine.

We have glanced at the circumstances attending the death of the fable, but our business is with its birth. As I have said, I do not propose to discuss the question whether it first took shape on parchment in 750 or 770; whether the first scribe who wrote the Donation intended a harmless romance or planned a wicked forgery. All these discussions are beyond my present purpose, which is to deal with what the Donation tells us as to the state of men's minds in Rome about the middle of the eighth century. We are conscious at once of a great gulf separating the ideas of that age from those which were prevalent at the beginning of the seventh century. We then saw a Pope, perhaps the greatest of all the Popes, Gregory the Great, struggling for liberty, almost for life, 'between the swords of the Lombards'. The necessities of his position forced him sometimes to over-step the strict limits of his spiritual realm, to appoint a tribune of soldiers, to rebuke a careless general, to conclude a provisional treaty; and his contest with the Patriarch of Constantinople extorted from him sometimes bitter cries and complaints against the Emperor into whose ear the Patriarch was whispering. But through all I think we may say that Gregory the First bore himself as the loyal, though often the deeply-dissatisfied subject of the Emperor, and there is never a hint of a disposition on his part to claim temporal dominion as against his Sovereign or to pose as the rightful civil ruler of Italy. Now we see that there is a change. In the middle of the eighth century it is evidently the feeling of the clerics of the Lateran, not only that they should ride on horses covered with white saddle-cloths—that they probably did in the days of Gregory;—not only that the Pope, since he waived the right of wearing the imperial diadem, ought to wear a tiara with a circlet of gold, the mark of his clerisy, and should be waited upon by janitors, chamberlains, guards, in imitation of imperial magnificence; but also that he ought to govern, as a king or an emperor, 'the city of Rome, and all the provinces and cities of Italy and of the West', whatever extension of his rule might be intended by these last words of awful and ambiguous import.

Henceforth when we hear, as we often shall do, of the rights and claims and privileges of Peter, we must remember that, at least in the thoughts or the aspirations of some Roman ecclesiastics, these words include a large measure of temporal sovereignty for their head, the Bishop of Rome. The claim to undisturbed possession of the property with which the Papal See has been endowed, the so-called 'Patrimonies of St. Peter', is included in these words as it was included in them during the pontificate of the first Gregory, but there is also something more, further reaching, more world-historical in their purport. We are dealing now not merely with estates, but with kingdoms. And in this connection we have to remember the nature of the process by which the Pope became Pope. Zacharias or Stephen, Paul or Hadrian, is not a hereditary ruler, he is the elected head of a mighty corporation, wielding the strongest moral and intellectual forces at that time existing in the world. When he seeks to establish and to extend his temporal dominion he is not merely 'fighting for his own hand', he is not merely seeking to gratify his own arrogance and ambition—though these very human qualities undoubtedly played their part—but he is also striving for the honour and glory of the great college of ecclesiastics which has chosen him for its head, and by means of which he has risen from obscurity to greatness. If we may borrow an illustration from modern politics, the jealousy of a British First Lord of the Treasury for the dignity and honour of Parliament represents the jealousy of an eighth-century Pope for the glory and aggrandizement of the chair of St. Peter.

As I have said, however, we shall find that the claims of Peter as urged by Stephen II are an entirely different quantity from those same claims as urged by Gregory I. Whence comes the change which has been wrought in those hundred and fifty years? Partly no doubt from the dense ignorance which has overspread Rome and the west of Europe and which has made such a fable as that of Constantine's Donation possible. We are moving now through a region of mist and twilight, and the few forms that we can discern loom larger through the darkness. The collapse of the Teutonic royalties in Gaul and Spain may have helped somewhat, leaving the Pope of Rome greater by comparison. The estrangement between Italy and Constantinople on the question of the worship of images undoubtedly was a factor in the problem, though its influence has been sometimes exaggerated. It seems possible that the uprise of the religion of Mohammed strengthened the position of the Papacy, exhibiting as it did great religious leaders such as the early Caliphs in command of mighty armies and lords of a worldwide empire. Moreover, the very danger at which Christian Europe shuddered when it saw Islam overspreading the world, may have suggested the necessity of discipline and the union of Christendom under one spiritual head.

But after all it was probably our own countrymen who bore the chief part in the exaltation of St. Peter's chair. The Gallican Church had been lukewarm, the Celtic missionaries had been all but hostile, but the new Anglo-Saxon converts, the spiritual children of Augustine and Theodore, could scarcely find words to express their passionate loyalty and devotion to the Bishop of Rome. We have seen a little of what Boniface and his companions were doing in Germany and Gaul. To these men whom I have already called, from this aspect of their work, the Jesuits of the eighth century, must in great measure be attributed the lordlier tone in which the Popes with whom we are now dealing utter their mandates to the nations.

One word in conclusion, not by way of polemic, but in order to make it possible to avoid polemic in the pages that are to follow. It will be seen that I treat the claims to temporal dominion urged in the name of St. Peter as absolutely fantastic and visionary.

The Apostle himself, the rock-like stay and support of his brethren in the first age of Christianity, is of course no myth, but a historical personage as real as Xavier or Livingstone. The theory that he was bishop of Rome, and that, in fulfillment of words spoken to him by Jesus Christ, supernatural gifts for the teaching and guidance of the Church have been bestowed on all his successors, is a theory which, though it finds no foothold in the mind of the present writer, has been held by too many generations of devout and earnest Christians to be mentioned here with anything but respect and sympathy. But the notion common in the Middle Ages, that the holy man, from his resting-place in the Paradise of God, is acutely interested in the precise delimitation of the boundaries of his successors' kingdom, and by supernatural means seeks to retain for them Perugia or Comacchio—this notion, which is I believe no part of the essential teaching of the Roman Church and which has faded or is fading out of the minds of men, seems to me mere mythology, as much so as the story of the intervention of Juno and Venus in the wars of Troy. But even mythology has often influenced history. It was in the name of the Delphic Apollo and to avenge the encroachments of the Phocians on the territory of the god that those Sacred Wars were waged which brought Philip of Macedon into the heart of Greece and indirectly gave Alexander the supremacy of the world.

CHAPTER VIII.

THE STRUGGLE FOR THE EXARCHATE.

A few months after the elevation of Pippin to the royal dignity a new and a most important actor appeared upon the scene of European politics. Towards the end of March, 752, Pope Zacharias died. A presbyter named Stephen was elected in his place, but on the third morning after he had taken up his quarters in the Lateran palace, on arising from sleep he was struck down by an apoplectic seizure, of which he died on the following day. The people were assembled in the basilica of S. Maria Maggiore, and chose as Pope another Stephen, who was immediately installed in the vacant see.

This Pope (more correctly known as Stephen II than as Stephen III, for the short pontificate of his predecessor ought not to enter into the calculation) was of Roman origin, and having been early left an orphan had been brought up in the Lateran palace. He was thus emphatically the child and champion of the Papacy, apparently a man of more combative spirit and more ambitious temper than his predecessor, and was destined during the five short years of his pontificate to battle more valiantly than any who had gone before him for the ideas of temporal sovereignty and worldly dominion with which the Lateran palace was teeming.

But indeed if any such visions as those dreamed by the author of the Donation of Constantine were to become realities there was no time to lose. Already, a year before the death of Zacharias, an event had taken place which altered the whole balance of power in Italy. This was the capture of Ravenna (A.D. 751) by Aistulf, king of the Lombards. As to this event, one of such vast importance for Italy and for Europe, we are left by all the chroniclers and biographers of the time in exasperating ignorance. We know not whether the city fell by blockade or by sudden assault; nor how the marshes and canals which had protected her for so many centuries were overpassed; we do not even know the name of her last imperial governor, though as no Exarch is named after Eutychius it is conjectured that he may have been the man. All that we can say with certainty is that an apparently genuine charter among the archives of the monastery of Farfa is given forth by 'Haistulfus rex' and dated by him 'Ravennae in palatio" on the 4th of July in the year 751.

We note with some surprise the date of the downfall of Byzantine rule over Italy as exercised from Ravenna. Under many weak and inefficient emperors that rule had endured, and now under a sovereign of the strong and warlike Isaurian race, under the stern, self-sufficing and energetic Constantine Copronymus, it comes to an end. Probably the iconoclastic controversy was the chief cause of this strange result. The revolts which about 730 broke forth in Italy had indeed apparently been suppressed, but the chasm between the ruler and the ruled had probably never been closed, and Constantine V may have felt that it was better for him to devote all his energies to the defence of the East against the Saracens than to waste troops and treasure in warding off the assaults of the Lombards on a city the inhabitants of which would hail the first opportunity for escaping from under his rule.

In another aspect the date of the fall of Ravenna is a memorable one. It differs only by three years from the date before the birth of Christ which is generally assigned to the foundation of Rome. Romulus founding his little city in 754 B. C.; the Roman Empire practically extinguished in Italy in 751 A. D.; such are the two landmarks on either side of the central event in the history of the world; and the length of the long uphill road from Romulus to Augustus makes us better appreciate the often foreshortened distance from Augustus to Aistulf.

It was assuredly a mistake in Aistulf's statesmanship, however tempting might be the looseness of the Byzantine hold upon Italy, to drive the Emperor's representative out of Ravenna. The balance of power was thus destroyed; a governor in whom Liutprand had found a useful ally was removed, the Pope was relieved from what had in past days been a galling dependence on the Exarch, and he and the Lombard were now left face to face to fight out their deadly duel.

What were the distinguishing characteristics of thetwo combatants who were thus entering the lists to strive for the sovereignty of Italy? On the one hand Aistulf, son of Duke Pemmo of Friuli and of that Griselda-like wife of his, Ratperga, who was so ashamed of her plain face and clownish figure that with exaggerated humility she begged, but vainly begged, her husband to divorce her. That Aistulf was a strong man and a brave soldier had been clearly shown on that great day of the battle of the Metaurus when he hurled the two Spoletan champions over the bridge. That he was a man of stormy and impetuous nature he manifested when, at Pavia, at the scene of his father's deposition, in his wrath at Liutprand's cold contempt he was on the point of murdering the Lombard king. But though he was such a sovereign as we might expect to find ruling over a still halfcivilized people, the historian discovers nothing in the recorded actions of Aistulf to justify the epithets 'cruelest,' 'wickedest,' ' malignant,' 'impious,' 'most atrocious,' which are hurled thick at his head by the passionate papal biographer. The student of these pontifical lives soon learns that adjectives like these only mean that the Pope and the man who is thus described were striving for mastery. The laws of this king seem to show a wise and statesmanlike care for the morals of his subjects; and his numerous grants to various religious houses in his dominions prove that we are not here dealing with a determined enemy of the Catholic Church such as the Gaiseric and Huneric of an earlier century. But that which was truly blameworthy in Aistulf was that, after he had provoked a struggle, he would not accept the consequences of defeat. He was willing to promise anything when the enemy's hand was upon his throat, but as soon as the pressure was relaxed and he was left to himself he at once began to cast about for excuses for delaying or altogether evading the fulfillment of his promise. Most of us have met such persons as this in actual life, and have generally found that all their shifts and evasions only make their final fall more calamitous.

On the other hand stands Stephen the Roman, Pope of Rome. If I read his character aright, he was less of an ecclesiastic and more of a politician than his predecessor. In the case of Zacharias the evangelization of Germany and the restoration of 'a godly discipline' in Gaul seem to have been the objects nearest to his heart; while to Stephen the establishment of his lordship over some of the fairest parts of Italy and the fulfillment in some degree at least of the splendid dreams of the Donation of Constantine seem to be the sole objects worth striving for. With this end in view, and knowing that he must thereby be brought sooner or later into collision with the Lombard ruler, he doubtless often meditated on the fact that his predecessor, even the unworldly and unambitious Zacharias, had provided him with a strong buckler of defence against his foes by the answer which he had given to the Frankish messengers; that Pippin, anointed king of the Franks in the name of St. Peter and by the hands of Boniface, was morally compelled to afford to the Papal See that protection which Charles Martel had refused to furnish.

The Lombard king on his side, as judged not by the passionate scribes of the Lateran but by the calm voice of History, may be held to have been pursuing not unworthy aims. The Byzantine Exarch and his train of Oriental foreigners once driven out of Italy, Ravenna and the Pentapolis firmly joined to the solid Lombard dominion north of the Po, the connection between the north and centre of Italy would be assured, the great duchies of Spoleto and Benevento would be restrained from their disloyal, 'centrifugal' policy which could only end in disaster to the Lombard name, and the successors of Aistulf might one day rule over a harmonious and united Italy such as had once been so nearly formed by the wise policy of Theodoric.

We have also to observe that in all that part of Italy which had been subject to the Empire there was probably a party not unfavourable to the claims of the Lombard king. Of Rome itself it is asserted by a chronicler, who though late has some pieces of valuable information intermingled with his rubbish, that 'certain wicked men, Romans, arose and sent word to king Aistulf that he should come and take possession of the Tuscan frontier and usurp the Roman Empire'.

However slender may be the authority for this statement, it corresponds in some measure with the probable course of events. The disturbances which will have hereafter to be related, following on the death of Pope Paul, clearly reveal the existence of a Lombardising party in the City of Rome. The two nations, Roman and Lombard, had now been in close contact for nearly two centuries. Relations of commerce, probably of intermarriage, must have grown up between them during the long years of peace. And moreover, even the rule of the Lombard king, harsh and irregular as it may have been and often exercised through corrupt instruments, may have seemed preferable to that of a college of priests or the representative of an absentee and practically powerless Emperor.

As for the *Ducatus Romae*, it seems clear that the Lombard king was bent on extorting from it at least the acknowledgment of his supremacy and the payment of a poll-tax by its inhabitants. Whether he would have gone beyond this and insisted on interfering with its internal affairs may perhaps be doubted, for these semi-barbarian conquerors were not generally great organizers or remodellers of the administration. To the Pope especially and to the Papal Curia we may believe that they would have left a large measure of independence if only they had been willing to acquiesce in the extension of Lombard rule over all that had been imperial Italy. But no such life on sufferance would satisfy the present mood of the Roman pontiffs. They were determined to assert their claim to rule over all those portions of Italy which had remained imperial at the time of the Lombard invasion. So much at least should be theirs, the question as to the Lombard portions of Italy being reserved for future discussion. And these portions of Italy seem to have been claimed on some such theory as the following, and by arguments which were independent of the Donation of Constantine, though they may have usefully buttressed up the weak places in that wonderful document. 'The Pentapolis and Exarchate have hitherto belonged to the Roman Empire, though the man who now bears the title of Roman Emperor has proved himself unable to preserve them. But the Roman Empire means the Roman Republic, and the true representative of the City of Rome, if the Emperor abdicates his power, is the bishop of that City. And the bishop of Rome is the successor of St. Peter, and the

Apostle from his high place in heaven watches over the interests of his successors. Therefore whosoever interferes with our claim to exercise temporal dominion over the fragments of Italy which of late were governed in the name of the Emperor at Constantinople, incurs the wrath of St. Peter, and will be shut out by the great Key-bearer from the kingdom of heaven'

The question was further complicated and an element of less shadowy right was given to the papal claims by the existence of the vast estates, the so-called ' Patrimonies of St. Peter,' which were scattered far and wide over Italy, and in which the Popes exercised undoubted rights, not as sovereigns, but as proprietors. Some account of these patrimonies has already been given in connection with the history of Gregory the Great, and we may well believe that as the same causes which had led to their creation continued to operate, the estates of the Church of Rome would be not less but far more extensive in 750 than in 600. On these estates a Lombard king, moving his armies backwards and forwards over Italy, was almost compelled to trample. Even a modern strategist, with the scientific maps of a military staff at his disposal, would not always find it easy to avoid marching through these wide-stretching patrimonies; and an army's march in those days, far more than in ours, meant inevitably more or less of devastation. Thus it would be not entirely without justification from a strictly legal point of view that after such a campaign the Pope should utter his shrill cries to his Frankish ally, calling upon him to take vengeance on the Lombard for his violation of the 'justitiae' or rights of St. Peter.

But in all this contest which is now looming before us there is not really any religious interest at stake. We must not of course look forward to the great religious wars of the sixteenth century; nor must we look back to the strife between Arian and Catholic in the fifth century. The Lombards are now in doctrine absolutely, in accord with the Roman Church. In their public documents they insist on calling themselves the Catholic and God-beloved nation of the Lombards; and their kings (no doubt by the advice of their clerical counsellors) continually express sentiments of the most edifying piety in their charters and edicts. The opposition is not religious, but it is political and racial; the antagonism of two sovereigns, each of whom yearns to make himself lord of Italy; the loathing mingled with fear and contempt which the dainty Roman entertains for the strong, unkempt, and (as he avers) uncleanly Lombard.

It has been necessary to give this sketch of the aims and feelings of the two contending parties, because for the next twenty eventful years we shall be practically dependent on one litigant alone for the story of the great law-suit. The lives and letters of the Popes are really our sole source for the history of the Frankish conquest of Italy. Each reader will have to judge for himself what amount of correction the statements thus delivered to us require in order to make them correspond with the veritable facts of history.

According to the papal biographer, while the newly elected Pope was attending to the philanthropic duties of his calling, founding and restoring alms-houses, and providing for the maintenance of one hundred of 'Christ's poor,' a great persecution was commenced by Aistulf, king of the Lombards, in the city of Rome and the towns surrounding it. Hereupon the most blessed Pope, in the third month from his ordination, sent messengers to conclude a treaty of peace with the Lombard king. The messengers were the Pope's brother Paul (himself one day to wear the Papal tiara), and Ambrose, a tried and trusty servant of the Lateran, who had held for many years the high place—highest among lay officials—of *Primicerius Notariorum*. They took large presents in their hands, and succeeded in concluding a treaty of peace (A.D. 752) with Aistulf for forty years, similar probably to that which Zacharias had concluded for twenty years with his brother Ratchis.

'But nevertheless,' says the biographer, 'that impudent king of the Lombards, tempted by the cunning of the Old Enemy, barely four months afterwards committed perjury and broke the treaty, inflicting divers insults on the most holy man and the whole Roman people, directing various threats against him. For in his God-abandoned blindness he longed to invade the whole of this province [the Ducatus Romae] and to inflict a burdensome tribute on the inhabitants of this City, yearning to exact a poll-tax of one solidus annually from every citizen, and indignantly asserting that this Roman City and the towns surrounding it were all subject to his jurisdiction'.

The reader will observe that so far we have not come to actual bloodshed. Aistulf puts forward claims to jurisdiction and taxation, which he perhaps alleges to be justified by the forty years' treaty, but he does not yet enforce them by the sword. He only 'desires' and 'yearns' to do so, and with that old passionate temper of his 'indignantly' asserts what he deems to be his rights.

Seeing how the storm of the king's anger was brewing, the Pope sent again two messengers to appease his wrath. This time they were the abbots of the two most celebrated monasteries in Italy, that of St. Vincent on the Vulturno, and that of St. Benedict on Monte Cassino. The foundation of the latter monastery was described in a previous volume. The monastery of St. Vincent had been founded about half a century before the accession of Stephen II by three kinsmen, young noblemen of Benevento, named Paldo, Taso and Tato, whose adventures when they set forth from their father's houses secretly in search of holiness and solitude are told with charming naiveté by the monastic author of the Chronicon Salemitanum. Their monastery was erected in the wild Abruzzi Mountains near the source of the Vulturno, and already as a home of austere saints it had acquired a renown only second to that of the great house of St. Benedict.

'When these two abbots,' says the biographer, 'bore to the most cruel king the Pope's request that the treaty might be observed and the people of God of both parties might be allowed to dwell in peace, he treated them with absolute contempt, spurning all their admonitions, and to the ruin of his own soul sent them back abashed and disappointed to their own monasteries, bidding them take notice that he would not bend in the least to the will of the aforesaid most holy Pope. Which when that eminent Father heard, he at once, according to his usual practice, commended to Almighty God his cause and the cause of the people committed to his care, suggesting his dolorous lamentation to the Divine '.

At this point, however, there appeared upon the scene the representative of one whom raging Lombard and weeping Pope were both in danger of forgetting, the *de jure* lord of Ravenna and all Italy, the Emperor Constantine V. 'While these things were being done there arrived at Rome John, imperial *silentiarius*, bringing a message to the most holy Pope, and at the same time a letter of command to the aforesaid impious king that he should restore to their proper lord those territories of the Republic which he had usurped with devilish ingenuity. This imperial messenger the Pope sent, along with his brother the deacon Paul, to the most wicked Aistulf at Ravenna. When they had been received he dismissed them with an empty answer, assuring the Emperor's messenger that he would order some nefarious man of his own nation, steeped in the counsels of the devil, to hasten to the Royal City. They therefore returned to Rome, were presented to the Pope, and reported to him the ill success of their mission. Then the holy man, perceiving the intention of the malignant king, sent his own emissaries and apostolic rescripts to the Royal City, along with the Emperor's messenger, earnestly entreating the imperial clemency that (as he had often prayed him before) he would by all means come into these regions of Italy and set free the city of Rome and the whole province of Italy from the bitings of this son of iniquity.'

This passage is important as showing that now in the year 752, twenty-six years after Leo III issued his iconoclastic decrees, the Pope still considers himself an imperial subject, and has even yet no matured design of breaking with the Byzantine Emperor, if only that Emperor will play his part properly and will deliver him from the swords of the Lombards.

The biographer continues : 'Meanwhile, the most atrocious king of the Lombards, persisting in his pernicious design, flamed into vehement fury, and roaring like a lion uttered his pestiferous threats against the Romans, vowing that they should all be butchered with one sword unless they would submit themselves to his dominion on the aforesaid terms. Then again the most holy father, having collected the whole Roman assembly, thus addressed them with paternal love : "I pray you, dearest sons, let us implore the pardon of God for our heaped-up transgressions, and He will be our helper, and in His merciful providence will deliver us from the hands of our persecutors." Then the people, obeying his healthful counsel, assembled with one accord, and all with streams of tears besought the help of the Almighty. On one these days he made procession, singing the Litany with much humility, and bearing on his own shoulder with the help of the other bishops the most holy likeness of our Lord and Saviour Jesus Christ which is named "the made without hands," at the same time exhibiting other sacred mysteries, and so with naked feet walked, followed by the whole commonalty, to the church of the Holy Mother of God which is called Ad Praesepe. Ashes were sprinkled on the heads of all the people, and they walked along with mighty wailings, calling on the most merciful Lord God. But the Pope had tied to the adorable cross of our Lord that covenant which the wicked king of the Lombards had broken.'

The biographer then goes on to describe how the Pope ordained that these solemn processional litanies should be sung every sabbath day; the goal of the processions being by turns S. Maria Maggiore, St. Peter's, and St. Paul's. He also assembled all his bishops and clergy in the Lateran palace and exhorted them to be diligent in the study of the Scriptures and in other spiritual reading, that they might have a ready answer for the adversaries of the Church of God. Nor was conduct forgotten. 'With ceaseless and strengthening admonitions he warned the people of God to live soberly and piously and to keep themselves from all wickedness.'

But while thus sharpening afresh all the weapons of his spiritual warfare, Stephen was preparing that appeal to the great power beyond the Alps for which both the Gregories and Zacharias had opened the way. By a returning pilgrim, whose name has not reached us, he sent a letter to the newly-crowned Pippin, begging him to despatch messengers bringing an invitation or a summons to the Frankish court. The king took the hint, and (probably in the spring of 753) Droctigang, abbot of Jumieges, appeared at the Lateran with a request for the Pope's presence in Frank-land. Another Frankish courtier arrived soon after to repeat the same invitation.

At this point of the negotiations we find two Papal important letters from the Pope in that great collection the *Codex Carolinus,* which will henceforward be one of our main authorities. They were written with the intent that they should be taken back to

Frank-land by the messengers whom Pippin had sent. In them the Pope expresses his high satisfaction with both of the envoys, and begs that one of them, 'Johannes vir religiosus' (who is perhaps the second unnamed messenger alluded to in the Liber Pontificalis), may accompany any future embassy that the king may send him. In the first letter, addressed to Pippin himself, Stephen assures him of the special protection of Peter, and exhorts him to persevere in the good course upon which he has entered. 'Because he that endureth to the end the same shall be saved. And for this thou shalt receive an hundred-fold in this life and shall inherit the life eternal.'

The other letter is addressed 'To the glorious men our sons, all the dukes of the Frankish nation'. The motive of this letter is revealed to us by some words of Einhard, the biographer of Charles the Great, in which he describes the intense dislike of many of the Frankish nobles to the proposal of a war with the Lombards. There were probably many reasons for this dislike. The relations of the two peoples had been for many generations friendly; the trouble and hardships of a Transalpine campaign were more obvious than the profit likely to result from it to anyone but the Pope; even the great ecclesiastics, still but half reconciled to the strict discipline which Zacharias and Boniface had imposed upon them, may have given but cold assent to the proposal to make their papal master yet more masterful.

To the Frankish nobles accordingly Stephen addressed himself, nominally asking for their advocacy of his cause with the king, really no doubt seeking to smooth away their opposition. 'We are confident that you fear God and love your protector the blessed Peter, Prince of the Apostles, since you may be certain that for every struggle which you undertake on behalf of your spiritual mother the Church, you shall receive an hundred-fold from the hand of God, and from the Prince of the Apostles himself the forgiveness of your sins. Therefore let nothing hinder you from aiding our petition to our son the God-preserved and most excellent Pippin, that so your sins may be blotted out, and the Key-bearer of the kingdom of heaven may open to you the door and introduce you into eternal life.'

The Frankish messengers probably returned from Rome with these letters about the beginning of July. Before the answer could be sent, Aistulf had taken a step further towards the attainment of his end by occupying Ceccano, a village on the Via Latina, southeast of Rome, and just inside the frontier of the Ducatus Romae. The learned and impartial editor of the Liber Pontificalis, Abbé Duchesne, aptly calls our attention to the fact that this occupation of Ceccano 'is the first act of hostility on the part of the Lombards. Till now the biographer has said a good deal about persecutions, menaces, broken treaties, citations, but he has not related any act of war'. However, it was undoubtedly a menacing deed. The old northward road by Perugia to the Exarchate, the Via Flaminia, was already of course closed, and now some stages on the southward road were to be occupied by the Lombards; the Ducatus Romae was to be more effectually barred from all possible communication with the imperial governor at Naples; the Pope might expect before long to see the Lombard standards on the south-eastern horizon moving towards the Lateran itself. Add to this the fact that Ceccano was cultivated by coloni of the Roman Church, and was therefore probably one of the 'patrimonies' of St. Peter, and we have reason enough for the Pope's resentment being fiercely kindled by such an invasion, though it was not, as far as we know, accompanied by bloodshed or any especial deed of violence

However, the Lombard king does not appear at from this time to have pushed his inroad further into the Ducatus Romae. The next event was the return of the imperial *silentiarius* John, accompanied by the papal messengers from Constantinople. Still the Byzantine Emperor clung with extraordinary tenacity to his belief in embassies as a means of inducing the hot-tempered Lombard to disgorge his conquests; and with equally strange ignorance of the schemes which were being revolved in the papal breast, he chose the Pope as the most fitting advocate of the desired restitution. Assuredly, one thinks, Constantine V cannot have read the alleged Donation of his great namesake. However, the Pope was still the Emperor's subject: he must go to the Lombard Court and demand restitution to the empire of Ravenna and the cities pertaining thereto: but as a preliminary he sent a messenger to Aistulf requesting a safe-conduct for himself and all his companions.

The return of that messenger with the safe-conduct coincided most fortunately with the long-desired arrival in Rome of the Frankish envoys who were to act as escort to the Pope. They were two of the most eminent men in the Frankish kingdom, 'the most glorious duke' Autchar, and—a yet more important personage—Chrodegang, bishop of Metz. This last-named ecclesiastic was sprung from a noble family in Brabant, and is even said, by one doubtful authority, to have been a cousin of the king. He was now a middle-aged mam; he had been for many years referendarius (practically equivalent to chancellor) to the Frankish sovereign, and for the last eleven years (since 742) he had been bishop of Metz, the capital of the Austrasian kingdom. Liberal, learned (according to the estimation of the age), and fervent in piety, he was after Boniface the most noteworthy churchman of his generation. Like Boniface, he was intent upon the greatly needed work of reforming the morals of the Gaulish clergy, and with this end in view he drew up, probably soon after his return from his mission to Rome, a Rule for the collegiate life of the clergy of his cathedral church. To Chrodegang more than to any other person may be attributed the institution of secular canons, the foundation of cathedral chapters, and not a few of the disciplinary rules which still survive in our English colleges. Chrodegang's main purpose was to introduce into the lives of the officiating clergy something of the same regularity and strictness which the wise moderation of the rule of Benedict had given to the lives of the monks. But several expressions in his Rule show that he was also impressed by the splendour and dignity of the ceremonial in the churches at Rome, and in ritual, and especially in music, he was a zealous advocate of the usages which he had observed during his Roman embassy.

On the 13th of October, 753, Pope Stephen II rode out of the Flaminian Gate on his fateful northward journey. Many of his own immediate flock, many too of the inhabitants of other cities, followed him for some miles along the road, beseeching him with tears to renounce his perilous enterprise. Doubtless the true goal of his journeyings was already an open secret in Rome. It was not merely the Roman bishop who as a dutiful subject of the empire was going to the palace at Pavia to plead the cause of Constantine Copronymus and to obtain the restitution of the Exarchate. It was the Patriarch of Western Christendom who, though in delicate health, was going to cross the Alps, to appear in Gaul, the first of the long line of Popes to tread the soil of that country, to invoke in person the help of the newly anointed king of the Franks, and bring that powerful piece upon the board to cry 'check' to the Lombard king. Notwithstanding the lamentations of the people, Stephen II held on his way, accompanied by a number of bishops and priests and by some of the chief officers in the little army of the Ducatus Romae. At the fortieth milestone, after night had closed in, just as they were entering the Lombard territory, they saw a great sign in heaven—even a globe of fire falling towards the south from the region of Gaul and of the Lombards; evidently a token of great changes coming from the northern lands upon Italy.

The Frankish duke Autchar went forward and heralded at the Lombard Court the approach of the sage from venerable ambassador. No sooner, however, had the Pope set foot in the city of Pavia than he was met by a messenger from Aistulf—whom we are inclined to call, not as the biographer does, 'most wicked,' but 'most foolish '—ordering him on no account to say one word by way of petition on behalf of Ravenna, the Exarchate, or any of the cities which recent Lombard kings had wrested from the empire. The Pope returned the sensible and manly answer that no such attempts at intimidation would avail to silence his remonstrances on behalf of those cities.

'When the Pope had arrived at Pavia and was presented to the wicked king he offered him many gifts, and besought him with copious tears that he would restore the Lord's sheep which he had taken away and would give back to every one his own'—a gentle hint as to the duty of recognizing the imperial claim. Then the imperial envoys unfolded their commission, and doubtless with true Byzantine pomp of words pressed for the same surrender. All was in vain: nor does the recital of the biographer convey the impression that the Pope himself expected or desired it to be otherwise. But then began the real battle of the day. The Frankish envoys, Chrodegang and Autchar, 'pressed heavily on Aistulf with the demand that he should relax his rules and allow the most holy Pope to travel to Frank-land'. At which he called the blessed man before him and asked him if he had any desire to hasten into Frank-land; whereupon the Pope by no means held his peace, but showed plainly his inclination to make the journey. Thereat Aistulf gnashed his teeth like a lion, and several times sent his creatures to him privately to try and divert him from his purpose. But when next day in the presence of Chrodegang the king again asked him if he wished to travel into Frank-land, the Pope answered, "If your will is to give me leave, mine is altogether to make the journey." '

The Pope had played a bold but skillful game. The request for his presence, coming from so powerful a neighbour as the king of the Franks, urged by his own ambassadors and heartily seconded by the himself, was one which Aistulf durst not refuse; and so the important journey was commenced. On the 15th of November Stephen set forth from Pavia accompanied by two bishops, four presbyters, an archdeacon, two deacons—Ambrose the *primicerius* and Boniface the *secundicerius* of the papal curia—two *regionarii*, and other attendants. They made the first stages of the journey as rapidly as possible, fearing (as proved to be the case) that Aistulf would repent of his granted leave and seek to hinder them on their way. They arrived, however, ere any messenger could stop them at the Italian end of the pass of the Great St. Bernard, no doubt the Val d'Aosta, which owing to the early and unsuccessful Lombard invasions of Gaul had remained for a hundred and eighty years in Frankish hands and was now called one of the Frankish passes. Arrived there, the Pope and his companions sang a psalm of praise to God who had so far prospered their journey. But to the dangers from men succeeded the dangers of Nature, the perils and the toils necessarily in that day accompanying the passage of a ridge more than 8,000 feet high in the month of November. That which is now the pass of the Great St. Bernard, but was then the Mons Jovis, rose before them, doubtless thickly covered with snow, and not crowned with that hospitable dwelling which for more than a thousand years has offered shelter to pilgrims, but perhaps still showing the dismantled and shelterless ruins of the temple of Jupiter. The biographer, who evidently was not one of the party, tells us nothing of the hardships of the ascent and descent, but they left their indelible impression on the mind of the chief pilgrim. Two years later, writing to Pippin, Stephen says, 'By St. Peter's orders my Unhappiness was directed to come to you. We surrendered ourselves body and soul to the mighty labours attending a journey into so vast and distant a province. Trusting utterly to your fidelity, by God's will we arrived in your presence, worn out by the frost and the snow, by the heat and the swelling of waters, by mighty rivers, and most atrocious mountains and divers kinds of danger'.

However, all these perils overpassed, the Roman ecclesiastics descended safely into the valley of the Rhone, and rested from their labours in the renowned monastery of St. Maurice at Agaunum, the scene of Burgundian Sigismund's devotion and despair. This religious house was under the government of the abbot Wilichar, formerly Archbishop of Vienne, who on the surrender of his see had gone on pilgrimage to Rome and there made the acquaintance of Pope Stephen. They were here therefore in the presence of old friends, and doubtless greatly enjoyed the calm and the shelter of the renowned convent. During the Pope's sojourn at St. Maurice, which probably lasted several weeks, Ambrose the *primicerius* sickened with fever and died. He was sixty years of age, and had probably never recovered from the fatigues of the mountain journey. Six years later his body was carried back across the Alps and buried in St. Peter's basilica.

The Pope had hoped to find the Frankish king waiting for him at St. Maurice, but the necessity of repelling a Saxon inroad had apparently deranged the royal plans. However, Pippin's confidential adviser, Fulrad, abbot of S. Denis, soon appeared at the convent, together with a duke named Roland, charged with a renewal of the invitation and with the duty of escorting the ecclesiastics to the palace.

King Pippin, who had been keeping his Christmas at the Villa Theudonis on the Moselle, received we are told with immense joy the tidings of the Pope's arrival in his kingdom, and journeyed, with his wife, his sons, and his nobles, to another 'villa publica,' or royal demesne, that of Pons Hugonis, to meet him. This place, from which apparently all traces of a royal palace have now vanished, is the little village of Ponthion in Champagne, not far from those Catalaunian plains on which Attila and Aetius fought their mighty battle. Looking at the map, we are somewhat surprised to find the place of meeting between the Pope, coming from Switzerland, and the king who had kept Christmas on the Moselle, fixed so far to the west, but evidently both potentates had in their mind an approaching solemnity in the neighbourhood of Paris, and shaped the course of their journeys accordingly.

From Ponthion Pippin sent his son Charles a hundred miles forward on the road to meet the pontiff. A meeting full of interest for after generations; for this Charles, a lad of fourteen years, is none other than the future Charlemagne, and this Pope Stephen is the first of a long line of pontiffs who were to crown kings while themselves exercising something like kingly rule. When news came that the Pope was approaching Pons Hugonis, the king rode forth to meet him at the third milestone from the palace, and dismounting from his horse prostrated himself before his papal guest, and then walked like a groom beside his palfrey. Forty-two years before, a predecessor of Stephen had entered in like triumphal guise the city of Constantinople; but only the Emperor's representatives, not the Emperor himself, then graced his triumph. This may therefore be considered the first of those exhibitions of ostentatious humility on the part of the Crown towards the pontifical Tiara which were to be so numerous throughout the Middle Ages. Thus in solemn procession, with the usual ecclesiastical accompaniment of loudly chanted hymns and spiritual songs, Pope and King moved onward to the gates of the palace of Ponthion.

The day of this fateful meeting was the sixth of January, 754, the feast of the Epiphany. The Christmas festivities at Thionville had probably therefore been summarily cut short by the tidings of the Pope's approach. When host and guest had entered the palace they proceeded to the royal chapel, and there, girded with sackcloth and with ashes on his head, the Pope fell prostrate before the King, and with the ever-ready accompaniment of tears besought him—to do what? Every word here is important, and the biographer shall therefore tell us the story himself.

'The blessed Pope with tears besought the most Christian King that by treaties of peace he would arrange the cause of St. Peter and the republic of the Romans. Who by an oath *de praesenti* assured the most blessed Pope that he would with his utmost energy obey all his commands and admonitions, and as soon as he should have convened a diet(?) by all means to restore to him the Exarchate of Ravenna and the rights and territories of the [Roman] republic'.

Winter was now making felt its full severity, and accordingly the King commended the Pope and his train of followers to the comfortable shelter of the abbey of S. Denis presided over by their friend Abbot Fulrad. There after the lapse of some time Pippin also appeared and there the solemn ceremony of his second coronation was performed by the head of Western Christendom. In that ceremony queen Bertrada, dressed in magnificent royal robes, and her two Charles and Carloman, the latter a little child of three years old, bore their part, and were all crowned together with the chief of their house. An important part of the ceremony was the anathema pronounced by the papal lips on any who should in after-ages presume to treat the race of Pippin as Pippin himself had treated the race of Clovis. 'At the same time,' says an unknown but well-informed writer, the Pope confirmed the chiefs of the Franks with his blessing and the grace of the Holy Spirit, and bound them all by such an interdict and threatened penalty of excommunication that they should never, for all time to come, presume to elect a king sprung from the loins of any other but of these persons whom the Divine Mercy had deigned to exalt, and in accordance with the intercessions of the holy Apostles to confirm and consecrate by the hands of their vicar the most blessed Pope.'

Vain was this attempt to establish a new doctrine of Divine Right on behalf of the posterity of Pippin. In a century and a half Henry the Saxon in Germany, in a little more than two centuries Hugh Capet in France, were to push the last Arnulfings from their thrones. Did St. Louis or any of the later Bourbon or Habsburg rulers who in their turn claimed Divine Right and papal sanction for their demand on the inalienable allegiance of their subjects ever remember that, according to the words pronounced by Pope Stephen in the chapel of S. Denis, they and all their house were under excommunication and interdict for presuming to violate the divine, apostolic, papal decree which settled the crown of the Franks on Pippin and his seed for ever?

It is to be observed that, according to the document from which I have just quoted, Stephen anointed Pippin not only to be King, but also Patrician. This was of course in no sense a Frankish but a purely Roman dignity, and pointed to the closer connection which was henceforth to subsist between Pippin and the City of Rome. Referring to previous pages of this work for the history of the title of Patrician, I may remind the reader that it had been of late years generally borne by the Exarch, and thus denoted authority over that part of Italy which was still imperial, an authority delegated from Constantinople. But when Pope Zacharias in the year 743 set forth on his journey of intercession to Ravenna, he, as we are told, 'left the government of the City to Stephen Patrician and Duke.' It would appear therefore that already ten years before the events which we are now considering, the Pope considered the *Dux Romae* as his subordinate, and that the Dux *Romae* bore the title of Patrician. It was probably in some such sense as this, and with the intention of conferring upon the Frankish king both a dignity, the first among Roman laymen, and a duty, that of guarding the territory of Rome from hostile invasion, that the Pope hailed his powerful friend in the chapel of S. Denis as not only King but Patrician. The title was bestowed upon the royal children as well as on Pippin himself, and is from this time forward sedulously used by the Pope in writing to his protectors, though Pippin himself does not seem to care about its adoption. From a strictly legal point of view probably no one but the Emperor at Constantinople had any right to confer the title, but neither Pope nor Frankish king seems to have troubled himself to enquire what were the strict legal rights of Constantine Copronymus.

At some time during this year 754 the Pope was seized with a serious illness, the result of the fatigues of the journey and of the rigour of a northern winter. His life was for a time despaired of, but he suddenly recovered, and was found by his attendants one morning convalescent when they had feared to find him dead.

And now all eyes were directed to the great *placitum* which was to be held at the royal villa of Carisiacum near to Soissons in the heart of the old kingdom of the Salian Franks. As has been already said, we know that there was a certain unwillingness on the part of some of the great Frankish nobles to fight the Pope's battles with the Lombard beyond the Alps. The strength of this opposition appears from the following words of Charles's biographer Einhard: 'The war against the Lombards was with great difficulty undertaken by Charles's father on the earnest entreaty of Pope Stephen, because certain of the chief men of the Franks with whom he was wont to take counsel so stoutly resisted his will that they proclaimed with free voices that they would desert the king and return to their own homes. Pippin, who was no Oriental despot, but the chosen leader of a free people, had to persuade and entice his subjects into granting the consent which was necessary for the fulfillment of his promises to the Pope. Stephen himself was apparently not present at this assembly. He was perhaps not yet fully recovered from his sickness, and he knew that he could trust his royal friend to plead his cause effectually. But when Pippin repaired to the place of meeting, where he was about to 'imbue the nobles with the admonitions of the Holy Father he was met by a powerful, perhaps an unexpected opponent. His brother Carloman, whom he had last seen in the barbaric splendour of a Frankish chief, and who had then been his equal, nay his superior in power, now appeared before him, barefooted, with shaven head, in the coarse robe of a Benedictine monk, to plead humbly—for what? That he would give prompt and effectual aid to the menaced head of the Western Church? No: but that he would live in peace with Aistulf, and not move one of his soldiers into Italy. The Papal biographer shall tell the story of this marvellous intervention in his own words:—

'Meanwhile the most unspeakable Aistulf by his devilish persuasions so wrought upon Carloman the brother of the most pious king Pippin, that he drew him forth from the monastery of St. Benedict in which he had dwelt devoutly as a monk for a certain space of time, and directed his course to the province of Frank-land, in order to raise objections and oppose the cause of the redemption of the Holy Church of God and the Republic of the Romans. And when he had arrived there he strove with all his power and vehemence to subvert the cause of the Church, according to the directions which he had received from the aforesaid unspeakable tyrant Aistulf. But by the grace of God he availed not to move the most firm soul of his brother the most Christian king Pippin: on the contrary, that excellent king, when he perceived the craftiness of the most wicked Aistulf, renewed his declaration that he would fight for the cause of God's holy Church as he had before promised the most blessed Pontiff. Then Pope and King with one accord taking counsel together, and remembering the aforesaid Carloman's own promise to God that he would lead a monastic life, placed him in a monastery there in Frank-land, where after certain days at the call of God he migrated from the light of day.'

This is all the information that we possess as to this startling reappearance of the princely monk on the political arena, save that the official annals inform us that Carloman undertook this journey unwillingly, being bound by his vow to obey the orders of the abbot of Monte Cassino, who again was under constraint, laid upon him by the stern orders of the Lombard king. This explanation, though accepted by many writers, does not seem to me sufficient to account for the facts. The abbot of Monte Cassino had not in past times shown himself thus subservient to the will of Aistulf, and a man occupying a position so venerated throughout Italy could not have been thus easily coerced into a course of which his conscience disapproved. Nor does the Papal biographer's own account of the vehemence with which the impulsive Carloman fulfilled his mission correspond with the chronicler's statement of the reluctance with which it was undertaken. To conjecture the motives even of our best-known contemporaries is often an unprofitable task, but if I may conjecture the motives of Carloman I would suggest that he had now seen enough of the Papal Curia of Italy and of the Lombards to know that the best thing for the country of his adoption, and even for 'the Holy Church of God' for which he had made such vast sacrifices, would be the establishment of a *modus vivendi* between the Bishop of Rome and the Lombard king, and that he may even have had some prophetic vision of the long centuries of sorrow which the Pope's appeal for aid from beyond the Alps would bring upon Italy.

The death of Carloman followed at no great interval his unsuccessful intervention in the cause of peace. It has never been suggested that this event was not due to natural causes, but among these, disappointment and chagrin at the discovery that he who could once have ordered peace or war with the certainty of obedience, must now plead and plead in vain for the cause of peace, may very probably have contributed to the fatal result. The continuer of the chronicle of 'Fredegarius' tells us that he remained at Vienne with his sister-in-law queen Bertrada, languished for many days, and died in peace in the year 755.

The mission of Carloman having proved fruitless, and the nobles assembled at Carisiacum having sufficiently signified their concurrence in the royal policy, Pippin proceeded to his work of obtaining, by negotiation if possible, if not by the sword, a promise from the Lombard king to respect 'the rights of St. Peter'. In order to state clearly what those rights were, a document appears to have been drawn up, in which Pippin set forth the territories which if he were victorious he was prepared to guarantee to the Pope. This is the far-famed Donation of Pippin, a document certainly less mythical than the Donation of Constantine, but one which has been the cause of almost as loud and angry a controversy, chiefly because, the document itself having disappeared, its contents have to be supplied by conjecture; and in this conjectural reproduction scarce two of the guessers altogether agree.

Twenty years later, when Charles the Great visited Rome in the midst of his victorious campaign against the Lombards, the then Pope Hadrian, as we are told, 'constantly prayed and besought him, and with paternal affection admonished him to fulfill in all things that promise which his father the late king Pippin of blessed memory, and himself the most excellent Charles with his brother Carloman and all the chiefs [lit. judges] of the Franks, had made to St. Peter and his vicar Pope Stephen II of blessed memory, when he journeyed to Frank-land : his promise namely to bestow divers cities and territories of that province of Italy and confirm them to St. Peter and all his vicars for a perpetual possession. And when he [Charles] had caused that promise which was made in Frank-land in a place which is called Carisiacum to be read over to him, he and all his nobles approved of all the things which were there recorded.'

    The authenticity of the passage here quoted has been itself gravely questioned, and great difficulties, as we shall hereafter see, encompass the question of the donation by Charles (in 774) founded upon this alleged donation by his father twenty years earlier. But upon a review of the whole evidence it seems to me clear that a donation of some kind was made by Pippin to the Pope at Carisiacum in 754. We call it a donation, but it was in strictness not a donation, but a promise to distribute in a certain manner the spoils to be taken from the Lombard king. And if we take into consideration the thoughts and desires of the Frankish king as far as these are disclosed to us by his words reported by the chroniclers, we may be able to make a probable conjecture as to the nature of the gift which he promised to make to the Pope in the event of victory. He was informed that the Lombard king—generally described to him as 'most wicked' and 'quite unspeakable'—had lately reft from 'the Roman Republic' certain territories between the Adriatic and the Apennines, that he was trying to subject the citizens of Rome to the payment of a poll-tax, and that in his marchings hither and thither through Italy he was trampling upon the Papal patrimonies and oppressing the coloni by whom they were cultivated. All this King Pippin has determined must come to an end. The *justitiae* or rightful claims of St. Peter must be vindicated; the patrimonies must be safe from molestation; the independence of the citizens of Rome must be maintained; the territories lately wrested from 'the Roman Republic' must be restored—not to the Byzantine Emperor, a personage about whom the Frankish king knew and cared but little, but to 'the Roman Republic,' that is to St. Peter, first bishop of Rom and keeper of the doors of the kingdom of heaven, that is to St. Peter's vicar, Pope Stephen II, now sheltering under the Frankish wing in the abbey of S. Denis, to whom moreover he, Pippin, owed a debt of gratitude for the confirmation of him and his sons in the kingdom of the Franks.

    Further than this it is not likely that the Pope's demands or the king's promises extended. The settlement of the Lombards in Italy was now near two centuries old, and might be considered as ancient history. The dukes of Spoleto and Benevento had not, as far as we know, assisted the designs of Aistulf, and had often of recent years been leagued with the Pope against the Lombard king. There was therefore no reason why they should be attacked in the impending Holy War. Restitution of the *status quo ante* Aistulfum, a return to the state of affairs which existed in Italy in the time of Liutprand, was the object which Pippin set before his eyes; only with this exception, that the Exarchate of Ravenna and the Pentapolis, the territories which had been torn from 'the Roman Republic' by Aistulf, were to be handed back, not to the lieutenant of Constantine Copronymus, but to Stephen II, bishop of Rome.

    It is probable enough that the 'Donation' may have been expressed in vague and large terms into which a later Pope might read more than was in the mind of either contracting party at the time of its first inception. In this connection it is important to remember—a fact of which the modern reader is too apt to lose sight—that the geographical information at the command of a statesman of the eighth century was enormously inferior to that which would be available for the humblest mechanic at the present day. Every man of moderate education now knows the configuration of Italy on the map, and can at once approximately estimate the probable effect of this or that cession of territory on the balance of power in the peninsula. If the Frankish king and his counsellors had access to any map either of Gaul or Italy, which may be gravely doubted, it would not be a better one than that which, under the name of the Tabula Peutingeriana, is preserved in the Imperial Library at Vienna, and which, however interesting to the historical student, so grotesquely distorts the shapes and alters the sizes of the countries composing the Roman Empire that any judgment formed on its evidence would be sure to be mistaken.

In fine, Pippin's interest in the affairs of Italy was only of a secondary kind. The scheme, which eventually ripened in his son's mind, of crushing the Lombard monarchy and annexing Italy to his dominions, never, we may safely say, suggested itself to this king of the Franks. All that he was concerned with was the consolidation of his dynasty and the salvation of his soul. To secure these ends he was willing to march into Italy, to defeat the Lombard king, and to assert the claims of St. Peter; but these ends accomplished, the sooner he returned to his own villa by the Marne or the Moselle the better. As we shall see, though he twice appeared and fought in Italy, he did not once visit Rome.

At first Pippin tried the path of negotiation with the Lombard king. Three successive embassies crossed the Alps charged to obtain from Aistulf by the promise of large gifts a recognition of 'the claims of St. Peter.' All being in vain, Pippin summoned the Frankish host to meet him at the royal villa of Brennacum, on the 1st of March, 755. The army moved southward; the 'wedges,' as we are told of the Frankish host, had accomplished nearly half their journey, when Pippin, at the instance of the Pope—sincerely anxious doubtless to prevent the effusion of Christian blood—sent yet one more embassy to Aistulf. It is probably to this embassy that the words of a slightly later chronicler refer, to whom we are indebted for something more definite than the sonorous platitudes of the Papal biographer:—

'Pippin therefore [being about to] cross the Alps, sending his ambassadors to Aistulf, demanded that he would not afflict the Holy Roman Church, whose defender he had become by the divine ordinance, but would render full justice for the property which he had wrested from it. But Aistulf, puffed up with pride, and even with foolish words heaping reproaches on the aforesaid pontiff, would not promise him anything except liberty to return through his dominions to his own proper place. The ambassadors, however, protested that on no other conditions would the lord Pippin depart from the borders of Lombardy unless Aistulf would do justice to St. Peter. "What is that justice of which you speak?" asked Aistulf, to the ambassadors made answer, "That you should restore to him Pentapolis, Narni, and Ceccano, and all the places where the Roman people complain of your injustice. And Pippin sends you this message, that if you are willing to render justice to St. Peter he will give you 12,000 solidi" (£7,200). But Aistulf, spurning all these offers, dismissed the ambassadors without any words of peace.'

On learning the rejection of the proposals for peace the Frankish host, which had marched by way of Lyons, Vienne and Grenoble, ascended successively the valleys of the Isère and Arc, and reached S. Jean de Maurienne, whence they would behold the snowy peaks of the mountains round Mont Cenis rising before them. Here the main body of the host seems to have halted, collecting its strength for the tremendous enterprise of crossing the Mont Cenis in the face of the opposition of a watchful foe. Suddenly and unexpectedly came the tidings that no such enterprise lay before them, that the peril, though not the labour, of the passage of the Alps was vanished. The Lombard king had collected his army and pitched his camp in the valley of Susa, 'with the weapons and engines of war,' says the chronicler, 'and the manifold apparatus which he had wickedly collected against the Republic and the Apostolic See of Rome, wherewith he now strove to defend his nefarious designs'. As the reader has been already reminded, the valley of Susa as well as that of Aosta had been included in the Burgundian-Frankish dominions ever since the early and unsuccessful inroads of the Lombards into Frankish territory. This fact and the consequent necessity of violating Frankish territory before he could even occupy Susa may explain the backward state of Aistulf's preparations for defence. Assuredly, however, he should not have contented himself with merely pitching his camp at the mouth of the pass, but should have occupied some of the heights, so as to harass the march of the invading Aistulf army. The result of this improvidence was too plainly seen. A small body of Frankish soldiers, sent probably with no other object than that of effecting a reconnaissance, were seen emerging from the pass. Aistulf moved at early morning with the whole Lombard army against them, but the Franks, confiding in the help of God and St. Peter, possibly also still enjoying the advantage of the higher ground and fighting with great valour, inflicted serious loss on the Lombard host. The proportion of deaths among the Lombard officers was especially severe, a feature of mountaineering warfare which is often observed at the present day. Almost all the dukes and counts and other nobles were slain in this engagement, and Aistulf himself narrowly escaped death by the fall of a rock. Casting away his armour he fled with the remnant of his host down the valley to Pavia, and shut himself up in that city. Rapidly did Pippin and his men now accomplish the dreaded passage of the Alps. They were in time to capture the deserted camp, to plunder it of its treasures of gold and silver and all the abandoned ornaments of regal magnificence, and to make its tents their own. Pippin then sat down with his army before the city of Pavia, laying waste with fire all the surrounding country, and carrying havoc far down the fertile valley of the Po.

Aistulf soon perceived that he was unable to cope with the might of the king of the Franks, and through the nobles and clergy in the besieging army began to make overtures for peace. They appear to have been seconded by him whom the biographer calls 'the most blessed and as it were angelic pope,' who was in the camp of the invaders, and who desired to stay the ravages of war and the further effusion of Christian blood. A treaty of peace was drawn up between the Romans, the Franks and the Lombards, in which Aistulf with all his nobles bound himself by a mighty and terrible oath to immediately restore Ravenna and divers other cities to the Roman Republic. Hostages were given to ensure the observance of the treaty and of Aistulf's promise that he would entertain no further hostile designs against the republic or the see of Rome; and the costly presents wherewith he had obtained their advocacy of his cause were handed over to the Frankish nobles. After these matters had been settled Stephen returned to Rome with the dignified ecclesiastics who formed his train, enriched with large presents by the generous Frankish king, and Pippin returned to his own land, carrying with him apparently no small part of the great Lombard hoard.

He had not, however, really settled the dispute by his intervention. Unfortunately, as already hinted, Aistulf seems to have been one of those irritating personages, like our Ethelred the Unready, who can make neither war nor peace, neither fight a good stand-up fight successfully, nor accept the consequences of defeat when beaten. Pippin had probably not long returned to his northern home when he received a letter in which Pope Stephen bitterly complained of the many tribulations inflicted upon him by the unjust king of the Lombards. 'That old enemy of the human race, the Devil, has invaded his perfidious heart, and he seems to make of no account the promises which he gave under the sanction of an oath, nor has he consented to restore one hand's breadth of land to the blessed Peter and the holy Church of God, the Republic of the Romans. In truth ever since that day when we [you and I] parted from one another he has striven to put upon us such afflictions, and on the Holy Church of God such insults, as the tongue of man cannot declare: nay, rather the stones themselves, if one may say so, would with mighty howlings weep for our tribulation... I especially grieve, my most excellent sons' (the young kings, Charles and Carloman, are addressed along with their father), 'that you would not hear the words uttered by our Unhappiness, and chose to listen to lies rather than to the truth, deceiving your own souls and making yourselves a laughing-stock. Wherefore without any effectual redress of the wrongs of St. Peter we had to return to our own fold and to the people committed to our charge'.

This is the theme to which Stephen II returns in this and many following letters. 'You have made peace too easily: you have taken no sufficient security for the fulfillment of the promises which you made to St. Peter, and which you yourselves guaranteed by writing under your hands and seals.' Remembering the eagerness for a peaceable settlement without further effusion of Christian blood, which his biographer attributes to the Pope, we are somewhat surprised to find him adopting this tone of remonstrance. It is of course possible that Stephen may have advised the Frankish king to insist on some surer guarantee than oaths and hostages for the fulfillment of Aistulf's promises; but on the other hand it may be suggested that the Churchman, unused to the sights and sounds of war and anxious for peace, urged on his royal friend terms of accommodation which he himself when he had returned to Rome found to be quite insufficient for his purpose.

'Better is it not to have vowed at all,' urges the Pope, 'than to vow and fail to perform the vow. The promised donation written by your own hand is firmly held by the Prince of the Apostles himself. Consider what a stalwart exacter of his dues is the blessed Peter, who through my intervention has anointed you and your sons to be kings; and fear lest when the just Judge appears to judge the quick and the dead and to consume the world by fire, that same Prince of the Apostles shall prove that your written promise failed to bind you. A severe account will you then have to settle with him. All the nations round believed that you who had received from Providence this shining gift, granted to none of your ancestors, of protecting the rights of the Prince of the Apostles, were going to obtain justice for him by your most mighty arm. But in this you seem to be failing, and great stupefaction has seized all hearts by reason thereof. "Faith without works is dead": therefore listen to our cry, and speedily and without delay obtain the restitution to St. Peter of all the cities and towns contained in your donation, as well as of the hostages and captives who are still detained'.

These piteous cries for help do not seem to have been immediately answered. It was probably too late in the year for the Frankish king to think of undertaking another Transalpine expedition. But meanwhile Aistulf, with incredible folly as it seems to us, as well as with scandalous disregard of his plighted word, took the field, and endeavoured to capture Rome in the winter months of the year 756, before Pippin could come to its rescue. On the 1st of January an army under the command of the Duke of Tuscany came down, like Porsena's Etruscans of old, clustering round the Janiculan Mount and blocked up the three gates of the City, on the right bank of the Tiber— Portuensis, S. Pancratii, and S. Petri. The Lombards of Benevento, who had made a levy *en masse,* marched from the South, and beset the gates of St. Paul and St. John, and the three gates between them. King Aistulf himself pitched his tents, like another Alaric, outside the Salarian Gate, and said (or was reported by the trembling citizens to have said), 'Open to me this Salarian gate, and let me enter the City. Hand over to me your Pope, and I will deal gently with you. Otherwise I will demolish your walls and slay you all with one sword. Then let me see who will deliver you out of my hands.'

The Lombard blockade of Rome lasted for three months. Of the events which marked its course we have no other information than that which is conveyed to us by the indignant Papal biographer and by the loud shrieks of Pope Stephen himself, who in two letters written to Pippin about the 24th of February describes, and perhaps exaggerates, the actions of the Lombard king. The farms of the Campagna are said to have been laid waste with fire and sword. The Lombards are accused of burning the churches, of throwing the images of the saints into the fire, of stuffing their pouches with the consecrated elements and devouring them at their gluttonous repasts, of stripping the altars of their altar-cloths and other adornments, of carrying off and violating the nuns, some of whom died of the ill-treatment which they received, of belabouring the monks, some of whom they lacerated with stripes. The farm-houses on St. Peter's property were destroyed by fire: so too were the suburban houses of all the Romans of every class. The cattle were driven off, the vines cut down to the roots, the harvests ' trampled down and devoured.'

All this catalogue of crimes is derived from the Pope's letters addressed to Pippin, passionately crying for help. The Papal biographer, while confirming in general terms the charge of wasting the Campagna with fire and sword, adds a more specific accusation, that of digging up the bodies of the saints and carrying them away. This lawless quest for sacred relics shows the strange mixture of savagery and devotion in the minds of the Christianized but only half-civilized Lombards.

The military operations of the Lombard army seem to have been confined to the re-capture of Narni (which had been previously handed over by Aistulf to the emissary of Pippin), and to frequent but unsuccessful assaults on the walls of Rome. In repelling these attacks the Pope saw with pleasure, conspicuous on the walls, the mail-clad figure of Abbot Warnehar, who had come to Rome as Pippin's envoy, and who now, says the Pope, 'watched day and night for the defence of the afflicted City of Rome, and like a good athlete of Christ strove with all his might for the defence and liberation of all of us Romans.'

Late in the second month of the siege the valiant Warnehar, along with two other of Pippin's envoys, returned from Rome, accompanied by George, bishop of Ostia. They travelled by sea, and they bore two letters from Stephen to the king, from which the foregoing particulars as to Aistulf's invasion have been quoted. These letters repeated in yet shriller key than their predecessors the entreaties, nay the commands, of the Pope to Pippin, if he valued his eternal salvation, to come speedily to the rescue of Rome. 'The Lombards taunt us in their rage and fury, saying, "Now we have surrounded you. Let the Franks come if they can and deliver you from our hands". On you, after God and St. Peter, depend the lives of all the Romans. If we perish all the nations of the earth will say, "Where is the confidence of the Romans which they placed in the kings and the nation of the Franks?". More than that, the sin of our ruin will lie on your soul; and in the last great day of judgment, when the Lord shall sit surrounded by the blessed Peter and the other Apostles to judge as it were by fire every class, each sex, and every one of this world's potentates, He will harden His heart against you, who now harden your heart against our prayers, and will say to you (0 God forbid that it should be so), "I know you not, because you did not help the Church of God, and because you took no care to deliver His own peculiar people when they were in peril." '

To add emphasis to these two letters a third brought containing and enforcing the same arguments, and putting them in the mouth of the awful holder of the keys of heaven, St. Peter himself. The letter is addressed to the three kings, Pippin, Charles, and Carloman; to the most holy bishops, abbots, presbyters; and to all religious monks; also to the dukes, counts, armies and people dwelling in Frank-land. In it the Apostle assures his correspondents that he has chosen them as his adopted sons for the deliverance from the hands of their enemies of the City of Rome in which his bones repose, and the people of Rome committed to his care by Christ. 'As if I, God's apostle Peter, were now standing in my bodily presence before you, even so do you firmly believe that you hear the words of my exhortation, because, though I be absent in the flesh, in the spirit I am not far from you. For it is written, " He that receiveth a prophet in the name of a prophet shall receive a prophet's reward." Moreover our Lady, the Mother of God, Mary ever a virgin, doth with us most solemnly adjure, warn, and order you : and the like do the thrones and dominations and the host of the heavenly army, the martyrs and confessors of Christ, and all who are in any way well-pleasing to God.

'Run! run! by the living and true God I exhort and summon you: run and help, ere the living fountain which has satisfied your thirst be dried up, ere the last spark of the flame which gave you light be quenched, ere your spiritual mother, the Holy Church of God, through whom you hope to receive eternal life, be attacked and foully ravished by impious men. ... I speak on behalf of that City of Rome in which the Lord ordained that my body should rest, that City which He commended to my care and made the foundation of the faith. Liberate that City and its people, your brethren, and do not suffer it to be invaded by the nation of the Lombards: so may your provinces and your possessions not be invaded by nations that ye know not of. Let not me be separated from my Roman people: so may you not be separated from the kingdom of God and the life eternal. I conjure, I conjure you, 0 my best beloved ones, by the living God, suffer not this my City of Rome and the people that dwelleth therein to be any longer tortured by the nation of the Lombards: so may your bodies and souls not be tortured in the eternal and unquenchable fire of Tartarus with the devil and his pestilential angels. And let not the sheep of the Lord's flock committed to my care by God, namely the Roman people, be any longer scattered abroad, so may the Lord not scatter you and cast you forth as He did unto the people of Israel.'

To address such a letter to the Frankish king in the name of the Apostle himself was certainly a daring stroke of rhetoric. It jars upon modern taste and feeling, it may perhaps have jarred upon the spiritual sensibilities of some men even in that day, to have the Prince of the Apostles introduced thus audaciously as an actor on the scene where Stephen, Aistulf, and Pippin were playing their respective parts. But if it was an offence against reverence and good taste, there is no reason to think that it was anything more. It would be perfectly understood by those to whom the letter was addressed that the words were the words of Stephen, though the superscription of the letter assigned them to Peter. It is surely through a deficiency of imagination and of insight into the feelings of a past age and its modes of expressing them, that some modern authors have seen in this document an attempt to impose on the credulity of Pippin by presenting him with a forged letter from the world of spirits.

These urgent entreaties, these promises of spiritual reward and menaces of spiritual perdition, produced the desired effect. It was probably as early in 756 as warlike operations could be undertaken that Pippin again marched by way of Châlons-sur-Saone and Geneva to S. Jean de Maurienne, and crossed the Mont Cenis, routing the Lombards, who seem to have been again stationed at the mouth of the pass, and upon whom Pippin's soldiers burst with Frankish fury, slaying many and driving the rest in flight before them down the valley. But on his march towards Pavia, he met, not Aistulf, but two unlooked-for visitors from Constantinople. George the first secretary and John life-guardsman (the same officer doubtless who had come on a similar mission two years before) had arrived in Rome charged with a commission to the Frankish king. Stephen had informed them of Pippin's intended movements, and had probably showed by his manner that he was no longer the subservient courtier of Byzantium, but that the 'Donation of Constantine' was about to take effect through the intervention of his powerful friend beyond the Alps. The Imperial envoys disbelieved the tale, but took ship for Marseilles, accompanied by an emissary from the Pope. On their arrival at Marseilles they found that the Pope's information had been too true, that Pippin was indeed already on his march for Italy; and probably the gossip of the seaport told that the expedition was all for the 'justice of St. Peter', with not a word about the 'justice of the Emperor'. Saddened by this discovery they strove to the utmost of their power to detain the Papal envoy at Marseilles, to prevent him from reaching the presence of the king. But 'though', we are told, 'they afflicted him grievously, by the intervention of St. Peter their crafty cleverness was brought to nought'. However, the Imperial ambassadors getting the start of the Papal envoy, travelled with rapidity to the camp of the Frankish king, whom they overtook not far from Pavia. With earnest entreaties and the promise of many presents George besought Pippin to restore Ravenna and the cities and villages of the Exarchate to the Empire.

'But in no wise,' says the biographer, 'did he avail to incline the firm heart of that most Christian and benignant king to any such surrender. Mild as he was, that worshipper of God declared [with emphasis] that on no account whatever should those cities be alienated from the power of the blessed Peter and the jurisdiction of the Roman Church and the Apostolic See, affirming with an oath that for no [living] man's favour had he given himself once and again to the conflict, but solely for love of St. Peter and for the pardon of his sins: asserting too that no abundance of treasure would bribe him to take away what he had once offered for St. Peter's acceptance. Having given this answer to the Imperial ambassador, he at once gave him leave to return to his own place by another way, and thus did the Silentiarius arrive at Rome, having accomplished nothing of his purpose.

As to the details of Pippin's second campaign in Italy we know scarcely anything. Aistulf probably abandoned the siege of Rome by the end of March, and returned to Pavia to defend himself against the threatened invasion. Pippin with his nephew Tassilo, the young duke of Bavaria, again ravaged the plains of Lombardy, and again pitched his tents under the walls of Pavia. Once more Aistulf saw himself compelled to beg humbly for peace, to renew his promise to surrender to the Pope the cities of the Exarchate and

Pentapolis, and to add thereto the town of Comiaclum which lay in a lagoon north of Ravenna, and may perhaps have made the occupation of Ravenna more secure. A written 'donation of all these territories' to St. Peter and the Holy Roman Church and all pontiffs of the Apostolic See for ever was given by Aistulf and laid up among the Papal archives. Assuredly also some stronger guarantee than this for the fulfillment of Aistulf s promises was taken by the Frankish king. According to one chronicler—not of the most trustworthy character—Aistulf had to surrender a third part of the great Lombard hoard to his conqueror, to promise fealty and a yearly tribute of 5,000 solidi to the king of the Franks, and to guarantee by the surrender of hostages the fulfillment of all previous engagements to St. Peter and Pope Stephen.

When Pippin returned to his own land he commissioned the faithful Fulrad, now by interchange of hospitalities doubly bound to the Pope, to see to the fulfillment of Aistulf's promises. Accompanied by the officers of the Lombard king, Fulrad 'entered,' says the biographer, 'each one of the cities both of the Pentapolis and Emilia, received their submission, and taking with him the nobles' of each city, together with the keys of their gates, arrived at Rome. Having placed the keys of the city of Ravenna as well as of the different cities of the Exarchate along with King Pippin's donation on the tomb of St. Peter, he handed them over to the same Apostle of God and to his vicar the most holy Pope and all his pontifical successors, to be forever possessed and disposed of by them.

The biographer then gives the names of twenty-three cities and towns, which will be found in a Note at the end of this chapter. It will be sufficient here to state that they did not comprise (as one might suppose from the previous sentence) all the cities of the two provinces of the Emilia and Pentapolis. Of the Emilia only about a fifth, in the extreme east of the province, was yet obtained by the Papal see. The whole of the Pentapolis however, with the important exception of Ancona, was included in the cession to the Pope of which Fulrad was the happy instrument. This cession therefore comprised all the coast-line of the Adriatic from Comacchio north of Ravenna to Sinigaglia north of Ancona. Inland it reached up to the great dorsal spine of Italy formed by the Apennine range, and was doubtless now connected with the Ducatus Romae by the western branch of the great Flaminian Way, on which 'the Republic' had long held the key-city of Perugia and now probably acquired whatever other towns or villages were necessary to establish a secure communication between the bishop of Rome and his new dominion on the Adriatic. Narni, we are expressly told, was now again restored to him, but Narni is on the eastern branch of the Via Flaminia, over which, since the Lombard duke of Spoleto occupied that important post of vantage, we can hardly suppose the Popes to have had any claim other than one of courtesy.

Thus then is the struggle at last ended. The keys of all those fair cities repose in the well-known crypt where, amid ever-burning candles, lie the martyred remains of the fisherman of Galilee. The territory between the Apennines and the Adriatic, ruled over of late by a Greek exarch, wrested from him by the Lombards and from the Lombards by the Frankish king, has been handed over, in spite of the 'Greek' Emperor's remonstrance, 'to the Roman Republic, to St. Peter and to his Vicars the Popes of Rome for ever.' The Pope does not yet assume the kingly title, nor must we commit the anachronism of calling him 'il Papa-Re', but it cannot be doubted that the old man at whose feet the keys of the twenty-three cities have been laid, and before whom the nobles of those cities have bowed, is recognized as their ruler, and that we behold in Stephen II the real sovereign of 'the Exarchate'.

NOTE A. List of the Cities ceded by Aistulf to Stephen II (756).

The following are the names of the ceded cities as given by the Papal biographer, with their modern equivalents, which are in some instances conjectural.

Ravenna
Rimini.
Pesaro.
La Cattolica, on the coast between Rimini and Pesaro. Fano.
Cesena.
Sinigaglia.
Jesi.
Forlimpopoli.
Forli.
Castro Caro (near Forli).
Montefeltro, now San Leo, S.W. of S. Marino.
Arcevia, near Jesi.
Mons Lucatium, in the territory of Cesena.
Serra dei Conti, between Jesi and Fossombrone.
The Republic of San Marino. Sarsina.
Urbino.
Cagli.
Cantiano.
Gubbio.
Comacchio.
Narni.

CHAPTER IX

THE PONTIFICATE OF PAUL I

We have again reached a point at which there is a clearing of the historical stage and some new actors appear upon the scene.

It was probably while Pope Stephen was still sheltering at S. Denis that the great champion of the Papacy, Boniface, received the crown of martyrdom. Revisiting the scene of his early labours in Friesland in the summer of 754, he had collected a number of recently-baptized converts on the banks of the river Boorn, in the flat land between the Zuyder Zee and the German Ocean, and was about to perform the ceremony of their confirmation. A party of Frisian heathens, revengeful for his old attacks on their idols, and coveting the ecclesiastical treasures, the vessels of silver and gold which he and his companions (for he had a long train of attendants) had brought, came upon them at daybreak on the 5th of June. Boniface forbade his followers to fight, held high the sacred relics, and said to his disciples, "Fear not them which kill the body. Anchor your souls on God, who after this short life is over will give you the prize of eternal life in the fellowship of the citizens on high". The barbarians rushed on with swords drawn. Boniface lifted a copy of the Gospels high over his head. A Frisian sword struck down the feeble defence. He was slain, and fifty-two of his companions with him. The barbarians rifled the tents, drank the sacramental wine, and hurled the precious manuscripts into the sluggish river, where long after, we are told, they were found uninjured. The very codex which the saint had used for a helmet showed the barbarian's sword-cut through it, but had all its letters visible. So perished the great apostle of Germany. The monks of Utrecht soon appeared upon the scene of the martyrdom, and carried off the precious relics of the martyrs to their own cathedral. The great prize of all, however, the body of Boniface himself, they were not permitted to retain. It was borne away up the Rhine-stream and the Main-stream to be laid in his own beloved monastery of Fulda.

It was only a few months after the surrender of the Exarchate and the Pentapolis that Aistulf, king of the Lombards, vanished from the scene. The Frankish chroniclers tell us that he was "meditating how to falsify his promises, leave his hostages in the lurch, and violate his oaths"; but no evidence is adduced of these fraudulent designs. All that we know with certainty is that he fell from his horse while hunting, was thrown violently against a tree, and died after a few days of the injuries which he had received. The accident probably happened at the end of December, 756, for in the letter which Pope Stephen II wrote to Pippin to inform him of the fact he says, "That follower of the devil, Aistulf, devourer of the blood of Christians, destroyer of the churches of God, struck by a divine blow has been swallowed up in the infernal whirlpool. For in the very days in which he set forth to devastate this City of Rome, after the year had come round, he was so stricken by the divine sword that at the very same season of the year in which he had committed so many crimes he finished his impious life".

The Lombard people, as might be expected, had gentler words to use in speaking of their departed king. Six years, nine years, fifteen years after his death he was still "our lord king Aistulf of good and holy memory".

On the death of Aistulf the Lombard state narrowly escaped the horrors of a civil war. One of the most powerful men in the kingdom was a certain Desiderius, a native probably of Brescia, who had been much favoured by the late king and advanced by him to the high dignity of Duke of Tuscany. At the head of the assembled forces of that important district he stood forth as a claimant for the crown. Desiderius, however, was apparently a man of undistinguished birth. There were other Lombard nobles who considered themselves to rank much before him in the kingdom; and above all, the late king's brother Ratchis in his cell on Monte Cassino, notwithstanding that for seven and a half years he had worn the monkish cowl, heard with indignation that the throne which had once been his was occupied by such an one as the low-born Desiderius. He escaped to Pavia, and there for three months, from December to March, ruled in the palace of the Lombards.

As to the elevation of Desiderius to the throne is thus given in the Legend of St. Julia from a MS. Chronicle of Bishop Sieard of Cremona (who died in 1215) : I follow the translation of Abel : 'There lived in Brescia a nobleman, pious and God-fearing, named Desiderius. When the barons and chief persons of the realm gathered together at Pavia to choose a king, Desiderius said to his wife Ansa, "I will go there too". She laughed and said, "Go, mayhap they will choose thee for their king". He went, and arrived on the first day at a place called Lenum, where he lay down to rest under a tree. While he slept, a snake stole forth and wound itself round his head like a crown. His servant feared to wake him, lest the snake should bite him. Meanwhile Desiderius dreamed that a royal diadem was placed upon his head. Then he awoke, unharmed by the snake, and said, "Arise, let us go, for I have had a dream from which I judge that I shall be king". When they came to Pavia they found the people standing about in the courtyard, waiting for the decision of the electors, who had consulted together for several days without being able to come to a decision. So the crowd said to Desiderius, "Go in to them, Desiderius, and tell them that we are tired of waiting". He went in and told them what the crowd said, and when they saw Desiderius, of whom nobody had thought before as a candidate, one of the assembly cried out, "This Desiderius is an honourable man, and though he has not large possessions, he is valiant in war. Let us choose him for king". So it was done: he was arrayed in royal robes and proclaimed king amid general rejoicing. But he forgot not the place where the serpent had wound itself round his head, but built there a glorious abbey in honour of Jesus Christ and St. Benedict, and enriched it with many gifts. His wife also built at her own cost a convent for nuns in Brescia, and endowed it with estates, meadows, mills, and springs of water, with many dependants and slaves in all the surrounding bishoprics, and with costly ornaments, as became a queen of the Lombards'.

Happily a civil war was avoided, mainly as it would seem through the influence of the Pope, who beheld, doubtless with genuine disapproval, this attempt of a professed monk to return to the world and the palace which he had quitted, and who saw an opportunity to extend his newly-won dominions by working on the Duke of Tuscany's eagerness for the crown. An agreement was come to between Desiderius and Stephen, which is thus described in a letter written by the Pope to his Frankish patron : —

'Now by the providence of God, by the hands of His Prince of Apostles St. Peter, and by thy strong arm, by the industrious precaution of that man beloved of God, thy henchman Fulrad, our beloved son, Desiderius, mildest of men, has been ordained king over the nation of the Lombards. And in the presence of the same Fulrad he has promised on his oath to restore to St. Peter the remaining cities, Faenza, Imola, and Ferrara, with the forests and other territories thereto belonging; also the cities Osimo, Ancona, and Umana, with their territories. And afterwards, through Duke Garrinod and Grimwald. he promised to restore to us the city of Bologna with its district, and he professed that he would always remain in quiet peace with the Church of God and our people. He declared that he was loyal towards your God-protected realm, and he begged us to entreat your Goodness that you would confirm the treaty of peace with him and the whole nation of the Lombards.'

This compact, as we learn from the Papal biographer (as well as from the letter just quoted), was framed on the advice of Fulrad, now evidently the accepted and permanent link between Pippin and Stephen, and it was made not only in his presence but in that of Stephen's brother Paul the deacon, and of Christopher, who had accompanied him as *regionarius* into France, who was now *consiliarius*, and who was thereafter to fill the higher office of *primicerius* and to play an important part in Roman politics. The object and motive of this stroke of Papal policy are clear. As stated by the learned editor of the Liber Pontificalis, the conquests of Aistulf from the Empire having been restored, it was now desired to go back a generation further and reclaim the conquests of Liutprand. These were 'the remaining cities' on the west and south of the already-ceded territory, which Pope Stephen now claimed, and some of which he actually obtained as the price of his support of Desiderius. In view of the relations which afterwards existed between this man, the last of the Lombard kings, and the Papal See, it is strange to find him here spoken of as 'mildest of men', and to remember that he was actually the favoured Roman candidate for the Lombard throne.

On receiving the document in which the promise and oath of Desiderius were contained, Stephen sent a letter of exhortation by the hands of the presbyter Stephen (one day to be himself Pope) to the monk-king at Pavia. The indefatigable Fulrad hastened with a detachment of Frankish soldiers to the help of Desiderius, who could also reckon on a contingent from the army of the *Ducatus Romae*. Ratchis saw that the scale was too heavily weighted against him. He could not fight the Franks, the Pope, and the Lombard duke of Tuscany all at once. He descended from his lately mounted throne, returned to Monte Cassino, and died there, when or how we know not. All that we know is that he, like so many other renowned sons of Benedict, lies buried on that famous hill.

In this connection it is interesting to observe that in the just quoted letter of Pope Stephen, the last that he wrote to his Frankish patron, there is a plea for pardon to the monks who had accompanied Carloman in his journey to the Frankish Court. This plea, which is preferred at the request of their abbot Optatus, shows how heavy had been the hand of Pippin on all who were concerned in that ill-starred intervention.

The promise so solemnly sworn to by Desiderius was not altogether made void. Apparently before the abdication of Ratchis was complete, the urgent Pope sent his messengers to obtain the surrender of the promised cities. They returned bringing with them the keys of Faventia, Tiberiacum, and Cabellum (Faenza, Bagnicavallo, and Cavello), together with all the towns in the duchy of Ferrara. This accession of territory rounded off the Papal dominions in the north, but the important cities of Imola, Bologna, and Ancona (with their neighbours Osimo and Umana) were still withheld by the Lombard king.

The letter in which Pope Stephen II announced to Pippin the accession of Desiderius described his friendly disposition towards the Roman See, and prayed the Frankish king to look favourably upon him, was one of the latest documents to which he set his hand. That letter seems to have been written in the month of March or April, and on the 26th of April, 757, he died. Many of his predecessors had been men of Greek nationality. In his five years' pontificate this essentially Roman Pope had done much to fasten down the great western Patriarchate to the soil of Italy. His is certainly one of the great epoch-making names in the list of bishops of Rome. As Leo the First had turned aside the terrible Hun and had triumphed over the Eastern theologians, as Gregory the Great had consolidated his spiritual dominion over Western Europe and rescued for it a great province from heathendom, so Stephen II won for himself and his successors the sovereignty over some of the fairest regions of Italy, gave a deadly blow to the hereditary Lombard enemy, and in fact if not in name began that long line of Pope-kings which ended in our own day in the person of the ninth Pius.

While Stephen was lying on his death-bed there was already hot debate going on in Rome as to his successor. A certain portion of 'the people of Rome' favoured the election of the Archdeacon Theophylact, and assembled daily in his house to discuss measures for his elevation. This party is called by some modern writers 'the Lombard', by others 'the Imperial' party. We have no evidence in support of either conjecture.

Another, and as it proved a more powerful section of the people, favoured the elevation of the deacon Paul, brother and chief counsellor of the dying pontiff. He, refusing to go forth into the City and court the suffrages of the electors, remained in the Lateran with a few faithful friends waiting upon his brother's death-bed. His fraternal piety was rewarded. After Stephen II had been solemnly entombed in the basilica of St. Peter, the adherents of Paul carried his election to the vacant throne, and the supporters of Theophylact dispersed, apparently without tumult.

We have already in the case of Silverius seen the son of a Pope chosen for the papacy, though not in immediate succession to his father. Now brother follows close upon brother as wearer of the Roman mitre, almost the only instance of the kind that has occurred in the long annals of the papacy. The choice in this instance seems to have been a good one, but it might have been a dangerous precedent. Considering the immense power which the Popes have wielded, it must be considered on the whole an evidence of statesmanship and courage on the part of the electors that mere family claims have so seldom determined the succession to the pontifical throne.

Of the new Pope's character and personal history we know but little. A Roman of course by birth, like his brother, and like him brought up in the palace of the Lateran, he was probably at this time still middle life, since his ordination as deacon dated only from the days of Zacharias (741-752). What little we hear of his character seems to indicate a man of kindly temper, paying nightly visits to the cottages of his sick neighbours, or with his servants relieving the wants of the destitute : visiting the gaols also at night, and often setting free their inmates who were lying under sentence of death. Moreover, we are told, 'if by the injustice of his satellites he had caused temporary tribulation to any man, he took the earliest opportunity to bestow on such one the comfort of his compassion'. Even these words of praise indicate already the characteristic defects as well as merits of a government by priests, but they are valuable as evidence that already the Pope exercised all the functions of a temporal sovereign in Rome, probably therefore also in the *Ducatus Romae* and the lately annexed Pentapolis.

The ten years of Paul's pontificate were an interval of peace between two political storms. He appears to have made it his chief aim to follow in all things the policy of 'my lord and brother of blessed memory, the most holy Pope Stephe '; and his copious correspondence with Pippin enables us to trace the workings of this policy in relation to the Empire, the Lombards, and the Frankish kingdom. We will consider each subject separately.

I. **The Empire**. Already in the last letter written by Pope Stephen II to Pippin we find a note of alarm sounded as to the hostility of the iconoclastic 'Greek' Emperor. 'And this,' says Stephen, 'we earnestly pray of your Exalted Goodness that you would order such measures to be taken with respect to the Greeks that the holy Catholic and Apostolic faith may through you remain whole and unshattered for ever'. This note becomes louder and more shrill throughout the correspondence of Paul, whose religious aversion to the image-breaking Emperor is mingled with his anxiety as a temporal ruler lest, either in conjunction with Desiderius or by his own unaided efforts, Constantine V should wrest from the Church its hardly-won dominions on the shore of the Adriatic.

A certain George, an Imperial secretary, had been sent from Constantinople on a roving mission to the West, to win over Pippin if possible to the cause of iconoclasm, to effect an alliance if possible with Desiderius, to recover Ravenna and the Pentapolis if possible for the empire, but at any rate and by all means to counter-work the schemes of the bishop of Rome, doubly odious at Constantinople as the great defender of image-worship and the rebellious subject who had by Frankish help obtained possession of the best part of Imperial Italy and was now holding it in defiance of his lord. The influence of this secretary George on Western statesmen was profoundly dreaded by the pontiff. A letter, which is quoted only in abstract, contained "lamentations and tribulations, because King Desiderius has been taking counsel with George the Imperial envoy, who has come hither on his way to *Francia* to the intent that the Emperor should send his army into Italy to wrest from us Ravenna and the Pentapolis and the City of Rome". Desiderius has had 'private and nefarious conversations' with George at Naples for the same purpose. And lastly, in some mysterious way George has won over a certain presbyter Marinus to his 'unjust operations against the holy Church of God and the orthodox faith' : that is, no doubt, to the iconoclastic crusade. A short time before, this Marinus had been high in favour with both Pope and Frankish King. He had been 'our most dearly beloved and faithful presbyter','to whom at Pippin's request Paul granted the *titulus* or parish church of St. Chrysogonus in the Trastevere at Rome. Now he is under the severe displeasure of the Pope and has to undergo a singular punishment. "Tell our brother bishop Wilchar", writes Paul to Pippin, "to consecrate presbyter Marinus bishop on our behalf. And order him to go and preside over some city in your dominions, which your most wise Excellency may decide upon, that he may there call to mind the wickedness which he has perpetrated and repent of his unrighteous deeds lest otherwise the Devil should lay hold of his wandering mind and raise him aloft to dash him down into utter ruin".

More than once we find the Pope repeating to his powerful patron the alarming rumours which have reached him as to the designs of 'the most wicked Greeks'. "Some of the most sincere subjects of your spiritual mother [the Roman Church] have intimated to us that six patricians, bringing with them three hundred ships, together with the navy of Sicily, have started from the Royal City [Constantinople] and are hastening to us here in Rome. What they want to do or for what cause they are being sent hither we are utterly ignorant. This only is told us, that they are directed to come first to us and afterwards to your Excellency in Francia".

This letter appears to have sounded a vain alarm. The six patricians, it would seem, did not make their appearance in Rome, nor were their three hundred ships descried in the offing from Ostia: but a letter from Pippin, which was probably a reply to the foregoing, informed the Pope that he was ready for the help and defence of the Holy Church of God 'when the necessity for such help should arise'; a gentle hint that it would be well not to harass a king, who had hard battles of his own to fight, with rumours of imaginary invasions.

About three years later, circa 763, (apparently) the rumour of a Byzantine invasion was revived, the tidings again coming from some of the faithful subjects of mother Church, probably some of the Roman party in Pentapolis or Ravenna. Again, 'The nefandissimi Graeci, enemies of God's holy Church and assailants of the orthodox faith, in direct opposition to God's will, are longing to make a hostile attack on us and on the region of Ravenna'. So great is the alarm into which the Pope is thrown by these tidings that he is willing to accept even Lombard help for his deliverance. Pippin is besought to send an envoy to Desiderius at Pavia, to the Lombard dukes of Tuscany, of Benevento, of Spoleto, ordering them all to hasten to the assistance of the Pope.

This too, however, was a vain alarm. The Emperor sent ambassadors, probably twice or thrice, to discuss the iconoclastic question with the Frankish king, to importune him for the restoration of the Exarchate, to wrangle with the Pope's envoys as to the wording of their master's letters, but no armed intervention of any kind was made by Constantine Copronymus in the affairs of Italy.

This exhibition of feebleness on the part of an Emperor of the strong Isaurian race, perhaps the toughest and most courageous of them all, may well surprise us till we look at the difficulties nearer home with which that Emperor had to contend. From 753 to 775 he was almost constantly at war with the Bulgarians, the near and still heathen neighbours of Thrace and Macedonia. Most of his campaigns were successful, but even a successful campaign imposed a great strain on his resources and those of his empire.

Nor did he altogether escape the fickleness of the fortune of war. In 759 he sustained a serious defeat in one of the passes of the Balkans. In 765 a great naval armament, consisting of 2,600 transport ships, was wrecked in the Euxine, and all the crews perished. This disaster was followed by a conspiracy, in which some of the chief nobles of the Empire were engaged, and which even Constantine's own iconoclastic Patriarch of Constantinople was suspected of having favoured.

Throughout, the Emperor's fiercest fight was with his own subjects, and was caused by his remorseless, relentless vigour in giving effect to the iconoclastic policy of his father. In the year 753, two years after the Lombard conquest of Ravenna, a great synod was held at Constantinople which condemned the worship of images. The Bulgarian wars and other embarrassments prevented the immediate outbreak of persecution. It began however in full violence in 761, and from that time onwards Constantine, fiercely hated by a large party among his subjects, frantically cheered by another party (which included probably the strongest portion of his army), was pursuing, with all the energy of his soul, the ruin of the monks and bishops who yet clave to the worship of images. It was the monks who especially attracted the wrath of the Emperor, and out of whose ranks came the most celebrated martyrs to the cause of image-worship. Such an one was Andreas, who, having insulted the Emperor by calling him 'a new Julian, a new Valens', was scourged through the Hippodrome, strangled, and cast into the Bosphorus. Such an one was Stephanus, who after spending thirty years in a cave in Bithynia and having afterwards become the abbot of a monastery of refugee monks, was forcibly removed from his cell and banished to the island of Proconnesus, then thrown into prison, and fed for eleven months on six ounces of bread weekly, and at last, with the connivance if not by the express orders of the Emperor, was pulled out of prison, dragged through the streets, hacked to pieces, and cast into the malefactors' burying-place.

It does not appear that there was much actual bloodshed in this iconoclastic persecution, but there was an insulting flippancy in the methods employed by Constantine V which made his tyranny harder to bear than that of more murderous persecutors. When he found it impossible to procure the adoption by the monks of the decrees of the Synod of 753, he turned them out of their monasteries, many of which he converted into barracks for his soldiers. Some of the expelled monks were compelled to walk up and down the Hippodrome, each holding the hand of a prostitute, amidst the jeers and spittings of the mob. The Patriarch Constantine, who as has been said fell under suspicion of being concerned in the conspiracy of the nobles and who had also grown cold in his iconoclastic zeal, was scourged so severely that he could not stand. He was then carried in a litter to St. Sophia, and compelled to listen to the reading of a long paper containing the history of his misdeeds, for each one of which he received a blow on the head from the reading secretary.

Then, after the hair of his head, beard and eyebrows had been shaven off, he was seated on an ass with his face to its tail, and exposed in that state to the insults of the populace in the Hippodrome. At last, after he had been compelled by all these cruelties to recant his condemnation of the iconoclastic synod, he was beheaded, and his truncated corpse was thrown into the pit of the suicides. This depth of degradation, into which imperial tyranny had hurled the second patriarchate of Christendom, is probably the best justification that can be offered for the Roman pontiff's eagerness to obtain the position of sovereignty, which, as he might think, could alone secure him from a similar downfall.

For Constantine Copronymus himself, whatever may be our judgment upon the iconoclastic controversy, it is impossible not to feel loathing and abhorrence. Of course his cruelties have been exaggerated by the ecclesiastical historians whose voices alone have reached posterity: but after making every reasonable deduction on this account, it is impossible to doubt that he was deliberately, wantonly, and insultingly cruel. And moreover, his antagonism to the Church was not confined to the iconoclastic controversy. He seems to have been one of the earliest instances of that free-thinking tendency which was the result of the contact of Christianity and Islamism. He spoke lightly of some of the names most venerated by Christians; he almost encouraged profanity in speech; his morals were undoubtedly licentious. A free-living as well as free-thinking ruler, bringing a round of joyous revelries into the solemn old palace by the Bosphorus, he no doubt achieved a certain popularity both with his soldiers and with the mob: but this very looseness of faith and of morality must have made his religious persecution all the more exasperating. The intolerance of a narrow bigot is hard to bear, but the intolerance of a man who is himself devoid of faith is yet more intolerable.

This Emperor, Constantine V, and these two Popes, Stephen and Paul, mark the final severance of political relations between Rome and Constantinople, to be followed in the next century by the great and final rupture of ecclesiastical relations between them. The harsh and violent character of Constantine Copronymus had something to do with this result; the fact that Stephen and Paul were Romans, while their two immediate predecessors, Gregory III and Zacharias, had been Orientals (the first a Syrian, the second a Greek), had perhaps even more to do with it: but obviously the chief determining factor was the capture of Ravenna by Aistulf, and its surrender at the command of Pippin to the Papacy. The sceptre had thus obviously departed from Constantinople and been transferred to 'Francia'. For a few years the Popes continued as a matter of form to date their letters by the year of the Emperor reigning at Constantinople, but after 772 even that survival from the old days of dependence faded away. Let us consider what this renunciation of dependence on the Eastern Augustus amounted to, for it gives a very peculiar character to the second half of the eighth century. From the time when bishops were first consecrated in Rome, down to—let us say—726, there could be no doubt that the bishop of Rome was a subject; nor (with some possible reservation for the short interval of Ostrogothic domination) that he was the subject of a Roman Emperor reigning at Rome, at Milan, at Ravenna, or at Constantinople. From 726 to 800 the Pope was practically ' amasterless man', the virtual ruler of the *Ducatus Romae*, and afterwards the acknowledged lord of the Exarchate and the Pentapolis. From the year 800 down to the French Revolution, the Pope, however great might be his spiritual pretensions, was, as regarded his temporal dominions, included, theoretically or practically, in that great, mysterious, loosely-compacted organization which was called the Holy Roman Empire. From the downfall of Napoleon to the seizure of Rome by Victor Emmanuel, a space of fifty-five years, the Pope-king was in theory as well as in practice an absolute monarch, owning no political superior however shadowy, as much a sovereign as the kings of France or Spain before the Great Revolution. Thus, from this point of view, the half-century between Waterloo and Sedan reproduced, as no intervening period had done, the half-century between Leo the Isaurian and Charles the Great.

II. ***The Lombards.*** We have next to consider the relations of Paul I with the new Lombard king, Desiderius. It need hardly be said that these relations soon became unfriendly, but they were scarcely interrupted by actual war. We have seen that Faenza and a little corner of territory round it were ceded to St. Peter. Further than that concession the gratitude of Desiderius for Papal help or his fear of the Papal anathema never went. On the contrary, he soon bestirred himself for the restoration of the power of a Lombard king to the fullness of its privileges in the days of Liutprand, and in doing so inevitably came into collision with the '*justitiae*' of St. Peter, and provoked the shrill outcry of the Pope.

In the last letter which Pope Stephen II wrote to Pippin (in March or April of 757), the letter in which he praised the excellent disposition of 'the mildest of men, Desiderius', were written these words:— "Moreover the people of the duchy of Spoleto, by the hands of St. Peter and your very strong arm, have appointed a duke for themselves. And both the Spoletans and the Beneventans all desire to commend themselves to your Excellency, preserved by God, and with panting breath are urgent to entreat your goodness".

Here was indeed an important change threatened in the political map of Italy. True it is that the Spoletan and Beneventan duchies had often stirred uneasily and mutinously against the rule even of a strong king like Liutprand; but if the Pope's letter accurately described the situation, if they were 'commending' themselves to Pippin, that meant, in the already current language of feudalism, that the two dukes desired to place their hands in his and to swear themselves the men or vassals of the Frankish king. Possibly the Pope's language is not to be understood thus in the fullness of its technical import, but at any rate it was plain that the two southern duchies, separated as they now were from the northern kingdom by a continuous stretch of Papal territory, were in great danger of being lost to the Lombard state.

    We must turn back for a few moments to consider what events had been occurring in these two duchies since the year 744. The fortunes of the Spoletan duchy during the years immediately following the death of King Liutprand are very obscure. From 745 to 751 Duke Lupus, known chiefly by his grants to the monastery of Farfa, seems to have reigned in the Umbrian duchy. After his death Aistulf perhaps took the duchy into his own hands, unless room has to be found for a certain Duke Unulf, who is doubtfully reported to have reigned for a few years. Apparently about this time the people of Spoleto took advantage of the troubles at Pavia following the death of Aistulf to choose for themselves a new duke, who (as we learn from a letter of Pope Paul) bore the great name of Alboin, and, as we have seen, they sought to secure their new independence of Pavia by placing themselves under the protection of Pippin. In Benevento, Gisulf II, who had been installed as duke by his great-uncle Liutprand, died in 751, in the prime of life, leaving a son, named Liutprand after his great kinsman, to inherit his dignity. For the young duke, who was probably but a child at the time of his father's death, his mother Scauniperga for some years acted as regent, but apparently before the year 757 Liutprand had assumed the reins of power. There are some indications that neither Aistulf nor Desiderius was heartily welcomed as king by the family of the great Liutprand; and possibly some especial dissatisfaction at the exaltation of the latter nobleman to the throne may have led the young duke and his counsellors to venture on the treasonable course of 'commending' themselves to the Frankish king. However this may be—and our information as to these two Lombard duchies is extremely meagre—it was soon clear that the new king had both the will and the power to compel their unwilling allegiance. Desiderius assembled his army, marched through the Pentapolis, probably not sparing its harvests and reached Spoleto in his victorious course. Here he arrested the new duke, Alboin, with his chief nobles, and threw them into prison. He drew near to Benevento: the young duke did not dare to await his attack, but fled to Otranto, along with his foster-father John. Unable to invest that sea-coast town without a fleet, Desiderius proceeded to Naples, and there concerted measures with the Imperial envoy George for the reduction of Otranto and—so the Pope was told—for the recovery of Ravenna. The Sicilian navy was to undertake the blockade of Otranto; the Lombards were to invest it on the land side; the young prince and his governor were to be handed over to Desiderius, but the city if captured was probably to be restored to the officers of the Emperor. How far this programme was carried into execution and what became of young Liutprand we know not. At this point he disappears from history, and his o, place is taken by a certain Arichis, whom Desiderius installed in the duchy of Benevento, and to whom he gave his daughter Adelperga to wife. The names of. both husband and wife, but that of the latter especially, will often recur in the later chapters of this history.

    As for Spoleto, Desiderius seems for a year or two to have retained it in his own hands, but in April, 759, he invested Gisulf with the ducal dignity.

    After this triumphant campaign Desiderius visited Rome. He came apparently not as a warrior but as a guest and a pilgrim, to pay his devotions at the tombs of the Apostles. He had, however, set his heart on obtaining the restitution of the hostages at the Frankish court (probably those who had been given by Aistulf at the end of the war of 756), and he hoped to accomplish this by the Pope's mediation. The price which he offered was the addition—or as the Pope called it the restitution—to the Papal territory of Imola, the next town westward on the great Emilian way after the recently acquired Faenza.

The result of this interview between Pope and Lombard King was seen in two remarkable letters dispatched by the hands of one Frankish and two Papal emissaries to the court of Pippin.

In one letter, the Pope, after thanking God for having raised to the pontificate one so humble as himself, and quoting the words of the Psalmist, 'I will take the cup of salvation and will call upon the name of the Lord', alludes to the blessing pronounced on the peacemakers, and then continues: "Let your most excellent Goodness know that our most excellent son, King Desiderius, has arrived at the threshold of the Apostles, peacefully and with great humility, and that with him we have held discourse which will be salutary to both of us. He has promised to restore to us the city of Imola: on this condition however, that we should send our *missi* to your Excellency, and that [by their mediation] he should receive back the hostages whom as it seems you have still with you, and that you should consent to confirm with him the peace [which was ratified with his predecessor]. Wherefore we pray you to restore those hostages to our aforesaid son Desiderius, to confirm your treaty of peace with him, and to correspond with him on terms of cordial friendship: so that, by the favour of God, His people of both nations may in your joyful times dwell in peace and great safety, and that Almighty God may grant you a long life on the throne of your kingdom".

So ran one letter, borne by Ruodbert, George and Stephen. The second was not like unto it. Therein the Pope details at considerable length the 'impious and cruel' deeds which have been perpetrated by Desiderius in the course of the campaign just described, and the 'nefarious' negotiations which he has been conducting with the Emperor's ambassador at Naples. After the conquest, or as the Pope calls it the 'dissolution' of the two duchies, he has come to Rome, and there "we have besought and exhorted him by the most holy body of St. Peter and by your God-protected Excellency to restore to us the cities of Imola, Bologna, Osimo and Ancona, as he once promised to do in our presence and that of your *missi* Ruodbert and Fulrad. But he was not at all inclined to assent to this. He shuffled like the trickster which he certainly is, and made several suggestions, as for instance that if he could recover his hostages who appear to be there in Francia he would then enter into relations of peace and concord with us. We have longed greatly to write to you, but could not do so on account of the Lombards hemming us in on every side. In fact we did privately, by the greatest exertion, send you two apostolic letters, which we fear may have been intercepted by them. It is for this reason that we now by the aforesaid *missi* send you another letter, written as if in compliance with the will of King Desiderius, desiring you to release his hostages and confirm the peace with him. But, 0 good and most excellent king, our spiritual kinsman, we so penned that letter solely in order that our messengers might be able to get through into Francia, since if we had not done so they would have had no chance of passing the Lombard frontier. But when you receive that letter do not pay any heed to its contents, and on no account consent to restore the said hostages to the Lombard party. Rather we adjure you to order the strongest pressure to be put upon Desiderius and the Lombard nation, so that he may restore those cities which he promised to your honey-flowing Excellency, and through you to your protector St.

Peter. For as to none of the things which he promised at the outset of his reign have we been able to come to a firm agreement with him".

These two interesting but contradictory letters slumber side by side in the pages of the Codex Carolinus, as they once slumbered in the Frankish archives; but it is one of the tantalizing results of this one-sided correspondence that we do not know what answer Pippin made, nor with which of them he complied. The whole tenour of the letters, however, shows that he was determined not to undertake another Italian campaign, if it were possible to avoid it, having already wars and fightings enough on his hands on the other side of the Alps. Had Desiderius indeed attempted to wrest the already surrendered cities out of the hands of St. Peter, Pippin might have been bound in honour to interfere, but if only the status quo could be maintained, he did not feel himself called upon to take up arms for the further enlargement of the Church's territory. Thus in a letter, of which it is much to be regretted that we cannot determine the date, the Pope acknowledges that Pippin has recommended him to live in peace and love with Desiderius, king of the Lombards, and actually proceeds thus, "Now if that most excellent man shall be willing to remain in that true love and fidelity which he hath promised to your Excellency and the Holy Church of Rome, we too will remain in firm charity and stable peace with him, observing that injunction of the Lord, 'Blessed are the peacemakers, for they shall be called the children of God'."

These pacific counsels of the Frankish king and his obvious reluctance to draw the sword a third time on behalf of Peter, seem to have produced the desired effect; and Desiderius, if not harassed with entreaties to restore the remaining cities of the Pentapolis and Aemilia, appears to have been willing to remain at peace with Rome. There was indeed one interruption to this peace in 761, when he made an attack on Sinigaglia and sacked a city of Campania, but this does not seem to have been a long or serious campaign. On the whole, one would say from a perusal of the correspondence that there was something like a gradual reconciliation between Paul and Desiderius. The increasing bitterness of feeling between the Eastern and Western Churches perhaps contributed to this result, the *nefandissimi Graeci* having now taken the place of the *nefandissimi Langobardi* as chief enemies of God and His Church.

In one letter the Pope says to Pippin: "You tell us that you directed Desiderius to return to us our runaway slave Saxulus. But I ought to tell you that Desiderius came here himself to pray at the tombs of the Apostles, and that he brought Saxulus with him and restored him to us. At the same time we arranged with Desiderius that he and our *missi* should make a tour through the various cities and there settle our claims. This has now been satisfactorily accomplished for Benevento, Tuscany, and partly for Spoleto. In a postscript you told us that you had admonished Desiderius to constrain the men of Naples and Gaeta to restore the patrimonies of St. Peter situated at Naples, and to allow their bishops-elect to come hither for consecration. We thank you for this".

Everything seems to show that by the end of Paul's pontificate a *modus vivendi* had been arrived at between the Lombards and the Roman pontiffs.

III.

The Frankish Kingdom.

The relations of Pope Paul with the Frankish king, as disclosed to us by the Codex Carolinus, consist chiefly of a lavish outpouring of spiritual compliments, of an exhibition of that gratitude which is 'a lively sense of favours to come', and of frequent entreaties for help which never arrives. Not once nor twice, but in almost every letter, and often many times in a letter, Pippin and his boyish sons (who are always coupled with him) are reminded that St. Peter has anointed them to be kings. Pippin is the new Moses, the new David, a man specially protected by God, who has laid up for himself infinite treasures in the starry citadels, where neither moth nor rust doth corrupt the treasures prepared for the righteous. "The name of your Excellency", says the enthusiastic pontiff, "sparkles on the book of life in the sight of God. No tongue can express the thanks which the holy Church of God and the Roman people owe to your Excellency for all the benefits conferred upon them. None of this world's rewards can be an adequate remuneration. There is but the one only God, consisting in three substances, who can fittingly reward your Excellency with the joys of the heavenly kingdom. Pray continue steadfast in that good work of our protection which you have begun. Right well has your Christian Excellency perceived how great is the impious malice of the heretical Greeks, who are eagerly plotting to humble and trample down the holy Catholic and Apostolic Church and destroy the holy orthodox faith and the tradition of the holy fathers. Do you manfully resist these impious heretics. Our strength is in your arm, and we will say, 'O Lord! save the most Christian king Pippin, whom Thou hast ordered to be anointed with holy oil by the hands of Thine Apostle, and hear him in the day when he calleth upon Thee'."

The glory of the pious king is reflected upon his faithful people. In an ecstatic psalm of thanksgiving addressed 'To the Bishops, Presbyters, Abbots, Monks, Dukes, Counts, and to the whole muster of the army of the Franks, God-protected and Christ-beloved', the Pope thus salutes them: "You, dearest ones, are a holy nation, a royal priesthood, a peculiar people, whom the Lord God of Israel hath blessed : therefore joy and exult because your names and the names of your kings are exalted in heaven, and great is your reward in the sight of God and His angels. For Peter is your protector, the Prince of the Apostles to whom our Redeemer has granted the power of binding and loosing in heaven and on earth".

As the *missi* went backwards and forwards between Mutual Rome and the Frankish villa, they generally bore with of Pope them some costly present, an emblem of the friendship which united Pope and King. A table (perhaps inlaid with precious stones) had been presented by Pippin to Stephen II, 'and through him to St. Peter'. "This table", says Paul, "we brought in with hymns and spiritual songs to the hall of that chief of Apostles, and laid it on your behalf on the shrine of that door-keeper of the kingdom of heaven. Then we anointed it and placed upon it the sacred oblation, which we offered up for the eternal welfare of your soul and the stability of your kingdom, laying our apostolic censure and anathema on any one who should dare to remove it from thence. In that same apostolic hall, therefore, it will remain for ever, as a memorial of you, and be sure that you will receive a fitting reward from God and St. Peter in the heavenly kingdom".

After the baptism of Pippin's infant daughter Gisila (who was born in 757), the king sent to his venerable friend the napkin which had been used in the ceremony. The Pope gladly accepted the offering, and considered himself to be thereby constituted godfather of the royal child. From that time forward his favourite epithet for Pippin, one never absent from his letters, is '*spiritalis compater*', our spiritual co-father. "With great joy", he says, "and accompanied by a whole cohort of the people, we received this napkin in the chapel where rests the holy body of the blessed Petronilla, the helper of life; which chapel is now dedicated to keep in eternal memory the praises of your name".

The story of the discovery of the body of Petronilla is told in the *Liber Pontificalis*, from which we learn that long before this time a marble sarcophagus had been discovered with these letters engraven upon it, AVREAE PETRONILLAE FILIAE DULCISSIMAE. It was not doubtful (thought the scholars of that day) that these letters had been carved by the hand of the Apostle Peter himself, to express his love for his 'sweetest daughter'. Pope Stephen II had erected a chapel in honour of Petronilla close to that of her uncle St. Andrew in the great basilica which bore the name of her father. The dedication of this chapel had been in some way connected with the name of Pippin, and its erection was regarded as a visible monument of the league of eternal friendship between the Pope and the Frankish King. One of the first acts of Paul I on his elevation to the papacy had been to transport the body of Petronilla on a new wagon to the home prepared for her by his brother, and thither, as I have said, he now in solemn procession bore the baptismal napkin of the infant Gisila.

The Pope on his part frequently accompanied his plaintive petitions for help with some ornament or cunningly-wrought article of apparel, which may perhaps have been designed in the old days of splendour before the barbarians came, and which, secure in the treasury of St. Peter, had escaped the soldiers of Alaric and Totila, or the yet more penetrating quest of the Byzantine logothete. "I send you", he says, "by way of benediction, one *apallarea*, a sword set with jewels, with the belt belonging thereto, a ring holding a jacinth, a quilted mantle with peacocks' feathers embroidered upon it. Which little blessing we beg that you may receive uninjured. To the lords Charles and Carloman, with our great apostolic blessing, we send a ring apiece containing jacinths".

At another time the Pope sends "to your Excellency such books [probably on certain subjects named by the king] as we have been able to meet with; that is to say, a book of antiphons and responses, a grammar, a copy of Aristotle, a copy of Dionysius the Areopagite, a geometry, an orthography, and a grammar, all written in Greek, and also a clock for use at night"

In this way the intercourse of rulers was helping forward the cause of civilization, even when their own motives were not altogether pure or unselfish. Constantine Copronymus, harshly dissolute Emperor as he was, may rightly claim a high place in the musical history of Western Europe. No fewer than six of the chronicles add to their notices of the year 757 (the year of Paul I's accession) this naive sentence : "And the organ came into Frank-land". They often differ strangely from one another as to the date of wars and councils, but this one date, that of the year when the deep voice of the organ was first heard in a Frankish cathedral, seems to have fixed itself indelibly in their remembrance. And from those, which may be called the state-chronicles, we learn the fact that this wonderful organ was one of many presents sent by the Emperor Constantine to the king of the Franks.

In the still rude and barbarously furnished villa of a Frankish prince it was not perhaps easy to find a suitable present to submit to the critical gaze of the courtiers of Rome or Constantinople. This was probably the cause of a letter (unfortunately known to us only by the reply) in which the young princes Charles and Carloman expressed to the Pope their regret that they had not sent him any present. "By the same letter", says the Pope in answer, "you inform us that you are extremely ashamed that you have not been able to send us any gifts by the hands of your messengers who brought it. But why, sweetest and most loving sons, why, most victorious kings, should you yearn to gladden us with your gifts? We desire no other gifts than always to learn of your safety and prosperity, and to be able to congratulate you on your attainments, that is our enriching: your exaltation, that is the exaltation of God's holy Church : your defence of the orthodox faith; these are the best presents that we can receive".

And yet notwithstanding this lavish outpouring of sweet words, the deeds for which they were to be the payment were never done. During all the ten years of Paul's pontificate no Frankish warriors again threaded the passes of Mont Cenis in order to strike another blow for the 'justices' of St. Peter. To understand the causes of this negative result we must glance very briefly at the occupations and anxieties of the Frankish king during the same period.

In 758, the year when the first note of dissatisfaction with 'the meekest Desiderius' was sounded by Paul, Pippin was engaged in a tough struggle with the Saxon tribesmen on his north-eastern frontier, making a breach in the rampart which they had cast up for the defence of their country, fighting many battles, slaying a great multitude of their warriors (probably not without severe loss among his own men), and at last reducing them to submission and to the promise of an annual tribute of three hundred horses.

In 759 Pippin achieved the important result of expelling the last Saracen invader from Gaul. The campaign was, it is true, not an arduous one. Having marched his troops to Narbonne and formed the siege of that city, he opened secret negotiations with the descendants of the Visigoths, who formed doubtless the bulk of its inhabitants. When they had obtained an assurance that if they became once more subjects of the Frankish king they should be allowed to live by their own national law and should not be compelled to come under the Salian or Ripuarian code, they agreed to Pippin's terms, slew the Saracen garrison, and opened the gates of their city to the Franks. Thus was ended the Moorish domination north of the Pyrenees. But though the campaign was not an arduous one, it may well have left Pippin little leisure for redressing the importunate and ever-growing claims of St. Peter.

The next year, 760, saw the commencement of a struggle which, with little intermission, occupied Pippin's whole energies for the remaining nine years of his life, which evidently brought him sometimes into serious danger, and which by its toils and anxieties probably shortened his days. This was the war with Waifar, duke of Aquitaine. That great region between the Loire, the Atlantic, and the Pyrenees, which had once belonged to the kingdom of the Visigoths and which became subject to the Franks in 507 (when the pious Clovis could no longer endure that the Arian heretics should possess so large a portion of Gaul), had probably never been so thoroughly incorporated with the Frankish monarchy as the rest of what we now call France, and had certainly of late yielded but an insecure and shadowy allegiance to the *fainéant* Merovingian kings. As we have already seen, Duke Eudo assumed an almost independent position in his wars and treaties with Charles Martel; and now his grandson, Duke Waifar, was probably unwilling to own himself the 'man' or vassal of one who had no royal blood in his veins. Doubtless if Francia was to become one coherent state, Aquitaine must be made to own the absolute sovereignty of the Arnulfing king : and it was upon the whole the greatest service which Pippin rendered to his country, that by severe toils, undertaken probably in failing health and amid many distracting cares, besides the piteous appeals of the Roman pontiff, he did succeed in accomplishing this great result.

The pretext—it may have been more than a mere pretext—for the war, was found in Waifar's refusal to restore to some churches under Pippin's special protection the property which belonged to them in Aquitaine. War was declared, and was carried on, probably with varying success, though the chroniclers record only Frankish victories, for the four years from 760 to 763. Then came a new and a threatening development of the struggle. Tassilo, sister's son to Pippin, now a young man of twenty-one years of age, who had for fifteen of those years held the dignity of duke of Bavaria, who had followed his uncle to the Italian war in 756, and had in the following year at Compiegne sworn tremendous oaths of fidelity on the holiest relics of the saints, now in the fourth year of the Aquitanic campaign flatly refused any longer to follow the Frankish standard, and falsely feigning sickness returned to his own country, from whence he sent a message that he would see his uncle's face no more. Thus did the young duke definitively renounce his allegiance to his Frankish overlord, and, what was a more outrageous offence in Teutonic eyes, by the time and manner of his defection he committed the unpardonable crime of *harisliz*, or desertion of his lord in the presence of an enemy. This act changed all the after-life of Tassilo, darkened its close, and exercised an important if indirect influence on the fortunes even of the Lombard people.

It is probable that Tassilo's defection caused the failure of the campaign of 763, and it is possible that Pippin himself may have been thereby brought into a situation of peril. If so, we may safely refer to this period two letters from Pope Paul, in the first of which he expresses his anxiety for the king's safety, seeing that so long a time has elapsed since he heard news of him, and that gloomy tidings concerning him are arriving 'from your and our enemies'—who are probably the Greek iconoclasts.

In the second letter the Pope announces that he has heard from various pilgrims to the thresholds of the Apostles that the king has returned in safety to his home, tidings which fill his soul with joy and call forth his fervent thankfulness to God.

In a letter written some years later the Pope informs Pippin of some faint overtures towards reconciliation which Tassilo desires him to communicate to his offended overlord; but nothing seems to have resulted from this mediation.

For two years Pippin remained in his own land pondering the situation, distracted by the double war which seemed opening out before him, and collecting his forces for either event. At length he decided, no doubt wisely, that the Aquitanic enterprise alone must be proceeded with, and that the chastisement of his rebellious nephew must for the present be postponed. The three years from 766 to 768 were devoted to the prosecution of the war, evidently with ever-increasing success. At length in the midsummer of 768 Waifar, who had been for many months wandering up and down in Perigord, a hunted fugitive, was slain, apparently by one of his own followers; and the war of Aquitaine was at an end.

Theological discussions occupied some of Pippin's leisure in the interval between these triumphant campaigns. In January, 767, the Byzantine ambassadors appeared before a synod of Frankish bishops which was convened at Gentilly near Paris. As described by the chroniclers, it was assembled to decide 'questions concerning the Holy Trinity and the worship of images'. The purely theological question was the everlasting argument between Easterns and Westerns as to 'the procession of the Holy Spirit' and the words 'Filioque' surreptitiously (said the Easterns) added to the Nicene confession of faith. It is suggested that this old grievance was brought up by the Byzantine envoys in order to counterbalance the iconoclastic innovations objected against them by the Latins. The synod, however, appears to have dispersed without arriving at any harmonious conclusion—the predecessor of many equally fruitless discussions of a similar kind between the Eastern and Western Churches.

We read in the Codex Carolinus some letters in which apparently the Pope, in expectation of the holding of this synod, speaks confidently of the result, and praises the unshaken firmness of Pippin in all his dealings with the shifty and heretical Greeks, but we have none expressing the satisfaction which he must certainly have felt if he heard the result. The chronicler informs us that after his victorious campaign of 767 Pippin sent his army into winter quarters and spent his own Christmas at Bourges, where he heard the tidings of the death of the Roman Pope. The news must have travelled slowly, for the death of Paul the First actually took place on the 28th of June, 767. On account of the summer heats he had retired to the church of his namesake, S. Paolo Fuori le Mura. He was seized with sickness, and his death followed in a few days. His body, at first buried in that basilica, was after an interval of three months transported by a multitude of Romans and foreigners, with psalms and hymns, to the regular resting-place of the Popes at St. Peter's.

'And the bishopric of Rome lapsed for one year, one month [and ten days]'. So writes the Papal biographer. That lapse of the episcopate is the Church's way of describing the wild scenes of faction and disorder which will form the subject of the next chapter.

NOTE.

On the Offices of the Papal Household.

These officers, who formed practically the ministry of the Pontifical State, are thus enumerated by a MS. of the twelfth century found in the Lateran and published by Mabillon.

"In the Roman Empire and in the Roman Church of today there are seven Palatine Judges, who are called *Ordinarii*, who ordain the Emperor, and with the Roman clergy elect the Pope. Their names are as follows :—

I. *Primicerius*, and II. S*ecundicerius*, who receive their names from their offices themselves. These two, walling in the Emperor on the right hand and the left, seem in a certain way to reign with him : without them no decision of importance is taken by the Emperor. Moreover, in the Roman Church in all processions they lead the Pope's palfrey, taking precedence of the bishops and other magnates.

II. The third is the *Arcarius*, who presides over the tribute.

IV. The fourth is the *Sacellarius*, who hands forth to the soldiers their pay, gives alms to the sick on the Sabbath day, and bestows upon the Roman bishops and clergy and persons in orders their *presbyteria* [stipends],

V. The fifth is the *Protoseriniarius*, who presides over the *scriniarii* whom we call *tabelliones* [scriveners].

VI. The sixth is the *Primus Defensor*, who presides over the *defensores*, whom we call advocates.

VII. The seventh is the *Adminiculator*, whose duty it is to intercede for orphans and widows, for the afflicted, and for captives.

In criminal cases these men do not judge, nor do they pronounce a capital sentence on any man, and at Rome they are clerics who are never promoted to any other rank. But the other magistrates, who are called *Consuls*, conduct trials and punish those who are amenable to the laws, and pass sentence on the guilty according to the magnitude of their crimes.''

In the four centuries which elapsed between Paul I and Alexander III many changes may have taken place, but there seems reason to suppose that the officials here enumerated were to be found in Rome in the eighth century. I would suggest, however, a doubt whether they were necessarily all ecclesiastics at the period with which we are now dealing. Christopher and his son Sergius seem to me more like laymen than clerics.

As Hegel points out, the full title of the *Primicerius* and *Secundicerius* should include the addition *notariorum*; and they may be considered as the President and the Vice-President of the Papal Chancery.

The statement that they with the Roman clergy elected the Pope would of course not be true for the eighth century, in which there was still a semblance of popular election. Savigny, however, suggests that these seven *Judices Palatini* directing the election of the Pope may have furnished the type for the seven cardinal-bishops of a later day, and may even have had some influence on the selection of seven as the number of the Electors in the Holy Roman Empire.

CHAPTER X

A PAPAL CHAOS.

The death of Paul I brought out in strong relief the difficulties which result from clothing a religious leader with temporal power. The arguments in favour of that course are obvious, and have already been often referred to. The cruelties inflicted on Popes who dared to differ from the Eastern Augustus on questions of religious dogma, the transportation of Silverius to the desolate Palmaria, the attempt to drag Vigilius from the altar to which he clung for refuge, the death of the persecuted Martin at inhospitable Cherson, the attempts on the liberty of Sergius and on the life of the second Gregory, might not unreasonably suggest, even to an unambitious Roman pontiff, that if he was to be safe he must be also sovereign; nor can we deny that the happy device of interweaving the claims of St. Peter and his Vicar with those of the Holy Roman Republic seemed to offer a plausible means of obtaining this sovereignty without too obviously abandoning the position assumed by Christ when He said, "My kingdom is not of this world".

But, however the truth might be veiled by the festoons of pious rhetoric, the substantial fact remained that the bishop of Rome was now virtually king over the central City of the world, and over fair domains touching both the Tyrrhene and the Adriatic Seas; and this proud position naturally attracted the ambition of men for whom the spiritual prerogatives of the successor of St. Peter would have had no fascination. In later centuries this motive was to be made miserably manifest when the Papal See became for a time almost an appanage of the Counts of Tusculum. We have some faint presage of those evil days in the scenes which were now enacted before the bewildered gaze of the citizens of Rome.

The little town of Nepi, about thirty miles from Rome, was, as we have already seen, one of the frontier towns of the Ducatus Romae looking towards Lombard Tuscany. Here dwelt an ambitious citizen of doubtful nationality, named Toto, who had by means unknown to us acquired the dignity of dukedom. Conspiring with three of his brothers, named Constantine, Passivus and Paschalis, and with a troop of rustics, drawn apparently from both sides of the border and devoted to his will, this adventurer conceived the daring design of giving a Pope to Rome and of ruling the new Papal territory in his name,

Pope Paul was still lingering on his death-bed under the shadow of his namesake's great basilica when Toto, his brothers, and his accomplices appeared upon the scene. They intended—so we are told—to hasten events by cutting short the feeble thread of the pontiffs life, but were prevented by the *primicerius* Christopher, who invited them and the rest of the Roman nobility into his house and gave them 'strong and salutary' counsels as to abstinence from crime. He even succeeded (so he averred) in inducing them and the heads of the opposite party to bind themselves by mutual oaths not to elect any Pope save from among the bishops, priests and deacons of the Roman Church, and not to introduce any of the suburban rustics into the City in order to carry the election. All this advice however was in vain, and the oaths solemnly taken were only so many perjuries. Scarcely had Paul I sighed out his latest breath, when Toto and his brothers with a horde of rustics from the towns of Tuscany rushed into the City through the Gate of St. Pancratius on the Janiculan height, held a tumultuary election in the house of Toto (who seems to have possessed a palace within the walls of Rome), and chose as Pope, Constantine the layman, the brother of the invading chief.

This tumultuary election took place apparently on the evening of Sunday, the 28th of June, 767, and was followed by the march of Toto, his brothers and his rustics to the Lateran palace of the Patriarchate, where George, bishop of Praeneste, was ordered to admit the new Pope to the minor orders, which were so to speak the threshold of the ecclesiastical state. The bishop at first refused, cast himself at the feet of Constantine, and begged him by the holy mysteries to cease from his presumptuous attempt and forbear from introducing such an unheard-of innovation into the Church of God. But the rough men who had just taken part in the election in Toto's palace gathered round him, and with fierce threats ordered him to do as he was bid. Terrified, the bishop consented, and ordained Constantine, who, now a cleric, stalked in and seated himself in the patriarchal chair.

When Monday dawned the same unfortunate bishop George, who had now no choice but to cast in his lot with the usurper, admitted Constantine to the successive degrees of subdeacon and deacon in the oratory of St. Laurence at the Lateran—otherwise called the Sancta Sanctorum—and presented him to the people to receive their oath of obedience. On the following Sunday, Constantine proceeded through the streets of Rome with his usual train of armed men (doubtless marshalled by his truculent brothers), entered the great basilica of St. Peter, and was there consecrated Pope by George of Praeneste and two other bishops, Eustratius of Albano and Citonatus of Porto.

The elevation of Constantine to the pontificate was certainly irregular, for though there had been many instances (notably the case of the great Ambrose of Milan) in which laymen had been suddenly raised to the presidency of other sees, in Rome the practice was so rare as to be almost unknown, and the Pope, by a rule which had not been broken for more than two centuries, ought to be chosen from the ranks of either the deacons or the presbyters. But however manifest the irregularity of the whole proceeding, the necessary formalities had been in some fashion complied with. There had been a popular election, the candidate had passed through the ecclesiastical grades up to that of deacon (higher rank in the Church was not necessary), had been consecrated Pope by three bishops of the Roman Church, and could now sit in the chair of St. Peter and call himself 'Servant of all the servants of God'. He did in fact for thirteen months preside over the Apostolic See, though he is not reckoned in the number of the pontiffs, nor is his face to be found in the long series which gaze down upon the beholder from the walls of the great church of St. Paul's Without the Gates.

Early tidings of these strange proceedings were brought by a notary named Constantine to his official chief Christopher, who as *Primicerius Notariorum* should in due course have presided over the election and formed one of the board of threewhich should have ruled Pome during the vacancy of the Holy See. Terrible were the threats of which Constantine the notary was the bearer from his namesake unless Christopher would assist in making him Pope. This however he steadfastly refused to do, betaking himself instead to tears and prayers to Almighty God for the preservation of His Church from the impending scandal.

A certain Duke Gregory, a dweller in Campania, who probably attempted to resist the usurping Pope by force of arms, was put to death, and Christopher hearing that his own death also was decreed took refuge with his sons in the church of St. Peter. He was at last induced to emerge from his place of refuge on receiving from Pope Constantine a solemn assurance, confirmed by an oath before St. Peter's tomb, that he and his sons should be allowed to dwell peaceably in their homes till the approaching Easter-tide. After that he was to be allowed to retire with his son Sergius to the monastery of the Saviour near Rieti, in the district of Spoleto.

Meanwhile the new Pope had addressed two letters of the orthodox pattern set him by his predecessor, to 'his dear son Pippin, king of the Franks and patrician of the Romans'. The ordinary phrases about the starry realms, the honey-flowing Excellency of the Frankish king, his God-protected kingdom, the duty which he owes to his protector St. Peter, and so forth, flow from the pen of this suddenly-exalted layman as smoothly as from that of the 'child of the Lateran' who preceded him. Many no doubt of these sentences were 'common forms' which would be supplied by any of the clerks in the Papal chancery to his employer. The solecisms in grammar and spelling, even more outrageous and more frequent than those which we meet with in the letters of Pope Paul, suggest the idea of a pattern set by such a clerk and imperfectly copied by an illiterate rustic. The allusions, however, to the circumstances of his own elevation to the pontificate are peculiar, and if there be any truth in the account of the matter given by the Liber Pontificalis, are audacious:—

"We expect you have already heard that our predecessor Paul, of blessed memory, has by the call of God been withdrawn from the light of day, and that the inhabitants of this City and of the surrounding towns have chosen my Unhappiness to preside over them as their pastor".

The allusion to the share which 'surrounding towns' have had in the election is a slight tribute to veracity.

"When I seriously consider with myself what are the duties of the office into which I have crept, in respect of tending the rational sheep of the Lord, I must confess that unbearable sadness fills my secret soul". (The 'office into which I have crept' sounds like a very candid confession of the truth, but is probably due to the new Pope's ignorance of the meaning of the words, which some crafty clerk dictated for his adoption.)

"But I who am greatly weighed down and perceive that by no virtues or attainments of my own have I been advanced to this dignity, conclude that the Divine compassion working on the hearts of the people has brought about this result : and therefore, like one awakened from a heavy sleep, I perceive with stupefaction and ecstasy that an honour has been conferred upon me which I never desired, which I never even thought of, and to which my little faint heart never aspired. For suddenly being seized by the violent hands of an innumerable multitude of people who all agreed in this thing, I was borne as it were by a mighty blast of wind up to the great and awful height of this pontificate. . . . Oh, how great and fearful a thing art thou, the responsibility of the pastor! And how can I, unhappy one, fulfill the onerous duty of the cure of souls!"

The Pope then goes on to make a short confession of faith in order to show his absolute orthodoxy. He alludes to Christ's converse with sinners, and (with some dexterity) to the call of Matthew the publican from the tax-gatherer's table, and he announces the arrival of a presbyter from Jerusalem bringing the patriarch Theodore's synodical letter addressed to the late pontiff Paul, from which it is clear that the patriarchal thrones of Jerusalem, Antioch and Alexandria, all agree with that of Rome in upholding the worship of images. Upon the whole this rustic brother of Duke Toto plays his part so well and imitates so admirably the language of his predecessor—the rough Esau this time counterfeiting the bland voice of the peaceful Jacob—that one almost expects to see that he will succeed in carrying off the Church's blessing.

That consummation was prevented by the energy of the two men, Christopher and Sergius, father and son, who had held the two highest offices in the Papal chancery, and who, whether from personal ambition or from honest loyalty to the traditions of the See, were determined that Constantine's usurpation of the papacy should not be legitimatized by success. We have seen that they obtained leave to retire to a monastery near Rieti after Easter, 768. The Papal biographer, who has his own reasons for disliking the two men, though he approves their deed, says that they feigned the desire to become monks, and swore that they would assume the monastic habit, in order to obtain from Constantine the required permission to depart from Rome. Instead of resorting to the convent of the Saviour at Rieti, where the abbot was waiting to receive them, they made their way to Spoleto and besought the Duke Theodicius to escort them across the river Po to the court of Desiderius. He did so, and the two ministers having been admitted to the presence of the Lombard king, earnestly besought him to lend his aid 'that the error of such a novelty might be cut off from the Church of God'.

Desiderius appears to have authorized the Duke of Spoleto to interfere in the Roman troubles, but not to have sent any troops of his own for that purpose. Probably the power of this suburban 'Duke' Toto was inconsiderable, and no great display of force was needed to crush him. In fact, the only persons of whom we hear as sharing in the invasion of Rome are the inhabitants of Rieti and Furcona, two insignificant towns in the Apennine highlands belonging to the duchy of Spoleto. Under the command of Sergius and a certain presbyter Waldipert, who probably came as envoy from the Lombard king to control the impending revolution, the rustic army marched suddenly on Rome by the Via Salara, and reached the bridge over the Anio at twilight on the 29th of July (768). Next day they crossed the Ponte Molle, and worked round on the north and north-west of Rome, first to the Gate of St. Peter's and then to the Gate of St. Pancratius. Some relations of Christopher opened the gate to his son, and there the Lombards stood on the Janiculum, near the site of the present church of S. Pietro in Montorio, overlooking the outspread City. They displayed the Lombard banner, but 'stood trembling on the walls, fearing the Roman people, and not daring to descend'. So says the Papal writer, but it is more probable that Sergius and Waldipert, knowing that they had friends in the enemy's camp, determined to avoid the odium of a victory won by the swords of the Lombards, and preferred to wait for the course of events. Duke Toto with his brother Passivus mounted up to the gate, having in their train two of the ministers of the Papal household, Demetrius and Gratiosus, whom they believed to be their friends, but who were secretly in league with the assailants. One of the Lombards named Racipert rushed upon Toto, but was stoutly resisted, and met his own death from Toto's weapon. The Lombards wavered, and were in act to flee, when Secundus and Gratiosus attacked Toto from behind with their lances and slew him. Thereupon Passivus rushed across the City to the Lateran palace and told his brother the Pope what things were being done on the Janiculan hill. Then Constantine and Passivus, with the bishop Theodore, the Pope's delegate, hastened to the great basilica of the Lateran, and fled from chapel to chapel seeking some inviolable refuge. In vain : after they had undergone some hours of suspense the officers of the Roman militia came and dragged them forth from the oratory of St. Caesarius and put them in ward, perhaps in one of the dungeons of the palace.

On the next day, which was a Sunday, Waldipert, without consulting his confederate Sergius, gathered together a number of Roman citizens, proceeded to the monastery of St. Vitus, and invited forth from thence a certain priest named Philip, whom the crowd greeted with the acclamation, 'St. Peter has chosen Philip, Pope'. They then led him in state to the Lateran basilica : a bishop offered the customary prayer; the new Pope bestowed his blessing on the people from the balcony of the church, and entered the palace of the pontiffs. Here he sat at the head of a banqueting company, among whom were some of the great ecclesiastical dignitaries and officers of the Roman militia.

But Philip, who was doubtless looked upon by the Lombard faction in the City as one of their own partisans, was, though a priest, not one of the regular parish-priests of Rome, and his election therefore, though not as irregular as that of Constantine, was contrary to the established custom of the Roman Church. As soon as Christopher (who had apparently travelled more slowly than his son) appeared upon the scene and was informed of Philip's election, he waited outside the gates of the City, and swore with a great oath in presence of the assembled Romans that till Philip was expelled from the Lateran he would not enter Rome. His word was recognized as decisive. Gratiosus the chartularius, the slayer of Toto, with no very large troop of Roman citizens following him, marched to the Lateran and ordered the new Pope to depart thence. Philip, who seems to have deserved a better fate than to be made Pope at such a time, calmly descended the great staircase of the Lateran palace, and returned amid the reverent greetings of the crowd to his monastic seclusion.

The election of the new Pope was thus taken definitely out of the hands of the Lombard faction, and was to be carried through by the *primicerius* Christopher alone. He convened an assembly of all the orders of the state at the *Tria Fata*, the northeast corner of the Roman Forum, in front of the church of S. Adriano, which probably occupied the site of that which was known in republican times as the Comitium. Here then, where once the Roman people had listened to the orators who expounded to them the policy of the Senate, was now gathered the strangely-mingled assembly which is thus described by the Papal biographer : "All the priests and leaders of the clergy; the chiefs of the militia and the whole army, and the honourable citizens and a concourse of the whole Roman people from great to little".

This assembly, unanimously as we are told, elected Stephen, priest of S. Cecilia in Trastevere, to the vacant see. He was a Sicilian by birth, son of a man named Olivus. He was not more than fifty years of age, and had come as a boy to Rome in the time of Gregory III, who placed him in his own recently-founded monastery of St. Chrysogonus. Zacharias transferred him from thence to the Lateran 'patriarchate', and gave him a place in his household, at the same time consecrating him as priest of S. Cecilia. He thus became one of those 'cardinal-priests' (as men were beginning to call them) from whose ranks and those of the cardinal-deacons the Pope was now usually chosen. He is said to have been learned (according to the very moderate standard of that age) in the Scriptures and in the traditions of the Church, and he was probably a person of some ability, as he was sent by Paul I on an important mission to Pippin.

Such was the man who was now raised by the influence of the *primicerius* Christopher to the vacant patriarchate. The Lateran had again a lawful possessor: the interval of chaos was ended.

CHAPTER XII

THE PONTIFICATE OF STEPHEN III.

The new Pope, however skillful he may have been as a diplomatist, was not a man of any strength of will or singleness of purpose. In his short tenure of the Papacy—only three years and a half—he performed some extraordinary political evolutions and was guilty of some acts which at least resemble treachery and ingratitude. Altogether he is one of the poorest figures in the Papal annals of the eighth century.

The first business of the new reign was to decide as - to the fate of the invader of the Papacy' and his abettors. George, bishop of Praeneste, who had been, with his will or against his will, the chief instrument in Constantine's elevation, had been stricken with paralysis soon after that event, and was now either dead or so much enfeebled by disease as not to seem worth punishing. Strangely enough, we hear nothing of proceedings against the two bishops, of Albano and Porto, who also concurred in the consecration. The direst fury of the successful champions of the purity of Papal election was reserved for Theodore, the *vice-dominus* who had acted as ecclesiastical prime minister during the thirteen months of chaos, and who with his master sat trembling in the Lateran when the Lombards poured into the City. Some of the more lawless men of Stephen's party, whose cruelty is unsparingly condemned by the Papal biographer, laid hold of Theodore where he was kept in ward, and plucked out his eyes and tongue. Passivus, the brother of Constantine, also had his eyes plucked out, and then, as the biographer says, 'they showed themselves so unpitying towards the men whom they had thus barbarously used, that they did not even allow them to be removed to their own homes that they might be tended by their servants, but taking away from them all their goods and their household retinue, they sent Passivus to the monastery of St. Silvester and Theodore to the monastery of Clivus Scauri' (which occupied the site of the palace of Gregory the Great on the Coelian Hill). Here suffering agonies of hunger and thirst, and vainly crying out for water, the unhappy *vice-dominus* soon after expired.

As for Constantine himself, he was brought forth from his prison; a heavy weight was attached to his feet, he was seated on a horse upon which, no doubt in derision, a lady's saddle had been prepared for him, and was thus led in ignominious triumph to the monastery of S. Saba on the Aventine.

A week had now passed since the entry of the Lombards into the City. The new Pope was to be consecrated on Sunday, but on the previous Saturday, the 6th of August, certain of the bishops and other clergy were assembled in the Lateran basilica, and Constantine being brought before them was, after the reading of the canons, formally deposed. Maurianus a sub-deacon tore the pallium from his neck and cast it at his feet, and then proceeded to cut off his pontifical shoes. Further proceedings against him seem to have been postponed to the meeting of a council. On the next August 7, day, as had been arranged, took place the consecration of Stephen III, whereat a general confession was made by the Roman people of their sin in submitting without resistance to the impious invasion of the Apostolic See; and this confession was read again in a loud voice by the scrivener Leontius from the ambo of St. Peter's.

One of the first acts of the new Pope was to send a messenger to his powerful Frankish patrons with the tidings of his elevation and a request for the summoning of a council of the Church. The messenger chosen for the purpose was naturally the all-powerful Sergius, who was now again *secundicerius*, and also *nomenculator* in the Papal court. But when Sergius arrived in Frank-land he found that the old king was already dead.

The last time that Pippin's name was mentioned he was resting at Bourges in the autumn of 767 from his eighth Aquitanian campaign, and was receiving the tidings of the death of Pope Paul. His intervention in the affairs of the distracted Papal See was, as we have seen, solicited by the intrusive Pope Constantine, but apparently the application received no reply. In the spring of 768 he again set his face south-westwards, determined once for all to make an end of the resistance of Waifar, duke of Aquitaine. A certain Remistan, Waifar's uncle, who after taking oaths of fealty to Pippin had treacherously gone over to his nephew's side and surrendered to him the towns which Pippin had entrusted to his guardianship, was captured, apparently not without guile, and hung on a gallows at Bourges. The mother, sister, and nieces of Waifar were next brought in as captives to the king's camp at Saintes. Still, however, the chief quarry escaped. Though utterly beaten, Waifar wandered hither and thither through the cave-lined valleys of Perigord, and though Pippin divided his followers into four bands and sent them in quest of the fugitive, they failed to capture him. At last however on the 2nd of June, 768, the hunt was ended, in unsportsmanlike fashion, by the murder of the quarry: Waifar was assassinated by some of his own followers, as one of the chroniclers tells us, not without suspicion of the king's privity to the crime. The action of Pippin in striving so persistently for the incorporation of Aquitaine with the Frankish monarchy was probably wise and statesmanlike, but there is nothing knightly in his treatment of the champion of her independence.

The conqueror took up his quarters at Saintes, and there held an assembly at which he regulated the affairs of Aquitaine, now virtually a new, or at least a recovered possession of the Frankish kings. The great ecclesiastics on whose behalf the contest with Waifar had been originally entered upon were restored to the full enjoyment of all their estates; new *beneficia* were carved out for the behoof of Pippin's loyal followers; yet according to the wise policy of the Austrasian kings, no attempt was made to force the unique and time-hallowed civilization of Aquitaine into the rigid mould of the half-barbarous jurisprudence of the Northern Franks. It was enacted 'that all men, Romans and Salians alike, should keep their own laws, and that if any man should come from another province he should live according to the law of his own fatherland'. We have seen a similar privilege accorded to the Visigoths of Septimania, who on passing from under the Moorish yoke were assured by Pippin that they should still retain their own laws; and thus we find already in action that curious system of 'personal laws' which was so marked a feature of Carolingian administration, especially in Italy.

But even while Pippin was thus wisely settling the affairs of his new conquest the hand of death was upon him. It was during his residence at Saintes that he began to sicken with fever. He journeyed towards the Loire; he visited the tomb of St. Martin, greatest of the saints of Gaul, and besought the intercession of the canonized soldier. In vain; but one more journey was left him to accomplish, the journey to his place of sepulture, the venerable abbey of St. Dionysius at Paris. He was still living when he reached it, but he died on the 24th of September (768). He had attained only the 54th year of his age. The Arnulfing princes were far tougher and healthier than the short-lived Merovingians, but even they did not attain to great length of days. Probably in Pippin's case the fatigues and anxieties of his nine Aquitanian campaigns hastened his end.

Pippin is one of those historical personages of whom we know just enough to be tantalized with a desire to know more. Even as to his personal appearance we have no trustworthy information. The belief so prevalent in the Middle Ages, that he was a man of short stature, perhaps originated in a confusion between him and his grandfather Pippin of Heristal, but the contrast between the little father and the giant son was so tempting that the fallacy easily took root. Already little more than a century after his death Saga was busy with his exploits. The monk of St. Gall (884-887) tells us that having discovered that the chiefs of his army were privately casting imputations on his courage, Pippin ordered a wild bull to be let loose, and then a fierce lion after him. The lion made one spring, fastened his claws in the bull's neck, and pulled him to the ground. Thereupon the king shouted to the by-standers, 'Either drag the lion off the bull or slay him on the top of him'. With hearts frozen with fear the courtiers faltered out, "Master! there is not a man under heaven who dare attempt such a thing as that". Thereupon the king leapt from his throne, drew his sword, cut through first the neck of the lion, then the neck of the bull, sheathed his sword, and calmly resumed his throne. "Do you feel now", said he, "that I can be your master? Have you not heard what little David did to the mighty Goliath and the short-statured Alexander to his stalwart chiefs?". As if struck with thunder, the courtiers fell to the ground, saying, "Who but a madman would contest your right to rule?"

The story, pure Saga as it evidently is, may be accepted as pointing to an early tradition that Pippin was of short stature, and (which is of more importance) to the difficulties which sometimes beset his path from the insubordinate conduct of some of the leading men of his kingdom. Like our own Henry VII, he had to walk warily in the presence of men who remembered the time when he was only one of themselves. The chroniclers say but little expressly concerning these tendencies towards insubordination; but in one very important case, the debate on the Italian expedition, they admit that such tendencies existed, and we can see that they exerted an important influence on the course of affairs.

King Pippin left but three children—the little princess Gisila, of whose birth and baptism we have already heard in the correspondence of Pope Paul—and her two brothers, who had already reached man's estate, Charles and Carloman.

It is an illustration of the fragmentary and unscientific character of the Frankish chroniclers of this period that they give us no clear information of the uncertain date of so important an event as the birth of Charles the Great. His friend and biographer Einhard gives virtually three different dates—742, 743, and 744. Two annalists place it in 747, but it is hardly possible to reconcile so late a date with the commission entrusted to the young prince to meet Pope Stephen II in December, 753, nor with a document of 7603 in which he is already spoken of as a man. On the whole, the most probable conclusion is that Charles the Great was born in 742, and was therefore twenty-six years old when he succeeded his father.

As to the date of Carloman's birth we have scarcely more information. One annalist places it in the year 751, and if he is correct, Pippin's younger son was a little child of three years old when he, along with his father and brother, received the often-mentioned anointing from the Papal hands in the abbey of S. Denis. On that basis of calculation he would be seventeen years old at the time of his father's death.

The strange obscurity which hangs over the birth and infancy of the greatest of Frankish sovereigns may possibly be due to the fact that he was not born in wedlock. Even this cannot be positively asserted; but there is some authority for dating the marriage of Pippin with Bertrada, daughter of Charibert, count of Laon, in the year 749, which was certainly after the birth of Charles, though before the birth of Carloman. The sovereigns of Arnulfs line, though not licentious, were notoriously irregular in their matrimonial relations, and seem generally to have kept for some years as a mistress the woman whom they afterwards married with the rites of the Church. According to Frankish law, even on this theory, the subsequent marriage of his parents rendered Charles legitimate, but in the relation which existed between the two brothers, and especially in the somewhat contemptuous tone which Carloman occasionally assumed towards Charles, we may perhaps see indications of the fact that the younger brother prided himself upon the strict legitimacy of his birth and looked upon the elder as little better than a bastard.

The division of his dominions between his two sons had been one of the last occupations of the dying king. The details of that division cannot be quite accurately his sons, stated, but we may say generally that the dividing-line ran more nearly east and west and less from north to south than in some previous partitions. Thus we are told that Austrasia fell to the share of Charles; Burgundy, Provence, Septimania, Alsace and Alamannia (Swabia) to that of Carloman. The allocation of Neustria is not mentioned, but it seems probable that it was allotted to Charles. As to Aquitaine, the authorities differ irreconcilably; the historian whom we have just quoted declaring that it was divided between the two brothers, while the author of the Annales Einhardi says that it was all included in the lot of Charles. Bavaria is not mentioned in the scheme of partition, a striking illustration of the virtually independent position obtained by its Duke, Tassilo.

We find with some little surprise both the two young kings fixing their residences in the northern part of the realm. Samoussy near Laon and Attigny on the Aisne are the places from which Carloman dates his charters in the spring of 769, while Charles celebrated the Christmas of 768 at Aquae Grani (Aix-la-Chapelle or Aachen), the first and last love apparently of the great Austrasian.

As has been already hinted, the relation between these two brother sovereigns was very unlike that brotherly harmony which prevailed in the previous generation between the elder Carloman and his brother Pippin. The blame of Carloman's ill-temper is laid by one annalist on 'evil counsellors among his nobles', and it is hinted that at one time there was a danger of actual civil war between the two brothers. As Carloman disappeared early from the scene, we do not of course hear the story as it would have been told by his partisans. Probably, besides the motives of personal pique and thwarted ambition, there may have been working in the minds of the counsellors of the two young kings some of those 'centrifugal' tendencies, the rivalries between Frank and Burgundian, between the men of pure Teutonic descent and their Gallo-Roman competitors which led a century later to the disruption of the Frankish monarchy.

The first event which disclosed to all the world the gaping chasm between the two brothers was the war in Aquitaine. Almost immediately after the death of Pippin a certain Hunold, probably related to the family of the dethroned duke, raised once more the trampled standard of Aquitanian independence. Charles marched southwards in the spring of 769 to suppress this revolt, and called on his brother for aid; but though Carloman came to meet him at a place called Duasdives, he brought no troops with him, and entirely refused to assist in the reconquest of Aquitaine; an unbrotherly act if the province had been assigned to Charles alone, an incomprehensible one if it was held by the two brothers in partnership.

After all, the revolt of Hunold proved to be but a feeble affair. The old king in his nine campaigns had crushed the spirit of the men of Aquitaine too thoroughly to leave much work to be done there by his son. Charles marched to Aquitaine, and Hunold was soon fleeing before him. He fled to Gascony, and placed himself under the protection of Lupus, duke of that remote corner of Gaul. At the threat of war, war which, as Charles declared, should be continued till Gascony was reduced to the same condition of dependence as Aquitaine, Lupus surrendered his guest, together with that guest's wife, and promised implicit obedience to all the commands of the Frankish king. What became of Hunold and his wife we are not told; but Charles was through life, except on one or two occasions of special exasperation, a merciful conqueror. He built a strong fort at Fronsac near the junction of the Dordogne and Garonne, and returned in triumph to his Austrasian home.

While these events were occurring in Gaul, Pope Stephen III, having obtained the consent of the two young kings, was holding a synod in the Lateran basilica in order to obtain the solemn judgment of the Church on the recent anarchical proceedings at Rome. The synod was not ecumenical; it did not even represent all the countries of the Western Patriarchate; but the presence of twelve Frankish bishops 'very learned in the divine Scriptures and the ceremonies of the holy canons', along with forty ecclesiastics from the various districts of Northern and Central Italy, was a wise precaution to give dignity to the proceedings of the assembly and to prevent its seeming the mere mouthpiece of a vindictive Roman faction.

The bishops being all assembled in the great basilica, and Pope Stephen III having taken his place as president of the synod, Constantine, the late Pope, now sightless, and having endured for eight months the hardships of a dungeon, was brought in and placed in the midst of the assembly. It was sternly enquired of him, 'why he, a layman, had presumed to invade the Apostolic See and to do a deed so new and wicked in the Church of God'; whereupon he declared that he had been forced into that deed by the people of Rome, weary of the exactions and injustices of the late Pope, Paul—an important hint as to some of the causes that had been at work in the recent revolution—and, as he averred, after the vote of the peoplehad been taken by show of hands he had been laid hold of and forcibly inducted into the Lateran palace. Then falling to the ground and stretching forth his hands on the marble pavement, he confessed with tears that he had been guilty of sins more in number than the sand of the sea, for which he implored the merciful forgiveness of the synod. They caused him to be raised from the ground and sent back to his dungeon, adjourning their decision for a day.

On the morrow, when he was again questioned as to the 'impious novelty' of his deed, Constantine, who seems to have recovered a little of his lost self-confidence, replied that for a layman to be consecrated bishop was no novelty at all. He might have appealed to the well-known case of the election of Ambrose of Milan, but he chose more recent instances. Only seventeen years before, Sergius, a layman, whose wife was still living, had been consecrated archbishop of Ravenna, and though it was true that he had been cited to Rome on account of the alleged irregularity, and even imprisoned there, the irregularity had been condoned by Paul I, and he had been allowed to return to his see, an archbishop in full communion with Rome.

So too, only three years before the date of the Lateran synod, Stephen, a layman and governor of Naples, who had earned the enthusiastic love of the Neapolitans, had been at a time of terrible pestilence chosen bishop by the people, and had gone to Rome, where he received episcopal consecration at the hands of the same Pope Paul.

When Constantine urged these examples in mitigation of his offence the whole assembly was filled with fury. Unmoved to pity by the vacant gaze of those poor sightless eyes, they buffeted him on the face, they forced him to bow his neck, and finally thrust him out of the church. As to his ultimate fate the Papal biographer is silent. The members of the synod then brought the registers of Constantine's Papal acts and the records of the council which had been held under his presidency and burned them all in the midst of the presbytery. This done, Pope, priests and people cast themselves to the ground, chaunting *Kyrie Eleison*, with floods of tears—those copious ecclesiastical tears!—confessed their grievous sin in having received the communion from Constantine's hands, and all submitted themselves to the penance due for so great an offence.

The Papal biographer relates at great length the deliberations of the synod concerning the difficult question of ecclesiastical orders bestowed by the hands of the intrusive pontiff. The practical result was this, that the ecclesiastics who had been raised by Constantine to the rank of bishop were deposed from the episcopal office, but, after submitting themselves to a second election by the clergy and people, were reconsecrated by Stephen. Those men, on the other hand, who had been but laymen before and had received consecration as deacons or presbyters from the intruder, were thrust down from their clerical office (to which Stephen vowed that he would never again raise them), but not being allowed to return into the world and resume the duties and privileges of laymen, were ordered to retire into monasteries and spend the rest of their lives in religious meditation. Unhappy victims, these, of the revolution which in the eighth century corresponded to a change of ministry in the nineteenth!

The usual decree that 'with great honour and affection the sacred images should be venerated by all Christians', and the usual anathema on 'the execrable synod which has been lately held in the regions of Greece for the deposition of those sacred images', received the probably unanimous assent of the council. More important than these, however, as affecting the constitution of the Church for the eleven centuries which have since passed over it, was the solemn resolution framed under anathema by the council, 'that no layman nor man of any other order should presume to be promoted to the holy honour of the Pontificate, unless ascending by distinct steps he had first been made [cardinal] deacon or cardinal presbyter'. We here meet, for the first time apparently, with the term cardinal applied to the parochial clergy of Rome, those hinges of the ecclesiastical organization of the Metropolis. They shared it with the 'sub-urbicarian' bishops of the territory in the immediate vicinity of Rome; and from this time forth it was established as a sacred principle of the Church that only from one of these three orders, cardinal-deacons, cardinal-priests, cardinal-bishops, could a bishop of Rome be chosen. Thus the cardinals were now the alone eligible persons; but it was not till three centuries later that they became the alone electors.

It was probably some months, it may have been a year, after this synod of the Lateran, that Stephen III addressed to the two young Frankish kings a letter in which he congratulated them that the dissensions between them, rumours of which had evidently reached even to Rome, were now at an end, and exhorted them to turn their re-established harmony to good account by vigorously urging the assertion of all the just claims of St. Peter. 'If any one tells you that we have already received satisfaction of these claims, do not believe him'.

Harmony was indeed for a short time in the course of the year 770 re-established between the two Frankish kings, but it was by means of which Pope Stephen little dreamt, and which drove him nearly wild with anger and alarm when he discovered their nature.

The chief agent in this reconciliation was the dowager-queen Bertrada, who now after her husband's death emerges from the comparative obscurity of her earlier career, and plays with statesmanlike prudence and sagacity that part of all-controlling, all-counselling queen-mother with which we are so familiar in later chapters of French history. The policy which she advised, and which doubtless found many other advocates in the Frankish council-chambers, was not precisely that of the earlier years of her late husband, though towards the close of his reign he had seemed to be tending thitherward. "Is it wise", we can imagine the counsellors of Bertrada's party to have questioned,— "is it wise to spend the energies of the loosely-compacted Frankish kingdom in expeditions across the Alps, in order to enforce these shadowy, ever-growing, never-satisfied claims of St. Peter? We thereby make the Lombard our deadly enemy, him who so lately as in the days of Liutprand and Charles Martel, was our cordial, our ancestral ally. And not only the Lombard, but with him goes the young duke of Bavaria [for Tassilo a few years before this time had married Liutperga, daughter of Desiderius, and formed a strict alliance with his new father- in-law]; and Tassilo's relation to the monarchy is one of the darkest spots in our horizon. The late king never ventured to punish him for his great *harisliz* in 763. What the old hero dared not attempt, his young and inexperienced sons are not likely to succeed in. Were it not better to renounce the thoughts of vengeance and to have at least a friendly, an allied, if we cannot have a humbly obedient Bavaria? Aquitaine is but just tranquillized; she is still heaving with the turmoil of the nine years' war of her subjugation. Then on the north-eastern frontier of the realm hover the fierce, still heathen Saxons. There in those trackless forests, in those wide-spreading marshes between the Weser and the Elbe, lies the real danger, and also the true vocation of the Frankish monarchy. Even the Church can be better served by forcing those wild heathen tribes to bow their necks to the yoke of Christ, than by wresting a few more Italian cities from the Lombards and handing them over to the successor of St. Peter. But before all things peace is the present need of the Frankish kingdom; peace instead of strife between the two royal brothers, peace with the Lombard and peace with the Bavarian. And if the Pope should storm and threaten us with the wrath of St. Peter and the terrors of the Day of Judgment, let him storm and let him threaten. He has been already paid handsomely enough for that holy anointing at S. Denis of which we have heard so much. It is time now for the sons of Pippin to think of themselves and their own country, which is Frank-land, and not 'the province of Italy'."

Probably by some such reasonings as this was that great change in Frankish policy brought about, which was signalised by the journey of queen Bertrada to Italy in the year 770. The point which to us is left in the greatest obscurity is how the reconciliation with the Lombards was connected with that which was undoubtedly the object nearest to Bertrada's heart, the reconciliation between Charles and Carloman. That there was some such connection is clear from the words of the annalists, but it would be mere guess-work to say in what way it was brought about.

Intent on carrying through this scheme of reconciliation, Bertrada undertook the labours and not inconsiderable hardships of a journey from the north of Gaul into Italy. Starting probably from her son Charles's court at Liège, she met Carloman by appointment at a little place called Selz in Lower Alsace. There, doubtless, mother and son conferred on the new course of policy, and she obtained his consent to the projected alliances. Journeying thence to Bavaria, she no doubt conferred with Tassilo as to the best means of securing the future friendship of Franks, Bavarians, and Lombards. Having crossed the Alps, she probably visited the court of Desiderius at Pavia and there opened the purport of her journey. "Friendship between the Frankish and Lombard courts : more than friendship, matrimonial alliances : your daughter Desiderata for my eldest son: my little daughter Gisila, now twelve years old, to become hereafter the wife of your son Adelchis"; this was the flattering, the surprising offer made by the widow of the pious Pippin to the 'most unspeakable' Lombard king. Even in making it, however, Bertrada did not wholly forget the claims of St. Peter. Certain additional cities were to be handed over to the Pope; a condition to which Desiderius gladly consented. Though all is left painfully vague as to this part of the negotiation, it appears that some cities—how many we know not—were actually ceded by the Lombard at this time to the Papal See. Bertrada, who as we are told, when she had finished her business, went to worship at the threshold of the Apostles probably took to the pontiff the soothing news of this surrender. We may say almost with certainty that she said nothing at Rome of the projected double marriage. Having probably called on her return journey at Pavia, she recrossed the Alps, taking with her the intended bride. Desiderata arrived at Charles's court; the existing lady of the palace, Himiltrud, was divorced if she was his wife, or simply dismissed if she was his concubine, and the daughter of Desiderius was hailed as queen of the Franks, while some of the chief men of the kingdom swore to the observance of the treaty of peace and friendship which Bertrada had concluded between them and the Lombards.

When the news of this astounding alliance, either actually accomplished or about to be accomplished, reached Rome, the rage of the outwitted Pope knew no bounds. He seized the pen and wrote to the two brothers one of the fiercest, haughtiest, most scornful letters that ever proceeded even from the Papal chancery, a letter which already seems instinct with the spirit of Hildebrand rather than with the meek submissiveness of a bishop just emancipated from the heavy yoke of Byzantium.

After dilating on the virtue of constancy in the faith as exhibited by God's chosen servants, and alluding to the fall of man, which through the wiles of the Ancient Enemy was brought about by the weak nature of woman, Pope Stephen proceeds :—

"Now a thing has been brought to our hearing which we cannot even speak of without great pain in our heart, namely, that Desiderius, king of the Lombards, is seeking to persuade your Excellencies, that one of your brotherhood should be joined in marriage to his daughter. Certainly if that be true, it is a veritable suggestion of the devil, and not a marriage, but rather a most wickedly imagined concubinage. How many men, as we learn from Holy Scripture, through unsanctified union with a woman of another nation, have departed from the commandments of God, and fallen into grievous sin! But what indescribable folly is this, O most excellent sons and mighty kings, that your illustrious Frankish race which shines supreme above all other nations, and that most noble royal line of yours, should be polluted—perish the thought—by union with the perfidious and foully stinking race of the Lombards, which is never reckoned in the number of the nations, and from which it is certain that the tribe of lepers hath sprung!

No one in the possession of his senses would ever suspect that such renowned kings would entangle themselves in such hateful and abominable contagion. For what fellowship hath light with darkness, or what part hath he that believeth with an infidel?".

The Pope then alludes to the fact, of which he appears to speak without any hesitation, that both the young kings have already, by the desire of their father, married fair and nobly-born wives of their own Frankish nation. This positive utterance of his seems to force us to the conclusion, opposed as it is to the statements of most of the chroniclers, that Himiltrud, the mother of Charles's eldest son (afterwards known as Pippin the Hunchback), was his awfully-wedded wife and not a concubine. But who shall unravel the mysteries of the marriages of these most Christian kings of the Franks?

The Pope proceeds with his passionate exhortation : "None of your ancestors ever accepted a woman of another kingdom and a foreign nation as his wife", an assertion which he would have found it hard to justify from history. "And who of your most noble house ever condescended to contaminate himself by mixing with the horrid nation of the Lombards, that you should now be persuaded to defile yourself with that horrible people?".

Knowing doubtless the share which Bertrada hadt aken in these hateful negotiations, he reminds her, through her son, that his predecessor Pope Stephen II had dissuaded Pippin from divorcing her—we know not on what pretext—and expresses his hope that the sons will imitate the obedience which the father then manifested towards the Holy See. The same obedience had been shown in rejecting, under Papal advice, the offer of a brilliant alliance for the little Gisila with the son of the Byzantine Emperor.

The Pope then returns to his strongest argument. "You have promised firm and lasting friendship with St. Peter's successors. Their enemies were to be your enemies; their friends your friends. That league of mutual friendship was the reward of my pious predecessor Stephen II's journey across the Alps, a journey which he would have done well never to have undertaken if the Frank, whose aid he invoked, is going to join the Lombard against us. He reminded you of that promise in a letter which he wrote to you on his death-bed. Where is that promise now?

"Wherefore the blessed Peter, Prince of the Apostles, who received the keys of the kingdom of heaven from the Lord, adjures you through my unhappy mouth; and with him all the bishops and presbyters, the nobles and judges, and all the rest of the clergy and people of Rome adjure you, by the majesty of God and by the tremendous day of future judgment, that by no manner of means shall either of you two brothers presume to receive in marriage the daughter of the aforesaid Desiderius, king of the Lombards : nor shall your sister, the noble lady Gisila, dear to God, be given to Desiderius' son : nor shall you dare to put away your wives.

"This warning of ours we have placed upon the tomb of the blessed Peter, and have over it offered sacrifice to God, and we do now with tears direct it to you from the same sacred sepulchre. And if (which God forbid) any one shall presume to act in opposition to this our adjuration and exhortation, let him know that by the authority of my lord the blessed Peter, Prince of the Apostles, he is fast bound in the chain of our anathema, and is banished from the kingdom of heaven, and with the devil and all his horrid crew and the rest of the wicked ones is sent down to be burned in the everlasting fire. But he who shall keep this word of our exhortation, being honoured with celestial benedictions from the Lord, shall be counted worthy to receive the rewards of eternal joy with all the holy ones, elect of God.

"May the heavenly grace keep your Excellencies in safety".

This extraordinary letter, as we have seen, failed to produce any effect. The policy of Bertrada and her counsellors was for the time triumphant. Desiderata, the Lombard princess, was enthroned in Charles's palace and received on her head the precarious crown-matrimonial of the Austrasian Franks. Seeing this, the Pope, though doubtless bitterly enraged, concealed his resentment and bided his time. The next two letters from him that we find in the Codex Carolinus are full of words of cloying sweetness, towards Bertrada, towards Charles, and towards Carloman. He announces to Charles and his mother that their envoy Itherius, who was dispatched for the restoration to the Holy See of its patrimonies in the duchy of Benevento, has accomplished his mission with admirable prudence and fidelity, and prays that he may be rewarded according to his deserts. He rejoices at receiving the greatly desired 'syllables' from the God-protected Carloman which announce the birth of a son, and craves to be allowed to act as godfather to the infant Pippin, that there may be the spiritual relationship of co-fatherhood established between them, to the great joy both of the Pope and the people of Rome.

But all this time events were ripening for a new and astonishing change in Italian politics. "Since my Frankish patrons have deserted me", Stephen seems ° to have said to himself, "since they have left me alone to face the fury of the now omnipotent Lombard, what hinders me from following their example, and making my peace, unknown to them, with the common foe?". There were indeed two great living hindrances to the adoption of this tempting policy—Christopher and his son Sergius, *Primicerius* and *Secundicerius* of the Papal household, and all-powerful in the Lateran palace. These men by accepting the aid of Desiderius against the intruder Constantine and then seating their own candidate, not his, on the Papal throne, had sinned too deeply against the Lombard king for any hope of forgiveness. Moreover, in all the subsequent demands for the recognition of the *justitiae* of St. Peter their voices had ever been the loudest and the most importunate. But probably the weak and vacillating Sicilian Pope was weary of the domination of these men, and his weariness made him listen gladly to the suggestions of another of his servants, the chamberlain Paulus Afiarta, who had been gained over by Desiderius and stood at the head of the Lombard faction in the City. The sacrifice of Christopher and Sergius was therefore resolved on, and when in the season of Lent (771) Desiderius came with an army, professedly to worship at the tombs of the Apostles, and when Pope Stephen went forth to meet him and ostensibly to confer with him concerning the restitution of St. Peter's rights, all Rome probably suspected, and Christopher and Sergius knew, that what would be called in modern phrase a change of ministry was impending. It happened that a certain envoy of Carloman named Dodo was then in Rome, probably at the head of a body of troops. Some of the peasants of Tuscia and Campania, and even from far-off Perugia, had also been gathered together for the defence of Rome, when it was known that Desiderius was on his way. The gates of the City were closed, new ones were hung on their hinges where the old were too rotten to resist attack, the citizens were called to arms, and (again to use a modern phrase) the City was proclaimed to be in a state of siege.

The contemplated defence of the City of Rome against the Lombards had this peculiarity, that the man who should have been the representative of all that was most Roman and national among the besieged was supposed, not untruly, to be in league with the besiegers. We know from many instances in modern history how ill it fares with a king or a commander-in-chief in such circumstances, and what a menacing shape the indignation of the mob can assume against a half-hearted or traitorous general. In this case, Christopher and Sergius, with their Frankish ally and Dodo and a troop of armed men at their heels, rushed to the palace of the Lateran; 'intent on murdering me', writes the resentful Pope. That is most improbable, but that they meant to put pressure on Stephen to compel him to renounce his alliance with Desiderius is not to be doubted. "They entered with arms" (he continues)"the sacred *patriarchium* of the Lateran, they smashed the doors and tore the curtains of the palace with their lances, and entered with their coats of mail and their spears into the basilica of Pope Theodore, where we were sitting, and into which no one had till then penetrated with so much as a knife in his hand".

The Pope, we are told, sharply chided the insurgents for coming armed into the holy *patriarchium*, but he condescended to take an oath, 'by all the sacred relics that were contained in the Lateran basilica', that he would have no secret dealings with Desiderius, and thus quieted them for the time. Next day, however, he contrived to elude their vigilance by some ingenious device, and made his way, attended by certain of his clergy, to the great basilica of St. Peter, which was practically the headquarters of Desiderius. In the conference which there took place the Lombard king appears to have promised to satisfy all the claims of St. Peter, if only those evil counsellors, Christopher and Sergius, might be delivered into his hands. Meanwhile St. Peter's was closed to prevent the egress of the clergy who had come with the Pope; closed too and rigorously guarded were all the gates of the City; everything seemed to portend a bloody encounter.

The Lombard party was, however, undermining the position of Christopher and Sergius by promises, threats and gold. The great authority of the Papal name was freely used to discourage the citizens who were holding the City against their own bishop. Two bishops, Andrew of Praeneste and Jordanes of Signia, presented themselves before the Porta Sancti Petri, bringing to the two chief rebels the Pope's fatherly advice that they should either enter some monastery for the salvation of their souls, or at once come forth and meet him at St. Peter's. Though Christopher and Sergius knew the Lombard's resentment against them too well to trust themselves to his mercy, others less deeply involved began to waver. The Pope's envoys again approached the gates and cried with a loud voice, "Hear ye what Pope Stephen orders by the command of God. Do not wage war against your brethren, but expel Christopher and Sergius from the City, and free the City, yourselves and your children from peril". With that, many began to swarm down the walls that they might make their way to the besieging army. A certain duke Gratiosus, who was a kinsman of Sergius, feigned to depart to his own house, but collected a band of citizens and went to the Porta Portuensis, hoping to be able to open it. Finding it hopelessly barred, they wrenched it from its hinges, and so went forth by night to the Papal presence. And now all the City was in an uproar; everywhere men were trying to open the gates and pass out through them; the two ministers saw that they were surrounded by traitors and the game was lost. When the hour of Vigils sounded from the great bell of St. Peter's, Sergius climbed down the wall and hastened to that basilica, but was arrested by the Lombard sentinels and carried off to their own king. Christopher followed, was also captured, and brought into the presence of the Pope, who promised that his life and that of his son should be preserved if they would quit their public career and enter a convent.

Next day the Pope celebrated mass in the presence of Desiderius, and returned (apparently) to the Lateran palace after giving orders that Christopher and Sergius, whom he left at St. Peter's, should be quietly brought back into the City at nightfall. But as soon as the sun began to set, Paulus Afiarta, with a band of reckless partisans and with at least the connivance of Desiderius, forced his way into St. Peter's, carried off Christopher and Sergius, and brought them to the gate of the City. Here, in accordance with that barbarous practice which the New Rome had taught to the Old, his men plucked out the eyes of both prisoners. The aged Christopher, who was carried to the monastery of St. Agatha, died in three days of the torment which his brutal captors had inflicted upon him. Sergius, imprisoned in Pope Gregory's monastery on the Clivus Scauri and afterwards transferred to the *cellarium* of the Lateran, lingered there in blindness and misery till the death of the reigning Pope.

It is impossible not to feel, in conning these pages of the Liber Pontificalis, what a wave of barbarism has swept over the leading citizens of Rome, both lay and ecclesiastical, since the days of Gregory the Great. Partly no doubt this is due to the long descent into ignorance and superstition during the course of the seventh and eighth centuries, but it seems to have become more rapid and more fatal since the two Gregories and Zacharias vanished from the scene. Is it an unwarranted conjecture which would connect this increasing ferocity of Roman politics with the acquisition of temporal power by the Roman pontiff?

When the revolution was accomplished the question naturally arose, 'What will the kings of the Franks say when they hear of the deeds that have been done?'. In order to propitiate their resentment Stephen wrote a long letter to Bertrada and her son Charles, in which he described the whole affair from the point of view of Paulus Afiarta and Desiderius. The Lombard king, once so 'unspeakable' and 'stinking', is now 'our most excellent and God-preserved son, King Desiderius, without whose aid we and all our clergy and all the faithful members of God's Church would have been in peril of our lives'. "The most unspeakable Christopher and his most wicked son took counsel with Dodo, the envoy of your brother Carloman, to slay us. Behold what villainies and devilish machinations the aforesaid Dodo put in operation against us, but we are sure that our most excellent son his master will at once disavow his proceedings. It was the enemies of Christopher and Sergius who rushing upon them plucked out their eyes, without our will or counsel, as we call God to witness". (When Stephen lay upon his death-bed he did not assert his innocence of this crime quite so positively.)

Lastly, "let your Religiosity beloved by God"— this to Bertrada, "and your most Christian Excellency"—this to Charles—"recognise how in the name of the Lord the most excellent and God-preserved king Desiderius has met us with all good will. And we have received from him full and entire satisfaction of all the claims of the blessed Peter". (On this point also, when Stephen lay at the point of death, he told a different tale to his successor.)

From this time, the Lent of 771 to February 772, Paulus Afiarta, a bold, unscrupulous man, probably reigned supreme in the Papal council, and Stephen was fain to live in outward amity with Desiderius, veiling his fear and his dislike of the unspeakable one as well as he could. Scarcely had this great change in his policy been accomplished when he learned that with a little patience it might have been avoided. Charles the Frank was not after all irrevocably committed to friendship and alliance with Desiderius. It was probably in the summer of 771 that he sent back Desiderata to her father's court, a woman scorned and a repudiated wife. No reason seems to have been given for this insulting breach of the marriage covenant, but its cause was probably personal rather than political. The Monk of St. Gall (writing it is true more than a century after the event) says that she was in delicate health and unlikely to bear children, and therefore, in accordance with the judgment of the holiest ecclesiastics, was deserted as if she were dead.

We may perhaps reasonably conjecture that this delicate Italian flower bore but ill her transplantation to the keen air of Brabant and Westphalia, and that Charles, who was a man of brisk and joyous temperament, spending most of his life in the open air and expecting his wife and his children to follow him to the chase and on the campaign, came to the speedy conclusion that the pale Lombard princess was no wife for him, and cut the knot with as little ceremony as our own Henry Tudor.

There were not wanting voices and remonstrance in his own palace against this selfish desertion of a lawfully wedded wife who had done him no wrong. Bertrada, who had arranged the marriage and had brought the young bride across the Alps, was deeply mortified by the divorce, which caused the only serious dissension that ever separated the mother and the son. His young cousin Adalhard also, though still only a page in the palace, boldly condemned the divorce, which, as he declared, would make the king an adulterer, and all his nobles who had sworn fidelity to the new queen, perjurers. Having thus delivered his soul, Adalhard retired from court life into a monastery.

Politically, of course, such an event could have but one result. As close as the alliance between Desiderius and Charles might have been had they remained kinsmen, so deep and impassable was now the chasm between the injured father and the faithless husband of Desiderata. Only, between the dominions of the two kings stretched the wide realm of Carloman, and it is by no means clear what would have been his attitude towards either. The line of policy pursued by his envoy Dodo at Rome looks like hostility to the Lombard, who, as we shall see, expected him to take a bloody revenge for the murder of Christopher and the blinding of Sergius. But on the other hand, Einhard expressly tells us—and his words seem to point to this period of their history—that many of Carloman's partisans strove to break the bond between the two brothers, so that some purposed to engage them even in civil war. And it would seem certain that at this crisis, after the repudiation of Desiderata, any one who was the enemy of Charles must have been the friend of Desiderius.

But all such speculations were set at rest for ever by the death of Carloman, which occurred on the 4th of December, 771. We know nothing of the cause or the manner of this untimely ending of a life which had lasted but twenty years. Nor is the character of the young king, or what might have been the possible future of his career, at all made clear to us. A far less forcible and far less pathetic figure than his uncle the elder Carloman, he seems to us—but herein we may do him wrong—only a somewhat petulant and querulous young man, the impracticable partner of his heroic brother. Like the dark star which, as some astronomers tell us, circles round Sirius, so Carloman interests us only by the question how long he will continue to obscure the transcendent glory of Charlemagne.

Two months after Carloman, died Pope Stephen III, after a short and troubled pontificate of three years and a half. What passed between him and his successor Hadrian, when he was lying on his death-bed, will be related in a future chapter.

CHAPTER XII

RAVENNA AND ROME.

Before we enter upon the memorable pontificate of Hadrian I, which lasted twenty-three years and witnessed great changes in the political aspect of Italy and the Papacy, it will be well to give a glance at the ecclesiastical relations existing between Rome and the dethroned capital of Ravenna. Our information on this subject is fragmentary, obscure and confusing; but, even in its confusion, it evidently reflects the troubled and uncertain state of men's minds whenever the relation of the two cities came under discussion.

If we consider their previous history we shall see that there was sure to be some such trouble and uncertainty. Here was Rome on the one hand, which had first obtained her high ecclesiastical position as the political capital of the world, and had then languished for three centuries under the neglect of the great Imperial absentee, but was now virtually throwing off the yoke of Constantinople and winning for herself a new, a temporal, and an Italian dominion by her opportune alliance with the great Austrasian house. Ravenna, on the other hand, which had been the seat of the Imperial lieutenants for two centuries, had now lost all the pomp and splendour which they had conferred upon her. No more now would an Exarch fresh from Constantinople, surrounded by his life-guards and followed by his obsequious eunuchs and chamberlains, ride through the streets of Ravenna to hear mass sung in the basilica of St. Ursus or St. Vitalis. The Exarch gone, the Archbishop of Ravenna felt his own importance diminished and power slipping from his hands. Was Ravenna to be only one of the many cities of the Lombard kingdom? Or, yet worse, was it to be politically subject to the see of Rome; the Pope not merely an ecclesiastical superior whose claims to the Universal Patriarchate of the West might be decorously admitted in theory and on suitable occasions evaded in practice, but an actual sovereign, with power of life and death, able to enforce his edicts, and in the last resort judging all causes, civil as well as temporal, at Rome? Even in the days of the great Gregory, when the see of Ravenna was held by his own friend and disciple Marinianus, things had not always gone smoothly between the two pontiffs. Since then, apparently, the estrangement had increased rather than diminished; and now this claim on the part of the Roman Pope to rule Ravenna as a subject city was as much as possible waived aside, and always bitterly resented by the Archbishop and people of Ravenna.

It is this contention which gives sharpness to the tone of the ecclesiastical historian of Ravenna whenever he has occasion to mention the see of Rome. Long ago I ventured to bring before my readers some of the strange, often puerile legends which Agnellus, abbot of St. Mary's and St. Bartholomew's, told of the archbishops of Ravenna in that extraordinary book, his Liber Pontificalis. We have now come to a different portion of his history. Though still inaccurate and blundering, he has no longer so much need to draw upon his imagination for facts. As we are now within thirty-five years of his birth within seventy years of the composition of his history, we may take his narrative as almost that of a contemporary, vouched for as it is by such notes of time as 'this man was my predecessor at four removes in the government of my monastery' and 'my grandfather was concerned in that rebellion'. Above all, the dislike of the Papal claims to sovereignty, which is shown in every page, is an important symptom of the times. We shall certainly follow the counsel of the good Benedictine Editor, who tells us that all these calumnies against the Holy See are to be read with caution, but the existence of the antipathy which prompted the calumnies is itself a fact of which we are bound to take notice.

It was an archbishop John, sixth of that name, who occupied the see of Ravenna during the eventful reign of the Lombard Liutprand and for ten years after his death. Agnellus mentions the siege of the city by Liutprand and the act of treachery on the part of one of its citizens by which the Lombard king effected its capture. But he says nothing expressly as to its subsequent surrender to the Byzantines, though he implies it by his mention of the Exarch as again ruling in the city. Nor (which is more extraordinary and in fact inexcusable) does he make the slightest mention of the final capture of Ravenna by the Lombards under their king Aistulf in the year 751. To atone for his silence on these important events, he retails some of the ecclesiastical gossip of the city. Archbishop John having become unpopular with the citizens was banished to the Venetian territory for a year. Then Epiphanius the *scriniarius*, lamenting the widowed condition of the Church of Ravenna, persuaded the Exarch to order his recall. On the archbishop's return Epiphanius suggested that he should offer a handsome present to the Exarch and prevail upon him to issue process against the enemies who had procured his banishment. "If you will do this covertly", said Epiphanius, "I will conduct the suits, while you can preserve the pontifical character and appear to have no desire for the punishment of your foes". It was done: the accusers were summoned before the judgment-seat, and to each one the *scriniarius* said with righteous indignation, "What sort of a sheep was you who, when thy shepherd was leading thee through grassy meads, didst strike him with thy horn and prepare a bill of indictment against him?". Thus by the terrors of the law large sums of money were collected, the promised *honorarium* was paid to the Exarch; possibly something remained over for the ingenious *scriniarius*, and the archbishop was never again molested by his foes.

During the same pontificate, says Agnellus, an Imperial *ministrategus* came against Ravenna, thinking to ravage it. And then follows the strange story about the battle in the Coriander-field between the the 'Greeks' and the men of Ravenna which has been briefly given in a previous volume. Have we in this wild and somewhat childish legend a remembrance, however distorted, of some genuine engagement between the men of Ravenna and the troops of the iconoclastic Emperor? Were Agnellus a more trustworthy historian, we might question whether after all Ravenna was wrested by the Lombards from the Empire, whether it had not succeeded in throwing off the yoke of Byzantium and was a small but independent state when Aistulf conquered it and annexed it to his kingdom.

On the death of John VI (in 752) Sergius was elected to the vacant see. The cause of the election of this young man, whom Agnellus describes as 'short of stature, with a smiling face, grey eyes and comely figure, and sprung from very noble ancestors', is an unsolved enigma. For Sergius was a layman, who by reason of his youth can hardly have won the confidence of his fellow-citizens as did Ambrose of Milan and Stephen of Naples when they were invited or constrained to exchange high office in the State for high office in the Church. Moreover, Sergius was married, and his wife Euphemia was still living, though now consecrated as a deaconess by the husband from whom she was thus strangely separated. The sole explanation that can be suggested for these irregular proceedings is that Ravenna was still in the throes of a revolution, only just annexed to the Lombard kingdom, suffering many vexations (as Agnellus tells us) from the Lombards and Venetians—this incidental notice of war with the maritime islanders is perhaps significant—and that there may have been some political reasons for placing the representative of one of the noblest families in Ravenna at the head of the Church, the only institution which seemed to have a chance of maintaining Ravenna's independence.

However, the expedient answered but poorly. Sergius had long disputes with his clergy, most of whom refused to communicate with him, whereupon he consecrated other priests in their places whose claims very nearly caused a schism in his Church. This dispute, however, was healed by smooth words from the young archbishop of the smiling countenance, and by some mutual concessions in the important matter of vestments. Then, however, came a struggle with Rome. Though Sergius had received consecration at the hands of the Pope he was summoned to Rome by Stephen II on that pontiff's return from his memorable journey across the Alps. We are told that he had trusted in the King (doubtless King Aistulf), that he would lend him his aid, and being deceived by him was fraudulently led to Rome by some of his own fellow-citizens. Probably the meaning of all these obscure hints is that the semiindependence of the see of Ravenna was an obstacle to Pope Stephen's designs of obtaining temporal dominion over the Exarchate and Pentapolis, and that the irregularity of the election of Sergius, though condoned at the time, now furnished a useful pretext for beating down a dangerous rival.

The enquiry into the cause thus cited to Rome seems to have lingered, for Sergius is said to have been detained there for three years. At last a synod was assembled which was ready to cast him down from his 'pontifical' rank. The Pope (whom Agnellus calls the *Apostolicus*) thus addressed him: "Thou art a neophyte; thou didst not belong to the fold, nor serve according to the canons in the Church of Ravenna, but didst creep in like a thief into the episcopal chair, and hast repelled the priests who were worthy to taste the honours of the Church, and by main force and the favour of secular persons thou hast kept possession of the see". To this Sergius answered: "It was not by my presumption, but because the clergy and all the people elected me. Thou didst thyself put to me all the canonical questions, and I disclosed everything to thee; that I was a layman, that I had a wife, that I had [suddenly] come into the clerical status. All this I made known to thee, and thou saidst that there could be no obstacle [in the way of my consecration]. After thou hadst heard all these things concerning me, why then didst thou consecrate me?"

After this defence the assembly was divided, but all—says Agnellus, probably untruly—asked with anxiety, "How can we who are disciples judge him who [as archbishop] is our master?". Then the Pope in anger declared that he would on the morrow tear off the pallium from the neck of Sergius.

All that night the exiled archbishop passed in prayer, with floods of tears, at the altar of St. Nicholas. In the morning all Rome knew that Pope Stephen II had died suddenly and peacefully in his bed; 'by the judgment of God' says the apologist of the pontiffs of Ravenna. At dawn, Paul, the brother of the deceased Pope and his destined successor, entered the cell of Sergius, and said to him, "What wilt thou give me for leave to return in peace and with augmented honour to thy home?". Delighted at the prospect of being thus liberated from captivity, the archbishop said, "No small rewards will I give thee. Come to the archbishop's palace at Ravenna and examine the treasures stored up there—gold, silver, vessels of price, hoards of money. All shall be given thee; only whatsoever thou likest to leave me as a *benedictio*, thou canst leave". To this compact they both swore. On that very day the late Pope's brother was raised to the papacy, and celebrated his accession by releasing all captives [Sergius among them] and pardoning all criminals. He sent for Sergius and received him with all honour. When the archbishop of Ravenna fell prostrate on the ground before him—it is a marvel to find Agnellus admitting even that confession of inferiority—Paul raised him therefrom, fell on his neck and gave him the kiss of peace, and ordered his seat to be placed next his in the hall of audience.

After receiving from the new Pope words of peace and comfort, Sergius returned to his own see in the third year after he had quitted it. He was received with moderate congratulations by his flock, and moderate peace reigned in the City. Possibly this lukewarm reception was the cause why the returning exile proceeded to the church of St. Mary in Cosmedin and after singing mass prostrated himself before the altar of his patron, St. Nicholas, where he prayed for a very long time, and shed tears, 'which,' says Agnellus, 'are preserved unto the present day', that is to the eighty-fourth year after their first effluxion.

In course of time the Pope appeared at Ravenna to claim the fulfillment of the archbishop's compact. The ecclesiastics of the city, knowing that he was coming to rifle their treasury, took counsel together. Some said, 'Let us suffocate him'. Leo the deacon, *vice-dominus* of the archbishop, said, 'Not so; let us beckon him away to yonder cistern, as if we were about to show him some more treasures, and then push him in, so that he may appear no more among men'. At this moment Wiliaris, archdeacon and abbot of St. Bartholomew (Agnellus' predecessor at the fourth remove), came up, saw their plotting, and heard their diverse voices. Thereat he cried out, 'O my brethren, what are you planning? To slay the Pope? God forbid! Nay, but when night covers the sky, and the Romans, weary of eating and drinking, are stretched in slumber, then let us extinguish the lights, and stow away all the treasures of the church, or as many as we may be able to hide, without the archbishop's knowledge'. So said; so done; but ere they had finished their task, the Pope at dead of night appeared upon the scene, ordered the keys to be brought him by the *vestiarii* (vergers), and opened all the doors of the church. He carried off the relics, which they had not been able to hide, and many precious vessels of gold and silver to Rome. The citizens of Ravenna, when they heard of the robbery of their church, set off in pursuit of the waggon that bore the precious vessels, but the charioteers, alarmed, turned into Rimini for shelter, whereupon the men of Ravenna returned home disconsolate.

After his return to Rome the Pope sent letters couched in flattering terms to the archbishop and nobles of Ravenna, praying for the surrender of the men who had plotted against his life. This was granted; the men were all sent to Rome (the grandfather of Agnellus being one of them), and remained there in prison till they died.

'Now Sergius', says Agnellus, 'judged all the Pentapolis from Pertica as far as Tuscany and the table of Walanus just like an Exarch, and arranged all things as the Romans of old had done. He made a league with the Venetians, because he misliked the king of the Lombards and feared that evil might befall him from that quarter. In order to carry through this negotiation he gave seven purses of money apiece to each of the chief nobles among them.

On the death of Sergius, which occurred on the 23rd 01 August, 769, there was a dispute as to the succession to the see of Ravenna, of which Agnellus tells us nothing, but the Roman *Liber Pontificalis* makes it one of the articles of accusation against Desiderius and the Lombards. There was apparently an attempt to turn the election of Sergius into a precedent, and once more to seat a layman in the archi-episcopal palace of Ravenna. Michael, a *scriniarius* or registrar of the church, a man with no sacerdotal rank, obtained the help of Maurice, the duke of Rimini, who in his turn leant upon the aid of Desiderius, and this coalition succeeded by main force in installing Michael as archbishop of Ravenna, instead of Leo the archdeacon of the church, upon whom the election would otherwise have fallen. As Maurice, the duke of Rimini, by whom this state-stroke was accomplished, is characterized by the papal biographer as 'unspeakable', and as he acted in cooperation with Desiderius, he was probably a Lombard; and in any case his attitude appears to have been one of entire independence of Rome and even of actual opposition to the Holy See. Yet Rimini was one of the places which thirteen years before had been solemnly surrendered to Abbot Fulrad, and by him handed over to Stephen II. Thus we have in this event one proof the more how precarious and shadowy were the rights secured to the Pope by the great Donation of Pippin.

For a little time the intrusive archbishop seemed likely to establish himself in the see. Leo was shut up in prison, and a deputation was sent from Duke Maurice and the civil rulers of Ravenna to the Pope, praying him to consecrate Michael archbishop, and offering costly gifts to secure his compliance. Weak as he was, however, Stephen III utterly refused to take part in a ceremony which would have entirely stultified his protest and that of his brother ecclesiastics against the election of Constantine. The Church's treasures went to the Lombard at Pavia instead of to Stephen at Rome, and for a year the help of Desiderius thus purchased succeeded in keeping Michael on his archiepiscopal throne. Then the stubborn refusal of the Pope to consecrate and the terror inspired by a peremptory message from the Frankish king Charles, won the day. There was a popular insurrection at Ravenna. Michael was sent bound to Rome for judmnent, Leo was liberated and elected archbishop. He hastened to Rome with a long train of nobles and ecclesiastics, and was solemnly consecrated archbishop towards the end of 770, a little more than a year before the death of his champion Stephen III. Though he owed so much to Rome, his attitude during the eight years of his pontificate was generally one of stubborn opposition to the Papal claims.

The relations of the two Churches of Rome and Ravenna during the middle of the eighth century, which have been here briefly reviewed, vividly exhibit the uncertain nature of the Papal sovereignty over the Exarchate and the Pentapolis. It was one thing to get a 'page of donation', conferring wide-spread territories on the vicar of St. Peter; it was quite another thing to establish what modern diplomatists call 'effective occupation' of those territories. With such a royal or imperial mandate and with a full treasury, a Pope of the fifteenth century would probably have had but little difficulty in hiring a *condottiere* captain who would have made his claim effective. But though she had within her abundant elements of disorder, Italy was not cursed with *condottieri* in the eighth century.

CHAPTER XIII

THE ACCESSION OF POPE HADRIAN.

Pope Stephen III died, as we have seen, on the 3rd of February, 772. The waves of strife which had tossed him to and fro during his short and troubled pontificate were still raging round his deathbed. To the fierce and unscrupulous Paulus Afiarta it was a matter of life and death to preserve the ascendency of the Lombard faction and to crush any attempt of the Roman or Frankish parties to elect a Pope who would reverse the recently-adopted policy. Many of the clergy and civil magistrates of the City were sent into exile, even while Stephen III was dying, and a more terrible vengeance was taken on the hapless Sergius, who, though blinded and in prison, was still formidable to the imagination of Paulus. There seems to have been a *junta* of counsellors who at this time of crisis wielded all the power of the dying Pope. They were Paulus himself (who held the office of chamberlain), John the *dux Romae* (who was brother of the Pope, and whose implication in these deeds of violence renders it probable that Stephen himself had really concurred in the recent revolution), Gregory the *defensor regionarius*, and another chamberlain named Calvulus. These men signed an order to the warders of the prisons in the Lateran for the delivery of the body of the captive Sergius. In the of first hour of the night, eight days before the Pope's Sergius-death, Calvulus presented himself at the dungeon door with two men of Anagni, Lumisso a priest and Leonatius a military officer, and obtained possession of the person of the blind captive. The course of the narrative looks as if the two men of Anagni had some private resentment of their own to gratify by the murder of the fallen minister. However this may be, he was straightway slain and buried in a street close to the Arch of Gallienus.

Happily for the fame of the Holy See, these unscrupulous attempts to silence the voice of opposition to Paulus Afiarta and his party were not successful. We may perhaps conjecture that if there was a Lombard party in the Papal Curia represented by Paulus, and a Frankish party of which Christopher and Sergius had been the heads, there was also a Roman party representing the best traditions both of the City and the Church, who were determined that the most exalted office in Christendom should no longer be made the prize of victory in the bloody strife of *cubicularii* and *primicerii*. It was probably the voice of this respectable middle party which secured the election of one of the greatest Popes of the eighth century.

Hadrian I, son of Theodore, was a pure Roman by birth, born at a house in the Via Lata, near to where the modern Corso opens out into the Piazza di Venezia. His parents, who belonged to the highest nobility of Rome, died in his childhood, and he was brought up in the house of his uncle Theodotus, who had been formerly consul and duke, but afterwards filled the office of *primicerius* of the Roman Church. Hadrian grew up, a young man of handsome presence and generous and manly character, conspicuous while still a layman for his devout attendance at the neighbouring church of St. Mark, his almsgiving, his austerities, his study of the canons of the Church. Such a man, in the intellectual atmosphere of Rome, was naturally attracted within the ecclesiastical orbit. At the urgent invitation of Pope Paul he became first *notarius regionarius*, then sub-dean; and the succeeding Pope Stephen III advanced him to the rank of deacon, and admitted him to his intimate confidence. Though the biographer speaks of the devotion to study which marked him from his earliest youth, his learning, if measured by classical standards, would probably have been found woefully deficient. His letters, contained in the Codex Carolinus, swarm with grammatical blunders of which a schoolboy would be ashamed: and this is the more extraordinary, because (as was explained in an earlier volume) Hadrian was the Pope by whose orders the letters of his renowned predecessor Gregory I were collected into the great Register in which most of them have become known to later ages. And those letters, though not written exactly in the style of Cicero or even of the younger Pliny, are at least free from the solecisms which disfigure the letters of Hadrian. However, 'in the country of the blind the one-eyed man is king', and in the dense ignorance which prevailed at Rome in the middle of the eighth century Hadrian seems to have been reputed a learned man. He soon became a great and popular preacher, and this undoubted popularity caused him to be elected (9th of February, 772) as successor of Stephen III on the Papal throne.

The new Pope at once showed that he did not intend to be a mere instrument in the hands of Paulus Afiarta. On the very day of his election, even before his consecration, he ordered—and this prompt exercise of his power shows how truly monarchical was now the Papal character—that all the nobles of Church and State whom Paulus had banished from the City should be at once invited to return, and that all the political prisoners should be liberated. For the hapless Sergius, whom men doubtless expected to see now emerging from the dungeons of the Lateran, the order of release came too late.

Desiderius heard with concern that a new Pope who was not amenable to the counsels of his partisan was sitting in the palace of the Lateran. He sent an embassy, consisting of Theodicius duke of Spoleto, Tunno duke of Ivrea, and Prandulus the keeper of his wardrobe, to propose a renewal of the same friendly relations which had of late subsisted between Pavia and Rome. The speech in which Hadrian replied to the smooth words of these ambassadors was one of startling and undiplomatic frankness. "I for my part wish to live in peace with all Christians, including your king Desiderius, and in that covenant of peace which had been established between Romans, Franks and Lombards I shall study to abide. But how can I trust that same king of yours when I remember what my predecessor in this office, lord Stephen of pious memory, told me confidentially concerning his broken faith. For he told me that he had lied to him in everything which he had promised with an oath on the body of the blessed Peter, as to restoring the rights of God's holy Church: and further that it was only under the persuasion of the unjust arguments of the same Desiderius that he caused the eyes of Christopher and Sergius to be dug out, and executed the will of the Lombard on those two officers of the Church".

(It was not therefore wholly without the consent of Stephen III that that barbarous deed was done.)

"And in this way he caused us great harm and loss, for [the alleged reconciliation] brought no advantage at all to the apostolic cause. All this my predecessor, for the love which he bore unto me in my humble station, confided unto me: and moreover he shortly after sent unto him his own messengers, exhorting him to fulfill his promises to St. Peter. But this was the [insulting] reply which those messengers brought back with them:—

It is enough for the apostolic Stephen that I have cut off Christopher and Sergius from the world, since they were domineering over him. He need not talk about recovering the rights of the Church ; for if I do not myself help the apostolic man, he himself will soon be ruined, since Carloman, king of the Franks, the still surviving friend of Christopher and Sergius, is making ready an army to avenge their fate by marching to Rome and taking the pontiff himself captive.

"That was his reply. Lo! there you have the honour of King Desiderius and the measure of the confidence that I may repose in him"

After Hadrian had liberated his soul by this outburst, the Lombard emissaries assured him with solemn oaths that their master was this time in earnest in his desire for a league of amity with the Holy See, and would purchase it by the surrender of all the territory for which Pope Stephen III had striven. Once again the blandishments of the Lombard prevailed. Hadrian believed their words, and sent two ambassadors, of whom Paulus Afiarta was one, to receive the surrender of the desired territory.

Hardly, however, had the Papal messengers reached Perugia on their journey towards the Exarchate when they learned that Desiderius, far from preparing to cede any more cities to the Roman See, had appropriated Faenza, Ferrara and Comacchio, that is, had resumed possession of the cities which he surrendered in 757, and had added thereto Comacchio, which formed part of the territory ceded by Aistulf to Pippin's representative in 756. The faithlessness, and more than that, the inconsistency, the childish levity of purpose which characterizes these Lombard kings, exasperate the chronicler of their deeds and make him almost ready to acquiesce in the 'unspeakable' names hurled at them by Papal biographers.

It may be suggested with some probability that the cause of this sudden change of front on the part of Desiderius was the arrival of the widow and children of Carloman at the Lombard court. To understand the bearing of this event we must go back to the closing month of 771, in which the opportune death of Carloman relieved the Frankish world of the fear of a civil war between the two brothers. Charles's measures were taken with such exceeding promptitude as to suggest the thought that his plans had been matured while Carloman was dying. He hastened to Carbonacum, a royal 'villa' in Champagne, just over the frontier, and there met a number of the most eminent nobles and ecclesiastics of his late brother's kingdom. Chief among them were the venerable Fulrad, abbot of S. Denis, and Wilchar, archbishop of Sens, both of whom had often carried Pippin's messages to Rome. Carloman had left two infant sons, and the claims of both of these to share their father's inheritance were doubtless discussed in the assembly of Carbonacum. But the evil result of these divisions of the kingdom was too obvious, the lately impending danger of civil war was too terrible. The majority of the counsellors of the late king gave their voices for reunion under Charles, who celebrated his Christmas at Attigny as sole lord of all the Frankish dominions.

On learning the decision of the assembly, Gerberga, the widow of Carloman, taking with her the two infant princes, crossed the Alps and sought shelter at the court of Desiderius. With her went some, apparently not a large number, of the courtiers of her late husband, pre-eminent among whom was Duke Autchar, the same doubtless who eighteen years before had escorted Stephen II on his memorable journey Italy. King Charles, we are told, took very patiently his sister-in-law's flight to the court of his enemy, though he considered it 'superfluous', or, as a modern would probably express the matter, 'in bad taste'.

The arrival of Gerberga with her children and counsellors put a new weapon in the hand of Desiderius for revenge on the husband of his daughter. For to that revenge all calculations of mere policy had now to yield, the pale figure of the divorced and uncrowned queen of the Franks, 'not quite a widow, yet but half a wife', being ever in his sight and mutely appealing for the redress of her wrongs. Nor as a question of mere policy did the scheme which now shaped itself in his mind seem an unwise one. If he could have Carloman's children (the sole strictly legitimate heirs of Pippin, since Charles was not born in wedlock) confirmed in the succession to their father's kingdom; a barrier thus erected between him and the Austrasian king; his son-in-law Tassilo of Bavaria united to him, both by kinship and alliance; Desiderius might reasonably reckon on being left at liberty to pursue his designs for the subjugation of the whole of Italy, unhindered by meddlers from beyond the Alps. Obviously the doubtful element in the calculation was the degree of support which Gerberga could obtain in Frank-land itself for the claims of her infant sons. The chances of that support were no doubt overestimated both by her and by her right-hand man, Autchar; but when have the exiled pretenders to a throne rightly calculated the chances of a Restoration?

For the fulfillment of the designs of Desiderius it was desirable that he should make the Pope his confederate, in order to obtain the religious sanction conveyed by his consecration of the infant princes as kings of the Franks. The Lombard king evidently hoped to wrest this concession from the Pope by the same mixture of flattery and intimidation which had been so successful with his predecessor. He had yet to learn how different from the wavering will of Stephen III was the steadfast mind of Hadrian.

It was doubtless in order to execute these projects that Desiderius, not two months after the accession of Hadrian, made that fierce dash across the Apennines in the course of which, as already related, he wrested from the Roman See its newly-acquired cities of Faenza, Ferrara and Comacchio. At the same time the territory round Ravenna was ravaged by the Lombards, who ransacked the farms and cottages, and carried off the herds of cattle and the slaves of the farmers and the stored-up provisions of the peasants. Two tribunes brought to Hadrian from Leo the new archbishop of Ravenna the tidings of these outrages, with a piteous appeal for help, 'since no hope of living was left to him or his people'.

A fresh embassy from the Pope—since the mission of Paulus Afiarta and his colleague had proved so fruitless—brought to Desiderius the grave rebuke of Hadrian for these repeated outrages and violations of his promise. And now in his answer to this embassy the Lombard king showed at what he was aiming: "Let the Pope come to hold a conference with me, and I will restore all those cities which I have taken". The Papal messengers, who doubtless saw Gerberga and Autchar at the court of Pavia, perceived that this personal conference would involve a request or a command to anoint with the holy oil the children of Carloman.

Meanwhile what was Paulus Afiarta, so lately the omnipotent minister of the Pope, doing at the court of his friend Desiderius? He lingered on there, perhaps conscious of the peril which awaited him at Rome, but seeking by braggart words to reassure the king as to his undiminished credit at the Papal court: "You desire, O king, to have colloquy with our lord Hadrian. Trust me to bring it to pass. If needs be, I will tie a rope to his feet, but I will by all means bring him into your presence". And so saying he started on his return journey to Rome.

At Rome, meanwhile, in the absence of Paulus Afiarta, the murmurs and the suspicions caused by the disappearance of Sergius had grown stronger and stronger. At last the Pope summoned all the keepers of the *cellarium* in the Lateran and began a formal enquiry into the fate of their late prisoner. The warrant for his delivery to the chamberlain Calvulus was produced, and he, being questioned, admitted having transferred Sergius to the keeping of the two men of Anagni. They were sent for from

Campania, brought into the Papal presence, and, apparently, examined by torture Thus urged they confessed that they had slain Sergius, and were sent, under the guard of some of the Pope's most trusted servants, to show his place of burial. They came to the Merulana, to the Arch of Gallienus, near to which they dug for a little while, and then showed the guard the body of the ill-fated *secundicerius*, his neck bound tight with a rope and all his body gashed with wounds. Whereupon the beholders concluded that he had been suffocated, and then buried while still alive.

The bodies of the two fallen ministers Christopher and Sergius were now taken up and buried with honour in the basilica of St. Peter. The sight of the mangled body of Sergius stirred his late colleagues, the officials of the Church and State, to such a passion of indignation that they with a whole crowd of the commonalty of Rome rushed to the Lateran palace and clamorously besought the pontiff to take summary vengeance on the torturers and murderers of a blind prisoner. Accordingly Calvulus the chamberlain and the two men of Anagni being handed over to the secular arm, as represented by the Prefect of the City, were led down to the public prison and there examined in the presence of the people. The meaner criminals, the two men of Anagni, repeating the same confession which they had already made in presence of the Pope, were transported to Constantinople, there to be dealt with as should seem fitting to the Emperor. Of their further fate we hear nothing. Calvulus refused to confess his share in the crime, and, as we are told, 'expired by a cruel death in prison'. Probably this means that he died under the torture which failed to extract the desired confession.

Two men, who from their exalted position deserved the severest punishment of all, Duke John the late Pope's brother and Gregory the *defensor regionarius*, seem from the Papal biographer's silence as to then cases to have been left unmolested. But for Paulus Afiarta, the friend of the Lombard, the recreant servant of the Pope, another fate was in store. He had already left Pavia, and had been arrested by the Pope's orders at Rimini, the reason for that detention being apparently his treasonable practices with the Lombard. Now the minutes of the proceedings during the enquiry into the murder of Sergius were forwarded to Archbishop Leo at Ravenna, with instructions to deal with the case according to the ordinary course of justice. On receipt of these instructions the archbishop handed the prisoner over to the *consularis* of Ravenna, the officer who, now that the Exarch was gone, appears to have wielded the highest secular authority in the city. A public examination took place; the minutes forwarded from Rome were read; Paulus Afiarta confessed his guilt. The Roman pontiff expected that his brother at Ravenna would make a formal report of the case to him, but the archbishop having now got an old enemy into his power had no intention of allowing him to escape out of his hands.

In these circumstances, strange to say, Pope Hadrian, who seems to have been sincerely anxious to save the life of Paulus though desiring his punishment, tried the desperate expedient of an appeal to Constantinople. To Constantine Copronymus and his son Leo, now associated with him in the Empire, he sent a memorandum setting forth the crime of Paulus, and praying them to arrest him and keep him in close confinement in 'the regions of Greece'. A chaplain named Gregory, who was being dispatched to Pavia on one of the usual embassies of complaint to Desiderius, was instructed to halt at Ravenna and give to Archbishop Leo the necessary orders for the transmission of the culprit to Constantinople on board a Venetian vessel. The archbishop, however, somewhat insolently replied that it would be a mistake to send Paulus Afiarta to Venetia, since Maurice the duke of that district was in anxiety about his son, a captive in the hands of Desiderius, and would be tempted to make an exchange of prisoners, surrendering Paulus to his Lombard friend and receiving back his son. The Papal messenger proceeded on his journey, after giving a solemn charge to the archbishop and all the magistrates of Ravenna that not a hair of the prisoner's head was to be touched: but on his return from Pavia he found that the *consularis*, by order of the archbishop, had put Paulus Afiarta to death. Great was his indignation at this act of disobedience to his master, and sharply was expressed. Archbishop Leo, perhaps somewhat terrified by the thought of what he had done, wrote to Hadrian praying for a consoling assurance that he had not sinned in avenging the innocent blood. He received however only a curt reply: 'Let Leo consider for himself what he has done to Paulus. I wished to save his soul, by enjoining him to lead a life of penance, and gave my orders to my chaplain accordingly'.

The proceedings in this complicated affair are narrated in the Liber Pontificalis with a tedious minuteness which suggests the probability that the chaplain Gregory himself composed this part of the narrative and desired to clear himself and his master of all complicity in the death of Paulus Afiarta. The narrative however is not without its value, since it shows that still, so late as the year 772, the Pope was willing to recognize a certain jurisdiction over Roman citizens as vested in the Emperors at Constantinople, heretics and iconoclasts though they might be. It also illustrates the growing independence of the archbishops of Ravenna and their determination not to acknowledge the bishops of Rome as their superiors in any but purely ecclesiastical concerns.

The fall of Paulus Afiarta destroyed the last link between the Roman pontiff and the Lombard king. The latter now pursued without check or disguise his brutal policy of forcing the Pope to become his instrument by despoiling him of his domains. The summer 772 and autumn of 772 were occupied by a campaign—if we should not rather call it a raid—on two sides of the Papal territory. In the Pentapolis the Lombards seized Sinigaglia, Iesi, Urbino, Gubbio, Mons Fereti and several other 'Roman' cities. In fact, when we consider how much Desiderius had abstracted before, we may doubt whether in these Adriatic regions any city of importance was left to St. Peter except Ravenna and Rimini. This raid was accompanied, as we are told and we can well believe it, by many homicides, many conflagrations, and the carrying off of much plunder.

Even more insulting; and more ruthless were the proceedings of the Lombard ravagers in the near neighbourhood of Rome. Blera, only thirty miles north-west of Rome, was one of the four cities which thirty years before had been surrendered by the great Liutprand to Zacharias after the conference at Terni. It was assuredly the act of a madman, made 'fey' by the shadow of approaching doom, to harry the lands which his great predecessor had formally handed over to St. Peter's guardianship. Yet the word of command having been given, the rough Lombard militia of Tuscany poured into the territory of Blera, while the citizens, with their wives, their children, and their servants were engaged in the peaceful labours of the harvest. The invaders slew the chief men of the city (who were probably foremost in resisting the invasion), ravaged the country all round with fire and sword, and drove off a multitude of captives and of cattle into the land of the Lombards. Several other cities of the Ducatus Romae suffered more or less from similar depredations, and Otricoli on the Via Flaminia, a stage nearer to Rome than Narni, was occupied by the Lombard host.

While these deeds of lawless aggression were being perpetrated, the insolent diplomacy of Desiderius also held on its course. Several times did his messengers,

Andrew the *referendarius* and Stabilis the duke, appear at the Lateran desiring the Pope to come and talk with their master 'on equal terms'. The answer of Hadrian was firm and dignified: "Tell your king that I solemnly promise in the presence of the Almighty, that if he will restore those cities which in my pontificate he has abstracted from St. Peter, I will at once hasten into his presence wheresoever he shall choose to appoint the interview, whether at Pavia, Ravenna, Perugia, or here at Rome; that so we may confer together about the things which concern the safety of the people of God on both sides of the frontier. And if he have any doubt of my keeping this engagement, I say at once that if I do not meet him in conference he has my full leave to reoccupy those cities. But if he does not first restore what he has taken away, he shall never see my face". There spoke the worthy successor of Leo and of Gregory, the truly Roman pontiff, who showed that a citizen of the seven-hilled City had not quite forgotten the old lesson 'to spare the fallen and war down the proud'. In truth this year 772, which might have been the Lombard's great opportunity, had he known how to use it, was the year which brought out in strongest relief what there was truly heroic in Hadrian's character. We hear at this time of no cry for help to Frankish Charles. Both Hadrian and Desiderius knew full well that such a cry would have been uttered in vain, Charles had now begun that which was to prove the hardest and longest enterprise of his life, the subjugation and conversion to Christianity of the fierce Saxon tribes who dwelt in the regions which are now called Hanover and Oldenburg, on the north-eastern frontier of the Frankish kingdom. Though in the course of Charles's great career he was eventually carried across the Alps and the Pyrenees, though the Volturnus and the Ebro saw the waving of his standards, his heart seems to have been always in his own native Austrasia, and his conception of his kingly duties was connected much more with the civilization of Central Europe than with the extension of his dominions along the shores of the Mediterranean. Thus it was that, carrying forward the policy of his father and the preaching of St. Boniface, he determined that heathenism should cease throughout Saxonland, and devoted the first energies of his kingdom, when consolidated by the death of Carloman, to the attainment of that great object. Assuredly the work took longer time than he had expected. It began in 772, and was not completed till 804, after thirty-two years of almost incessant war. Possibly, had he known how long a road lay before him, he might never have entered upon the journey: but if so, it is fortunate for Europe that the future was hidden from his eyes, for however ruthless were some of his methods, however ghastly some pages of his slaughterous evangel, there can be no doubt that, in one way or another, the work had to be done, and that the world is better for the doing of it. If therefore, from an Italian point of view, Charles's action shall sometimes seem to us fitful, capricious, and lacking in unity of design, we must remember that during all the years of his vigorous manhood this arduous Saxon problem was absorbing the best energies of his body and his soul.

Intent on his great design Charles summoned his *placitum*—or, as we may call it, using the language of later centuries, the diet of his kingdom—to meet at Worms, probably in the early summer. From thence he advanced into the land of the Saxons, accompanied not only by his stalwart Frankish soldiers, but by bishops, abbots and presbyters—a numerous train of the tonsured ones. There were three great divisions of the Saxon people, the Angarii in the middle of the country, the Westfali on their western, the Ostfali on their eastern border. Charles marched against the Angarii, laid waste their land with fire and sword, and took their stronghold, Eresburg on the Diemel. From thence he marched to the Irminsul, a gigantic tree-trunk in a dense forest, which had been fashioned into a resemblance of the ash Yggdrasil of the Edda, the supporter and sustainer of the universe, and which was the object of the idolatrous veneration of the Saxons. Having hewn down the tree-idol he remained three days near the scene of his triumph. But a great drought prevailed in the land, and the army suffered grievously for want of water. The drought might be interpreted by the outraged idolaters as evidence of the anger of the gods; but the torrent which burst forth from the mountain's side and saved the whole army from perishing of thirst was a clear indication that the Christian's God was mightier than they. In these labours and dangers the campaigning season of 772 passed away: Charles having carried his standards triumphantly to the Weser, returned to Austrasia and celebrated his Christmas at Heristal in Brabant. The months of February and March (773) he spent at the villa of Theodo in the valley of the Moselle, sixteen miles north of Metz.

To this place (which is now called Thionville by the French and Diedenhofen by the Germans), in one of those winter months at the beginning of 773, came the Pope's messenger Peter with a piteous cry for help. Embassy after embassy had been sent in vain to Desiderius to beseech him to restore the captured cities, and had only been answered by further outrages on the Roman territory and by an announcement of his determination to march upon Rome itself. So closely were the roads beset that Peter found it necessary to make his journey by sea from the mouth of the Tiber to Marseilles.

Even while Peter was pleading the Papal cause at Thionville, Desiderius in fulfillment of his threat was moving towards Rome. Taking with him his son Adelchis, who had been for more than thirteen years the partner of his throne, and the widow and children of Carloman with their counsellor Autchar, he marched southward at the head of his army. He sent forward his messengers, Andrew and two other Lombard nobles, to inform the Pope of his approach, and received the answer, already repeated to weariness, "Unless he first repairs the wrongs done to St. Peter, he shall not be admitted to my presence". Still Desiderius pressed forward, and it seemed clear that an armed invasion of the Ducatus Romae was imminent. In Roman Tuscany, in Campania, and in Perugia, something like a levee *en masse* was made, and even from the cities of the Pentapolis, notwithstanding the presence of the Lombard garrisons, some men came to help in the defence of the threatened pontiff. The two great basilicas of St. Peter and St. Paul, being without the gates, were emptied of their most costly treasures, which were brought within the City, and the doors of St. Peter's were closed and barred with iron, to prevent the Lombard king from entering the church, as he probably intended, in order to carry the election of an anti-pope and the anointing by him of the infant princes. The great gates of the City had already some months before been closed, and small wicket-gates had been opened in them for the passage to and fro of the citizens.

Having made all these material preparations, Hadrian began to ply the spiritual artillery which had so often proved the best defence of Rome. Three ecclesiastics, the bishops of Albano, Palestrina and Tivoli, sallied forth from the City to the Lombard camp, which was fixed at Viterbo, fifty miles from Rome, and there presented to Desiderius the Pope's word of anathema, protesting against him by that word of command and exhortation, and adjuring him by all the divine mysteries that he should by no means presume to enter the territories of the Romans, nor to tread their soil, neither he nor any of the Lombards, nor yet Autchar the Frank.

Wonderful to relate, this 'word of anathema' was sufficient to foil the whole scheme of invasion. As soon as he had received this word of command from the aforesaid bishops, Desiderius returned immediately with great reverence and full of confusion from the city of Viterbo to his own home. Either he had overrated his own and his soldiers' courage in the face of the terrors of hell with which he and they were threatened, or he found that the *levée en masse* of Roman citizens would make his task more difficult than he had anticipated, or at last when too late he shrank from encountering the wrath of the Frankish king. For Charles was now evidently at liberty to attend to the affairs of Italy. In reply to the embassy of Peter he dispatched three envoys to Rome, the bishop George, the abbot Gulfard, and his own intimate the friend Albuin, to enquire into the truth of the Pope's charges against Desiderius. These men satisfied themselves that the Lombard king's assertions that he had already restored the cities and satisfied all the just claims of St. Peter were impudently false. They heard from his own lips the surly statement that he would restore nothing at all, and with this answer they returned to their master, who was probably at this time keeping his Easter-feast at the ancestral villa of Heristal. They carried also the Pope's earnest entreaties that Charles would fulfill the promises made by his father of pious memory, and complete the redemption of the Church of God by insisting on the restoration of the cities and the surrender of all the remaining territory claimed by St. Peter.

CHAPTER XIV

END OF THE LOMBARD MONARCHY.

At last the reign of the shifty and perfidious Desiderius was to come to an end. He had climbed to the throne by the help of a Pope whom he had deluded with vain promises. He had maintained himself thereon for sixteen years by a policy cunningly compounded of force and fraud. Now the day of reckoning was come.

Though we have really no Lombard history of this period—alas for the silent voice of the national historian Paulus—we have sufficient indications that the reign of Desiderius was unpopular with many of his subjects, and we may conjecture that the whole state was honeycombed by domestic treason. In November, 772, the young King Adelchis, enthroned in Brescia, signed a document by which he conveyed to the monastery of St. Saviour 'all the property and serfs of Augino, who has revolted and fled to Frank-land', together with all the farms, territories and serfs of eight other proprietors whose names are mentioned, and of other their accomplices, 'which they have lost for their disloyalty and which have thus become the property of our palace'.

We hear also of the avowed disaffection of Anselm, formerly duke of Friuli, who in 749 had laid down his ducal dignity, had assumed the monk's cowl, and had founded the monastery of Nonantula, a few miles north-east of Modena. Banished and proscribed by Desiderius, he was now living in retirement at Monte Cassino, but was using all the power which he had acquired by his deserved reputation for holiness to shake the throne of his royal antagonist. As he was a brother of Giseltruda, Aistulf's queen, we have in Anselm's disgrace probably another indication of the ill-will which existed between the families of the two last kings of the Lombards.

All these elements of weakness in the Lombard state were doubtless known to Charles, when, after deliberation with his Franks, probably at the Field of May, he determined to follow his father's example and invade Italy in the service of St. Peter. A levy of the nation in arms wag ordered and while it was proceeding Charles, still treading in his father's footsteps, sought by diplomacy to render the war needless. We are told that he offered Desiderius 14,000 solidi of gold, besides an [unnamed] quantity of gold and silver [vessels], if he would comply with the demands of Hadrian. The transaction looks suspiciously like a duplication of the similar offer of Pippin, but if the offer was ever made, it was this time also ineffectual. 'Neither by prayers nor by gifts did Charles avail to bend the most ferocious heart' of Desiderius.

The Frankish host was mustered at Geneva, and Charles then proceeded, according to a favourite strategic plan of his, to divide his army into two portions, one of which, under the command of his uncle Bernhard, was to march by the pass of the mountain of Jupiter, now called the Greater St. Bernard, while Charles himself was to lead the other over the Mont Cenis.

What next followed is told us in meagre and confused fashion by the annalists on one side and the Papal biographer on the other; and it is only by the help of one or two conjectures that we can combine the details into any harmonious picture. With that aid the story may be thus narrated. As before, there no fighting on the actual summits of the passes, but Desiderius prepared to meet the invaders in the narrow gorges on the Italian side before they had got clear of the mountains. He himself advanced from Susa to meet King Charles, while his son Adelchis, marching from Ivrea, awaited the approach of Bernhard. When Charles descended toward the valley of the Dora he found his further progress barred not only by the Lombard army, but by walls which they had built and by warlike engines commanding the pass. To force his way through seemed so difficult an enterprise that he again tried the path of diplomacy. He renewed his offer of the 14,000 solidi if Desiderius would restore the conquered cities. When this offer was refused he reduced his demand. Without the actual restoration of the cities he would be satisfied with the surrender of three hostages, sons of Lombard nobles, as a pledge for their future restitution. This too was met with a surly negative by Desiderius, and thereupon the young Frankish king was actually about to turn back and reascend the mountain. A dangerous enterprise surely with an embittered foe behind him! The question was then probably trembling in the balance whether the name of Charles the Great should ever be heard of in European history. But just at this crisis, on the very eve of the intended retreat, a panic seized the host of Desiderius. They left their tents, with all the stores that they contained, and fled in terror down the valley, at first pursued by no man, but soon followed by the Frankish soldiers, who slew numbers of them, though Desiderius and his nobles succeeded in making their escape to Pavia.

What was the cause of this sudden terror? Almost probably certainly the advance of Bernhard, who had succeeded in eluding or defeating Adelchis, and now, advancing on the flank of the army of Desiderius, threatened to cut them off from Pavia. The strategic operation planned by Charles, involving an attack by two converging hosts on an enemy in the centre of the circle, is admitted to be a very dangerous one for the assailant, but when it succeeds, the effect is crushing. It was the consciousness that they were thus utterly outmanoeuvred which drove Desiderius and his men in headlong rout down the valley.

Charles now meeting no obstacle in his onward march, in the beginning of October commenced the siege of Pavia. Seeing, however, that it was likely to be a long and tedious affair he returned to Frank-land, and fetched from thence his girl-wife Hildegard, an Alamannian lady of noble birth, only thirteen years of age, whom he had married immediately after his repudiation of Desiderata. She came with her infant son Charles and with his half-brother Pippin, the son of the first of all Charles's wives, Himiltrud. A boy of some seven or eight years old, probably, was this Pippin, born apparently to high destinies, but unhappily deformed in his person. The family affection, conspicuous in the Teutonic conquerors of Rome, shows itself in this young Austrasian warrior Charles, who must have his wife and children beside him if he is to endure the weariness of the long blockade of Pavia.

That blockade occupied eventually more than eight months, but not all of that time was spent by Charles himself before the walls of the cityon the Ticino. When he learned that Adelchis, son of Desiderius and partner of his throne, had fled with Gerberga and her sons to Verona, Charles marched thither with a chosen band of Frankish warriors, and, notwithstanding the strong position of Verona, appears to have taken it without much difficulty. Gerberga and her sons, with their chief adviser Autchar, surrendered themselves at once to Charles. All of them at this point vanish from history: a fact which may be interpreted differently according to our estimate of the character of the conqueror. To me, considering the clemency with which Charles usually treated his vanquished foes, it seems probable that all their lives were spared, though it is not unlikely that Gerberga and Autchar were recommended to embrace the monastic life, and that the sons were educated for the service of the Church. As for Adelchis, he escaped from Verona and began that life of wandering and exile which was his portion for the remainder of his days. Charles returned to the upper valley of the Po, and took many cities of the Lombards without relinquishing his grasp on Pavia.

Meanwhile, or perhaps even before some of the events just related, important political changes had been taking place in Central Italy. When it was seen that the throne of Desiderius was tottering, the Lombards of Spoleto, who had probably never heartily accepted the sovereignty of the Tuscan upstart, proceeded to make terms for themselves with him who seemed now likely to become the most powerful of Italian princes, the Bishop of Rome. "The leading men of Spoleto and Rieti", says the biographer, "ere yet Desiderius and his Lombards had arrived at the Alpine passes, fleeing for refuge to St. Peter, handed themselves over to Pope Hadrian, swore fealty to the Prince of the Apostles and the most holy Pope, and were tonsured after the manner of the Romans". Their example, we are told, would have been followed by all the inhabitants of the Spoletan duchy, but they were restrained by fear of Desiderius. After his defeat and flight to Pavia, and when his Spoletan soldiers had returned home, "immediately the whole body of inhabitants of the various cities of the duchy of Spoleto streamed together into the presence of the lovely pontiff, and rolling themselves at his feet earnestly besought his holy Thrice-Blessedness that he would receive them into the service of St. Peter and the Holy Roman Church, and would cause them to be tonsured after the manner of the Romans". Pope Hadrian marched with his new subjects to St. Peter's, administered the sacrament, received their oath of fidelity for themselves and their remotest descendants, gave them the desired Roman tonsure, and 'appointed them a duke whom they themselves had chosen of their own free will, to wit the most noble Hildeprand, who had previously taken refuge with the rest [of his followers] at the Apostolic See.'

At the same time, the citizens of Fermo, Osimo and Ancona, at the southern end of the Pentapolis, and the Tuscan town of Castellum Felicitatis, west of the Apennines, submitted themselves in similar manner to the Pope and his successors. Well may the biographer describe with exultation the extension of the Papal territory which Hadrian had thus obtained by his own unaided efforts. The commendation—for such the above transaction seems to have been—of the great duchy of Spoleto and the annexation of the other cities just mentioned, gave to the dominions of St. Peter the shape and extent which they retained down to our own day. The Adriatic provinces were now joined to the Ducatus Romae, not by the slender and precarious thread of Perugia and the Via Flaminia alone: a solid block of territory covering both sides of the Apennines and including the old Roman province of Picenum now gave roundness and symmetry to dominions which reached, nominally at any rate, from Ferrara in the north to Terracina in the south, a distance in a straight line of some two hundred and twenty miles.

The winter passed away, Eastertide was approaching, and Charles, who had probably a wider mental horizon than Pippin, determined to visit that great metropolis of Christendom which his father had never seen. Leaving of course all the working part of his army encamped round beleaguered Pavia, he started with a brilliant train of dukes, counts, bishops and abbots, and a sufficient body-guard of soldiers, on the road through Tuscany to Rome. He marched in haste, and was within a day's journey of the City, ere Hadrian heard of his arrival. 'Falling into an ecstasy of great astonishment,' the Pope directed all the magistrates of the City to go thirty miles along the north-western road to meet the great Patrician. They met him at the place called Ad Novas, the third station on the Via Clodia, near the shores of Lake Bracciano, and here they presented him with a standard, probably such an one as St. Peter is represented as granting 'Carulo Regi' in the mosaic outside the Lateran.

At one mile from the City the Pope had ordered that the illustrious visitor should be met by all the regiments of the little army of the Ducatus Romae, together with their officers and the boys who had come to Rome, probably from all the countries of the Christian West, to learn the language of the Church. The great crosses, which were, so to speak, the standards of the Church, were brought forth, as was the custom when an Exarch or Patrician entered Rome. All the Romans, men and boys alike, sang hymns of praise, in which Charles's Frankish soldiers joined with their deep Teutonic voices. As soon as Charles saw the crosses being borne towards him, he alighted from his horse, and in lowly pedestrian fashion, with the nobles who followed his example, accomplished the scene at rest of the journey. And now the venerable basilica of St. Peter—a building utterly unlike the domed Renaissance temple of Bramante and Michael Angelo—rose before them on the Vatican hill, and there in the long *atrium* outside the doors of the church stood Pope Hadrian and all his clergy, who had risen at early dawn to welcome their great deliverer. At the foot of the hill King Charles knelt down, assuredly in no feigned reverence, but overcome with emotion at the sight of the long dreamed of sanctuary, and kissed each step that led up to the crowded *atrium*. When he reached the summit, King and Pope clasped one another in a loving embrace—no Byzantine prostration of the ecclesiastic before his sovereign, no Hildebrandine abasement of the sovereign before the ecclesiastic—and so, while Charles cordially grasped the right hand of Hadrian, they together entered 'the venerable hall of St. Peter, Prince of Apostles', all the clergy and brethren of the monastic orders chanting the while with loud voices, 'Blessed is he that cometh in the name of the Lord.'

Let us pause for a moment to gaze at the figures of the two men, the highest types in their day of the old Roman and the new Teutonic civilization, who accomplish this fateful meeting on the steps of St. Peter's basilica. Hadrian, a Roman of the Romans, sprung of a noble stock, born almost under the shadow of the mausoleum of Augustus, bearing the name of the most artistic of Roman Emperors, 'elegant and very graceful in person', but a man of indomitable will and of courage that had never quailed before the threats of the brutal Desiderius—this man, as worthily as Leo or as Gregory, represents the old heroic spirit of the men of Romulus, transformed yet hardly softened by the teachings of the Man of Nazareth.

And Carl, not the majestic yet somewhat out-worn Emperor of medieval romance, but a young and lusty warrior who has not reached the half-way house of life. The very name of this grandson of Charles Martel has a Teutonic ring in it, and reminds us of the day when the unmannerly messenger burst into the second Pippin's presence as he was sitting by the solemn Plectrude and shouted out 'It is a Carl'. But though he is Teuton and Austrasian to the core, a descendant of untold generations of Rhine-land warrior-chiefs, and though the Frankish lawless love of women stains many pages of his history, he never forgets that he is also the descendant of the sainted Arnulf of Metz, and that his father was crowned by the not less saintly Boniface. The welfare of the Church is dear to his heart. If he be not a pattern of morality himself, he will not tolerate immorality in that Church's ministers. He has perhaps already begun to read the book which will be the delight of his middle life and old age, Augustine's great treatise 'On the City of

God'; and with the help of this great Roman, the Vicar of Peter, he has visions of one day bringing that city down to dwell on the earth, such wide spaces of which are subject to his rule.

A word as to the personal appearance of the great Austrasian. He was of commanding stature, probably not less than six feet five in height. His nose was long, his eyes large and sparkling, his face bright and cheerful. His hair, which when Einhard drew his picture was 'beautiful in whiteness,' we may imagine to have been at this time golden in hue, descending in long curls to his shoulders. His gait, even when he was an old man, was firm and martial: how much more when he now for the first time trod the soil of Italy at the head of his Frankish warriors.

Such were the two men who on Holy Saturday, the 2nd of April, 774, met in the atrium of St. Peter's. They marched together up the long nave, followed by all the bishops, abbots and nobles of the Franks, drew nigh to the *confessio* of the Apostle, and there, prostrate before the relics of the saint, offered up their loud thanksgivings to Almighty God for the victory which had been wrought by his intercession. Prayer being ended, Charles humbly besought the pontiff for leave to worship at the various churches in Rome. It was not the Patrician, come to set in order the affairs of the City, but the pilgrim from across the Alps come for the healing of his soul, who preferred this lowly request. Then they all went down the steps into the crypt and stood by the actual (or alleged) body of the Apostle, while Pope, King, and nobles gave and received solemn oaths of mutual fidelity.

We need not follow the enthusiastic biographer through his minutely-detailed description of the ceremonies which followed this 'joyous entry' of Charles into the City of Rome. On Saturday, the numerous baptisms usual on this day of the Calendar were administered by the Pope at the Lateran basilica. On Easter Sunday, a great presentation of Roman magistrates and officers to Charles was followed by a mass at S. Maria Maggiore, and then by a banquet at the Lateran palace. On Monday there was mass at St. Peter's, and on Tuesday at St. Paul's. But on Wednesday there was enacted, if the Papal scribe speaks truth, that great event the Donation of Charles to Hadrian, an event of such transcendent importance that the biographer must be allowed to tell it in his own words :—

'Now on the fourth day of the week, April 6, 774, the aforesaid Pope, with his officers both of Church and State, had an interview with the King in the church of St. Peter, when he earnestly besought and with fatherly affection exhorted him to fulfill in every particular the promise which his father, the late King Pippin of holy memory, and Charles himself with his brother Carloman and all the Frankish nobles, had made to St. Peter and his vicar Pope Stephen II on the occasion of his journey into Frank-land: this promise being that divers cities and territories of that province of Italy should be handed over to St. Peter and his vicars for a perpetual possession. And when Charles had caused this promise which was made at Carisiacum in Frank-land to be read over to him, he and his nobles expressed their entire approval of all things therein contained. Then, of his own accord, with good and willing mind, that most excellent and truly Christian Charles, king of the Franks, ordered another promise of gift like the former one to be drawn up by his chaplain and notary, Etherius. Hereby he granted the same cities and territories to St. Peter, and promised that they should be handed over to the pontiff, according to their defined boundaries, as is shown by the contents of the same donation, to wit, from Lima with the isle of Corsica, thence to Surianum, thence to Mount Bardo, that is to Vercetum, thence to Parma, thence to Rhegium, and from thence to Mantua and Mons Silicis, together with the whole exarchate of Ravenna, as it was of old, and the provinces of the Venetiae and Istria; together with the whole duchy of Spoletium and that of Beneventum. And having made this donation and confirmed it with his own hand, the most Christian king of the Franks caused all the bishops, abbots, dukes and counts to sign it also. Then placing it first on the altar of St. Peter, and afterwards within, in his holy *confessio*, the king and all his nobles promised St. Peter and his vicar Pope Hadrian, under the sanction of a terrible oath, that they would maintain his right to all the territories included in that donation. Another copy thereof, by order of the most Christian king, was made by Etherius, and to keep alive the eternal memory of his own name and the Frankish kingdom, was placed by Charles's own hands upon the body of St. Peter under the gospels which it is the custom to kiss in that place. Certain other copies of the same donation made by the bureau of our Holy Roman Church were carried away by his Excellency.'

By this transaction on the 6th of April, 774, if the Papal biographei1 is to be believed, the bishop of Rome became the actual or expectant sovereign of two-thirds of Italy. Actual or expectant, I say, because some part of the territory thus assigned was still in the hands of the Lombards, and yet more because the provinces of Venetia and Istria still, probably, owed allegiance to the Emperor Constantine. But in fact all enquirers who have carefully considered the question admit the impossibility of reconciling this alleged donation with the facts of history. The Pope of Rome never, we may confidently assert, was (as this donation would have made him) lord of all Italy with the exception of Piedmont, Lombardy, the immediate neighbourhood of Naples, and Calabria. The explanations of the difficulty are numerous. Forgery by the biographer, interpolation by a later hand, forgery by accepting a papal scribe, misunderstanding by the unlettered Frank, confusion between ownership of estates and lordship of territories, an early surrender by the Pope of rights which he found himself unable to maintain—all these solutions of the enigma have been suggested. For a slight and far from exhaustive discussion of the subject I must refer to a note at the end of this chapter. Only this much may be said at the present point, that the more completely the reader can banish from his mind the thought that in 774 Charles the Frank deliberately and of set purpose made Pope Hadrian sovereign of two-thirds of Italy and of the island of Corsica, the easier will he find it to follow the events of the next quarter of a century.

From Rome the Frankish king soon returned to Pavia, where the long siege was drawing to a close. Disease was rife within the city, and more men fell under its ravages than by the sword of the enemy. At last on a Tuesday in the month of June 1 the city surrendered, and Desiderius with his wife Ansa and a daughter whose name we know not became prisoners of the Frankish king. Recent events might well have embittered Charles against his Lombard father-in-law, but he displayed his usual clemency, and sparing his life sent him, apparently accompanied by the two royal ladies, to the monastery of Corbie in Picardy, the same holy house to which young Adalhard had retired when he refused to connive at repudiation of the Lombard princess Desiderata, and of which he was one day to be the venerated abbot. Here, we are told, the exiled king remained till the day of his death, passing his time in prayers and watchings and fastings, and many other good works. His wife, who had always been a zealous builder of churches and monasteries, doubtless shared this pious ending to that which had been in her husband's case a troubled and somewhat ignoble career.

The reader has now before him the historic facts as far as they are known, concerning the siege and fall of Pavia. He may be amused by seeing the transformation which, in the course of a century, these facts had undergone in the hands of monastic rhapsodists.

'There was in the court of Desiderius', wrote the Monk of St. Gall (in the book on the deeds of Charles which he dedicated to his great-grandson), 'a chief minister of King Charles named Otker, who having incurred his master's displeasure sought a refuge among the Lombards. When the war had broken out and the approach of Charles was expected, Desiderius and Otker together ascended a tower which commanded a very wide view. When the baggage wagons drew near which would have not misbeseemed the expeditions of Darius or Julius, Desiderius said to Otker, "Is Charles in this mighty army?". "Not yet," said Otker. The rank and file of soldiers collected from so many lands appeared: then the corps of guards, for ever intent on their duty: then the bishops, abbots and chaplains with their trains. At the sight of each successive company Desiderius asked, "Is not Charles with these?" and [for some unexplained reason] the appearance of the ecclesiastics filled him with more overmastering fear than all the rest, so that he longed to leave his tower and hide himself underground from the face of so terrible an enemy. But Otker said to him, "When you see an iron harvest bristling in the plain, and these rivers Po and Ticino which surround your walls black with the reflection of iron-clad warriors, then know that Charles is at hand." Even while he spoke a dark cloud from north and west seemed to overshadow the light of day. But then as the monarch drew nearer, the reflection from his soldiers' arms made a new daylight more terrible than night. Then appeared that man of iron, Charles himself, with iron helmet, gauntlets and breastplate, with an iron spear held erect by his left hand, for his right was ever stretched forth to his unconquered sword: the outer surfaces of his thighs, which for ease in mounting on horseback are with other men left bare, with him were encircled in rings of iron. Why speak of his greaves, for they, like those of all the rest of his army, were iron? Of iron too was his shield; and his iron-grey horse had the strength as well as the colour of that metal. Him, the great leader, all who went before, all who flowed round him on each side, all who followed him, imitated to the utmost of their power. The iron river filled all the plain, reflected the rays of the sun, struck terror into the pale watchers on the walls. "O the iron! alas for the iron!" so rose the confused murmur of the citizens. All these things I, a toothless and stammering old man, have told you at far greater length than I should have done, but then he, the truthful sentinel Otker, took them all in at a glance, and turning to Desiderius said to him, "Lo, now you have him whom you so earnestly desired to behold"; whereupon Desiderius fell fainting to the ground.'

The Monk then goes on to describe how, as there were still some among the citizens of Pavia who refused to open the gates to the Franks, Charles in order that the day might not pass over without some worthy deed, ordered his men to build a basilica in which they might render service to Almighty God outside the walls, if they could not do so within them. So said, so done. The men dispersed in all directions, some seeking stones, some lime for mortar, some timber, some paints and painters, and thus setting to work at the fourth hour of the day, before the twelfth hour thereof 'they had erected such a basilica, with walls and roofs, with ceilings and pictures all complete, that no one who looked upon it would have supposed that it could have been built in less than a twelvemonth'.

After this, that party among the citizens which was in favour of surrender prevailed, and on the fifth day of the siege, without shedding a drop of blood, Charles was master of the city.

Thus with the lapse of three generations had the story of the siege of Pavia been transformed, and the long and weary blockade of eight months' duration had become changed into a sudden capture, caused by the magic of his presence, a capture almost as marvellous and quite as unhistorical as the building in eight hours of the suburban basilica.

Passing from the realm of Saga, we are forced to ask ourselves the question why it was that the Lombard power went down so easily before the impact of the Franks. We ask, but our materials are so scanty that we must be contented with a most imperfect answer. We have seen that there were treachery and disunion in the Lombard camp, and that, from some disadvantage of birth or defects of character, Desiderius failed to win for himself the loyalty of the whole Lombard people. Moreover, throughout the two centuries of their history the 'centrifugal' tendency, which was the bane of so many of the new Teutonic states, was fatally manifest in the Lombard nation. Benevento and Spoleto were always bound by a very loose tie to Pavia, and at the least provocation Trent and Friuli were ready to fly off from the central power. Then there was probably the same want of cohesion between the Teutonic and the Latin elements of the population which led to the early downfall of the Burgundian and Visigothic kingdoms. The condition of the Roman *aldius* may have been, probably was, far better under Desiderius than under Alboin or Authari, but still he felt himself to be a subject where his fathers had been lords, and he saw no reason why he should fight for the maintenance of Lombard supremacy. To this must be added the inextinguishable and to us inexplicable animosity of the Church, to which, however orthodox their profession of faith, however lavish their gifts to convent and cathedral, the Lombards were still the same 'most unspeakable, most foul and stinking' race that they had been at their first entrance into Italy. Assuredly in this case the antipathy was one of race rather than of religion. The ecclesiastic who was perhaps the son of a Roman *aldius* hated the man 'who dressed his hair after the manner of the Lombards', not now as a heretic, but as the descendant of the invaders who had reduced his fathers to slavery.

And lastly, but perhaps not of least importance, we may suggest that the influence of climate was not unimportant in weakening the fibre of Lombard manhood. The soldiers of Alboin came, fresh and hardy, from the forests of the Danube and the glens of Noricum (very different countries assuredly from the pleasant lands which now represent them); they came into the softer climate of a land whose thousand years of civilization not all the ravages of the barbarians had availed wholly to obliterate. They came, they enjoyed, and probably they lost some of their ancient manhood.

Whatever the cause, it must be admitted that there is something which disappoints us in the meagrely-told tale of the downfall of the kingdom of the Lombards. Herein they differ from the Anglo-Saxons, their old neighbours, with whose history their own for so many years ran parallel. In both nations there was for long the same want of cohesion (till the Church, the enemy of Lombard unity, accomplished the unity of England); in both there was the same slackness, the same tendency to procrastination, the same absence of wide and far-seeing statesmanship. But the old Anglo-Saxon battle-songs found a fitting close on the well-fought field of Senlac, while the course of Lombard history trickled out to an unworthy end amid the famine and fever of Pavia.

NOTE

The Alleged Donation of Territory in Italy by Charles the Great to Pope Hadrian.

I. In the first place, let us have before us the actual words in Vita which the Papal biographer records this memorable transaction:

"At vero quarta feria, egressus praenominatus pontifex cum suis judicibus tam cleri quamque militiae in ecclesia beati Petri apostoli, pariterque cum eodem rege se loquendum conjungens, constanter eum deprecatus est atque ammonuit et paterno affectu adhortare studuit ut promissionem illam, quam ejus sanctae memoriae genitor Pippinus quondam rex et ipse praecellentissimus Carulus cum suo germano Carulomanno atque omnibus judicibus Francorum, fecerant beato Petro et ejus vieario sanctae memoriae domno Stephano juniori papae, quando Franciam perrexit, pro concedendis diversis civitatibus ac territoriis istius Italiae provinciae et contradendis beato Petro ejusque omnibus vicariis in perpetuum possidendis, adimpleret in omnibus. Cumque ipsam promissionem, quae Francia in loco qui vocatur Carisiaco facta est, sibi relegi fecisset, complacuerunt illi et ejus judicibus omnia quae ibidem erant adnexa. Et propria voluntate, bono ac libenti animo, aliam donationis promissionem ad instar anterioris ipse antedictus praecellentissimus et revera Christianissimus Carulus Francorum rex adscribi jussit per Etherium, religiosum ac prudentissimum capellanum et notarium suum : ubi concessit easdem civitates et territoria beato Petro easque praefato pontifici contradi spopondit per designatum confinium, sicut in eadem (sic) donationem continere monstratur, id est: A Lunis eum insula Corsica, deinde in Suriano, deinde in monte Bardone, id est in Verceto, deinde in Parma, deinde in Regio : et exinde in Mantua atque Monte Silicis, simulque et universum exarchatum Ravennantium sicut antiquitus erat, atque provincias Venetiarum et Istria: necnon et cunctum ducatum Spolitinum seu Beneventanum. Factaque eadem donatione et propria sua manu earn ipse Christianissimus Francorum rex earn conroborans, universos episcopos, abbates, duces etiam et grafiones in ea adscribi fecit: quam prius super altare beati Petri et postmodum intus in sancta ejus confessione ponentes, tam ipse Francorum rex quamque ejus judices, beato Petro et ejus vicario sanctissimo Adriano papae sub terribile sacramento sese omnia conservaturos quae in eadem donatione continentur promittentes tradiderunt. Apparem vero ipsius donationis eundem Etherium adscribi faciens ipse Christianissimus Francorum rex, intus super corpus beati Petri, subtus evangelia quae ibidem osculantur, pro firmissima cautela et aetema nominis sui ac regni Francorum memoria propriis suis manibus posuit. Aliaque ejusdem donationis exempla per scrinium hujus sanctae nostrae Romanae ecclesiae adscriptum ejus excellentia secum deportavit".

II. As to the geographical import of the donation the mention of Corsica is simple enough. That island at this time was possibly Lombard. At any rate it soon became part of the Frankish dominion. On the mainland of Italy the boundary traced begins from the gulf of Spezzia, and then runs nearly due north past Sarzana (Surianum), following upward the course of the river Magra till it strides across the Apennines at La Cisa (Mons Bardonis). Thence in a more north-easterly direction past Berceto (Vercetum) to Parma: along the Via Emilia for a short distance to Reggio, and thence at right angles to its former course till it reaches Mantua. From Mantua it goes nearly east till it reaches

Monselice (Mons Silicis), about fifteen miles south of Padua. From thence we must draw some conjectural line to include the two provinces of Venetia and Istria, though the mention of Monselice makes it hard to draw the line so as not to exclude the westernmost part of Venetia. When we have traced this northern frontier our work is done; for the Exarchate of Ravenna as it was anciently held (of course including the Pentapolis) and the two great duchies of Spoleto and Benevento practically include all Italy south of this line, unless we ought to make a reservation for the fragments of southern Italy which still belonged to the Empire, and which probably at this time consisted only of the territory immediately surrounding Gaeta, Naples, and Amalfi, the district which now bears the name of Calabria, and so much of the south-east of Apulia as went with the possession of Otranto—a district perhaps equivalent to the modern province of Lecce. Instead, therefore, of enumerating the portions of Italy which were included in the alleged donation, it will be simpler to consider what portions were excluded from it. They were (in modern geographical terms) Piedmont, the Riviera di Ponente and the Riviera di Levante as far as Spezzia, the late duchy of Piacenza, Lombardy north of the Po, Verona and (probably) Vicenza; Naples, Calabria, and Otranto. About two-thirds of Italy, as I have mentioned in the preceding chapter, were thus assigned to the vicars of St. Peter, and only one third was left for the Frankish King and the Empire to share between them.

III. Of this alleged donation, notwithstanding the statement by the biographer as to the copies deposited at Rome among the Frankish archives and elsewhere, no copy exists today, nor do we, I believe, ever find in any historian the slightest allusion to the production of such a copy. It is never once alluded to in the copious correspondence between Charles and Hadrian which is contained in the Codex Carolinus. And to fit it in with the course of dealing between the two powers, Frankish and Papal, during the forty years that intervened between the conquest of Italy and the death of Charles, is a task so difficult as to be all but impossible.

IV. In this dilemma various theories have been suggested, the discussion of which has filled many volumes. Here of course the discussion can be but very briefly summarized. We may divide the theories into two classes, those which uphold and those which deny the authenticity of the document contained in chapters the Vita Hadriani.

A. Upholders of the authenticity.

(1) Chief among these, and entitled to speak with preeminent authority, must be named the Abbé L. Duchesne, the distinguished editor of the Liber Pontificalis. He firmly maintains the authenticity and the contemporaneous character of the Vita Hadriani. The donation, wide as are its terms, is, he believes, a donation of territory, not a mere restoration of scattered 'patrimonies' violently abstracted by the Lombards. At the same time he admits, of course, that the Popes never really bore sway over the vast territories here conceded to them. He argues therefore that, after the conquest of Pavia, Charles changed his point of view. As he had now made himself king of the Lombards and was friendly to the Pope, there was no longer the same necessity for the Pope to be put in possession of such large domains in order that he might be protected against the malice of his enemies. Also Charles may have seen that now that the Lombard power was destroyed there was no longer, on the part of the Roman population, the old

willingness to come under the Papal rule. These changes in his mental attitude were taking place between 774 and 781, the date of his third visit to Rome. The Pope had also been discovering that he had not the power to rule such wide domains, and that even in the Exarchate and Pentapolis he could barely hold his own against the ambitious archbishop of Ravenna. In 781 therefore (presumably) an arrangement was come to, whereby, in consideration of some material additions to the Ducatus Romae in Tuscia and Campania, the Pope abandoned his vast and shadowy claims under the Donation of 774, which thenceforward passed out of notice.

The theory is ingenious and explains some of the facts. It is well argued for by Duchesne, but I find it difficult to believe that such an enormous abandonment of well-ascertained Papal rights would ever have been made, or being made would have left no trace in the Papal-Frankish correspondence.

(2) Another theory, which is advocated by Prof. Theodor Lindner with more elaboration but less lucidity than by Duchesne, is, virtually, that the document was not a donation of territory, but a restoration of 'patrimonies' within the limits described. Lindner's view is that both Pippin and Charles from the beginning had set before themselves no other object than the satisfaction of the just claims ('justitiae') of the successors of St. Peter. True it was that by a sort of legal fiction, according to which St. Peter represented the 'respublica Romana', the territories of the Exarchate and the Pentapolis, lately torn from the Empire by Aistulf, were looked upon as a sort of 'jacens hereditas' to which St. Peter was entitled, and so far Pippin's action had the result of conferring territorial sovereignty on the Pope. True also that the Ducatus Romae had by the force of circumstances, by the absenteeism of the Emperors, and the ever-present activity of the Popes, become in fact purely Papal territory. But as to all the rest of the lands and cities comprised within the boundary which started 'a Lunis', all that, according to Lindner's view, Charles promised to Hadrian was that those 'patrimonies' which had once belonged to St. Peter and had been wrested from him by the Lombards should, on production of the necessary evidences of title, be restored to the Holy See.

The theory is a plausible one. One may even go further and say that in all likelihood it represents with sufficient exactness what actually took place in St. Peter's on the 6th of April, 774. What Charles probably intended to do was to confirm in the fullest manner possible the Pope's sway (as ruler) over the Exarchate, the Pentapolis, and the Ducatus Romae, and to recover for him the possession (as landlord) of the estates in the rest of Italy of which he had been robbed by the ravaging Lombards. But the question now before us is not what Charles promised, but what the Papal biographer represents him as having promised. And here it seems to me that Lindner's contention fails. How can his statement of the character of the donation be got out of the words in the Vita Hadriani? Not a mention there of 'patrimonia', a large and unrestricted grant of 'civitates et territoria', no distinction drawn between the Exarchate or Pentapolis and other parts of Italy, for instance Tuscia, which had been Lombard for centuries: full words of grant of 'pro-vincias Venetiarum et Istriae et cunctum ducatum Spolitinum, seu [= et] Beneventanum'. Lindner battles bravely with this obvious difficulty, but if words are to have any meaning at all, these words cannot be taken in the limited sense which he would impose upon them.

It may be noted in passing that Abbé Duchesne, though fighting on the same side as Lindner in defence of the genuineness of the passage in question, entirely rejects the 'patrimonial' theory. He says 'Et ici je dois écarter l'idée que les régions limitées par la frontière *a Lunis—Monte Silicis* soient indiquées, non comme concédées dans leur entier et avec les droits de souveraineté, mais comme contenant des patrimoines revendiqués par l'Église Romaine'. But this often happens in this strange discussion. The champions on the same side destroy one another's arguments. As Faulconbridge says in 'King John'

'Austria and France shoot in each other's mouth.'

It may also be observed that Charles's promise, on Lindner's theory, would fall short of that which Hadrian had a right to expect. There was at least one large and important patrimony, that of the 'Alpes Cottiae,' situated north-west of the line traced by the donation. If it were merely a question of the restitution of plundered estates, why should that not have been restored along with the others?

Let us pass to some of the arguments advanced by

B. The opposers of the genuineness of the donation.

(1) In the first place, we ought to notice the possibility that the donation, though literally genuine, was in fact a forgery, having been obtained from Charles by some trick such as a skillful notary might practise on an unlettered sovereign. This is certainly not impossible. The Roman Court would contain at that time some of the most practised scribes in Europe, whereas Charles, as we are told by Einhard, though he tried hard to learn the art of writing, never succeeded in doing so, having begun too late in life. And though we know that he was not altogether illiterate, but greatly delighted in such a book as St. Augustine's 'De Civitate Dei', yet even this seems, from Einhard's account, to have been read to him at his meals, rather than by him in his library. But then Charles was not alone on this occasion, but was accompanied by all the great ecclesiastics as well as nobles of his realm, and it seems reasonable to suppose that among all of these there would be at any rate someone able and willing to detect any gross literary fraud practised upon his master.

Considerable stress has been laid on the mention of the name of Etherius, 'religiosus ac prudentissimus capellanus et notarius Caroli'. This is no doubt the same person as Itherius, abbot of St. Martin at Tours, who was sent in 770 to claim from Desiderius the return of the Papal patrimonies in Benevento on which he had laid hands, but all the theories founded on the personality of this man (some of them not very favourable to his loyalty to Charles) are mere baseless conjectures.

(2) It is suggested that the three chapters in the Vita Hadriani which record the donation are an interpolation of a later date into an authentic and contemporary document.

We may take Dr. Martens as the advocate of this theory, which he has maintained with much earnestness and diligence in his monographs 'Die Römische Frage' (1881).

Dr. Martens assigns the forgery of all three documents, the Donation of Constantine, the Fragmentum Fantuzzianum, and the three chapters in the Vita Hadriani, to about the same time, somewhere in the pontificate of Hadrian. All the rest of the Vita he looks upon as genuine and trustworthy, nor does he attribute to the Pope any complicity with this fabrication, but he thinks that it was probably imagined by some Roman ecclesiastic during Hadrian's lifetime—perhaps about 780 or 781—and then after his death was tacked on by him to the genuine Life (of which I suppose Martens considers the later chapters to have been at the same time suppressed). He thinks that this forger used for his purpose the slightly earlier Fragmentum Fantuzzianum, and built his romance upon it. His secret intention was to express his disappointment that Charles had so meagrely fulfilled the hopes of a great extension of the Papal dominion which had been founded on his anticipated victory over the Lombards. For this purpose, with malicious subtlety the author sketches the Frankish king in that attitude which the Roman clergy would have liked him to assume in 774, knowing all the while that in actual fact things turned out very differently. Charles really played his part as 'Defensor Ecclesiae' very coldly, only granting that which was of most urgent need and which it was scarce possible to withhold. The Vita, on the other hand, offers us the lying statement that Charles 'propria voluntate, bono ac libenti animo' bound himself by an utterly exorbitant promise, and swore a fearful oath for its fulfilment. As neither the Life of Hadrian I nor that of Leo III contains any account of the redemption of this promise, the king of the Franks stands before us in the pages of the Liber Pontificalis as a confessed oath-breaker. Thus to compromise the character of the great prince was the main object of the forger, but he may also have nourished a secret hope that some successor of Charles would deem himself bound to fulfil in its integrity the promise which here stood charged to the account of his ancestor.

(3) Such is the theory of Dr. Martens. Accepting, as I do, many of his arguments, I venture to go a little further and to suggest that the whole Life, as we have it, is the product of a slightly later age, and was composed in the hope, perhaps not a very confident hope, that the weak monarch who bore, not for nought, the title Louis the Pious, might be induced to acquiesce in its extravagant pretensions.

In this connection it seems to me an important fact that three times in the Vita Hadriani (though not in the now disputed chapters), Charles's name is mentioned with the addition Magnus, which he did not usually bear in his lifetime, but which was generally used soon after his death.

On the other side, in favour of the contemporaneous character of the Vita Hadriani, may be quoted undoubtedly the great authority of Abbé Duchesne, who thinks that the first forty-four chapters (that is the whole historical part of the Life) were composed in this very year 774. 'It is enough,' he says, 'to read these pages with some knowledge of their historic environment, to feel oneself in the presence of an absolutely contemporary narrative. It was not in 795, twenty years after the disappearance of the Lombard dynasty, that a writer would have dwelt so minutely on the details of the negotiations with Desiderius, on the punishment of Afiarta and his partisans, on the political correspondence with Constantinople, on the negotiations of the Spoletans with the Pope, even on the journey of Charlemagne to Rome in 774. At the death of Hadrian, men were already far from this earlier period: important events had succeeded, amongst others, two journeys of Charlemagne to Rome in 781 and 787, which have left their marks on the Papal correspondence, on the monuments, on the constitution of the Roman state : certain courses had been taken, new ways of looking at things had become necessary: of all which we find no trace in the narrative before us. It represents well enough what might be written, what ought to be written in 774, not what would be written after the death of Hadrian V

I can accept nearly all these statements of the eminent editor of the Liber Pontificalis, without accepting his conclusion that the Vita Hadriani, as we have it, is a contemporary document. Let me remind the reader of the extraordinary phenomenon which that work presents to us. Here we have a so-called life of the Pope which narrates with great minuteness the events of the first two years of his reign, which just leads up to the alleged donation by Charles, tells in a few lines the conquest of Pavia, and then is absolutely silent as to the last twenty years, most important years, of the same reign, giving us instead of history a most wearisome and diffuse catalogue of all the ecclesiastical rebuildings, and of all the articles of upholstery wherewith Hadrian enriched the Roman churches during his long pontificate. Surely there is something suspicious in this extreme loquacity as to two years and this utter silence as to the succeeding twenty. Whether there ever was or was not a life of Hadrian worthy of the name, must be I think a matter of conjecture. As to this production which is now before us, it appears to me to be what the Germans call a *Tendenzschrift*, having for its object the assertion of certain preposterous claims for papal sovereignty over two-thirds of Italy. I suggest that it was composed during the reign of Louis the Pious, that the compiler copied certain genuine and contemporary documents with reference to the collapse of the party of Paulus Afiarta and the negotiations with Desiderius, tacked on to them his absolutely fictitious account of the donation of Charles (perhaps to some extent copied from the Fragmentum Fantuzzianum), and they left the remaining twenty years of Hadrian's pontificate undescribed, knowing that at every step of the real history he would have been confronted with facts which proved the absurdity of his romance. To obtain the necessary length for his biography he has (like many other authors of the Papal lives but at greater length than they) ended that biography with the aforesaid catalogue of furniture, for which, very likely, trustworthy materials existed in the Papal *bureaux*.

We have thus three fictitious documents of great historical importance emanating from the Papal chancery or written in the Papal interest, during the hundred years between 750 and 850; possibly within a much shorter compass of time. They are the Donation of Constantine, the Donation of Pippin (Fragmentum Fantuzzianum), and the Donation of Charles.

One document of a slightly later date, the Privilegium of Louis the Pious addressed to Pope Paschal II in 817—a document which is now generally quoted as the *Ludovicianum* — after remaining long under a cloud of suspicion, has been of later years, chiefly by the exertions of two German scholars, Ficker and Sickel, rehabilitated as a genuine and trustworthy document. But this vindication of the Privilege of Louis does not help, but rather damages the alleged Donation by his father. For the Ludovicianum, though sufficiently generous towards the Popes, gives no more territory to them than is perfectly consistent with the course of historical events disclosed to us by the Codex Carolinus, and when it travels far afield beyond the limits of the three provinces (Exarchate, Pentapolis, and Ducatus Romae), it carefully introduces the word *patrimonia*. There is also a very distinct reservation of the Imperial supremacy over the duchies of Tuscany and Spoleto, accompanying the grant of certain revenues out of those provinces. Considering the characters of the men, it is almost inconceivable that the Popes would have accepted from the weak and pious son the limited grant of territories contained in the Ludovicianum if they had in their archives a document conferring far larger territories, bearing the signature of the strong and statesmanlike father. The Ludovicianum is therefore distinctly a witness against the Vita Hadriani.

There is no doubt, however, that in the course of the ninth century the fabrication had obtained extensive currency, being no doubt by that time fairly installed in the Liber Pontificalis. It is quoted in the False Decretals of Isidore, and it reappears in the Ottonianum, or 'Privilegium' granted to the Pope by the Emperor Otto I in 962.

After being in modern times generally discredited, the Caroline Donation has recently found some staunch and able defenders; but the qualifications and reservations, which even these authors have to make, show the extreme difficulty of the task which they have undertaken, and, at any rate in the judgment of the present writer, it is not probable that the cause which they have championed will finally prevail.

The whole discussion and the ever-expanding character of the Papal claims for territory at this period seem to be the best explanation of the forethought exhibited by the great Frankish ruler when he pinned down his Papal correspondents to certain positions by collecting their letters in the Codex Carolinus.

BOOK IX.

THE FRANKISH EMPIRE.

CHAPTER I.

THE PONTIFICATE OF HADRIAN I.

POPE Hadrian occupied the chair of St. Peter for twenty-three years, ten months, and seventeen days, a longer period than had fallen to the lot of any of his predecessors, except the twenty-five years which tradition assigns to St. Peter himself. That part of his pontificate which still lies before us was, as far as Italy was concerned, a long and level space, not marked by any such striking events as those with which the preceding thirty years had been thickly studded, nor will it require to be considered in so much detail.

Of course in Italy and all the western world the figure that loomed largest in the eyes of men was that of the great Austrasian, Charles, 'King of the Franks and Lombards and Patrician of the Romans'. His intervention in the affairs of Italy was necessarily fitful and intermittent, for (as has been already said) he had hard tasks to perform north of the Alps, tasks which sometimes well-nigh over-strained even his marvellous energy, and more than once exhausted his long-enduring patience. A very brief outline of these transalpine labours of his will serve to indicate that which lay in the background of Italian history during this quarter of a century.

The great, the Herculean labour of Charles during all the central portion of his reign was his Thirty Years' War for the subjugation of the Saxons. Subjugation, as Charles soon perceived, meant Christianization, and would not be accomplished without it. Christianization by moral and spiritual agencies was a slow process, too slow for the masterful Austrasian. There were therefore compulsory baptisms, fierce laws against obdurate heathens or relapsed converts, at last a terrible massacre. Then came great transportations of men, in the style of Sargon or Nebuchadnezzar; Saxons carried away into the heart of Frank-land; Frankish settlements planted in ravaged Saxonia. Thus at length, by harshest and least spiritual means, outward conformity to the religion which called itself Christianity was secured, and order reigned in Saxon-land.

Eighteen campaigns were needed to accomplish the work which was not ended at the time of the death of Hadrian. I here only lightly touch on the chief crises of that deadly struggle.

In 772 (as has been already related) Charles marched against the central tribe of Saxons, the Angarii, and hewed down their great tree-idol, the Irminsul. This act of defiance of the national faith was avenged by an invasion of the Saxons in 774. They entered Hesse, ravaged the country, sacked the abbey of Fritzlar erected by the holy Boniface, but were restrained— miraculously restrained said the monkish chroniclers—

from setting fire to the church. This invasion occurred while Charles was busy with his Lombard campaign. On his return across the Alps, during his winter residence at Carisiacum, he resolved that the Saxon truce-breakers should be either Christianized or exterminated. And in the great campaign of 775, notwithstanding a serious reverse which befell one of his generals, his arms were on the whole triumphant. The rebellion of Hrodgaud, duke of Friuli, called him across the Alps in the spring of 776, but he returned that same year, and prosecuted his military operations with such success that the great majority of the Saxons owned themselves beaten, surrendered to him their land, promised henceforth to live as his loyal subjects, and were baptized by thousands in the waters of the Lippe.

It was a deceitful calm, a mirage of victory. There was one chief, stronger and fiercer than all the others, the Westphalian Widukind, who had shared neither the baptism nor the homage to the conqueror, and he for eight years (777-785) waged obstinate war with Charles, leading his Saxons into the very heart of Austrasia while Charles was besieging Spanish towns and enduring the disaster of Roncesvalles, then retreating before the irresistible onset of the Franks, taking refuge with the heathen king of Denmark, returning to the fray, and guiding, evidently with some military skill, the movements of his insurgent countrymen. But in 785 even Widukind's stubborn soul bowed before the persistent energy of Charles. He surrendered, was baptized, and troubled his conqueror no more. A truce for six or seven years (785-792) followed, but war with the Saxons—now allied with the Frisians, a formidable combination—again broke out at the end of that time, and this war was taxing Charles's utmost energies, when the long pontificate of Hadrian came to a close. Undoubtedly this mighty conflict, not with enervated Lombards but with the grim, exasperated Teutons of the North, was always in the background of the great king's thoughts, even when the affairs of Italy and the Pope's appeals for help most imperiously claimed his attention.

Another war which, near the end of the period, called Charles with large armies to the banks of the Danube, was that which from 791 to 796 he waged against the nation of the Avars. We have seen, this Asiatic horde, successors of the Huns both in ethnological and in geographical position, enter Europe about the middle of the sixth century, ally themselves with Alboin, and afterwards invade and cruelly ravage the duchy of Friuli which was ruled by the descendant of Alboin's comrade. For some time they had ceased to be an overwhelming terror either to Italy or to Byzantium, and now, at the close of the eighth century, by a series of masterly campaigns, Charles succeeded in shattering their power, in storming their capital girdled as it was by nine concentric rings of fortification and carrying off the immense hoard which for two centuries had been accumulated there, the results of the ravage or the ransom of the fair lands to the south of the Danube. Chagan and Tuduns (such were the barbarous titles of the king and princes of the Avars) came humbly to Charles's court to ask for baptism and the favour of the mighty Frank. No greater deliverance did Charles work for Europe than this dispersal of the thunder-cloud which had so long hovered over its eastern horizon.

Almost equally important in its bearing on the formation of the future German *Reich* was the war in which Charles crushed the rising independence of Bavaria; but, as has been already hinted, the fortunes of the Agilolfing princes were so closely linked in prosperity and adversity with those of the Lombards, that the story of the fall of Tassilo, duke of Bavaria, may be fitly told hereafter in connection with the affairs of Italy.

Last to be mentioned here, but among the first of these events in the order of time, was Charles's passage of the Pyrenees in 778, his capture of Pampeluna. (previously held not by the Moorish misbeliever but by the Christian king of Asturias), possibly followed by the capture of Saragossa, but more certainly followed by his speedy return across the Pyrenees and by the disastrous defeat of his rear-guard at Roncesvalles.

We must now glance at the family relations of the great king during these central years of his life. We have seen how speedily the place of the divorced Lombard princess Desiderata was filled by the Swabian lady Hildegard (771-2). She is said to have been little more than a child, at most thirteen years of age, at the time of her marriage, and her married life lasted but for the same number of years, during which she bore nine children to her lord, four sons and five daughters. She was apparently of all Charles's wives the one who was most beloved both by her husband and by his people. She generally accompanied him on his campaigns, and thus it came to pass that her third son Louis (known to history by his surname the Pious or the Debonnair) was born, shortly before the disaster of Roncesvalles, in that country of Aquitaine of which he was to be during the first forty years of his life the nominal or real ruler.

Hildegard died in 783, and in the same year Charles lost his mother Bertrada, to whom he was fondly attached, and whose counsels, we are told, he had ever followed, except in the one matter of his repudiation of Desiderata, which was the only root of bitterness that ever sprang up between mother and son.

Not many months after the death of Hildegard the uxorious king took for his third wife Fastrada, the daughter of an Austrasian, Count Radolf. This was the least fortunate of all Charles's matrimonial ventures. Fastrada was a hard and cruel woman, whose influence, says Einhard, often urged her husband to actions contrary to the natural kindliness of his character. Two conspiracies against the throne (in one of which the hunchback Pippin, Charles's son by Himiltrud, was implicated) are attributed by the same writer to the resentment of the Frankish nobles at the cruelties of Fastrada. She died at Frankfurt on the 10th of August, 794, leaving two daughters, Theoderada of the golden locks and Hiltrud. At the end of the period with which we are now dealing, Charles was still a widower, but possibly living in concubinage with her who was to be his fourth and last wife, the beautiful Swabian lady, Liutgard.

While the Frankish king was thus travelling past the meridian of his days, marrying often and seeing a crowd of sons and daughters growing up around him, more than one change was passing over the palace by the Bosphorus, where dwelt the only Christian sovereign whose power could be likened to his own.

In August, 775, a little more than a year after the fall of Pavia, died the Emperor Constantine V, surnamed by his enemies Copronymus. His hereditary and inveterate hostility to the worship of images, his equally inveterate hostility to the monks and his attempts to degrade or to destroy them, the miserable life which the patriarchs of Constantinople (even though iconoclasts) led under his insulting tyranny, and the curious vein of artistic Paganism which blended with his Puritan iconoclasm, are the chief characteristics of a reign with which we need not now further concern ourselves.

Constantine was succeeded by his son, Leo IV, who was nicknamed the Khazar, in memory of the fact that his mother Irene was daughter of the Khan of the Khazars. His reign lasted but five years (775-780), and was distinguished by no important event. He was apparently a man of dull, unoriginal character, the sort of son that often grows up under the shadow of so masterful a character as Constantine Copronymus. In his dull way he carried on the iconoclastic policy of his father; he married a daughter of Athens, the energetic and ambitious Irene; he secured the succession for his son by that lady, and having done little else he died on the 8th of September, 780. He was succeeded by his widow and son, Irene and Constantine VI, reigning, not as regent and minor, but as joint sovereigns.

The character of Irene and her position both in political and religious history are so peculiar and so important as to require some special notice. An orphan, presumably beautiful, and certainly quick-witted, she had in some way fixed upon herself the affections of the young heir, Leo, who obtained his stern father's consent to marry her. Brought from Athens to a villa on the Sea of Marmora, she was escorted thence on the 1st of September, 769, with great pomp to Constantinople. The Bosphorus and the Golden Horn were covered with cutters and pinnaces bright with their silken sails, and all the nobles of Constantinople accompanied the exultant Athenian to the palace, where she was betrothed to Leo the Khazar. Three months later the marriage ceremony was performed, and at the same time she was crowned as Augusta, her husband already possessing the imperial dignity in association with his father.

The Isaurian dynasty had, however, committed a fatal blunder when it allowed its future chief to link his fortunes with those of the fair Athenian. To 'the City of the Violet Crown' the stern iconoclasm of Constantine Copronymus was supremely unattractive. When the man of Tarsus visited it seven centuries earlier he found it 'wholly given to idolatry', and it was a true daughter of those aesthetic loungers in the Agora who had now climbed up into the palace at Constantinople, though not the statues of Apollo or Athene, but the stern visage of the Saviour, the crowned Mother of God, and innumerable representations of apostles, martyrs and fathers, were the objects of her secret devotion. It was doubtless some distrust of her early educational environment which caused her father-in-law soon after her arrival in Constantinople to administer to her a solemn oath that she would never desert the iconoclastic party. She conformed outwardly through the remainder of his reign and through the reign of her husband, but during a fierce outbreak of Leo the Khazar (March, 780) against the worship of images by which he found that his own palace was invaded, the name of the Augusta herself was introduced as favouring the forbidden rites. Some of the proscribed images were found in her bed. She denied that she had ever worshipped them, but her angry and incredulous husband reproached her with her violation of the oath which she had sworn to his father, and banished her from his presence. He had apparently not taken her back into his favour when six months afterwards he died—a most opportune death for the lovers of the sacred emblems.

Irene having never been deposed from her imperial dignity succeeded now as joint sovereign with her son, Constantine VI, a boy ten years of age. Naturally, for some years, her will alone prevailed and she was sole ruler of the Empire. Her inclination towards the party of the image-worshippers might be inferred from the fact that she gave back a diadem which her husband had abstracted from one of the churches of Constantinople, and replaced in its own church the body of the virgin-martyr Euphemia which Constantine Copronymus, enraged at its alleged miraculous powers, had ordered to be thrown into the sea. Being, however, sufficiently occupied in quelling a revolt which was raised on behalf of the five princes, her late husband's half-brothers, she proceeded cautiously in the early years of her reign, and while tolerating, did not venture to enforce the worship of images.

It was at this period, while she still felt herself in need of external support, that she commenced negotiations for a matrimonial alliance between her family and that of the great monarch of the Franks. In the year 781, while Charles was spending Easter at Rome (his second visit to the Eternal City), he received there an embassy from

Constantinople, consisting of Constans the Treasurer and Mamalus the Grand Chamberlain, who came charged by Irene to negotiate a marriage between her son and the princess Hrotrud (whom the Greeks called Erythro), the eldest daughter of Charles and Hildegard. As the proposed bridegroom was only eleven and his intended bride only nine years of age, of course the contracting parties contemplated a long betrothal, but, such as it was, the proposal was accepted : the imperial boy and the royal girl were formally affianced to one another, and the Eunuch Elisha, an imperial notary, was sent to the Frankish court to instruct the future Augusta in the Greek language and literature and in the ceremonial observed in the 'Roman Empire'.

This alliance between the Isaurian and the Frankish dynasties is one of the great unrealised possibilities of history. It is probable that, had it been perfected, Charles would never have taken the title of Emperor of Rome. It is conceivable that the estrangement of feeling and eventual hostility between the Latins of the West and the 'orthodox Romans' of the East, which prepared the way for the Turkish capture of Constantinople, might have been avoided, if Elisha's lessons had borne their intended fruit, and the little princess Hrotrud had been eventually escorted as Empress by acclaiming multitudes to the palace of Constantine.

Side by side with Irene's negotiations for the Frankish alliance, she was also labouring cautiously tor a reconciliation with the See of Rome. In the year 783, on the abdication of the patriarch Paul, who declared that his conscience was disturbed by his iconoclastic isolation from the other Churches, Irene procured the election of her secretary Tarasius to the patriarchal throne of Constantinople. Tarasius was a layman, and admitted, nay emphasized the irregularity of his elevation, but stipulated for the convocation of a general council which should at the same time confirm his election and reverse the decrees against image-worship which had been passed at the so-called 'seventh ecumenical council' under Constantine Copronymus.

The messengers who brought to Pope Hadrian the tidings of this intended ecclesiastical revolution must have caused him some perplexity. Great on the one hand was the rejoicing over the prospect that the iconoclastic controversy which had raged for half a century was to be terminated by the triumph of the image-worshippers and of Rome; but on the other hand, the election of a layman to the patriarchal chair was a direct violation of the principle recently asserted in the synod of the Lateran; and this newly-made patriarch still claimed the title of 'ecumenical' which, two centuries before, had so grievously vexed the soul of Gregory. But on the whole, the advantages of the proposed change seemed to predominate. Hadrian addressed letters to Irene and to Tarasius, in which, while gently chiding that which seemed blameworthy, he praised their orthodoxy on the question of image-worship, and agreed to send representatives to the proposed council. He did not omit, however, to claim the restoration of the 'patrimonies of St. Peter' which had been confiscated by Leo III at the time of the first outbreak of the controversy.

An attempt to hold the desired ecumenical Council at Constantinople in August, 786, was foiled by the iconoclastic party. The war-worn veterans of Constantine Copronymus, still true to the memory of their victorious leader, rushed into the church where the ecclesiastics were assembled, and in fierce tones threatened to slay the new patriarch, the orthodox bishops, and the abbots. Vain were all attempts to quell the mutiny. The threatened churchmen were only too glad to dissolve the Council and to escape from the church, while the bishops (still numerous) of the iconoclastic party triumphantly shouted, 'We have conquered!'.

Their triumph was of short duration. Irene had the monks, and probably the mob of Constantinople, on her side. The soldiers who had taken the lead in the late disturbances were expelled from the city. More obsequious troops were brought from the 'themes' on the Asiatic side of the Bosphorus, and on the 24th of September in the following year (787), a Council which ranks in ecclesiastical history as 'the seventh ecumenical' and 'second Nicene' Council, was held at the venerated sanctuary of Nicaea.

At this Council Tarasius presided, and any irregularity in his election was therefore fully condoned. Numerous bishops who had joined in the iconoclastic movement recanted and were purged of their offences against triumphant orthodoxy. Most important of all was the 'definition' which received the assent of the Council at its seventh session (October 13, 787): 'As the figure of the Holy Cross, so also holy pictures, whether coloured or made of stone or any other material, are to be portrayed on vessels, on garments, on walls, or on tablets, in houses or by the road-side, especially pictures of Jesus Christ, of our immaculate Lady, of the venerable angels, and of all holy men. As often as these representations are looked at, the beholders are stimulated to think upon and imitate the originals, and therefore they are right in bestowing upon them salutation and honouring worship, but not that peculiar service which is due to the Godhead alone'.

The Second Nicene Council marks the great triumph of the image-worshipping party. It is true that there was a certain backwater of iconoclasm in the ninth century, but it does not seem to have ever after this had any chance of permanent victory in the Eastern Church.

Meanwhile, however, to turn from ecclesiastical to political relations, the correspondence about the Franco-Byzantine marriage was not proceeding smoothly. Great obscurity hangs over this abortive negotiation, and, strangely enough, each party to the contract seems to have desired to have the credit, or discredit, of its final rupture, which took place in the year 787. It was of course from the first a purely political arrangement, and as the years passed on, both parties discovered that it was not so suitable to their policy as they had supposed. The Byzantines wished to be free to support the Lombard exile, Adelchis; Charles was possibly already beginning to dream of an imperial crown. Female vanity and ambition concurred to the same result. Irene, who was becoming jealous of her son, feared the increase of power which he might derive from an alliance with the Frankish king. Possibly Fastrada also, who during the long course of the marriage treaty had taken the place of the dead Hildegard by Charles's side, disliked the thought that her young step-daughter would obtain a higher place in European ceremonial than her own, as the result of so splendid an alliance. Whatever the cause, the negotiations were broken off, bitter resentment took the place of the interrupted friendship, and the little Hrotrud grew up in her father's court, spent her life there, and died in 810 at the age of thirty-eight, a princess of rare charms and endowments, but, unfortunately for her reputation, a mother though not a wife.

As for Constantine, his mother sent for a damsel from Armenia named Maria, and ordered him to marry her. The youth obeyed, but his resentment at being deprived of his Frankish bride was, we are told, one cause of that estrangement from his mother and of that long duel between them which, though the beginning of it (789) falls within our present period, will be best related in a future chapter in connection with its terrible end.

It may have been partly a cause and partly a consequence of the estrangement between the two courts that Charles and Irene eventually took opposite sides in the iconoclastic controversy. Possibly the hard struggle which Charles and his servants had to wage against the stubborn idolatry of the Saxons made him impatient of these decrees, which on the strength of fine-drawn distinctions between 'veneration' and 'worship', or 'worship' and 'service', seemed to them practically to commit the Christian Church to the worship of idols. But we perceive also an element of personal antipathy to Irene, of Western antagonism to the East, working in the mind of Charles, when we find him remonstrating against the presumption of the Eastern sovereigns in calling themselves 'God's chosen instruments', and in styling their own edicts *divalia*; objecting to a woman dictating her decrees to the Church, 'since woman, as the weaker vessel and the one most easily deceived, ought to be in subjection and repressed by the authority of the man'; and lastly, when we hear his invectives against 'certain rulers and priests of the Eastern regions, who, leaving sound doctrine and forgetting the apostolic anathema on any who should bring to his Galatian converts another gospel than that which he had preached to them, by their infamous and most silly synods strive to bring into the Church practices which neither the Saviour nor His Apostles ever taught'.

These passages are taken from the celebrated *Libri Carolini*, in which Charles (or some learned man, probably Alcuin, writing by his authority) utters a long tirade—not unaccompanied by argument—against the acts of the Second Nicene Council. With some show of impartiality he censures the iconoclasts as well as the image-worshippers. There is no reason, he says, why there should not be pictures in the churches, in order to stimulate devotion, and preserve in the minds of the people the memory of the events recorded in Scripture; but it is a matter of indifference to the Church whether they are there or not. By no means ought their presence in the churches to be insisted on; still less should Christians under peril of anathema be commanded to venerate them, as they were commanded by the rash, impertinent and silly council lately held in Bithynia.

The *Libri Carolini* were composed in 790 : and four years later, in 794, at a Council of Frankish bishops held at Frankfurt, a solemn condemnation was pronounced upon 'the Greek synod at Constantinople', which was accused of directing that the same adoration and service should be rendered to the holy images which was rendered to the Trinity. This last statement was due to an utter misunderstanding, and probably to a mistranslation of the proceedings of the council thus condemned. The fact that this mistranslation was to all appearance the work of some scribe in the Lateran (since Hadrian forwarded to Charles a copy of the proceedings translated into Latin) is an evidence of gross carelessness or ignorance, or both, in the officials of the Papal chancery, and is a fact that has an important bearing on the question of the donation of territory, referred to in the preceding chapter.

About the same time as the holding of the Council of Frankfurt, Charles addressed to Hadrian a letter similar to, but not identical with, the *Libri Carolini*, in which he besought the Pope to join in his condemnation of the detested Council of Nicaea. Of course Hadrian, who saw in the proceedings of that Council the victory of the cause for which he and his predecessors had been striving for half a century refused to issue any such condemnation. With great patience, in a very lengthy letter, he answered Charles's objections, point by point, indicating some errors into which he had been betrayed by his ignorance of the past history of the controversy. But in Hadrian's mind all roads led eventually to the question of the patrimonies of St. Peter. As he said to Charles, 'When the controversy about the sacred images first broke out, they took from us our patrimonies [in the south of Italy and Sicily]. Now they have renounced, it is true, the errors of iconoclasm, but we cannot get any answer to our reclamation of these patrimonies which are ours by an undoubted title for the lighting of candles [at the tomb of the Apostles] and for the nourishment of the poor. Wherefore, with your approval, we propose to send the Emperor an answer, thanking him for again erecting the sacred images in their old places, but warning him that if he fails to restore its patrimonies to the Holy Roman Church, we shall decide him to be a heretic for thus obstinately persevering in his old error'.

As to the precise issue of this discussion we are not informed. Possibly Hadrian's death, which occurred soon after, prevented the proposed letter from being ever sent. But the whole of these negotiations are most important in their bearing on the historical question of the separation, political and ecclesiastical, of the East from the West. This separation is often attributed to the iconoclastic controversy as its sole cause. Doubtless the hostile attitude of Leo the Isaurian and Constantine Copronymus on the question of image-worship had much to do with estranging the Pope from the Emperor, but it must not bear the whole blame for the final separation. For here, during the years from 787 onwards, we have the Church of Constantinople absolutely reconciled to the Church of Rome on the question of image-worship, and the Empress Irene, the foremost personage in the Empire, the enthusiastic defender of that usage of the Church. On the other hand, Charles and his bishops take up a position, nominally of neutrality, but really of bitter opposition to the Second Nicene Council, advancing arguments which the Pope condemns, and defending positions which he considers heretical. Both sides might agree to ignore the question, yet far on into the ninth century the opposition still continued. Yet in the year 800 we shall find a Pope (not Hadrian but his next successor) taking the lead in the great revolution which severed Rome from Constantinople and broke the last links of allegiance that bound the Pope to the Eastern Caesar.

CHAPTER II.

THE PONTIFICATE OF HADRIAN I.

WHEN Louis XVIII recovered the throne of his ancestors after the downfall of Napoleon, he said—or some astute person said for him 'Rien n'est changé : il n'y a qu'un Français de plus.'

Something like this seems to have been the attitude of Charles the Great in 774 towards his new Italian conquest. There was no attempt to force the Lombard nation into the Frankish mould. Their laws were left substantially unchanged. Even the administration of those laws was often left in Lombard hands. Of the counts, who for the most part superseded the Lombard *gastalds*, many probably belonged to the conquered nation; nor does there appear to have been any extensive confiscation of the estates of the Lombard nobles. The authority which Charles now wielded (and which he doubtless meant, as he had leisure to extend his dominion, to wield over the whole peninsula) was appropriately expressed by the new title which he used for twenty-six years, till it was superseded by one yet more majestic. He was now *Carolus Rex Francorum et Langobardorum atque Patricius Romanorum*. He was king of the Franks by inheritance from his father; king of the Lombards by conquest, but also, as far as we can see, by the general consent of the Lombard people, tired of the passionate weakness of Desiderius and glad to have the great Teutonic hero for their king. But he also now began to make systematic use of that title 'Patrician of the Romans' which Stephen II had bestowed upon his father, but which, so long as they held no territory south of the Alps, had been rather a burden than a delight to the Frankish sovereigns. Now that Charles was a great lord in Italy, it was worthwhile to try what rights were slumbering in that venerable designation, which the Popes had almost forced upon his family, but which now might be available for keeping the Pope himself in his proper place, as well as for winning the obedience of the non-Teutonic population of Italy.

It is not easy to ascertain what had been the ideal reconstitution of Italy which the Popes had floating before them when they invoked the intervention of the Frankish kings, but it is clear that the addition of the word 'Langobardorum' to Charles's royal titles by no means corresponded with their anticipations. It was soon seen that any one, were he ever so loyal a client of St. Peter, who claimed the rights of a Lombard king, must come into collision with the kingdom-cleaving designs of the Roman pontiff; and though expediency dictated the continued employment of such epithets as 'mellifluus' and 'a Deo servatus' in Hadrian's correspondence with Charles, we may be pretty sure that there were times when a full-bodied 'nefandissimus 'or 'Deo odibilis' would have better expressed the Papal emotions. The history of Italy during the quarter of a century before us, is almost entirely the history of the strained relations between the two men, Charles and Hadrian, who had sworn eternal friendship over the corpse of St. Peter.

I. First of all in this correspondence we are met by Hadrian's complaints of the arrogance and cupidity of Leo, archbishop of Ravenna. "Soon after your return to Frank-land", says the Pope, "this man, with tyrannical and most insolent intent, turned rebel to St. Peter and ourselves. He has brought under his sway the following cities of the Emilia: Faenza, Forlimpopoli, Forli, Cesena, Bobbio, Comacchio, the duchy of Ferrara, Imola and Bologna, asserting that they, together with the whole Pentapolis, were given to him by your Excellency; and he has sent his missus, Theophylact, through the Pentapolis, desiring to separate the citizens thereof from their service to us. These men, however, are not at all inclined to humble themselves under him, but wish to remain loyal to St. Peter and ourselves, as they were when Stephen II received from your pious father the keys of the cities of the Exarchate. But now that nefarious archbishop, detaining those cities of the Emilia in his own power, appoints such magistrates as he chooses, expelling those whom we have appointed, and drawing all suits to Ravenna, to decide them according to his own pleasure.

"Thus, to our great disappointment, your holy spiritual mother, the Roman Church, sustains a severe rebuff, and we ourselves are brought into great contempt, since the very territories which even in Lombard times we were known to govern with full powers, are now in your times being wrested from us by perverse and impious men, who are your rivals as much as ours. And, lo! this taunt is hurled in our teeth by many of our enemies, who say with scorn, 'How have you profited by the wiping out of the nation of the Lombards and by their being made subject to the Frankish realm? Behold, none of those promises which were made to you are fulfilled, and even the possessions which were aforetime granted by Pippin to St. Peter are now taken from you".

Next year Leo made his appearance at Charles's court, and Hadrian, on being informed of his rival's visit, professed a joy which was certainly mingled with alarm. "The Truth itself bears witness that we are always glad when we hear of any one approaching your royal footsteps. Had he informed us that he was about to enter your presence we would gladly have sent one of our own envoys along with him". In the letter which follows this, a grave charge of disloyalty is brought against the detested archbishop. John, the patriarch of Grado, had sent an important letter to the Pope, probably announcing the imminent rebellion of Hrodgaud, count of Friuli. This letter as soon as it arrived in Rome was copied and sent off to Charles, both Hadrian and his clerk feeling the matter to be of so great importance that they would not touch meat or drink till they had despatched it to their patron. The letter however, on its way through Ravenna, had been tampered with by Archbishop Leo, who had broken the seals and redirected it to the Pope. Hadrian roundly accused him of having done this in order that he might communicate the contents to Arichis, duke of Benevento, and Charles's other enemies, an accusation which was probably quite destitute of truth. In a postscript to this letter Hadrian asserts that the archbishop of Ravenna was puffed up with intolerable pride on his return from the Frankish court. The old complaints about his lawless proceedings in the Emilia and his vain attempts to seduce the men of the Pentapolis from their loyalty to St. Peter are renewed, and it is asserted that some of the judges who had been appointed by the Pope in the cities of the Emilia are actually kept in bonds by the arrogant archbishop. In November of the same year these charges are repeated in a more definite manner:

"We sent our treasurer Gregory to bring the magistrates of those cities hither, and to receive the oaths of fidelity of the citizens, but Leo would not allow him to continue his journey. Then there was Dominicus [possibly a Frankish official], whom you yourself recommended to us in the church of St. Peter, and whom we appointed count of the little city of Gabellum, giving him our written authority to govern that city. This man was prevented from exercising his office by Leo, who sent an army, brought him bound to Ravenna, and still keeps him in custody there. Puffed up with pride, he refuses, as aforetime, to obey our commands, and by the strong arm keeps possession of Imola and Bologna, declaring that you did in no wise grant those cities to St. Peter, but to him : and as to the remaining cities of Emilia, namely Faenza, the Duchy of Ferrara, Comacchio, Forli, Forlimpopoli, Cesena, Bobbio and Tribunatus-decimo, he allows none to come forth or to bring their actions to be pleaded before us, though they were all ready to seek our presence.

"As to all the other citizens of both the regions called Pentapolis, from Rimini to Gubbio, all come freely to us to have their suits decided and abide loyally in our service. Only that archbishop stands aloof in his ferocity and pride".

Here, in November, 775, the correspondence leaves the question of the Exarchate. We see Hadrian, notwithstanding the cession of territory which was undoubtedly made by the Lombard king to his predecessor Stephen II, quite unable to assert his rights over Ravenna itself and the province of Emilia which lay to the west of it. In the Pentapolis, however, the provinces between the Adriatic and Apennines to the south of Ravenna, the Pope can reckon on the loyal subjection of the people, who probably, with that tendency towards municipal isolation and jealousy which was so marked a feature of the civic life of Italy, had their own reasons for hating Ravenna and preferring the distant Hadrian to the near and insistent Leo. There is no evidence that matters mended for the Papal jurisdiction during the rest of the life of Leo, but on the death of that 'ferocious' archbishop, which probably occurred in June, 777, a successor was appointed, John VII, who apparently arranged terms of reconciliation with the Papal See.

II. Another burning question at this time, and one in which the Papal rights are more obscure than in the case of the Exarchate, is that of the duchy of Spoleto. A review of the various statements about this Umbrian province, so important to the consolidation of the Papal dominions, leads us to the conclusion that there was here a genuine misunderstanding, in the literal sense of the word, between the Pope and his powerful friend. As far back as the spring of 757 both Spoleto and Benevento had made some sort of 'commendation' of themselves to Pippin, blending the Pope's name with his in a manner highly suggestive of future controversies. But Pippin, who in 758 had to lead an army against the Saxons, and from 760 to the end of his reign was involved in the arduous struggle with Waifar of Aquitaine, had no mind to leave these urgent affairs in order to cross the Alps and vindicate a shadowy supremacy over those distant Apennine provinces. Thus the matter remained, save that Desiderius made both Spoleto and Benevento feel the curb of their Lombard overlord more tightly than any prince since the days of Liutprand. In the crisis of the fate of the Lombard kingdom, the Spoletans deserted the cause of their nation and put themselves under the protection of the Pope, to whom the new duke Hildeprand swore fealty, his predecessor Theodicius having possibly fallen fighting for Desiderius against the Franks. This commendation of Spoleto to the Pope is, as we have seen, confirmed by a document of the year 774, which is dated by no regnal year either of Frank or Lombard, but 'in the times of the thrice blessed and angelic lord, Hadrian, pontiff and universal Pope'.

It was with the consciousness of this peaceful victory won by the Church that Hadrian met Charles on the steps of St. Peter's on the 6th of April, 774. It seems probable that whatever may have been left unsaid or undefined, the Pope did mention his recent acquisition of the lordship of Spoleto, and that Charles did at the time consent to his retaining it, or was understood by Hadrian so to have consented. Not otherwise, as it seems to me, can we explain the clear statement made by Hadrian in a letter written about eighteen months afterwards to the Frankish king: "Moreover you offered the duchy of Spoleto itself, in your own proper person, to St. Peter, Prince of Apostles, through our Insignificance and for the ransom of your soul". But to establish the Papal claim to Spoleto it was necessary that the new duke and his people should give their consent to its recognition, and this, notwithstanding their recent oath of fealty, they appear to have stubbornly refused. After the fall of the Lombard monarchy there was no longer any need to seek the protection of the Pope against the wrath of Desiderius, and both prince and people preferred to be under the yoke of the brilliant Teutonic warrior who called himself *Rex Langobardorum,* rather than under that of the unwarlike priest who could scarcely open his lips without showing his detestation of 'the unutterable Lombards'. Hence it comes to pass that in January, 776, we find in a donation to the monastery of Farfa 'Hildeprandus gloriosus et summus dux ducatus Spoletani' dating the document by the year of the reign of 'Charles, the most excellent king of the Franks and the Lombards, in the second year, by Divine favour, of his reign in Italy'. And the same mode of dating (a clear indication that Charles and none other was Hildeprand's overlord) is found in two other documents of 776 and five of the year 777.

III. Not only in Spoleto was the newly-won Papal power endangered. It will be remembered that near the sources of the Tiber, on the Tuscan side of the Apennines, the little 'Castle of Happiness' had commended itself to Hadrian's protection. Here too the claims of St. Peter were being trampled under foot. "We must tell you", wrote the Pope to the King, "that that perfidious man, sower of tares and rival of the great Tempter of the human race, Raginald, formerly *gastald* in the Castellum Felicitatis, who appears now to be duke of Clusium, is by his unjust proceedings doing great harm to your holy mother the Church. For he seeks to wrest from us all the possessions which your Excellency offered to the Prince of the Apostles for the ransom of your soul, and to bring them into bondage to himself. Hastening with his army to our city, Castellum Felicitatis, he has carried off its inhabitants. I can in no wise believe that your Royalty, strengthened by God, together with our most excellent daughter the queen and your sweetest children, and all the God-marshalled army of the Franks, wrought the late mighty change in Italy for the exaltation of this duke Raginald, and not rather for the support of the holy Church of God which loves you, that by your benign championship she may shine in perennial glory.

"Therefore I pray and beseech you, for the love of St. Peter, not to allow the aforesaid Raginald (who was of old time a sower of strifes and scandals under King Desiderius) to remain in the regions of Tuscany nor to hold any delegated functions from you".

This is a type of many letters from Hadrian which were addressed to the Frankish king during the first two years after his Italian campaign. Endless complaints of the unutterably wicked and diabolical neighbours of the Pope, perpetual reminders of the faith solemnly plighted over the body of St. Peter, words of honeyed sweetness for Charles himself, for Hildegard, for the little princes and princess, and the divinely-protected army of the Franks, but also faithful warnings of the punishment which will overtake the king at the last day if he has allowed any one of the rights of his patron St. Peter to fall to the ground,—such are the ever-recurring themes of the Papal correspondence.

There are indications that this monotony of grumbling severely tried the long-suffering patience of Charles. He had done as much for the Pope and for himself also in

Italy as suited his present purpose. The care of the Saxon war hung heavy upon his soul, and did not seem likely soon to be lifted from it. That also was surely an enterprise pleasing in the sight of God and St. Peter, for had he not solemnly vowed in his palace at Quierzy to prosecute ceaseless war with the Saxons till they should either become Christians or be swept from the face of the earth? And now when he returned weary and war-worn to his 'villa' on the Oise or the Roehr he was sure to find some smooth-shaven, dark ecclesiastic from Rome, bearing one of these querulous letters from the Pope, and importuning Charles to lead an army across the Alps in order to enforce the ever-growing 'justitiae' of St. Peter in the Exarchate or Spoleto or Tuscany.

IV. Not only were the letters irritating; the who bore them were not always well chosen, and sometimes failed in proper respect towards the most powerful prince in Europe. In 774, soon after Charles's return from Italy, the Pope sent as his representative his chamberlain Anastasius, commending him to the royal favour. How that mission sped we know not, but next year Anastasius was again sent on a similar errand, and this time he was accompanied by a certain Lombard named Gausfrid of Pisa, who had taken refuge in Rome with a story, probably untrue, of an attempt to assassinate him, at the instigation of a Lombard duke named Alio. "Pray receive Gausfrid kindly", said Hadrian, "for the love of St. Peter and because we ask it of you, and deign to grant him the help of your favour and protection. We add also this request, that the generous exercise of your authority should secure him in the possession of those farms which you have bestowed upon him".

This recommendation appears to have been a blunder on Hadrian's part. His next letter was in reply to one from Charles which told him that Gausfrid was a detected swindler, who for his frauds had been dismissed from the royal service and who had bribed the king's notary to issue forged letters of grant in the royal name, probably with reference to those very farms for his quiet possession of which Hadrian interceded. The Pope pleads, no doubt truthfully, his entire ignorance of these deceitful practices of his client, and hopes that no scandal may be thereby engendered between him and his royal friend, but the incident was not likely to improve the relations between the two potentates.

Even more serious was the difficulty caused at the same time by the insolence of the chamberlain Anastasius, who in pleading his master's cause (probably with reference to the affairs of Ravenna and Spoleto) used such 'intolerable' words that the anger of the high-minded king was raised, and putting him in custody he refused to allow the chamberlain to return to Rome. What were these intolerable words? It seems highly probable that they amounted to a charge of breach of faith on the part of the Frankish king, a charge which the Teutonic warrior would resent more fiercely than one of the crowned diplomatists of Constantinople, and of which perhaps even the Roman courtier scarcely felt the whole insulting significance. Here, as in the interview at St. Peter's and all the transactions between Pope and King which rested on oral communications, we have once more to remember that the difference of language opened a wide door to mutual misunderstandings. Charles could read Latin, it is true, but we have on evidence that he spoke it fluently, and Hadrian, a Roman of the Via Lata, of course never demeaned himself to learn the barbarous Frankish tongue.

The Pope bitterly complained of the detention of his envoy, which, as he said, lowered him in the eyes of the Lombards and the citizens of Ravenna, making them think that he had altogether fallen out of Charles's favour. "Never since the beginning of the world", as he averred, "had it been known that an envoy of St. Peter, great or small, had been detained by any nation" : an assertion which might safely be made for the centuries intervening between the creation of the world and the Christian era. He prayed that Anastasius might be sent back to Rome: "We will most severely enquire into the matter, and correct him according to his ascertained guilt".

We hear in a later epistle of the return of Anastasius, but have no hint of his trial or punishment. Probably when the hot blood of the Frank had cooled, Charles perceived that it was better not to insist on the punishment of the Pope's too zealous representative.

V. Towards the end of 775, Hadrian was thrown into alarm by the rumours of an impending combination of Lombards and Byzantines against himself and his Frankish patron. Hrodgaud, a Lombard whom Charles had allowed to remain as duke of Friuli, was probably the soul of this combination, perhaps its only zealous member: but Hadrian believed that Hildeprand of Spoleto, Arichis of Benevento, and his special foe Raginald of Clusium, were all working for the meditated revolution, and were all in communication with the Emperor at Constantinople, at whose court Adelchis, the dethroned son of Desiderius, was residing, an honoured guest. It is possible that some such combination was being formed, and that the death of Constantine Copronymus (which happened on the 14th of September, 775) struck the keystone out of the arch and relieved Charles from serious peril: but we have as yet only the word of Hadrian for the fact, and as far as Hildeprand and Arichis are concerned, it is probable that he accused them unjustly.

Evidently Charles thought, and had reason for thinking, that if he could free himself from the embarrassing schemes of the ambitious Hadrian he could settle the affairs of Central Italy by negotiation, better than by the sword. He sent two envoys, the Bishop Possessor and the Abbot Radigaud, into Italy, but not in the first place to Rome. Hadrian, who knew that such an embassy was coming, waited for it (as he told Charles) through September and October, on into November, but waited in vain. He wrote to the governor whom Charles had installed at Pavia, and received only the chilling reply, "The king's envoys are not coming to you" : a reply which filled him with sorrow. The next article of his indictment against the ambassadors (for he persisted in professing to believe that the ambassadors were in fault and not their master) must be told in his own words:—

"We were very desirous to receive your Excellency's envoys with due honour, and through them to be satisfied of your safety. Wherefore we made all the preparations which became your royal dignity, and sent horses on the road to meet them. But they, when they had arrived at Perugia, instead of coming right on to us—as you had enjoined them and as your letters to us set forth—despising us, went to Hildeprand at Spoleto, sending us word to this effect: 'We are only going to converse with Hildeprand, and then, according to our orders, we will visit you at [the shrine of] our Apostolic Lord'.

"Afterwards, when they had talked with the aforesaid Hildeprand and were tarrying long time with him, we directed to them our apostolic letters to this effect: 'By Almighty God and the life of our most excellent son the great King Charles, pray come to us at once that we may talk over the things which concern the exaltation of the Church and the praise of our King. Then we will leave you to go according to your orders to Benevento'. But they, we know not on what errand, went immediately from

Spoleto to Benevento, leaving us in great disgrace, and have thereby increased the insolence of the Spoletans towards us.

"We pray you to remember, sweetest and most loving son, with what extreme kindness you addressed us, when you had hastened to the thresholds of St. Peter and St. Paul, saying that it was not in quest of gold or jewels, or silver, or letters (?), or men, that you and your God-protected army had undergone so great labour, but only to insist on the recovery of the rights of St. Peter, the exaltation of Holy Church, and our safety.

"As if actually present before your royal honey-flowing glances, we beg of you speedily to comfort and gladden us in the deep depression into which we have been thrown by the conduct of your envoys. Moreover, you yourself offered the duchy of Spoleto to St. Peter through us for the ransom of your soul. Therefore we earnestly pray you speedily to deliver us and the aforesaid duchy of Spoleto from this affliction, that by the intercession of St. Peter you may receive your due reward from our most merciful God".

At last the long-expected messengers, Possessor and Radigaud, arrived in Rome, charged by Hildeprand with apologies and entreaties for forgiveness. Far from obtaining his pardon, they had doubtless enough to do to shield themselves from the storm of Hadrian's reproaches. He sent a messenger, his treasurer Stephen, to Spoleto, who returned with more circumstantial accounts of the great impending invasion.

All the four dukes, in combination with the mob of the Greeks and the exiled Adelchis, were going to swarm over land and sea to the attack on the *Ducatus Romae*. The City was to be stormed, all the churches to be sacked, the precious jewelled canopy of St. Peter's tomb was to be carried off, "we ourselves—which God forbid!—to be carried captive", the kingdom of the Lombards to be restored, and Charles's power in Italy to be destroyed.

Hadrian sent up a piteous cry for help: "Do not leave us alone, nor postpone your consolation : lest the nations that are in all the world should say, 'Where is the confidence of the Romans, which after God they placed in the king and kingdom of the Franks?'. Redeem those pledges which with your own hands you offered to God for the salvation of your soul, that in the great day of future judgment you may be able to say, 'O my lord Peter! Prince of Apostles! I have finished my course; I have kept my faith towards thee; I have defended the Church of God committed to thee by Almighty goodness, and have freed her from the hands of her enemies. And now standing without spot before thee I offer to thee thy sons, whose deliverance from the power of the enemy thou didst commit to my hands. Lo! here they are, safe and sound'. Thus shalt thou, who holdest the reins of power in this present life, be permitted to reign with Christ in the life to come, hearing that welcome voice of His, 'Come, ye blessed of My Father, inherit the kingdom prepared for you from the foundation of the world'."

VI. Charles did march into Italy in the early part of 776, but his campaign, of which we have most meagre notices from the annalists, was all conducted within sight of the Alps. It seems to have been while he was keeping his Christmas (775) at Schlettstadt in Alsace that news was brought to him that 'Hrodgaud, the Lombard whom he had himself given as duke to the men of Friuli, was making a rebellion in Italy, had declared himself king, and that many cities had revolted to him. He judged speed to be necessary for the repression of this uprising, and accordingly, having collected his bravest soldiers, he marched with haste into Italy, slew Hrodgaud, recovered Friuli, Treviso, and all the other cities which had rebelled, established

Frankish counts in them, kept his Easter at Treviso, and then returned into Frank-land with the same speed with which he had come. Scarcely had he recrossed the Alps when he heard that the fortress of Eresburg had been taken by the Saxons, and the garrison of Franks expelled therefrom. Then followed one of Charles's splendid storm-sweeping marches over the land, his arrival at the sources of the Lippe-stream, and his meeting there with a vast number of the natives, who, cowering in fear, prayed his pardon for their rebellion, and were baptized by thousands in the waters of the Lippe. A conversion on a larger scale than any that rewarded the preaching of the first Apostles, but less durable in its results.

It was probably in part the fear of impending troubles in Saxon-land which caused King Charles to hasten his return across the Alps without paying the often-talked-of visit to Rome. Yet not entirely: the diplomacy which detached Spoleto and Benevento at this critical conjuncture from the threatened anti-Frankish confederacy had probably accomplished its purpose at the cost of some sacrifice of the Papal claims. As to Benevento, indeed, it is impossible for us to say what were the precise relations existing at this time between him who now called himself Prince of that city, Arichis, son-in-law of Desiderius, and the Frankish sovereign. But as we have already seen, Hildeprand of Spoleto seems to have remained satisfied with a condition, practically, of vassalage under Charles, and the negotiations carried on with him through the medium of Possessor and Radigaud had probably guaranteed him against any enforcement by Frankish arms of the claims of Papal sovereignty which he now set at defiance.

VII. It can hardly be doubted that at this time the relations between Pope and Emperor were strained almost to the point of breaking. There is an ominous interval of more than two years in the correspondence copied in the Codex Carolinus. Either no letters between the estranged allies in the period between February 776 and May 778, or those which were written and received were so bitter in their tone— like the 'insupportable' words of Anastasius—that, when the reconciliation took place, they were by common consent blotted out of the book of remembrance.

It is to this interval that a recent enquirer assigns the signature of a convention whereby Hadrian claim to renounced all claim to sovereignty in Spoleto and Tuscany, in consideration of certain yearly revenues to be paid to him out of the taxes of those two provinces. The evidence for this 'convention' rests on the alleged confirmation contained in the grant of Louis the Pious to Pope Paschal in 817, which has been before referred to. It is certainly possible so to interpret that document, but its language is perhaps intentionally obscure, and would be consistent with an entirely different series of transactions between Pope and King, nor is there anything which fixes the date of the 'convention' to the year 777 or 778. But however we may by our conjectures fill up this mysterious interval in the correspondence of the two statesmen, it is certain that after that interval is passed the correspondence begins again on an entirely different footing. Still is the Pope urgent for the satisfaction of the claims of St. Peter, still are the joys of heaven and the terrors of hell invoked to keep the Frankish sovereign up to the required pitch of devotion to the Apostolic service, but from this point onward the word 'patrimonies', for which we have hitherto looked almost in vain in the earlier letters, is of continual occurrence. Claims of territorial sovereignty seem to be tacitly abandoned, and the one constant demand of the Pope is that the landed estates, which have been violently torn from him or his predecessors in the days of the Lombard oppression, shall now be restored to the Holy Church of God, which is ready to produce the necessary vouchers and title-deeds to show that they are rightfully hers.

VIII. Yet, though this is the general character of the correspondence, we find with some surprise, in the very first letter after communications are re-opened, an allusion—the first allusion in any authentic document—to the imaginary donation of Constantine. After expressing his regrets that Charles has not been able to fulfill his promise of coming to Rome at the Easter of 778 and bringing his infant son Carloman to be baptized, Hadrian continues: "And as in the time of St. Silvester the Holy Catholic and Apostolic Church of Rome was exalted by the generosity of the most pious Constantine, the great Emperor, of holy memory, and he deigned to bestow on it power in these regions of Hesperia, so in these times, which are so prosperous for you and for us, may the Holy Church of God, that is of the blessed Apostle Peter, grow and flourish and be more than more exalted, that all the nations when they hear of it may shout, 'O Lord, save the King, and hear us in the day when we call upon Thee, for, lo, a new and most Christian Emperor Constantine has arisen in our day, through whom God has been pleased to bestow all gifts on His Holy Church'."

We surely cannot be mistaken in thinking that this passage, with its pointed allusion to 'the regions of Hesperia', refers to the celebrated fictitious document which was discussed in a previous chapter. But the Pope in this same letter goes on to claim, not widespread territorial sovereignty, but the restitution of "those possessions which Emperors, Exarchs, and other God-fearing men have for the good of their souls bestowed on the Church in the regions of Tuscany, Spoleto, Benevento and Corsica, together with the Sabine patrimony. Let these possessions, which have been abstracted by the unutterable Lombards through long periods of years, be restored in your days. We have many deeds of donation relating to these in our bureau at the Lateran; and these for your satisfaction we have sent by our aforesaid *missi*. We pray your Excellency therefore to order the patrimonies in their entirety to be restored to St. Peter and ourselves. So may the Prince of Apostles plead before the tribunal of Almighty God for your safety and long life and the exaltation of your kingdom".

The language of such a letter seems quite clear. It is specific estates—of vast extent it is true—secured by special title-deeds, not the sovereignty of two-thirds of Italy, for which the Pope here pleads in the name of St. Peter.

IX: The Pope speaks here of "these days of your and our prosperity". The times seem to have been less prosperous for the people than for their rulers. There was a terrible earthquake (778) in the territory of Treviso, by which many persons perished; forty-eight, we are told, in a single night in one village. "Great tribulations", says a ninth-century chronicler, "fell upon Italy after the Frankish conquest: by the sword, by famine, by wild beasts many persons perished, so that some towns and villages were left altogether bare of inhabitants". Hadrian himself in a singular way bears unconscious witness to the same fact, the misery of the people. It seems that Charles had enquired as to an ugly rumour which had come to his ears that Roman citizens were engaged in selling slaves to 'the unspeakable Saracens'. Such a charge in the honey-flowing letter of his illustrious friend was passionately repelled by Hadrian: "Never have we fallen into such wickedness, nor has any such deed been done with our permission. It is true that the unspeakable Greeks have traded along the Lombard shore and bought families from thence, and have formed a friendship for slave-trading purposes with the

Lombards themselves. Wherefore we ordered duke Alio to prepare many ships that he might capture the Greeks and burn their fleet, but he refused to obey our commands. As for us, we have neither ships nor sailors to catch them with. But God is our witness that we have done all that we could to repress this mischief, for we ordered the ships of the Greeks that were in our harbour of Centumcellae to be burned, and we detained the crews in prison for a long time. But the Lombards themselves, as we have been told, constrained by hunger, have sold many families into slavery. And others of the Lombards have of their own accord gone on board the slave-ships of the Greeks, because they had no other hope of a livelihood".

The chronological order of the letters which relate to the seventeen years now before us is so uncertain that it will be better to deal with them in their geographical relations.

X. We begin with the province of Istria, that long peninsula studded with cities which crowns the Adriatic gulf, and which played such an important part in the long controversy concerning the Three Chapters. Here, as we learn from a letter of Hadrian, the bishop Maurice, a loyal adherent of the Roman See, was employed to collect certain revenues due to St. Peter and transmit them to Rome. A suspicion arose that in his journeyings to and fro on these errands he was secretly stirring up the inhabitants to throw off the Byzantine yoke and acknowledge themselves subjects of Charles. The 'most nefarious Greeks' together with some of the natives of Istria arrested him, and in Byzantine fashion plucked out his eyes. He escaped to Rome, and the Pope sent him to Marcarius, duke of Friuli, at the same time addressing a letter to Charles begging him, as he valued his soul, to order Marcarius to reinstate him in his bishopric. As Istria was still a province of the Empire, it is not easy to see how this could be done without an actual declaration of war.

XI. We pass from Istria to the Venetian Islands, not yet the Venice of medieval history, for the city on the Rialto was still unbuilt, and Heraclea and Equilium were the chief cities of the confederation After the fall of the Exarchate, followed by the overthrow of its Lombard conquerors, the Venetians seem to have clung more tightly than ever to their connection with Constantinople, and to have been willing, in their loyalty to the Empire, to brave even the anger of the Pope. "We beg to bring to the notice of your Excellency", writes Hadrian to Charles, "that as you in your day of triumph directed that the Venetian traders should be expelled from the regions of Ravenna and the Pentapolis, we immediately sent our orders to those regions that we might give effect to your royal will. Moreover we have directed our precept to the archbishop of Ravenna, that wherever, in the lands subject to our sway, the Venetians hold either forts or property, he should absolutely expel them from thence, and resuming such possessions keep them in his own hands as property of the Church".

XII. The expulsion of the Venetians, it will be seen, extended to Ravenna as well as to the Pentapolis. As we have no more complaints of the usurpations of the archbishop of Ravenna, it may be inferred that the successors of Leo were during this period accepting quietly the yoke of St. Peter. Here, however, as well as elsewhere, we have evidences of the extreme difficulty with which the Popes, with the scanty material forces at their command, maintained the dominion which in theory was theirs. Strangely helpless is the letter which Hadrian addresses to Charles in 783 concerning the wicked deeds of 'those foolish and useless triflers' Eleutherius and Gregory, who appear to have been magistrates at Ravenna. "In their insolent obstinacy they have been grievously oppressing the poor and weak inhabitants in their district, selling men into slavery among the pagan natives, and greedily devouring their bread without compassion. Moreover, collecting a crowd of base and bloody men, they have not ceased daily to perform shameful murders. Once, when mass was being celebrated in the church, at the same hour when the deacon was preaching the Gospel to the people, these most impious men were shedding innocent blood in the self-same sanctuary, accomplishing the murder of men instead of sacrifice to God. These men, puffed up in arrogance, are about to appear in your royal presence, and dare to cherish the hope that they will separate you from St. Peter and ourselves. Pray let their impertinence not be permitted to behold your glorious countenance smiling upon them, but send them back to us, dishonoured and disgraced, under the charge of your most faithful *missi*, that so you may be rewarded in the day of judgment by your patron St. Peter".

The whole tenour of the communication indicates the strange, the almost indescribable, relation which existed between the Pope and the Frankish King of the Lombards and Patrician of the Romans. Ravenna was undoubtedly one of the cities included in the Donations of Pippin and Charles. Here, if anywhere, the Pope, unless thwarted by the archbishop of the city, might claim to exercise jurisdiction as a sovereign. Yet even here he seems to be unable by his mere authority to punish magistrates who have so flagrantly abused their powers as Eleutherius and Gregory have done, and there is evidently a virtual right of appeal from his decision to that of the Frankish king.

In ecclesiastical matters, however, as we might expect, Hadrian takes a different tone. He absolutely refuses to admit Charles's claim to interfere in the election of a new archbishop of Ravenna; he repels, almost with acrimony, the charge of the king's *missi* that he has connived at simoniacal practices in that church; but on the other hand (though this is not a purely ecclesiastical affair), he graciously concedes to his royal friend the right to transport some of the mosaics of Ravenna to his palace at Aachen. The letter giving this permission is so curious that it deserves to be quoted :—

"We have received your bright and honey-sweet letters brought us by Duke Arwin. In these you expressed your desire that we should grant you the mosaics and marbles of the palace in the city of Ravenna, as well as other specimens to be found both on the pavement and on the walls [presumably of the churches]. We willingly grant your request, because, by your royal struggles, the church of your patron St. Peter daily enjoys many benefits, for which great will be your reward in heaven. By the hands of the same Arwin we have received one sound horse sent to us by you. The other, which was despatched at the same time, died on the road. For your remembrance of us in this thing we return you thanks.

"But in consideration of the love which in our inmost heart we do bear towards your glorious kingdom, pray send us such splendid horses, shapely in bone and fullness of flesh, as may be worthy of our riding. Such animals, in all respects worthy of praise, will cause your illustrious name to shine in triumph; and for this you will receive your wonted and worthy reward from God's own apostle, so that after reigning in this world with the queen and your most noble progeny, you may deserve to obtain eternal life in the citadels of heaven".

XIII. Travelling southward along the great Flaminian Way we come to the Umbrian duchy of Spoleto, where the Lombard Hildeprand, first the client and afterwards the pertinacious opponent of the Pope, held sway for fifteen years after the fall of the Lombard monarchy. We have seen that, though recalcitrant to the yoke of St. Peter, he was willing, perhaps eager, to profess himself the loyal adherent of Charles. This dependent relation (which it is hardly permitted us yet to speak of technically as vassalage) was owned and emphasized when, in 779, Hildeprand, having crossed the Alps, presented himself before Charles at the villa of Virciniacum and offered great gifts to his lord. We may reasonably conjecture that then at least, if not before, the Frankish king assured the Spoletan duke that his act of 'commendation' should protect him from all claims of a similar kind that might be urged against him by the bishop of Rome. With this state of things Hadrian had perforce to rest content, though it was certainly not without a pang that he saw himself constrained to abandon the project of adding the duchy of Spoleto to the territories on the Adriatic and Tyrrhenian seas which it would so admirably have welded together. But that he did thus accept his defeat seems to be shown by a letter in which he submissively begs for the supply of certain woods which could be furnished only in the regions about Spoleto, and which were required for renewing the wainscotings in the basilica of St. Peter.

We shall find Duke Hildeprand in the year 788 taking part with other Lombards and Franks in resisting a Byzantine invasion, probably on the coast of Apulia. In the next year (789) he died, and was succeeded, not by any Lombard, but apparently by a Frankish warrior named Winichis, who had taken a leading part in resisting the same invasion. This man was ruler of Spoleto during all the rest of the life of Charles, and at last, in 822, he resigned his ducal rank and retired into a monastery.

XIV. At Rome itself the chief events during the twenty-one years that we are now reviewing were the second and third visits of Charles to 'the threshold of the Apostles', which took place in the years 781 and 787 respectively, each time at the great festival of Easter. We will deal here with the first of these visits. He started from Worms in 780 to fulfill his long-delayed project of presenting his son Carloman to the Pope for baptism. He was accompanied by Hildegard, and by his two younger children, Carloman and Louis, the former three, and the latter two years old. In the four years which had elapsed since Charles was last in Italy, quelling the revolt of Hrodgaud of Friuli, memorable events had happened. Besides the endless invasions of the land of the Saxons, he had removed his court and his army into the province of Aquitaine (April 778), had crossed the Pyrenees, besieged Saragossa, and suffered in his retreat at Roncesvalles, that great disaster to his rear-guard which will forever be as world-famous in song as it is insignificant in history. Having crossed the Alps, Charles took up his quarters in the old Lombard palace of Pavia, where the new *Rex Langobardorum* kept his stately Christmas. He lingered for some time in Upper Italy, where there were doubtless many disorders which needed his strong, reforming hand. On the 15th of March (781) he was at Parma, giving a charter to the merchants of Mantua, where, (according to the generally received opinion,) he held a solemn *placitum* for the enactment of the decree which goes by the name of the *Capitulare Mantuanum*. By Easter Day, 15 April, he was in Rome, face to face with Hadrian after seven years of absence and chilling correspondence.

We have no such detailed account of his entry into Rome as on his first and last visits to the City, but assuredly the Roman populace had no lack of gorgeous ceremonies on the occasion of this visit. In the first place, there was the baptism of the four-year-old son, who entered the baptistery as Carloman and emerged from it as Pippin, having received that royal name from his godfather Hadrian. Why the name was thus changed we are not informed, but it seems probable that it was in order to publish to the world that Pippin the Hunchback, son of Charles and Himiltrud, was on account of his deformity excluded from succession to the throne. It is noteworthy that after this ceremony Hadrian always studiously addresses Charles as his spiritual co-father, and Hildegard as spiritual co-mother, a designation which helps us to distinguish between the letters written before 781 and those subsequent to that date.

After the baptism of Pippin, he and his baby brother Louis were crowned by the Pope, to denote that they had been named by their father as kings of Italy and Aquitaine respectively. It was perhaps not altogether politic on the part of Charles to give the Pope so prominent a place in the investiture of his sons with the regal dignity. A few more precedents of like kind, and the opinion might grow-up that no one could be a rightful king of the Franks and Lombards who had not received his crown from the hands of the pontiff.

Again another sight for the spectacle-loving citizens of Rome. It was while Charles still abode in the City that the ambassadors of Irene, Constantine the Treasurer and Mamulus the Grand Chamberlain entered it, doubtless with imperial pomp, in order to conclude the treaty of marriage between their young lord Constantine and the Frankish maiden Hrotrud. One marvels how Hadrian comported himself between the representatives of the old and the new regime; between the ambassadors of the sovereign *de jure* and the visible sovereign *de facto*. It was indeed a strange complication. Here was the eunuch Elisha, whose name went back to the days of Hebrew prophets, come to instruct a daughter of the Franks in 'the language and literature of the Greeks and the customs observed in the monarchy of the Romans'. Hebrew, Greek, and Latin, the three languages of the superscription on the cross, were blended in the commission of this envoy from Constantinople.

'The monarchy of the Romans'; that was still the name borne by the state whose centre was the city of Constantine, a name to which it could prove its right by an unquestioned pedigree. And here was the bishop of Rome, who till nine years before this time had dated all his documents by the year of the Byzantine sovereign, who had never been formally released from his allegiance to the Roman Emperor, who could not now plead that heresy unloosed all bonds (for Irene was an orthodox image-worshipper), treating probably the envoys from Constantinople as the representatives of a foreign though friendly power, and professing himself the comrade, friend, or subject of a certain 'Patrician of the Romans' who was also king of a German tribe settled on the lower Rhine. Alas! that no historian has recorded for us the artifices by which diplomacy veiled this strange entanglement.

Soon after Easter, Charles appears to have left Rome and to have journeyed leisurely through Upper Italy, visiting the monastery of his late uncle Carloman on Mount Soracte, settling disputed claims in the neighbourhood of Florence, making grants to ecclesiastics at Pavia and Brescia, assisting at the baptism of his youngest daughter Gisila at Milan, and finally returning across the Alps about the month of August. This year 781 was one of those which were more especially dedicated by the great monarch to Italian affairs. He doubtless perceived that many disorders had crept into the Frankish administration of the country during the seven years that it had been deprived of 'the master's eye'. He now left it under the nominal vice-royalty of his son

Pippin, the newly-crowned king of Italy. The child-king, still only four years old, was destined to grow up into a strong and capable if somewhat hot-tempered man. Meanwhile the kingdom was probably administered in his name by Frankish regents or governors, the name of one of whom, Rotchild, has been preserved to us. We hear very little as to his deeds or character, and that little is not favourable.

XV. Some weeks after Charles had left Rome and while he was still in Italy he received an interesting letter from the Pope. "We have greatly rejoiced", says Hadrian, "to receive your wise and God-inspired letters in which you say that your cause is ours and ours is yours. We trust that this truth, which has certainly been taught you by divine inspiration, will shine forth manifest to all men". The Pope then goes on to describe the disputes which had arisen between the monks of the great monastery of St. Vincent on the Vulturno and their abbots. Of these abbots, one, Autbert, had by Charles's command been summoned to Rome to justify himself before the Papal tribunal, but had died suddenly, worn out by the fatigues of the journey. A synod was then held at Rome to investigate a charge of treason against his rival and successor, Abbot Potho. Before this synod appeared the monk Rothgaud, and gave testimony as follows : "My lord, when we were performing the service for Sexts, and according to custom were singing, for the safety of the king and his progeny, the psalm 'Save me, 0 God, by Thy name', suddenly the abbot stood up and refused to sing. Afterwards, as we were walking together, the abbot began to say, 'What do you think of our cause, for I expected to see a sign and have not seen it?'. Rothgaud uttered a pious commonplace about God's power to humble the heart of man, and the abbot (according to his statement) answered, 'If it were not for the monastery and my Beneventan land, I would hold him [King Charles] of no more account than one dog'. Then he added, 'There are only as many Franks left [in the country] as I could carry on my shoulders'.

"Abbot Potho being asked what he had to say in answer to this charge, said, "Of course our congregation always prays for his Excellency and his children. But while I was at the service, when the prayers were ended and the boys began to sing *Domine in nomine tuo salvum me fac*", I suddenly rose in order to attend to some business for the good of the monastery. As for our talk on the road, what I said was, 'If it were not that it would seem like desertion of the monastery and its property, I should certainly go to some place where I need not care for anybody'. As for the Franks, I said nothing at all of the kind which he alleges against me".'

Rothgaud was re-examined, and could produce no testimony in confirmation of his charge. He was alone with the abbot when the conversation took place. Evidence was given that he was himself a man of bad character, who having committed incest with his niece had been obliged to leave the priesthood and turn monk.

Then three monks who had belonged to the party of Autbert complained that they had been illegally detained and imprisoned to prevent them from resorting to Charles's court for justice. Potho replied that he certainly did station guards upon the bridge [over the Vulturno] to prevent these and all other monks from violating their rule and 'going back to their vomit in the world'.

The result of the trial was that Potho was acquitted on the oath of ten monks, five Franks and five Lombards, that they had never heard him utter any treasonable sentiments against King Charles's Excellency.

XVI. Many letters passed soon after this about the great affair of the Sabine Patrimony. Unfortunately neither they nor any of the chroniclers of the time appear to give us any precise indications of what this Sabine territory was. All that can be said is that it was situated in the neighbourhood of Rieti. We saw that Liutprand restored to Pope Zacharias a Sabine territory of which the Popes had been despoiled thirty years before. Possibly it had again fallen back into Lombard hands. What we know is that Charles during his second visit to Rome appointed two *missi*, Itherius and Maginarius, to go with the Pope's envoys to investigate St. Peter's claim to the territory in question. They went, and assembled about a hundred men, who swore on the Virgin's altar that this patrimony had of old belonged to St. Peter and the Roman Church. But 'perverse and unjust men', as the Pope complained, hindered the restitution of the patrimony. Letter after letter was sent. Hadrian declared that the imperial envoy, Maginarius, had seen the whole claim of St. Peter to the territory, as it resulted both from old Imperial donations and from grants made by the insolent kings of the Lombards themselves, indicating the territory in question and the farms belonging to it; a claim which even the faithless Desiderius himself had not dared to dispute in its totality, though he had denied it as to some individual farms. Hadrian quoted Scripture, 'Thy God hath commanded thy strength', from the 68th Psalm, and—not too reverently—applied the opening verses of the Epistle to the Hebrews to God's marvellous working 'in these latter days' by the hand of Charles in favour of St. Peter. At last after five letters had been written, and probably a couple of years had elapsed, the royal *missi* were successful in completing the transfer of the Sabine patrimony to the Pope and setting up boundary-stones to mark off its precise limits where it touched the territory of Reate.

XVII. The chief anxiety of Hadrian during all these years came from the principality of Benevento on his southern border. Here was one of the hated Lombards, a son-in-law of the arch-enemy Desiderius, reigning in glory and in virtual independence. Extension of the *Ducatus Romae* in the direction of Campania, recovery of some of the lost patrimonies in the south of Italy, were both difficult while that strong and detested Lombard held the 'Samnite' principality. There was also a fear, perhaps a genuine fear, that someday, when Charles, the champion, was fighting far away in the forests of Saxon-land, the prince of Benevento might join forces with 'the most wicked' Greeks, besiege Rome by sea and land, 'and even carry us captives—God forbid!—into their own land.

Prince Arichis, who now ruled in Benevento, and had held sway there since 758, was in some respects the finest specimen of a ruler whom the Lombard race produced. Brave in war, capable in administration and diplomacy, able to hold his own and to guide his bark through the troubled sea of Italian politics, he was also a man of considerable intellectual culture, generous towards the Church (like so many others of the 'unutterable' Lombards), and able to share and sympathize with the literary interests of his wife, the accomplished Adelperga.

This princess, the daughter of Desiderius, was apparently the pupil of Paulus Diaconus, who for her composed that history of the Roman Empire (the so-called Historia Miscella) which has been so often quoted in the foregoing pages, and the object of which was to continue the work of Eutropius and to enrich it with those notices as to ecclesiastical history which Adelperga looked for in vain in the pages of the heathen historian.

Though not apparently descended from the dukes of the old Beneventan line whose names were borne by himself and his sons, and though originally planted in the Samnite duchy as the friend and relation of Desiderius, Arichis seems to have been gladly accepted by the inhabitants of that duchy as their sovereign, and to have rooted his dynasty deep in their affections.

He was evidently a great builder, and we may well suppose that the splendid Roman monuments which adorned the city (some of which, like Trajan's noble arch, remain to this day) had an influence in directing the minds of the prince and princess of Benevento towards the literature of the wonderful race who had spanned the Calore and the Vulturno with their bridges, and had carried the Via Appia straight over hill and dale to Brindisi from Rome.

But not only were the princely pair attracted towards the literature of the Latins. With the Greeks of Constantinople (*Romans* as they persisted in calling themselves) they had, after the revolution of 774, a strong tie, in the fact that Adelperga's brother Adelchis was now living at the Imperial court, slowly subsiding into middle age and the condition of a great Byzantine noble, but ever and anon making desperate attempts, with the help of Greek soldiers and sailors, to recover his lost Lombard throne. It was probably this Byzantine influence which caused Arichis to build what Erchempert calls "a most wealthy and becoming temple to the Lord, which he named after the two Greek words *Hagia Sophia*, that is Holy Wisdom; and having founded there a monastery and endowed it with most ample farms and various wealth, he handed it over for ever to the Order of St. Benedict V".

The church and the monastery still remain, and the cloister of the latter, with its pillars bearing capitals of strange devices, is one of the loveliest in Italy, but successive earthquakes ruined the stately building of Arichis, and two tombs and a few columns are all that now remain thereof, save a bas-relief in the tympanum over the church-portal, depicting St. Mercury in soldier's attire presenting to the Saviour the kneeling Arichis, who wears the crown and the princely mantle.

The fortification of Salerno on the sea-coast was doubtless significant of this altered attitude of Benevento towards Constantinople. Hitherto the Lombard had looked upon the sea as his enemy, fearing invasion by the fleets of the Emperor or the Caliph. Now, however, that the Frank was the dominant power in Italy, and that help in resisting his menaces might come from a friendly Byzantium, it was important to have a stronghold upon the sea-coast. For this purpose Arichis fortified with massive walls the city which gives its name to the beautiful bay of Salerno, which at the same time he adorned with stately buildings seen from afar by mariners, and turned into a second capital of his principality.

About the year 778 the Pope found himself confronted by the allied Greeks and Beneventans in his attempt to retain his hold on some part of Campania. "Know" (he says to Charles) "that your and our rivals, the most unutterable Beneventans, are trying to seduce our people in Campania from their allegiance, working to this end in concert with the [Imperial] Patrician of Sicily, who is now residing at Gaeta and to whom they have bound themselves by strong oaths, as well as with the men of Terracina. We have, by means of the bishops, ordered the Campanians to come into our presence or to send five of the principal men of each city to your Excellency. This they refuse to do, though we have sent another urgent message to that effect by Bishop Philip and our nephew Paschalis. We have therefore decided to send our militia thither in order to compel their obedience. We pray you in the presence of the living God to order these most unutterable and God-hated Beneventans to cease from thus tempting our Campanian subjects. We for our part will hold no communication with them, nor will we receive their envoys or have aught to do with the consecration of their bishop, since they have become contrary to St. Peter, to us, and to you".

Hadrian seems, perhaps by means of his *generalis exercitus*, to have recovered possession of Terracina for a short time; but it was soon again wrested from him by 'the most wicked Neapolitans, together with the Greeks hateful to God, Arichis, duke of Benevento, giving them his malignant counsel.' This manner of speaking of the Neapolitans seems to show that Naples, though essentially a Greek city and nominally belonging to the Empire, was beginning to take a somewhat independent position in South Italy, as Venice was doing in the North.

Hadrian implored Charles to send his officer Wulfin speedily to his aid, so as to arrive before the 1st of August. "Let him order all the Tuscans and Spoletans and even the wicked Beneventans who are in your service and ours to come and recover Terracina, and if possible to capture Gaeta and Naples also, recovering our patrimony in that territory". He proceeds to describe a scheme, so clever as to be almost unintelligible, by which he had hoped apparently to get hold of Naples without losing his claim on Terracina :—

"We made a compact with the false Neapolitans last Easter through their envoy Peter, by which we sought to recover the patrimony of St. Peter which is in that city, and at the same time to subdue them to your service. It was agreed that they should give us fifteen hostages of the noblest of their sons, and that we should abandon our claim to Terracina. Then they were to go to their Patrician in Sicily [to obtain his permission to] hand over to us our patrimony, which being done they should recover both the city and their hostages. But we on our part could not give up either the city or the hostages without your sanction, and so we hoped to keep these hostages for your service. All this, however, was hindered by that most unfaithful Arichis, duke of Beneventum, who, continually entertaining the envoys of the most wicked Patrician of Sicily, prevented our receiving the hostages from the aforesaid Neapolitans. For he is daily expecting; to his own perdition, the son of Desiderius the long-ago-not-to-be-mentioned king of the Lombards, that together with him they may attack both us and you. Pray let nothing cool your love to St. Peter. We care nothing for the city of Terracina itself; we only wish that the faithless Beneventans may not in this thing find the desired loophole for escaping from their allegiance to you".

XVIII. As I have before said, it is the misfortune of a history compiled from a one-sided correspondence like the *Codex Carolinus* that it is always describing the beginning of transactions of whose end it is ignorant. We know nothing as to the final settlement of the disputes last recorded, save that it is clear that the Pope's schemes for obtaining a footing in Naples were not successful.

As far as Beneventan affairs are concerned, there is an eventless interval of about seven years (780-786). This lull in the storm is doubtless due to the death of Leo the Khazar (September, 780), the accession of Irene and her son, and the friendly relations which were almost immediately established between the Greek and Frankish courts. Not even on the occasion of Charles's second visit to Rome (Easter, 781) do we hear of any direct communications, friendly or unfriendly, between him and Arichis of Benevento.

The years which intervened between the second and third visits of the Frankish monarch to Rome were some of the most memorable ones in his Thirty Years' War with the Saxons.

In 782, supposing the subjugation of the Saxons to be complete, he convened an assembly at the sources of the Lippe, and there promulgated that stern and rigorous Act of Uniformity which was called *Capitulatio de Partibus Saxoniae*, and which denounced death, not merely on those who were guilty of sacrilege or other obvious crimes such as the murder of a priest; not merely on those who still openly celebrated the old heathen sacrifices; but even on those who only negatively disobeyed the rule of the Catholic Church, for instance by not fasting in Lent or by hiding in order to escape from baptism.

Soon did Charles discover that he had not yet quelled the spirit of Saxon heathenism. Widukind returned from Denmark and preached everywhere revolt against the tyranny of the new lords. At Mount Suntal three Frankish generals were defeated by the Saxons; two of their number, together with four counts and twenty other nobles, were slain, and the Frankish army was almost annihilated. Then came Charles's terrible campaign of revenge, and that atrocious massacre of 4,500 Saxon prisoners by the banks of the Aller, which is in Charles's history what the massacre of Drogheda is in that of Cromwell, the one fatal blot on a career otherwise noble and magnanimous. Before this invading army Widukind fled, and after two more years of Frankish triumph he came in, made his full submission to Charles, and underwent the rite of baptism (785), the Frankish king himself acting as his godfather.

So, for a time, the Saxon storm was laid, but during these later years the relations with Constantinople had been growing steadily worse, the marriage treaty was collapsing, and, as an inevitable consequence, trouble for Charles and the Pope was brewing in Southern Italy.

In 786 (apparently) Hadrian wrote to Charles with a requisition for 1,000 pounds of tin for the roofing of St. Peter's, and informed him that Arichis was trying to wrest Amalfi—that near neighbour of Salerno— from the duchy of Naples and add it to his dominions. The Neapolitans resisted by force of arms, and many Beneventans were slain. Soon, however, Arichis, hearing rumours of an impending visit of Charles to Italy, decided to end this quarrel and to close up the ranks of the dwellers in Campania ere the Frank approached their borders. He made over to the Neapolitans some long-desired lands and revenues in the Terra di Lavoro and the district of Nola, strengthened the fortifications of Benevento and Salerno, and probably re-opened the long-closed negotiations with the Greek Empress and her son.

XIX. The time had evidently come, after more than five years' absence, for another visit of the *Rex Langobardorum* to Italy. Accordingly at the end of autumn (786) he crossed the Alps, and, apparently without visiting his palace at Pavia, journeyed straight to Florence, where he spent his Christmas. He came not now, as on his previous visit, accompanied by wife and children. The much-loved Hildegard was dead, and the proud and difficult-tempered Fastrada had for three years shared his throne. Possibly he was not unwilling to escape from her harsh companionship for some months, while his paternal heart was gladdened by the thought of seeing again the young king Italy, Pippin, now a bright boy in the tenth year of his age.

Early in the year, Charles arrived in Rome, and probably remained there a month or more, but of his entry into the City and his interviews with Hadrian we have nothing recorded. With reference to both his second and third visits we have good reason to complain of the utter silence of the so-called Vita Hadriani in the Liber Pontificalis, which is in fact only a history of two years of that long pontificate. We learn, however, from the annalists that while he was in Rome, Romwald, the eldest son of Arichis, a youth of great intellectual promise, the joy and stay of his parents, appeared in the presence of Charles, offering on his father's behalf great gifts and a promise of perfect obedience to the will of his overlord if only he would refrain from invading the territory of Benevento. The submission seemed sufficient to the Frankish King, but the Pope, ever hostile to the Lombard duchy, counselled war, and the fiery nobles in Charles's train echoed his words. Into the Beneventan territory he accordingly marched, visiting the venerable monastery of Monte Cassino on his way, and by the 22nd of March he had taken up his quarters at Capua. According to one late and doubtful authority a battle followed between Charles and Arichis, but it seems more probable that no battle was fought. Arichis shut himself up in his strong city of Salerno, and looked doubtless over the sea for the hoped-for Grecian galleys. Meanwhile the Frankish host was quartered in the land, and, 'like locusts', were eating up the fruits thereof. The prince of Benevento saw that his case was desperate, and sent another humble message to Charles, offering as before "that he and his people would willingly obey all Charles's commands, that he would pay a yearly tribute of 7,000 solidi, and, as a pledge for his fulfillment of these conditions, he proposed the surrender of thirteen noble Beneventan hostages and two of his children, his younger son Grimwald and his daughter Adelgisa". The last condition, as both poets and annalists agree in telling us, was especially hard to the paternal soul of Arichis. Erchempert tells us that it was included in the conditions that the Beneventans should shave their beards after the manner of the Franks, and that all charters and coins should bear the name of Charles.

Large treasure was at the same time brought by the ambassadors. Charles accepted their terms, being as we are told, especially desirous to spare the churches and monasteries of the land from the ravages of an invading army. Romwald, who had hitherto been kept a prisoner, was released and allowed to return home. Grimwald followed in Charles's train beyond the Alps. Adelgisa, on her father's earnest prayer, was restored to her parents.

It was apparently during Charles's stay in Capua that he received the Imperial ambassadors who came to make the final demand for the hand of the princess Hrotrud, and to whom he gave his final answer, that he would not allow his daughter to be carried away from him into that distant land.

At the end of March he left Capua for Rome, kept his Easter there (April 8, 787), then visited Ravenna (where he was the guest of the Archbishop Gratiosus), spent the early summer in Upper Italy, and, before the middle of July, had crossed the Alps and was back in his own Rhine-traversed city of Worms. So ended this Italian journey. Thirteen years were to pass before he again appeared in Italy to make his fourth, his last and his most famous pilgrimage to Rome.

XX. Soon after these events death laid a heavy hand on the princely house of Benevento. On the 21st of July, 787, died the heir of the house, Romwald, in the 26th year of his age. A month later (August 26, 787) died Arichis himself, after living fifty-three years and reigning thirty. Another son, Gisulf, had apparently died some years before. Only Grimwald remained, and he was a hostage and a captive in the hands of the Frankish king. Now all the efforts of the widowed Adelperga's diplomacy were put forth to obtain the surrender of Grimwald, that he might return and take his place on his father's throne, and all the efforts of Hadrian's diplomacy were put forth to prevent that surrender.

The story is complicated by the fact that Hadrian, ever mindful of the interests of St. Peter, had asked for and apparently obtained from Charles a concession of certain towns in the Beneventan territory. It seems probable that the consent of Arichis to this diminution of his principality had been one of the conditions of the treaty which was the price of Charles's withdrawal from his land. The names of these towns (if we may trust the enumeration of them in the grant which is called the *Ludovicianum*) were Sora, Arce, Aquino, Arpino, Teano and Capua—certainly a goodly addition to the *Ducatus Romae* on its eastern and south-eastern border.

As to Capua, there was clearly a party in that city, headed by a certain presbyter Gregory, which was willing to accept the Papal yoke. In January, 788, Gregory came with nine of his fellow-citizens (who, it Capua, is to be observed, nearly all bore Lombard names) to swear allegiance to St. Peter.

Hadrian evidently had some fear of offending his great patron by accepting the proffered allegiance, but in any case, as he shrewdly remarked, "our doing this will sow dissension among them, and when they are thus divided they will be more easily overcome by our excellent son, for his benefit and St. Peter's". The purport of the oath was "to keep fealty to Peter the Apostle of God, and to the royal power of the Pope and the Frankish King".

After the oath had been administered, Gregory sought a private interview with the Pope, saying, "I have a secret which I must impart to you after swearing that oath". The secret was that immediately after Charles's return from Capua the preceding year, the late prince Arichis had opened disloyal negotiations with Constantinople, praying for the honour of the Patriciate, the addition of Naples to his dominions, and an armed force to protect him from the anger of Charles and to replace his brother-in-law Adelchis on the Lombard throne. In return for these concessions he was willing to become a subject of the Empire, and, as the outward sign of his submission, to adopt the Grecian garb and the Grecian mode of trimming his hair and his beard. On receiving these overtures, the Emperor, according to Gregory, had sent two of the officers of his guard along with the governor of Sicily, bearing gold-enwoven robes, a sword of honour, and a comb and tweezers for the important operation of dressing the converted Lombard's hair. They were at the same time instructed to claim the surrender of Romwald as a hostage for his father's good faith.

All these elaborate negotiations however—for which we have only the word of the intriguing Gregory, and which are probably untrue as far as Arichis is concerned—were snapped in twain by the sudden deaths of Arichis and his son. The Greek ambassadors however—and here we have no reason to doubt the truth of Gregory's statement—had landed at Acropolis in Lucania, had thence journeyed by land to Salerno (January 20, 788), had had an interview with Adelperga and the nobles of Benevento, but had been adjured by them not to bring them into trouble with Charles (whose envoy, Atto, was then in their city) by their presence at Salerno till the much-desired Grimwald was safe at home again. They had therefore betaken themselves to Naples, where they had been received by the Neapolitans with banners and standards—(why should they not, since Naples was still an Imperial city?)—and were there watching their time for the renewal of negotiations with the young Grimwald as soon as he was once more in his father's palace. Adelchis meanwhile was hovering about the Adriatic: 'at Treviso or Ravenna' said one account, 'at Taranto' said another, which added that Adelperga was meditating a pilgrimage, in company with her two daughters, to the shrine of St. Michael on Mount Garganus, doubtless not for the sole purpose of kissing the Archangel's footprints, but in order to creep round to Taranto—only eighty miles distant from Sant' Angelo—and greet her brother on his landing.

Such was the tangled web of truth and error which was laid before Charles in the early months of 788 by the successive letters of the importunate Hadrian. The one piece of advice which he urged with most monotonous pertinacity was, 'Do not let young Grimwald go'; and next to that was the exhortation to move his troops into the south of Italy before the 1st of May, and not to allow the Beneventans to put him off with excuses and perjured promises till the spring season, which was most suitable for warlike operations, should be passed.

Charles however, who had spent so large a part of the year 787 in Italy, was by no means disposed to undertake an expedition thither in 788 in order to soothe the nervous fears of the Pope, or assist him to nibble off some further portions of the Beneventan principality. As for keeping the young prince Grimwald in captivity and so making his father's house desolate, there was something in Charles's nature too magnanimous to accept so mean a policy. Moreover, Paulus Diaconus, who had been the constant companion of his leisure for the last six years, had probably instilled into his mind some of his own love and admiration for Adelperga and her children. And though it was manifest that the Court of Constantinople was making desperate efforts to bring about the restoration of Adelchis and so overthrow the Frankish dominion in Italy, it was by no means clear to the statesmanlike intellect of Charles that the best way of guarding against such an attack was to refuse the reasonable request of the Beneventans for the return of their prince, and so drive them into irreconcilable hostility. He held his hand therefore for the present, and meanwhile despatched two successive embassies to Italy in order to examine the state of affairs in that country and report to him thereon. The first embassy consisted of a deacon, named Atto and Guntram the Keeper of the Gate in the royal palace. The second embassy included Maginarius, abbot of S. Denis, a deacon named Joseph, and Count Liuderic. Maginarius had already been often sent to the Papal Court, and had been especially concerned in the affair of the restoration of the Sabine patrimony. Atto had been before engaged in Beneventan business, and it is perhaps allowable to suppose that he had some leaning towards Adelperga's, as Maginarius had towards Hadrian's side of the controversy. However this may be, it is worthwhile to glance at two letters written by the Pope and one by Maginarius, which relate the somewhat adventurous story of the two embassies, and which shed a valuable light on the political condition of South Italy in the year 788.

The two embassies apparently arrived in Rome at the same time, but Maginarius and Joseph had not yet been joined by their colleague Count Liuderic. The other two envoys, Atto and Guntram, went forward to a little place called Valva, while Maginarius and Joseph, after they had been joined by their belated companion, travelled by way of the river Sangro to the Beneventan territory. There seems to have been some misunderstanding between the two parties as to the rendezvous, and thus it happened that, in spite of Hadrian's earnest entreaties that they would all keep together, the Atto embassy reached Benevento four days before the Maginarius embassy, and after waiting some little time, pushed on to Salerno, where the princess was abiding, and where alone they could discharge their commission. What happened to Maginarius when he in his turn arrived at Benevento shall be told in his own words, as he described it to his royal master:—

"But when we arrived at the Beneventan frontier, we perceived that the inhabitants had no loyal feeling towards your Excellency. We therefore wrote to the other envoys, begging them to wait for us at Benevento, that we might act in concert as the Apostolic Lord [Hadrian] had counselled us, and if we found the men of Benevento loyal, proceed together to Salerno, and if not, consult together what was best to be done. We had been told that they wished to wait for us, and thus take counsel together before proceeding to Salerno. But when we had passed through the ranks of the people disloyal to you (God be contrary to them!) and had arrived at Benevento, hoping there to find our comrades and to consult with them as to the discharge of your commission, we found that one day before our arrival they had departed for Salerno.

"This brought us into great tribulation, both because we had not got our comrades with us, and because the men who were loyal to you told us that if ever we reached Salerno we should be detained there till they knew what was to be done with Grimwald and with their envoys to you. And they assured us that if we could not give them a sufficient guarantee that you would let them have Grimwald for their duke and that you would restore to them those cities of theirs which you had given to St. Peter and the Apostolic Lord, they would not fulfill your orders, but would keep us fast bound as their prisoners. If we could make these promises, however, then they would obey all your orders.

"On receipt of this intelligence, I, Maginarius, pretended to be very sick, so that it was impossible for me to journey to Salerno. Then in order that we might have our colleagues restored to us, I wrote a letter to Adelperga and the other Beneventan nobles to this effect; that I, Maginarius, wished to forward Joseph and Liuderic on their journey to her, but that they entirely refused to go without me. Let them therefore send to us Atto and Guntram, and twelve or fourteen, or as many as they pleased, of the nobles of Benevento. We would then disclose to them the nature of our commission, and discuss as to the best course to be pursued for your advantage and the safety of their land. After I had recovered my health, if it were possible, I would go with them to Salerno, but if not, the other four would all revisit Salerno and there treat of all things with the nobles.

"Adelperga, however, refused to send any of the nobles to us, but Guntram alone was allowed to rejoin us at Benevento. Then when we had learned from your faithful subjects that they were determined to ruin us, we told Guntram all that we had heard of their disloyalty to you, and he told us the same story. And Guntram wished for Atto's sake to return to Salerno; but we said that it was better that one should be detained prisoner than two.

"Having heard much more about the disloyal designs of the Beneventans, and seeing that we could in no wise serve your interests by remaining, we departed at cock-crow without their consent, and by the help of God fought our way through till we reached the territory of Spoleto in safety".

The same story substantially is told by the Pope, with this additional information, that the plan of the ruling party at Salerno had been, if the envoys went thither, to entice them out to some spot by the seaside, and there to have a sham-fight with their neighbours of Amalfi, Sorrento and Naples, in the course of which Charles's envoys might be slain as if accidentally, while no blame for their death would attach to anyone. The story of this plot, like so much else to the discredit of the Beneventans, came from that marvellous story-teller, Gregory of Capua. He was probably also responsible for the statement, admitted to be made only on loose hearsay, that the envoy Atto, when he heard that his colleagues had fled, took refuge at the altar in the church of Salerno. "But the Beneventans", said Hadrian, "persuading him, and as I think dissembling their real intentions, soothed his fears, and hypocritically sent him back to your Excellency, professing themselves your faithful subjects in all things".

On a review of the whole story it seems probable that there was no justification for the fears, in their extreme form, of the nervous and timid Maginarius. There was evidently a strong anti-Frankish party at Benevento and Salerno, and men's minds were in an excited state, so long as it was deemed possible that Charles would abuse the advantage which he possessed in the possession of the person of young Grimwald, to terminate the line of the princes of Benevento. But, guided by the advice of his one brave envoy, Atto, Charles adopted the nobler course. In the spring of 788 Grimwald returned to his native land and was received by his subjects with great joy. It was of course stipulated that he should accept the same position of dependence towards Charles which his father had occupied in the last year of his reign. He swore that deeds should be dated and coins engraved with the name of the Frankish king, and in the important matter of hair-dressing that the Lombards should shave their beards in Frankish fashion, wearing only the moustache.

XXI. Doubtless the dependence of the Beneventan prince on his Frankish overlord was of a somewhat slight and shadowy character. The coins and the deeds did not always bear the name of Charles, nay, in later years there was actual warfare between Grimwald and his young overlord Pippin. But, in the main, the generous policy of the king was proved to be also true statesmanship. Especially was this made manifest in the autumn of 788, when the long-threatened Greek invasion of Italy at last became a reality. The exiled prince Adelchis, with Theodore the administrator of Sicily, and John, treasurer and paymaster of the Imperial army, having landed their troops in Calabria (which still designated the district near Brindisi, the 'heel' and not the 'toe' of Italy), moved westwards and began to ravage the territory of the Beneventans. To meet them, advanced a mingled armament of Lombards and Franks. Hildeprand, duke of Spoleto, and Grimwald of Benevento—loyal to Charles though the invader was own brother of his mother—fought under the generalship of Winichis, who, notwithstanding his Lombard-sounding name seems to have been an officer on the staff of Charles, and at any rate commanded the detachment—not a large one—of Frankish troops. The battle may very likely have been joined somewhere in Horace's country, within sight of the volcanic cone of Monte Vulture. It resulted in the complete defeat of the invaders, a defeat admitted by the Greeks, as it is claimed by the Frankish historians. Four thousand of the Greeks were slain, and one thousand taken prisoners. John the Sacellarius probably fell on the battle-field. It is clear that the Franks alone could not have won this victory, and that the policy of King Charles in dealing tenderly with the great Lombard dukes was abundantly justified by the issue of this campaign.

As for Adelchis, he appears to have escaped from the field of battle and returned to Constantinople, where he probably reached old age in inglorious ease, a well-fed Byzantine patrician. Charles Edward Stuart had played his part and was transformed into the Cardinal of York.

XXII. The return of the young Beneventan prince to his father's palace was regarded with much disfavour by Pope Hadrian. He wrote to Charles, saying, "We beg of your Excellency that no man may be allowed to hinder your own holy desires, and that you will not treat Grimwald, son of Arichis, better than your own patron Peter, the blessed key-bearer of the kingdom of heaven. That Grimwald when he was at Capua in the presence of your envoys congratulated himself thus: Our lord the king has ordered that any one, whether great or small, who wishes to be my man shall without doubt be my man or any one else's whom he may choose'. [That is, there was to be no compulsory allegiance to the Pope, but anyone who pleased might change his service for that of Grimwald.] And, as we have heard, some Greek nobles residing at Naples said with howls of insulting laughter, 'Thank God! all their promises [that is the promises of the Franks] are brought to nought'. For our part we care nothing for their laughs and their mockeries, though the Greeks themselves remarked that the apostolic envoys had now twice returned without effect".

How the question of the Beneventan cities was left is not clear from the Papal correspondence, but it seems doubtful whether Capua at any rate was firmly bound over to the Papal service. In the letter just quoted Hadrian complains that the fair words of Charles as to Populonia and Rosellae and the Beneventan cities are not backed by corresponding deeds on the part of Charles's envoys: "We sent dukes Crescentius and Hadrian together with your envoys into the regions of Benevento to accomplish your royal wishes; but [the latter] would not hand over to [our representatives] anything except bishops' houses, and monasteries, and court-houses, and at the same time the keys of cities without the men, for the men themselves have it in their power to go in and out as they please. And how can we keep the cities without the men, if their inhabitants are allowed to plot against [our rule]? But we want to have freedom to rule and govern these cities in the same way and by the same law as we do the other cities in Tuscany which are comprised in your gift".

Evidently there was a fault in the working of the political machine, for which neither Charles nor Hadrian could be considered altogether responsible. It was admitted that certain large portions of Central Italy were to be held and governed by the Pope—possibly with a certain reservation of supreme rights to the Patrician of the Romans—but the Pope had no army worth notice under his command, no organized system of police, and as his orders were thus destitute of material sanction, his dominions from Ravenna to Capua were constantly on the point of slipping from his hold.

XXIII. In order to continue the story of 'the Samnite Duchy' it may be stated that Grimwald began gradually to disregard the command to date his charters by the years of his lord paramount and to stamp his effigy on his coins, and that his attitude towards the Frankish king became more and more obviously that of a revolted subject. He also obtained in marriage the hand of a 'Greek' princess, named Wantia, said to have been the niece of an Emperor. The marriage indeed did not turn out happily, and eventually his love was turned into such bitter hate that (as the chronicler tells us) 'he made the opposition of the Franks an excuse for sending her in Hebrew fashion a writing of divorcement', and forcibly transporting her to her own home. That quarrel may, however, have happened some years later. Meanwhile the Greek alliance and the signs of impending revolt caused Charles to send one, or perhaps two, hostile expeditions into the Beneventan territory. In 791, we are told, Charles, on his return from a victorious expedition against the Avars, ordered his son Pippin to march into the land of Benevento and lay it waste with fire and sword. In the following year two of the young princes were sent against the rebellious duchy. Louis, then a lad of fourteen, who had been staying with his father at Ratisbon, was ordered to return to his own kingdom of Aquitaine, collect troops, and march over the Mont Cenis into Italy. He accomplished the journey in the autumn, reached Ravenna, spent his Christmas there, and then, with his Aquitanians, joined his brother Pippin. Together they invaded the Samnite duchy, and at least succeeded in ravaging it so thoroughly that their own soldiers were well-nigh reduced to starvation, and had to receive the Church's pardon for eating flesh in Lent, no other victuals being accessible. No victories, however, are placed to the credit of the young invaders, and the campaign was probably an inglorious one, as it is not even mentioned by the official chroniclers.

XXIV. The remaining seven years of Hadrian's pontificate (788-795) have not left any great mark on the *Codex Carolinus*. These were the years of great and victorious campaigns against the Avars (791-795), and of a revival of the long duel with the Saxons, who took the opportunity of Charles's absence in the Danubian lands to attack and to inflict a crushing defeat on the Frankish general Theodoric (793). Their land, in reprisal for this attack, was again laid waste by Charles's armies (794), and they had to submit to the transportation of more than 7,000 men—a third of the whole population—from Bardengau (the old home of the Lombards on the left bank of the Elbe), and to their replacement by colonists of pure Frankish blood (795).

To this period also belong the commencement of one of King Charles's most magnificent undertakings, the digging of a canal in North Bavaria between the Danube and the Rhine (793), and the assembling of a general council of bishops from all parts of Charles's dominions, held at Frankfurt-on-the-Main (794). At this council Charles presided like another Constantine, the heresy of the Adoptionists was condemned, and the declaration against image-worship was promulgated in defiance of the decrees of the Second Nicene Council.

As to the domestic relations of the great king during the interval before us, the one most conspicuous and most sorrowful event was the conspiracy of his eldest son Pippin the Hunchback, the offspring of his marriage with Himiltrud. This conspiracy, which was hatched during Charles's absence in Bavaria, in connection with his Avar campaigns, was partly caused by the cruelty and arrogance of queen Fastrada, but was joined by many noble Franks, both old and young, and aimed we are told at nothing less than the murder of Charles himself and all his sons by Hildegard, that Pippin might be his unquestioned heir. It was discovered through the information given by a Lombard named Fardulf, faithful now to Charles, as he had been to his former sovereigns Desiderius and Adelchis. On its detection the chief offenders were put to death, all save the Hunchback himself, who received the tonsure and passed the remaining nineteen years of his life (792-811) in monastic seclusion at Prum, in the Moselle country. Three years afterwards (795) Fastrada died, little regretted by the subjects of her husband.

As has been said, few important letters passed between the Pope and King during this last period of seven years. We find with interest and some surprise that Hadrian has to reassure himself with the text "If God be for us who can be against us?" on hearing of an alleged scheme of our own countryman, Offa, king of Mercia, to thrust him down from the papacy and elect another in his stead. Offa's own relations with Charles were generally but not uniformly amicable. Here too the breakdown of a marriage treaty produced a temporary rupture between the two courts. Offa's daughter was sought in marriage for the young Charles, but when he proposed to enlarge the treaty so as to obtain the hand of Charles's daughter Bertha for his son, the Frankish king, indignant and always averse to his daughter's leaving him for any husband, broke off the negotiations, and for a time put an embargo on all the English merchant-ships. But the dispute was ere long settled, probably by the mediation of Alcuin, Offa's subject and Charles's friend.

In a letter written about the year 791 the Pope exhorts Charles not to listen to any complaints made against his administration by the men of Ravenna and the Pentapolis, and insists that, even as he does not receive any of Charles's 'men' coming without their lord's licence to the thresholds of the Apostles, so Charles shall not give admittance to any of the Pope's 'men' who seek audience at his court unless they bring the Pope's licence and letters dismissory. In the same letter he uses the following remarkable words:

"We pray your Excellency not to allow any change to be made in that whole burnt-offering which your sainted father offered and you confirmed to St. Peter. But even as you assert that the honour of your patriciate has been irrefragably guarded and ever more and more increased by us, similarly may the patriciate of your patron St. Peter, granted in writing in its fullness by lord Pippin and more amply confirmed by you, remain ever his by irrefragable right".

This expression 'the patriciate of St. Peter' has been much commented on by scholars, and has been thought by some to express in juristic terms the relation of the Pope to that part of Italy which was under his sway. It is perhaps safer, however, to look upon it as a mere rhetorical phrase employed by the Pope to urge his suit with Charles. "You are Patrician, and I have ever honoured you as such; but I too, as representing St. Peter, and the rights which you have conferred upon him, may claim to be in a certain sense a Patrician, and I claim that you shall respect those rights as I respect yours".

At length the long pontificate of Hadrian came to an end. He died on Christmas Day, 795, and was buried in St. Peter's on the day following. Charles, who was on the point of despatching for his acceptance certain rich presents, part of the vast treasure taken from the Ring or circular city of the Avars, had now to send them to his successor, Leo III, who was elected on the very day of Hadrian's funeral and enthroned on the day following (December 27, 795).

As we have seen, the relations between the Frankish King and the Roman Pope had not been uniformly of a friendly character, but we are assured by Einhard, Charles's friend and biographer, that when he heard of Hadrian's death he wept for him, as if he had been a brother or the dearest of his sons.

CHAPTER THREE

TASSILO OF BAVARIA.

In order not to interrupt the current of Italian, and especially of Papal history, I have postponed to the present chapter all mention of one of the most important of Charles's enterprises, and one too which very closely concerned the fallen Lombard dynasty. I allude to his long duel with his rebellious vassal, Tassilo, duke of Bavaria.

In a previous chapter we have glanced at the history of the Agilolfings, the ducal house of Bavaria, during the seventh and eighth centuries. We have seen them drawing into closer and closer ecclesiastical connection with Rome, but at the same time we have seen their political connection with the Frankish monarchy growing weaker and weaker, and in spite of Charles Martel's intervention in their affairs, in spite of his marrying the daughter of one duke and Tasilo's refusal to follow Pippin into Aquitaine giving his own daughter in marriage to another, we have seen the position of the great lord who reigned at Ratisbon approximating more and more nearly to absolute independence. This tendency towards independence manifested itself in the most audacious manner when, in 763, the young duke Tassilo flatly refused any longer to follow the standards of his uncle and overlord Pippin in his campaign against Waifar of Aquitaine. With the Teutonic ideas as to the obligation of military service, and especially as to the duty of the 'companion' to follow his lord to battle, and if need were to die in his defence in the thickest of the war-storm, this was to commit an almost unforgivable offence, the grievous crime of *harisliz*. Politically too such a desertion was of evil omen for the future unity of the widespread Frankish realm. Thereby the young duke of the Bavarians seemed to say, "What is it to me whether the men of Aquitaine obey the rule of my Australian uncle at his palace in Champagne, or whether they set up for themselves as an independent kingdom? Perhaps they will do well if they can accomplish this. We too, I and my Bavarians, are not too deeply enamoured of the rule of these domineering Franks".

But however insolent was the defiance thus thrown in the face of Pippin, that monarch, now waxing old and infirm, was too closely occupied by the long war with Aquitaine to have leisure to accept the challenge of Tassilo. At his death in 768, Bavaria under its Agilolfing duke must be considered as having been practically independent. Tassilo was probably already at that date married to Liutperga, daughter of Desiderius.

Then came the good queen Bertrada's journey to Ratisbon and to Pavia (770), the marriage-treaty which she concluded for her son with the delicate daughter of Desiderius, the short-lived league of friendship between Frank, Lombard and Bavarian. It seems that, as far as Charles and Tassilo were concerned, the way had been prepared for this reconciliation by Sturmi, abbot of Fulda, successor of the great Boniface. Intent on his great work of the Christianization of the Saxons, he desired that the energies of the Frankish king by whom that work had to be accomplished should not be frittered away on needless wars in the south of Germany. Himself a Bavarian by birth, he undertook a mission from Charles to his native prince, and was 769 (?) so successful in his diplomacy that he established a peace between the two cousins which lasted for many years, and which apparently was not shaken by the repudiation of Desiderata, perhaps not even by the overthrow and exile of Desiderius. One evidence of the long continuance of this friendship is furnished by the fact that in 778 he sent a detachment of soldiers to serve under Charles in that Spanish campaign which ended in the disaster of Roncesvalles.

But during all this time Tassilo was assuming the style of an independent sovereign. He summoned synods, over which he presided; he left out the name of Charles and inserted his own in public documents; he even ventured to speak in them of "the year of my kingship". Through the whole of this period Bavaria seems to have been prospering under his wise and statesmanlike rule. In the East he subdued and converted to Christianity the rough Sclovenes of Carinthia; in the South he recovered, probably by friendly arrangement with Desiderius, the places in the valley of the Adige which had been taken from his ancestors by Liutprand. As a reward for his acknowledged services to Christianity, Tassilo's son Theodo (whom he made the partner of his throne in 777) was in 770 baptized at Rome by Hadrian.

On all this increase of reputation and territory, however, Charles was not likely to look with favouring eye, so long as he must entertain the painful thought that this fair Danubian land, which had owned the sovereignty of the weakest Merovings, was daily slipping from his grasp. On his second visit to Rome (781) he appears to have discussed Bavarian affairs with his Papal host, and the result of their conversation was the despatch of a joint embassy to Tassilo (two bishops sent by the Pope, a deacon and grand butler by the king), to remind Duke Tassilo of the oaths which he had sworn long ago, and to warn him not to act otherwise than as he had sworn to the lords Pippin and Charles. And when these ambassadors in pursuance of their instructions had spoken with the aforesaid duke, so greatly was his heart softened, that he declared his willingness at once to proceed to the presence of the king' (who had by this time returned to Frankland), if such hostages could be given as would leave him no doubt of his safety. On receipt of these hostages he went promptly to the king at Worms, swore the prescribed oath, and gave the twelve hostages who were required at his hands for the fulfillment of his promises, and whom Sindbert, bishop of Ratisbon, brought into the king's presence. But the said duke returning to his home did not long remain in the faith which he had sworn.

The hollow truce thus concluded lasted for six years, A hollow till Charles's third visit to Rome. By this time, 781-787, he had, as he thought, thoroughly subdued the Saxons. Widukind had been baptized, and for the time there was peace in North Germany. In Italy, too, Arichis of Benevento had without bloodshed been brought to his knees, nor had his brother-in-law of Bavaria apparently stretched out a hand to help him. Yet Tassilo seems to have known that his position was insecure; he sent accordingly two envoys, Arno, bishop of Salzburg, and Hunric, abbot of Mond See, to beg the Pope to reconcile him with King Charles.

The Pope seems to have honestly done his best to bring about the desired reconciliation earnestly besought Charles to renew friendly relations with his cousin of Bavaria. "The very thing that I desire", answered Charles: "I have been long seeking for the re-establishment of peace between us, but have not been able to accomplish it". The envoys were called in, but when the Pope proceeded to examine them as to the conditions which Tassilo was willing to accept, it appeared that they were in no sense plenipotentiaries, and had no other commission than simply to hear and carry back to their master the words of the king and pontiff. At this Pope Hadrian, not without cause, lost his temper. "Unstable and mendacious, false and fraudulent" were the words which burst from his lips: and he proceeded to pronounce the anathema of the Church on Tassilo and all his followers unless he fulfilled to the letter the promise of obedience which he had sworn to Pippin and his son. "Warn Tassilo", said he to the envoys, "that he prevent effusion of blood and the ravage of his land by manifesting entire obedience to his lord King Charles and his sons. If otherwise, if with hardened heart he refuse to obey my apostolic words, then King Charles and his army will be absolved from all peril of punishment for sin, and whatever shall happen in that land, burning or homicide or any other evil that may light on Tassilo and his partisans, lord Charles and his Franks will remain thereafter innocent of all blame".

The annalist then describes King Charles's return to his own land, his meeting with his queen Fastrada, and his convocation of a synod in Worms (July, 787), before which he declared all that had recently been done in the matter of the Bavarian duke. Once more an embassy was sent to remind Tassilo of the obligations of his oath and to summon him to the presence of his lord. On his refusal to obey the summons Charles prepared for the invasion of Bavaria, and according to his favourite system of strategy, divided Charles his army into three parts. He himself entered the Bavaria, country from the west by way of the river Lech and the city of Augsburg. The united forces of the Austrasian Franks, the Thuringians and the Saxons (for Charles already ventured to employ Saxons in his army) entered from the north-west, by way of Ingolstadt. The boy-king Pippin with his Italian forces came by way of the duchy of Trient and advanced as far as Botzen. Tassilo, seeing himself Tassilo surrounded on all sides and conscious that many of his own nobles wavered in their fidelity (preferring doubtless the distant Frankish overlord to the near Agilolfing duke), threw up the game, came into the presence of Charles, confessed that he had sinned grievously against him, resigned into his hands the ducal dignity which he had received from Pippin and received it back again on confessed terms of vassalage. He again swore the oaths of fealty and gave thirteen hostages, his son Theodo being one of them, for the faithful performance of his promises. Satisfied herewith, King Charles returned to his palace at Ingelheim on the Rhine and there celebrated Christmas and Easter.

The accord between the two cousins, the lord and the vassal, was of short duration. It was again proved that

'Never can true reconcilement grow
Where wounds of deadly hate have pierced so deep'

The early part of 788 was an anxious time for the Frankish king. War both with the Greeks and the Avars was evidently impending, and this was the time moreover when Hadrian was plying him with perpetual insinuations as to the hostile designs of Adelperga and her Beneventans and beseeching him not to surrender his hostage Grimwald. Tassilo it is true was humbled, but was not his very humiliation dangerous? Was he likely ever to forget that he came of an older and nobler line than that cousin who claimed him as his vassal; that his ancestors were dukes and all but kings of Bavaria, when the ancestors of Charles were but head-servants in Austrasia? And there were not only his own wrongs, but his wife's also, rankling in his mind. Liutperga's father had been dethroned and shut up in a monastery, her mother and sister had been forced to take the veil, her brother was wandering in hopeless exile; all these injuries cried aloud for vengeance, and smarting under their bitter memory she was—so men believed—even now urging on her husband to dangerous and treacherous designs.

Charles determined to deal first with the suspected rebel at home ere he struck at the enemy abroad. He called a general assembly of all his subjects, Franks and Bavarians, Lombards and Saxons, to meet him at Ingelheim. Tassilo was summoned and did not dare to disobey the call. Sundry of his own Bavarian subjects appeared to bear witness against him. They accused him (1) of having opened treasonable communications with the Avars, (2) of having summoned to his court men who had 'commended' themselves as vassals to King Charles and then laid snares for their lives, (3) of having ordered his men when they swore [oaths of fealty to Charles] to practise 'mental reservation' and swear deceitfully, (4) of having said (doubtless with reference to the fact that his son Theodo was hostage for his fidelity), "If I had ten sons, I would lose them all rather than stand by my sworn compact with the king. It is better for me to die than to live on these terms". To none of these accusations, we are told, was Tassilo able to offer a denial, and in truth the gravest of them all, the accusation of treasonable correspondence with the Avars, was confirmed by an expedition of that barbarous people against Friuli and Bavaria, only a few months later. Pondering these charges, and taking account also of the old and never-atoned-for crime of *harisliz* against King Pippin in 763, the assembled nations judged the Bavarian duke guilty of death. Charles however, "for the love of God and because he was and kinsman", commuted the sentence to deposition from his ducal rank and confinement in a monastery.

Tassilo bowed to the inevitable doom: he is even represented by the chronicler as entreating permission to enter a convent that he might there repent of his many sins. This, however, is doubtless the invention of the courtly historian. A more natural and more probable turn is given to the narrative by another annalist who tells us that "with many prayers he besought the king that he might not be shorn of his locks then and there in the palace, but might be spared the shame and humiliation of having this thing done to him in sight of all the Franks". The king hearkened to his prayers, and he was sent to the place where the body of St. Goar reposes on the banks of the Rhine. There he was made a 'cleric', and after that he was banished to the monastery of Jumieges. His two sons, Theodo and Theotbert, his two daughters, and his wife, the Lombard Liutperga, were all sentenced to the same religious seclusion. Charles was averse, for the most part, to the shedding of blood, but he highly valued, for his enemies, the opportunities for meditation and prayer afforded by the monotonous stillness of the cloister. At the same time some persistently loyal adherents of Tassilo were banished the realm.

Six years after these events the monk Tassilo was once more brought out into the light of day and obliged to face his victorious kinsman. At the synod of Frankfurt "appeared that Tassilo who aforetime was duke of Bavaria, to pray for pardon for all the faults which he had committed whether in the time of King Pippin or King Charles, at the same time with pure mind laying aside all wrath and bitterness of spirit for the punishment which had been inflicted upon him. As to his claims to property in Bavaria which had belonged to him or to any of his children, he utterly renounced them all, and declared that no demand in respect of them should ever be made in future. And he commended his sons and daughters to the compassion of the king. Upon this the king, moved with pity, freely forgave the aforesaid Tassilo for all the faults that he had committed against him, and promised him that he should live thenceforward in his favour and on his alms"; but did not apparently let him out of the monastery. He had probably been brought forth from its seclusion only in order to cure some technical defect in the former acts of deposition and confiscation. Herewith the once magnificent Tassilo vanishes out of history, even the year of his death being unknown: and with him ends the great Agilolfing line which for two centuries had seen its fortunes so closely interwoven with those of the Lombard kings of Italy.

CHAPTER FOUR

TWO COURTS : CONSTANTINOPLE AND AACHEN.

I
Constantinople.

THE Imperial palace at Constantinople at the period of which we are treating was a building already more than two centuries old, the *Chrysotriklinion* or Golden Hall reared by Justin II in 570. Its garden front looked south-eastward to the near waters of the Bosphorus. North-westward it looked towards the building which was still called the roman Senate-house, to the great Imperial forum known as the *Augusteum*, peopled with statues, and over that to the Hippodrome, where the charioteers of the Blue and the Green factions engaged in their maddening rivalry.

It was a building already haunted by some gloomy memories. From hence, if the popular legend were true, the Empress Sophia had sent the fatal distaff to Narses. Hither came Heraclius to die, heart-broken by the Mohammedan conquest of Jerusalem, and here probably his widow Martina suffered the barbarous mutilation which was the punishment of her audacity in aspiring 'to reign over the Romans.' From this palace Constans was driven forth to his Cain-like wanderings over the world by the spectre of his murdered brother; and here Justinian II, last scion of the race of Heraclius, spent the strange seventeen years of his mad misgovernment. In this palace reigned, as we have seen, in the year 790, a woman and a young man—Irene, widow of Leo the Khazar, Irene, and her son Constantine VI Irene was a woman in middle life, and Constantine was a youth of twenty.

She was keen-witted, fond of power, with something perhaps of the old Athenian brilliancy, and certainly, as has been already said, with the old Athenian tendency to be 'wholly given to idolatry'. But as her image-loving propensities fell in with that which was finally the prevailing fashion in the Orthodox Church, the atrocious crimes which she committed were glossed over by the scribes of the convent, and they have even dared to speak of her to posterity as 'the most pious', 'the God-guided', 'the strong-souled and God-beloved Irene'.

It is a sore temptation to an ambitious woman to find herself in command of the great machinery of a despotic government, with only a boy, and that boy her own son, for her future rival. The formation of that son's character lies almost entirely in her own hands, and without forming at first any deliberate schemes of wickedness, it is easy for the mother to foster the boy's natural disposition to indolence or pleasure, or extravagance, and thus to destroy his chances of ever successfully competing with her for power. The instances of Catherine de' Medici and Catherine of Russia will at once occur to the reader's mind; but Irene was prepared for the sake of power to wade far deeper into crime than either of the Catherines.

In the year 790 the long-repressed discontent of the young Emperor with his present position began to display itself. Over and above his disappointment at being commanded to marry the Armenian Maria instead of the Frankish Hrotrud, there was the daily annoyance of perceiving that while his presence-chamber was almost deserted, crowds of suppliants thronged the halls of Stauracius the logothete, the confidential adviser of his mother. Constantine was now twenty years old, and there were not wanting men of eminence in the state (among them his tutor was chief captain of the guards, Peter the commander-in-chief, and two patricians, Theodore and Damian) to urge him to assert his rightful position, banish Irene to Sicily, and reign as sole Emperor. But on the 9th of February (790) it happened that the city was shaken by a great earthquake, which so alarmed the inhabitants that they all went and lodged in tents in the fields outside the city. Irene and her son took up their quarters in the precincts of the church of St. Mamas, north of the city wall and looking across the Golden Horn towards the Valley of Sweet Waters. Apparently this change in the arrangements of the imperial party led to the discovery of the plot.

The coarse energy of Stauracius successfully asserted itself against the high-born conspirators. The nobles were flogged, tonsured, and shut up in their own palaces, and the tutor was banished to Sicily. Constantine himself, the young man of twenty, was beaten and scolded by his mother like a naughty child, and forbidden for many days to show himself in public.

In order to guard against any similar attempts in future, Irene caused an oath to be administered to all the regiments in the capital and its neighbourhood: "So long as thou livest we will not suffer thy son to reign, and we will always put thy name before his". But by this monstrous demand she prepared her own downfall. When the imperial messengers presented themselves to administer the new oath to the soldiers in the Armeniac 'theme', those men, mindful of many a victorious battle fought under the leadership of the father and grandfather of Constantine, flatly refused thus to disinherit the lawful heir for the benefit of the Athenian woman. Irene sent a certain Alexius, colonel of the palace-guards, to quell the mutiny, but the Armeniacs, shutting up their own general, gave the command to Alexius, and with jubilant shouts proclaimed Constantine sole Emperor. When the news of this *pronunciamento* reached Constantinople, all the other regiments, little hampered by their oaths, followed the example of the Armeniacs. On the 14th of October the legions were collected together in a place called Atroa, and insisted on Constantine coming forth to meet them. Irene did not dare to refuse their request. He came, and was unanimously acclaimed sole Emperor. Irene was allowed to retire to a palace of her own building, in which she had stored the greater part of her wealth. Stauracius suffered the usual fate of unsuccessful politicians at Constantinople, being flogged, tonsured, and sent into exile in Armenia. At the same time Michael Lachanodrakon, a war-famed veteran of the old Isaurian time, was made commander of the household troops.

In the following year Constantine engaged in two somewhat unsuccessful expeditions against Cardam, king of the Bulgarians, and against the generals of the Caliph Haroun-al-Raschid in Cilicia. His absence from the capital, perhaps also his obvious inefficiency in war, encouraged the party of Irene once more to raise their heads, and in January of 792 the feeble young Emperor found, or imagined, himself compelled once more to associate his mother with himself in the government of the empire, and to receive again with her the acclamations of the multitude, 'Long life to Constantine and Irene'. With Irene came back Stauracius to help her in playing a slow, patient game for her son's ruin.

In July, 792, the young Emperor, yearning to emulate the great deeds of his ancestors and misled by the vain prediction of a certain 'false prophet and astronomer' named Pancratius, attacked Cardam in a strong position which he held with some of the bravest of his troops. The attack failed disastrously, and Constantine had to fly headlong, leaving his tents, his horses, and his royal furniture in the hands of the Bulgarians, and many of his best officers (including the brave old Lachanodrakon) dead on the field of battle. That the futile astronomer Pancratius shared the fate of the brave men whom he had lured to their ruin was the least part of the disaster.

The ignominious end of the Bulgarian campaign made a great rent in the popularity of Constantine. Still worse for his fame was the severity with which he repressed an attempt to place his uncle Nicephorus, son of Constantine Copronymus, on the throne. Nicephorus was blinded, and his four brothers, two of whom had borne the title of Caesar, suffered the cruel Byzantine punishment of amputation of the tongue.

If there was one man more than another to whom Constantine owed his attainment of imperial power it was Alexius, who at a critical moment had headed the troops in the Armeniac theme when they acclaimed Constantine sole Imperator. Now, listening to the evil surmisings of Irene and Stauracius, who suggested that Alexius was aiming at the diadem, he refused to accede to the demand of the Armeniac soldiers that their beloved commander, then detained in honourable captivity at Constantinople, should be restored to them; and on the repetition of the demand with shrill urgency, he ordered Alexius to be blinded. At the news of this infamous act of ingratitude, which showed too plainly that all the supporters of the son would be sacrificed to the vengeance of the mother, the Armeniac soldiers rose in rebellion. From November, 792, till the 27th of May, 793, there was civil war in the Armeniac theme, and it was only by mustering all his forces, and at last by employing the base services of traitors, that eventually, on the date just mentioned, Constantine prevailed over his old allies. The chief officers and an iconoclastic bishop who had headed the revolt were put to death. The other leaders were severely punished with fines and proscriptions; and as for the rank and file, one thousand of them were brought chained into the city of Constantinople through the gate of Blachernae, and led ignominiously through the streets, bearing on each of their foreheads the words, tattooed in ink, 'Armeniac Conspirator'. Such were the rewards which the weak youth at his cruel mother's instigation conferred on his old supporters.

Grievously indeed, in the three years since he grasped the reins of power, had Constantine declined in the favour of his subjects, and he now proceeded to an act which brought him into hostility, not merely with the Church, but with all that was best and healthiest in the lay world of Constantinople. He had always disliked his wife Maria, and now 'by the advice of his mother, who in her longing for power wished that he should be condemned by all', he constrained that wife to enter a convent, and in August, 795, crowned as Augusta his paramour Theodote, one of the ladies-in-waiting on Irene. The next step, after the coronation and the avowed cohabitation, was to obtain the sanction of the Church to the marriage, and this, even with the submissive Church of Constantinople, was not an easy matter. The patriarch Tarasius refused to perform the ceremony, but consented at last to stand aside and allow another ecclesiastic, the abbot Joseph, to officiate in his stead. In September, 795, Constantine and Theodote were solemnly married in the palace of St. Mamas.

The Church of the Middle Ages, whether in Eastern or Western Europe, never seems more worthy of our respect than when she is upholding the rights of an injured wife and refusing to allow powerful princes to treat the sacred laws of marriage as of no account for persons in their high position. The part which Innocent III played as champion of Ingeberga, the repudiated wife of Philip Augustus, was taken in the case of the divorced Maria by Plato and Theodore, an uncle and nephew, heads of the renowned monastery of Saccudia on the flanks of the Bithynian Olympus. On Theodore, as the younger man, fell the brunt of the battle, but Plato also felt the heavy hand of the imperial bigamist, for announcing to Tarasius that he could no longer hold communion with him on account of his connivance at an adulterous union. It is true that Constantine and his new Empress—herself a cousin of Theodore's—resorted to almost abject entreaties in order to disarm Plato's just indignation but when these proved fruitless the imperial thunderbolt fell on the inmates and the neighbours of the Bithynian convent. Plato was brought to Constantinople and shut up in a narrow cell in the precincts of the palace, while Theodore, his brothers, and the other monks were sent under an imperial escort into exile at Thessalonica. In a long and interesting letter to his uncle, Theodore: describes the incidents of this journey. The letter does not give one the impression of any great hardships endured or severity displayed, but what it does show us is that in every town there was a large number of persons who sympathized with the monkish martyr and were indignant at his punishment. Assuredly some rivets in the ship of the state were loosened by the imprisonment of Plato and the exile of Theodore Studita.

In the embittered and unnatural relations which now existed between Irene and her son, even the events which should have consolidated the dynasty hastened its downfall. In October (796) the young Emperor, while taking the warm baths at Broussa, heard the joyful news that his wife, who remained at Constantinople, had borne him a son. He hastened off to the palace eager to welcome the longed-for heir, to whom he gave the name of his father, Leo. Meanwhile Irene, who had gone with him to Broussa, began to tamper with the allegiance of the soldiers, and by all sorts of gifts and promises to form a party among the officers, pledged to destroy her son and make her sole Empress. In March (797), Constantine, who had returned to Bithynia, set forth with a body of picked campaign, light-armed soldiers, amounting to 20,000 men, to fight the Saracens. The expedition ought to have achieved a great success, but the old intriguer Stauracius, knowing that victory would make Constantine's position impregnable, bribed the imperial scouts to bring in a lying report that the Saracens had fled and were nowhere to be seen. The easily-fooled Emperor returned home again inglorious, and deep discontent doubtless pervaded the whole army at such a display of military inefficiency on the part of the grandson of the great Copronymus.

On the 1st of May the child Leo died, and was bewailed by his tender-hearted father with floods of tears. On the 17th of June, after a great chariot-race in the Hippodrome, the Emperor sought the shade and sea-breezes of the shore below St. Mamas. On the road an attempt, an unsuccessful attempt, was made by the conspirators to seize him, but being warned in time he embarked hastily in the imperial gondola and escaped to the opposite shore of the sea of Marmora, intending to flee to the Anatolic theme, where the descendant of the great Isaurians was sure to find a welcome and a shelter. But the very companions of his flight, though he knew it not, were traitors. The people began to rally round their fugitive sovereign. Irene, who felt that it was now a fight to the death between her and her son, became alarmed. She feigned a desire for reconciliation, sent mediators, sent bishops to beg for a guarantee of her own personal safety, and offered, if that were given, to retire into a corner of the palace and spend the rest of her days in obscurity. Meanwhile, however, she was writing to her fellow-conspirators, "If you do not find some means to hand him over to me at once, I shall reveal to the Emperor all that has passed between you and me". Alarmed, the conspirators arrested Constantine early on the 15th of August, the festival of the

Assumption of the Virgin, hurried him on board the imperial boat, and carried him across to Constantinople. There he was imprisoned in the same Purple Chamber of the palace in which, twenty-seven years before, his birth-cry had been heard by the woman who was now consenting to his death. With brutal violence the conspirators plucked out his eyes, desiring that he should perish under the ghastly operation. He did not however die, but lingered on for at least twenty-three years but so broken and miserable in his blindness that in all the many palace-revolutions of the time no one thought of restoring to the throne 'the last male descendant of Leo the Isaurian'.

So terrible a deed as this, the worse than murder of a son by the order of his own mother, shocked even, the courtiers and ecclesiastics of Constantinople, inured as they were to tidings of barbarities from the imperial palace. On the one hand, men noted, that as it was at the ninth hour (3 P.M. on Saturday the 15th of August) that Constantine VI was blinded and all but slain, so it had been on the ninth hour on the same day of the week in September, live years before, that his uncle Nicephorus had been blinded and his four other uncles mutilated by the order of the young Emperor. But again, after this deed of wickedness was done, "the sun", says Theophanes, "was darkened for seventeen days, and did not give forth his rays, so that ships wandered about and drifted hither and thither, and all men said and confessed that on account of the blinding of the Emperor the sun withheld his beams. And thus did Irene his mother acquire the sovereignty".

She was indeed "cursed with the burden of a granted prayer", this devout Medea, who had had no pity for the fruit of her body, when maternal love was weighed in the balance against the lust of empire and found wanting. The history of her short reign is only a record of disastrous defeats and provinces ravaged by the Saracens, of attempts cruelly suppressed to set one or other of the mutilated sons of Copronymus on the throne, of bickerings between Irene's eunuch-ministers, Stauracius and Aetius, each of whom, watching with hungry eyes the failing health of his imperial mistress, was scheming to secure the splendid prize of the diadem for some relation of his own.

On Easter Monday, 799, the Empress made a solemn procession through the streets of Constantinople, starting from the great Church of the Holy Apostles, where all the Emperors and Patriarchs who had ruled the State and Church for near five centuries lay entombed. Irene sat aloft on a golden car, drawn by four milk-white steeds; and four patricians, groomlike, walked by the side of the horses. Imitating the custom of the old Roman consuls, she scattered money among the crowd as she moved along, and doubtless their venal throats became hoarse with cries of 'Many years to the new Helena! Long life to the August Irene!'. But under all this show of devotion there was evidently a feeling that a new and a monstrous thing had happened in 'the Empire of the World'. It was not merely that the pious idolater had stained herself, Athaliah-like, with the blood of her own offspring. It was that no woman, however virtuous or however beloved, had a right to sit alone on the throne of the Caesars. It was true that Pulcheria, that manly-minded woman, had been hailed as Augusta on the death of the brother whose counsels she had guided, but that was with the implied condition that she should make Marcian the partner of her throne. True that Theodora and Sophia had at the request of their doting husbands received from the Senate the same splendid title, but that was only as consorts of the reigning Emperor, nor had the influence of either Theodora or Sophia been obviously beneficial to the Empire. But the latest and the most striking instance of the foiled attempt of a woman to occupy the imperial throne was the case of Martina, widow of Heraclius, to whom, when she stood forth in the Hippodrome claiming to rule along with her son and step-son, the populace shouted, "O Lady, how can you receive the ambassadors of the barbarians or exchange words with them when they come to the imperial palace? God preserve the polity of the Romans from ever coming into such a condition as that."

The fact was, that there was ever a lingering consciousness that the Roman Imperator had come to his power in a different way and was altogether a different kind of ruler from the despotic kings and queens of the East. True, those Oriental monarchies might have had their Semiramis or their Dido, their Tomyris or their Queen of Sheba; but these were no precedents for the Roman State, which was still in theory a republic, and whose head was in theory—however absurdly different might be the customary fact—a brave general who, having won a victory over the enemies of Rome, was saluted by his enthusiastic soldiers with the title Imperator.

Thus the outcome of the whole matter was that at the close of the eighth century there was a generally diffused feeling that a wonderful and a horrible thing had been done in the polity of the Romans, and that the woman who called herself Augusta and rode in her golden chariot through the streets of Constantinople had no right to the name or the magnificence of the Emperors of Rome.

II.
Aachen.

We now turn from the Bosphorus to the Rhine; from the dull splendour of the Byzantine palace to the fresh if somewhat rude magnificence of the Frankish *villa*; from that Fury-haunted abode where a widowed mother plotted the ruin of her only son, to the joyous cavalcade of Charles and his daughters, as they rode with mirth and song from palace to palace of the beautiful Rhine-land.

The list of Charles's resting-places after his campaigns were ended, shows us in the clearest manner where his heart was fixed. He had inherited sovereignty over the country which we now call France, but apparently he only once visited Paris He completed the conquest of Aquitaine, but he spent only one Easter in that region. He made himself master of Italy, yet only thrice after his conquest did he visit Rome, and then half-reluctantly, on the urgent invitation of the Pope to settle the troubled affairs of the peninsula or to take part in some great religious ceremony. He had been born a Ripuarian Frank, and Ripuarian he remained to the end of his days, never happy when far away from the banks of the great German river by whose shores rose three of his great palaces, at Worms, at Ingelheim, and at Nimwegen, and which was lined with the stately Romanesque churches that told of his pious munificence. It was not actually by the banks of the Rhine, but in its neighbourhood, between it and the sister stream, the Meuse, that Charles built the last, perhaps the stateliest of his palaces, certainly the one which was longest connected with the memory of his greatness. Unmentioned in the literature and even in the road-books of the Romans, but certainly known to some of the Roman officers, the warm sulphur-springs of Aquae Grani bubbled out of the hills overlooking the Meuse, forty miles south-west of that city on the Rhine which was emphatically called Colonia. The earliest name of the town which grew up around these springs was derived from a surname of Apollo which was widely known in the north of Europe, though here again the classical authors are silent concerning it. This is the place which the Germans call Aachen, and the French, from the memory of Charles's great Christian temple, call Aix-la-Chapelle.

It was in 788, just after the Byzantine invasion of Italy, that Charles kept his first Christmas at Aachen, and from this time onwards it begins to dispute with Heristal in Brabant and Worms on the Rhine the honour of being his favourite place of abode. From 795 the end of his life it held the undisputed preeminence, thirteen out of his twenty remaining Easters and fourteen Christmases being spent beside the healing waters of Grannus. For the great attraction of the place, though it has a fresh and salubrious air, lay in those thermal waters heated by Nature to a temperature varying from 82° to 99° (Fahrenheit), and richly laden with salt, sulphur and carbonic acid. At the time when Charles began to pay more frequent visits to Aquae Grani he was entering the sixth decade of his life, and was probably beginning to feel those rheumatic or gouty pains which so often hang about the vestibule of old age, and which saline or sulphurous waters generally alleviate. One of the poets of his court describes the occupation of the labourers employed in searching for new hot springs, surrounding them with walls, and fixing magnificent seats on the marble steps. Charles himself, who was a strong and swift swimmer, would often invite, not only his sons but his friends and ministers of state, sometimes even his men-servants and body-guards, to accompany him to the bath, so that there would often be a hundred men or more swimming about together in the wide, warm pools of Grannus.

Thus then it came to pass that a Westphalian watering-place became the favourite residence of the Frankish king, and afterwards the second city of his empire. The minster of Aachen was the regular crowning-place of the Western Emperors for seven centuries, and in it thirty-seven kings and ten queens received the sacred diadem. In the sixteenth century this privilege was transferred to Frankfurt; a terrible fire which broke forth at Aachen in 1656 destroyed two-thirds of the city; it underwent a rapid decline, and though its cloth factories and the high repute of its thermal waters have restored some of its old prosperity, it has of course never regained the importance as a political centre which it possessed in the long ages from Charles the Great to Charles the Fifth.

The palace which Charles built at Aachen, and to which he transported the great brazen statue of Theodoric from Ravenna, has long since perished. In 881 the fire kindled by the invading Danes injured it; in 978 a degenerate descendant of Charles, the Frenchman Lothair, allowed his soldiers to plunder it. In the twelfth and thirteenth centuries it was twice ruined by fire. Finally, in 1353, a Town-hall, which again in our own days (1883) has suffered from fire, was built over its ruins.

But the great basilica which Charles founded at Aachen in honour of the Virgin, and which according to Einhard "he adorned with gold and silver, and candelabra and *cancelli* and gates of solid brass, and with columns and marbles brought from Rome and Ravenna", still stands, at least the most important part of it. This is the octagonal chapel, built after the model of S. Vitale at Ravenna, to which an atrium at the west end and a splendid choir at the east were added in the fourteenth and fifteenth centuries. Thus Charles's church with its remembrance of S. Vitale stands supported on either side by its younger and taller brethren, as if marking the beginning and the end of the Middle Ages.

The palace stood on the edge of a vast pleasaunce, green with woods and bright with waters, through which herds of deer wandered, and in which Charles and his courtiers often enjoyed the pleasures of the chase, or watched the evolutions of the young horsemen of the court in games which almost anticipated the medieval tournament. It was doubtless in this wide-stretching park that one Oriental visitor passed most of his European life. This was the great elephant Abulahaz (a present from the

Caliph Haroun-al-Raschid), whose arrival in Frank-land in 802 and death in 810 on a campaign of its master against the king of Denmark are solemnly recorded by the chroniclers.

Of Charles himself, the centre of the busy scene at Aquae Grani, and his manner of life there, a vivid picture is given us by his biographer Einhard. Of his commanding stature, bright eyes, long hair, and manly carriage this biographer has already told us He further informs us that his neck was somewhat too short for symmetry, and his belly prominent; but the shapeliness of his other members concealed these defects. His voice was clear, but hardly so loud as one would have expected from his giant frame. His health till he had passed his sixty-eighth year was excellent; but for the last four years of his life he suffered from frequent fevers and limped with one foot. All these troubles, however, lie yet ahead of us. We are still only at the date 795, and the Frankish hero has reached but the fifty-third year of his life. We hear with some amusement that, sick or in health, he insisted on regulating himself according to his own notions, rather than by the counsel of his physicians, whom he well-nigh hated because they always recommended him to eat boiled meat instead of roast.

Except on the memorable occasions of his visits to Rome he wore the national Frankish dress—shirt and drawers of linen, a tunic fastened by a silken girdle, and leggings. His thighs were bound round with thongs, his feet with [laced-up] shoes. In the winter he protected his chest and shoulders with a vest of otter-skins and ermine. Over all he wore a blue cloak, and he was ever girt with a sword, whose hilt and belt were either of gold or silver. Sometimes, but only at high festivals or when he was receiving the ambassadors of foreign nations, he wore a jewelled sword. At these festivals also he wore a robe inwoven with gold, shoes bedecked with jewels, a golden clasp holding his cloak together, and a diadem of gold adorned with precious gems. On all other days, his dress varied little from the ordinary costume of his people.

On rising, Charles appears to have held something in the nature of a *levée*; for while his clothes were being put on and his shoes fastened, not only were his friends admitted to his presence, but if the Count of the Palace had any hard case which required his decision, Charles would call the litigants before him and pronounce sentence as if he were sitting on the judgment-seat. So too, at this time, he would give the necessary orders to any of his ministers or the heads of his household.

He was very temperate in the matter of drink, holding drunkenness in uttermost abomination, especially in himself and those nearest to him. In the matter of feeding he was also temperate, but hardly came up to the Church's standard of abstinence, complaining that her rigid fasts were injurious to his health. After the midday meal in summer time he would eat an apple and take some cooling drink, and then doff his upper garments and shoes, and sleep as if it were night for two or three hours together. The evening banquet was evidently the chief meal of the day. On high festivals he invited a large number of guests, but generally he supped alone with his family. The ordinary meal consisted of only three or four courses besides the roasted game, to which he was most partial, and which the hunters were wont to bring in on spits. While he was dining, he listened either to music or to the reading of a book, especially a book of history telling of the deeds of the past, or the works of St. Augustine, among which the treatise on the City of God was his chief favourite.

His sleep at night—perhaps partly owing to his long *siesta* in the day—was not sound. He would often wake four or five times, and he sometimes beguiled the wakeful hours by trying to form letters on the tablets which for this purpose were always placed under his pillow. But he began the study of calligraphy so late in life that he never therein achieved any great success.

He had a fine flow of natural eloquence, and could, when he chose, express his thoughts with perfect clearness. In fact, so great was his readiness in speaking that it sometimes almost amounted to loquacity. He studied foreign languages, and was accustomed often to pray in Latin. Greek he could understand fairly well, though he never mastered its pronunciation. But after all, his own native Teutonic tongue was dearest to his heart. He began to compose a grammar of the Frankish language, and he wrote down and committed to memory the ancient and (as Einhard deemed them) 'barbarous' songs in which the deeds and wars of the old kings were celebrated. Would that his successors had taken the same interest in the true national literature of the German races! But Charles's successor Louis, himself more than half a monk and bred up in latinised Aquitaine, cared not for these spirit-stirring songs of his Ripuarian forefathers, and so they soon for the most part died out of the memory of men. Truly we at this day find it harder to forgive the 'debonnair' Louis for the loss of his father's ballad-book than even for the ruin of his father's Empire.

Somewhat anticipating the modern tendency of our German kinsfolk to use only home-grown words even in scientific terminology, Charles invented Frankish names for the twelve months, and enlarged the number of names of the winds from four to twelve.

We do not need the biographer's assurance that Charles 'most reverently and with the utmost piety cultivated the Christian religion with which he had been imbued from infancy', nor that 'beyond all other holy places he venerated the church of the blessed Apostle Peter at Rome.' Morning and evening, and at all hours of the day or night when the sacrifice of the Mass was being offered, he was zealous in his attendance at church so long as his health permitted.

He was extremely careful that all things pertaining to divine worship should be done decently and in order, and would often admonish the vergers not to allow anything common or unclean to be brought into the church or remain within its precincts. He made lavish provision of gold and silver vessels for the service of the sanctuary, and his supply of vestments was so liberal that even the doorkeepers were clothed in them. He took a keen interest in the subject of the Church's psalmody, following herein the example of his father, who had introduced the Gregorian music into the churches of Gaul; but he gave even more attention to the lectionary and homilies of the Church, eradicating to the utmost of his power the barbarisms which a succession of ignorant priests had introduced into their reading and preaching to the people

But vivid as was Charles's interest in ecclesiastical affairs, and zealous as was his championship of the faith against pagans and heretics, the contrast between the professions and the practice of churchmen did not escape his keen intelligence. "We wish", he says in one of his capitularies, "to ask the chief ecclesiastics and all those who are engaged in teaching from the Holy Scriptures, who are those to whom the Apostle saith, "Be ye imitators of me"? or what he meant when he said, "No one who is a soldier of God entangleth himself with the things of this world"? How is the Apostle to be imitated? How is any one to be a soldier of God? Pray let them show us truly what is meant by that "renouncing the world" of which they so often speak, and explain how we are to distinguish between those who renounce and those who follow the world. Is the difference only in this, that the former do not bear arms and are not publicly married? I would enquire also if that man can be said to have renounced the world who is unceasingly striving to augment his possessions by drawing persuasive pictures of the blessedness of heaven, and by threatening men with the everlasting punishments of hell? or that man who, in the name of God or of some saint, is for ever stripping simpler people, rich or poor, of their possessions, disinheriting the lawful heirs, and driving men thus unjustly deprived of their paternal estates to robbery and all sorts of crimes, the result of the dire necessities of their position?"

One asks oneself in reading such sentences as these whether Charles was thinking of certain letters of Hadrian, in which all the machinery of the joys of paradise and the terrors of hell was brought into action in order to add Comacchio or Capua to the Papal territory.

We must not, however, enter here on the wide question of the great king's relation to the Church. It is with Charles as head of a family and centre of a court that we have here to deal. At the date which we have now reached most of Hildegard's children were grown up. Hrotrud, the once-destined bride of Constantine, was twenty-three years of age. Nearly as old was her brother Charles, Pippin king of Italy was eighteen, Louis king of Aquitaine was seventeen years old. Probably that antagonism between the younger Charles and Pippin which was to embitter some of the later years of their father's life had already declared itself, but the two young kings of Italy and Aquitaine grew up each in his own kingdom, and only occasionally formed part of their father's court. Fastrada was now dead, but had left two daughters, probably little more than children. The Alamannian lady Liutgard, once mistress, afterwards wedded wife of Charles, was perhaps already sitting as queen in the palace at Aachen. Of the young tribe of princes and princesses whose mirth was dear to their father's heart Einhard gives us an attractive picture, yet one that is not without its shadows :—

"He determined that his children should be so educated that sons as well as daughters should be trained in liberal studies, to which he himself also gave earnest heed. The sons, as soon as their age permitted, were taught to ride after the manner of the Franks, and were practised in the use of arms and in the exercises of the chase. The daughters were ordered to learn to use the distaff and spindle, and to busy themselves with wool-work that they might not grow slothful through too much leisure.

"He took so keen an interest in the education of his sons and daughters that he never supped without them when at home, and never deprived himself of their company when travelling. On such journeys his sons rode beside him, and his daughters followed behind with a strong rear-guard of soldiers.

"As these daughters were most beautiful and he loved them dearly, it was strange that he never gave one of them in marriage, either to one of his own people or to a foreigner, but kept them always with him in the house till the day of his death, declaring that he could not dispense with their daily companionship. On this account, prosperous as he was in other respects, he had to endure the malignity of adverse fortune, but he so concealed his feelings that no one could ever tell that he was aware of any shadow of disgrace having fallen upon the good name of his daughters".

The scandals thus gently hinted at by Einhard have not grown smaller in the gossip of posterity, which has even (apparently without justification) coupled Einhard's own name with that of a supposed daughter of Charles, named Emma, in a well-known story of illicit love. But some of these domestic 'misfortunes' of Charles left unmistakable traces in Carolingian pedigrees. Princess Hrotrud herself, who died in her thirty-ninth year (810), though never married, left a son Louis, who was afterwards abbot of S. Denis, and prothonotary to her nephew Charles the Bald.

Much as he loved the merry talk of his daughters, Charles in the midst of his warlike and peaceful cares delighted none the less in the companionship of the most learned men of his age whom he succeeded in gathering round him. Indeed, this is beyond all his other achievements the distinguishing glory of his character and his reign, that he, though himself imperfectly educated, knew how to appreciate the learning of others, and, turning back the tide of barbarism and ignorance which had submerged Gaul since the days of Clovis, made himself the centre and the rallying-point of a literary and scientific movement, hardly less important than the great Renascence of the fifteenth century. It is one of the many points of resemblance between these two periods of Renascence, that the little literary and ecclesiastical *coterie* which gathered round Charles at the end of the eighth century took names—for the most part classical names—by which they were known to one another in their correspondence, instead of the rough Teutonic ones which they had received from their fathers, and of which they were perhaps partly tired and partly ashamed

Charles's own *sobriquet* was not classical, but biblical. He was King David, a name well chosen to symbolize the great conqueror, the wide-ruling king, and also the man who had such large and irregular experience of the 'love of women'. But David with his blood-stained hands was not allowed to build the temple of the Lord, and therefore, as Charles did build the stately basilica of Aquae Grani, he was sometimes addressed by his friends under the name of Solomon.

An honoured guest at the Frankish palaces before Charles took up his abode at Aachen was the Lombard historian who has been so often quoted in previous volumes, Paulus Diaconus. He came, probably in 782, when he was himself about fifty-seven years of age, to plead the cause of his brother Arichis, who had incurred the displeasure of the Frankish king. In an elegiac poem Paulus thus laid bare to Charles the misery that had fallen upon him and his family:—

'Hear, great king, my complaint and in mercy receive my petition;
Scarce in the whole round world will be found such a sorrow as mine.
Six long years have passed since my brother's doom overtook him,
Now 'tis the seventh that he, a captive, in exile must pine.
Lingers at home his wife, to roam through the streets of her city
Begging for morsels of food, knocking at door after door:
Only in shameful guise like this can she nourish the children,
Tour little half-clothed babes, whom she in her wretchedness bore.
There is a sister of mine, a Christ-vowed virgin of sorrows:
Wellnigh with constant tears quenched is the light of her eyes.
Reft of its scanty equipment is now the home of our fathers;
Us in our utmost need no neighbour will help or advise.
Gone is the pride of our birth. Thrust forth from the acres paternal,
Now we are equalled in rank with those, the slaves of the soil.
Harsher doom we deserved: I own it. Yet, merciful monarch,
Pity the prayer of the sad. End our distress and our toil.
Give but the captive back to his fatherland and his homestead,
Give him the modest estate, his family's portion and stay:
So shall our mouths sing ever the praises of Christ the Redeemer,
Christ, who alone for your grace fitting rewards can repay'.

Taken literally this metrical petition would suggest the thought that Paulus had himself been concerned in hostile designs against the Frankish power. It is possible however, and is generally considered probable, that he here but speaks of 'us' and 'our deservings' in order more effectually to move the pity of the conqueror by associating himself with the guilt of the condemned man. Amid the many uncertainties which surround the life of the Lombard historian, one thing seems tolerably clear, that he had been for some years an inmate of Monte Cassino before he sought the court of King Charles to plead for his exiled brother From the favour which was shown to Paulus during the four years of his stay at the Frankish court there can be no doubt that his petition on behalf of his brother was promptly granted. He seems to have generally followed the court in all its peaceful promenades, and it was probably in one of these progresses that he found himself at the Villa Theodonis, where, as the reader may remember, he was interested in measuring the length of his shadow on Christmas day. Being himself a Greek scholar, he gave lessons in that language to the ecclesiastics who were chosen to accompany the little princess Hrotrud to Constantinople. He wrote the history of the bishops of Metz, duly glorifying Charles's sainted ancestor Arnulf. He also wrote epitaphs in respectable elegiacs on Charles's queen Hildegard, on two of his daughters and two of his sisters, and he was in fact during the four years of his stay in Frank-land a kind of literary prime minister of Charles the Great, entrusted by him with that work of revising the lectionaries and homilies of the Church to which allusion has already been made.

It was probably about the time of Paulus' arrival at the Frankish court that another literary man of some eminence made his appearance there. This was the aged Peter of Pisa, who many years before had become famous by a disputation which he held at Pavia with a certain Jew named Lull, and who now was invited across the Alps to teach grammar to the young nobles of the court, the great king himself often forming one of his audience. Between these two men, Paul the deacon and Peter the grammarian, there was an interchange of banter and half-ironical compliments, which seems to have amused their royal master as much as it perplexes the modern student, who after an interval of more than a thousand years strives to recover the meaning of these fossil *facetiae*.

Peter (who writes on behalf of Charles) in high-flown strains salutes Paul, "most learned of poets, who rivals Homer among the Greeks, Virgil among the Latins, Philo in his knowledge of Hebrew, Horace in his use of metre, Tibullus in eloquence. ... A glory which we hoped not for has now risen upon us. You have heard that at the bidding of Christ our daughter [Hrotrud] is about to cross the seas under the escort of Michael in order to wield the sceptre of the Eastern realm. For this cause you are teaching our clerics Greek grammar, that they may go thither, while still remaining in our obedience, and may seem to be learned in the rules of the Greeks".

Paulus answers that he perceives that all this is said ironically, and that he is "derided with praises and oppressed by laughter", all which makes him very miserable. He has never thought of imitating any of those mighty ones who have trodden the trackless road to fame; rather is he like one of the little dogs that have followed at their heels. "I do not know Greek", he says with untruthful modesty, "and I am ignorant of Hebrew. I have heard, and I exult in the news, that your fair daughter, O king, is to cross the seas and grasp the sceptre, so that through your child the power of your kingdom will spread over Asia. But if in that country your clerics who go from hence shall speak no more Greek than they have learned from me, they will be as dumb as statues and will be derided by all".

It was apparently the king's habit to send by an, officer of his guard a riddle or a sort of acrostic charade to one or other of these two grammarians, and humorously press for an immediate answer. Each of these riddles, as far as we can understand them, seems to be vapidity itself, but they have been the means of procuring for us vivid pictures of the handsome soldier from the palace who brought at sunset to Paulus what he calls 'the fire-tipped arrows' of Charles, and of the youth with beautiful body, in whose beard the dew-drops were hanging, when he stood at daybreak charged with a like perplexing message at the door of Peter.

The reader finds it difficult to repress his impatience when he reads the records of these elaborate trivialities. Yet even the nonsense of the court seems to bring us nearer to the Frankish hero than the bare record of his campaigns or the disputed text of his donations to the Pope. And at least this is the real Austrasian Charles with whom we are thus brought in contact, not the shadowy and unreal Charlemagne of romance.

About 786 Paulus seems to have returned to Italy, possibly in the train of Charles, who, as we have seen, spent Christmas of that year in Florence and the following winter at Rome. We hear very little about his old age, but there can be little doubt that he returned to Monte Cassino, for which retreat his heart yearned even in the midst of the splendours of Charles's court, and that he there in the end of his days composed his invaluable History of the Lombards, dying in one of the closing years of the eighth century.

About the same time when Paulus first visited the Frankish court, another learned ecclesiastic, a country man of our own, made his appearance there, a man destined to make a much longer stay and to exercise a more powerful influence than the Lombard historian. This was Alcuin, or (as he preferred to write his name) Albinus, a man already of much renown for his learning when in the year 781 he met King Charles at Parma and was persuaded by him to enter his service.

Alcuin was born probably about the year 735. He was sprung from a noble family in the Anglian kingdom of Northumbria, was of the same stock whence half a century earlier had sprung the sainted Willibrord, and if not actually born at York, was sent thither in very early childhood to be trained for the priesthood. The kingdom of Northumbria had not yet lost all its ancient glory, the glory of Edwin and Oswald; and York, the successor of the Roman Eburacum, was not only a great political centre, but was in fact the predecessor of the university towns of later ages. The venerable Baeda, the most learned man in Europe, was no more, having died perhaps in the very year of Alcuin's birth, but the tradition of his great attainments was kept alive by Egbert, who was archbishop of York from 732 to 766, and who took a keen interest in the education of the young Alcuin. Already when a boy of eleven years old, Alcuin had felt the exceptional charm which Virgil possessed for the students of Latin in the Middle Ages, and already, as with Jerome and Augustine, the influence of the great Mantuan was in some degree antagonistic to that of prophets and apostles. Though regular in his attendance at the morning service, he seldom visited the church after sunset. The rough and ignorant monk in whose cell he slept was equally lax in his midnight devotions. One night, says the biographer, when the porter at cockcrow called the brotherhood to rise for vigils, the monk, unaroused, continued in his snoring sleep, and the bright boy who shared his cell was also slumbering. Suddenly the cell was filled with black spirits, who surrounded the old monk's bed, saying, "Thou sleepest soundly, 0 brother!". He awoke and heard their taunting cry, "When all the brethren are keeping their vigil in the church, why art thou alone snoring here?" Thereat the spirits began to chastise him with cruel blows. The boy meantime was praying hard for deliverance: "O Lord Jesus, if ever after this I neglect the vigils of the church and care more for Virgil than for the chanting of psalms, then may such stripes be my lot. Only I pray Thee deliver me now". The spirits, when they had finished chastising the clown, cast their eyes round the cell. "Who", said the leader of the fiends, "is this other, sleeping here in the cell?" They answered, "It is the boy Albinus, hiding under the bed-clothes". "We will not chastise him with stripes because he is still raw, but we will punish him somewhat on the hard soles of his feet, and make him remember the vow which he has just made". They pulled the clothes from his feet, but Alcuin made the sign of the cross and repeated fervently the 12th Psalm. Thereupon the spirits disappeared, and the terrified monk and boy rushed into the church for shelter.

The story seems worth telling, however little belief we may have in the spiritual nature of the monk's tormentors, because it indicates the character of Alcuin's education, and his position midway between literature and theology. There can be no doubt—every letter from his pen proves it—that he was deeply imbued with the knowledge and the love of the great literature of heathen Rome. Yet he was also a loyal and devoted son of the Catholic Church, well acquainted with the Scriptures and with the works of the chief Latin fathers and he devoted the best powers of his trained and cultivated intellect to the defence of Catholic doctrine against heretics. In this capacity he fought as chief champion of the Church against Felix of Urgel and Elipandus of Toledo, who taught that Jesus Christ might be properly described as the adopted Son of God. In this capacity also he was probably engaged in the composition of the Libri Carolini, the celebrated treatise in which Charles endeavoured to define the true Via Media as to the worship of images.

The part which Alcuin played in these controversies is fully explained when we turn to his letters and poems and compare them with the letters and the biographies which proceeded from the Papal chancery. While Paul and Hadrian and their biographers express themselves in a Latin so barbarous, grotesque and ungrammatical that it would have seemed like a foreign language to Virgil or Seneca, the prose and poetry of Alcuin, and we may add of most of his companions in the literary *coterie* which gathered round the Frankish king, are grammatically correct and sometimes elegant. Doubtless there is in most of this Caroline literature a lack of freshness and spontaneity; the writers tend towards bombast and set too high a value on mere prettinesses of expression; in their poems especially, some of them borrow so extensively from the great Latin authors that they remind one of an idle school-boy trying to fill up his required number of lines by pilfered and unacknowledged quotations. Still, what these men wrote is Latin, if not always of the purest and noblest kind, and that is more than can be said of the letters in the *Codex Carolinus* and the lives in the Liber Pontificalis.

To return to the history of Alcuin. He was brought into close relations, as a pupil or friend, with three successive archbishops of York—Egbert, Aelberht, and Eanbald. While still a young man he seems to have accompanied the second of these on a journey to Italy, in the course of which he stayed at Pavia (then probably still the residence of a Lombard king), and there was present at the memorable disputation between Peter of Pisa and the Jew Lull, to which allusion has already been made. On Aelberht's elevation to the archbishopric (767), he succeeded him as head of the school attached to the church of York. On the death of Aelberht, he was sent by his friend Eanbald, who was elected to the vacant archiepiscopal throne, to receive his pallium from Rome. It was probably in the course of this journey that he met Charles at Parma and was earnestly entreated by him to take up his residence at the Frankish court. He refused, however, to do this without first obtaining the leave of his king and archbishop. That leave obtained, he repaired, about the beginning of 782, to Charles, then residing at Quierzy-sur-Oise, and at once received from him the gift of two rich abbacies.

With the exception of an interval of about two years spent in his native land, Alcuin remained till 796 at the court of his patron, organizing the school for the court-pages, renaming the courtiers with names taken from the classical poets, probably advising as to the services of the royal chapel, always acting as the literary and sometimes as the ecclesiastical prime minister of the great king.

In 796 he obtained permission to retire to the great monastery of St. Martin at Tours, of which he was made abbot, and there he spent the remaining eight years of his life (796-804), dying 'full of days' on the 19th of May, 804. For us this absence of Alcuin from the Frankish court is the most fruitful period of his life, because to it belong the bulk of the letters which he addressed to his royal patron, and from these we may infer what manner of counsels he gave while still dwelling under his roof.

I have been thus precise in stating the years of Alcuin's companionship and correspondence with Charles, since it is clear that he exercised a quite extraordinary influence on the mind of the Frankish hero, and to Alcuin's love of the Latin classics and close familiarity with their pages must in large measure be ascribed the specially Roman turn taken by Charles's policy in the great year 800.

The correspondence between Alcuin and Charles gives us a pleasant impression of the characters of both men. The scholar does not fawn and the king does not obviously condescend; and, most agreeable trait of all, there is an occasional exchange of banter between 'David' and 'Flaccus,' that being the Horatian name which was assumed by the British ecclesiastic. Thus, when Charles has asked Alcuin a question, not easy to answer, about the reason for the names given by the Church to the Sundays before Lent—Quinquagesima, Sexagesima, and Septuagesima; and when Alcuin has given an answer which is obviously an attempt to hide his ignorance under a cloud of words, Charles, after consulting some of the young clerks in the *Schola Palatii*, sends an explanation which is at any rate more intelligible, and probably nearer to the truth, than that given by Alcuin. But as Charles had apparently adopted the Alexandrian method of beginning the year from the autumnal equinox, Alcuin says, "I left Roman lads in the palace-school: how have Egyptians crept in there?". And with jokes about Egyptian darkness and frequent hits at the too great cleverness of 'your Egyptian lads' he tries to cover his retreat, though he admits that "I, the loiterer, I, forgetful of my former self, have perhaps rightly borne the scourge of your striplings states".

In serious matters the influence of Alcuin on the mind of the Frankish king seems to have been generally exerted in favour of a broad and tolerant policy. A favorable specimen of his by style is furnished by a letter which he wrote soon after his retirement to Tours, in the autumn of 796. After congratulating the king on his victories over the Huns [Avars], 'a nation formidable by their ancient savagery and courage', he goes on to recommend that to this new people there be sent pious preachers, men of honourable character, intent on following the example of the holy Apostles, who may feed them with milk, and not disgust their 'fragile minds' with 'more austere precepts'.

"After weighing these things, let your Piety, under wise advice, consider whether it is good to impose on a rude people like this at the beginning of their faith the yoke of tithes, exacted in full amount and from every house. It is to be considered whether the Apostles, who were taught by Christ Himself and sent forth by Him for the evangelization of the world, ever ordered the exaction of tithes, or demanded that they should be given to them. We know that the tithing of our property is a very good thing; but it is better to forego it than to lose the faith. Even we, who were born, bred, and trained up in the Catholic faith, scarce consent to the full tithing of our substance; how much less will their tender faith, their childish intellects, and their covetous dispositions consent to such large claims on their generosity? But when their faith is strengthened and their Christian habits are confirmed, then, as to perfect men, may be given those stronger commands which, their-minds braced by the Christian religion, will no longer reject with loathing".

Around Alcuin as a centre gathered a school of learned and nimble-minded men, his disciples, who helped forward the civilizing and educating work of the king of the Franks. Two of these may be noticed here, Angilbert, abbot of S. Riquier, and Theodulf, bishop of Orleans.

Angilbert was sprung from a noble Frankish family, and was brought up, almost from infancy, in the palace of Charles. His teachers were Alcuin, Peter of Pisa, and another grammarian named Paulinus. He accompanied the young Pippin into Italy, and was apparently one of his chief counsellors, having probably then already taken orders. He returned to the Frankish court, and in 790 was made by Charles abbot of the monastery of S. Riquier in Picardy. It was probably about the same time that he was appointed archchaplain to the king.

Angilbert was three times sent on important missions to Rome. The object of his second mission was to obtain from the Pope that condemnation of the Second Nicene Council which Hadrian, being himself an ardent image-worshipper, could not grant. But though thus engaged in serious ecclesiastical affairs, Angilbert was essentially a *littérateur* and a man of the world. The abundance of his poems (only a few of which are preserved to us) obtained for him in the literary club at the palace the *sobriquet* of Homer. He became enamoured of Charles's daughter Bertha, and though marriage was doubly impossible on account of his profession and her royal birth, she bore him two sons, to whom he seems to have been a loving father. Nor does Charles appear in any wise to have withdrawn his favour from his irregular son-in-law.

To Alcuin, who followed the fortunes of his pupil with anxious interest, Angilbert's intense fondness for the pleasures of the theatre caused some uneasiness. "I fear", he said, in writing to his friend Adalhard, "that Homer will be made angry by the edict forbidding spectacular entertainments and devilish figments. All which things the Holy Scriptures prohibit: insomuch that I find St. Augustine saying, "Little does the man know who introduces actors and mimics and dancers into his house, how great a crowd of unclean spirits follows them." But God forbid that the Devil should have power in a Christian home. I wrote to you about this before, desiring with all my heart the salvation of my dearest son, and wishing that you might accomplish that which was beyond my power".

Writing again two years later to the same friend, Alcuin rejoices over Angilbert's reformation. "I was much pleased to read what you have written about the improved morals of my Homer. For although his character was always an honourable one, yet there is no one in the world who has not to "forget the things which are behind and to reach out to the things which are before" till he attains the crown of perfectness". Now one of "the things that are behind" for him related to the actors, from whose vanities I knew that no small peril impended over his soul, and this grieved me. Wherefore I wrote him something on this subject, to prove the genuine sincerity of my love. And I was surprised that so intelligent a man did not himself perceive that he was doing blameworthy deeds and things which consisted not with his dignity".

One or two of the extant poems of Angilbert give us some interesting glimpses of life at Charles's court. He seems to have been always especially devoted to his former pupil Pippin, and, on that prince's return from Italy in 796, he greeted him with a poem of effusive welcome. He pictures the young Charles and Louis looking anxiously for their brother's arrival. The impatient Charles wonders if he is hindered by the badness of the roads. Louis, though he loves Pippin quite as dearly, is of more placid temperament (how like the future 'Debonnair' Emperor!) and comforts his brother by the recital of a dream, in which Pippin stood by him and assured him that ere the moon was at her full he would be with them.

Then Pippin arrives, and is greeted by father, stepmother, brothers, sisters and aunt. (Gisila 'the bride of heaven') with various manifestations of joy. The poem ends with pious aspirations, unhappily not fulfilled, for the fraternal union and concord of the three brothers, Charles, Pippin and Louis.

Another poem of more historical importance, which now bears the name of 'Carolus Magnus et Leo Papa', is attributed, though with some hesitation, to Angilbert. It opens with high-flown praises of Charles's qualities (among which we note especially his easy, genial manners, his love of the study of grammar, and his oratorical fluency), and then, after a description of the rise of the new capital of Aquae Grani, the poet proceeds to depict with some fluency, though at portentous length, the events of a day's boar-hunting in a vast wooded chase between the city and the hills. Charles himself is called 'the Pharos of Europe'. His horse, with heavy gold trappings, delights to be bestridden by the greatest of kings. Charles's sons are described with a monotony of laudation which savours too much of 'fortemque Gyan, fortemque Cloanthum'. The dress of Queen Liutgarda and of Charles's six daughters is minutely described, and if we could trust the poet's accuracy we should have here a valuable piece of evidence for the attire of Frankish dames of high station : but when we find that each of the ladies goes hunting with a gold coronet on her head, in which emeralds, or chrysolites, or jacinths are blazing, we are forced to suspect that the picture is conventional, and that each princess insisted on being described in the most gorgeous of her court costumes.

We may, however, accept from the poet his description of the flaxen, or yet paler than flaxen hair of several of the young Frankish princesses. And we note with interest his elaborate portrait of the brilliant Bertha, surrounded by her girl-friends; Bertha, whose voice, whose manly courage, whose quick-glancing and expressive face recalled the image of her father. For this was that one of Charles's daughters who was one day to be the unwedded wife of the poet.

After the boar-hunt the tents were pitched in the middle of the forest, and a splendid banquet followed, which was attended not only by the young sportsmen who had followed Charles, but by the grave and reverend seniors invited thither from the city.

The poet then proceeds to relate the interview between the King and Pope which will be the subject of the next chapter.

One word deserves our especial attention in this poem. It was composed probably in the year 799, certainly not later than June, 800, for it speaks of Queen Liutgard as still living : yet twice Charles is spoken of as 'Augustus', the name appropriated beyond all others to the Emperor of Rome. Certainly Angilbert had heard some whispers of the event which was to make the Christmas of 800 memorable.

Theodulf, the other great poet of Charles's court, the most copious of all save Alcuin, was born about 760 in the old Gothic province of Septimania, which since the middle of the century had formed part of the Frankish kingdom. After taking deacon's orders he seems to have made his way to Charles's court, where his learning and his zeal for reform of manners in Church and State obtained for him a high position. It is thought, however, that he never sat as a pupil in the *Schola Palati*, nor formed one of the innermost circle of the friends of Alcuin, and consequently he has no Latin nickname like the members of that *coterie*. About the year 798 he was consecrated bishop of Orleans, with the right of holding three or four rich abbacies along with his see. In this year he was also sent together with Leidrad (afterwards bishop of Lyons) as *missus dominicus* to hold synods, reform manners, and execute justice in the region of Gallia Narbonensis. Of this journey he has given us a valuable account in his longest and most important poem addressed 'Ad Judices.' In 801 and 802 he had a sharp dispute about right of sanctuary with Alcuin, who had then recently retired from the headship of the monastery of St. Martin at Tours. A certain accused person had fled from Theodulf's jurisdiction and taken refuge at St. Martin's shrine. Theodulf demanded, Alcuin passionately refused, the surrender of the criminal. Our countryman was probably in the wrong, since Charles, intervening in the dispute, gave judgment in Theodulf's favour, and strongly condemned the angry tone of Alcuin's letters.

After Charles's death Theodulf was for some time in high favour with his successor, Louis the Pious, to whom he addressed a poem of welcome on his passage through Orleans to Aachen. He was accused, however, of taking part in Bernard's rebellion against his uncle Louis, and was banished to Angers. It is not quite clear whether he was ever pardoned. According to one, somewhat late, authority he received permission to return, but was poisoned on the road home (821).

The style of Theodulf's Latin poems is considered by some critics to be superior to that of any of his contemporaries. To me he seems often intolerably diffuse, and I find it difficult to admire the poetical taste of a man who could spend weeks (as he must have done, if not months) in composing thirty-five vapid (necessarily vapid) verses of 'prayer for King Charles', which when read perpendicularly, horizontally, and along the lines of an inscribed rhomboid, give eight other acrostic verses to the same purport. Still his Latin is generally correct, and when he is clear of literary artifices like this and free from the enervating influences of the court, it is sometimes even forcible. His poems, with fewer plagiarisms than those of Angilbert, show an extensive acquaintance with the works of the Latin classical poets, especially with those of Ovid, whose fate as an exile vainly pleading for the return of court favour, that of Theodulf was, at the end of his life, so closely to resemble. It would be an interesting question to enquire where, at a distance from Charles's court, the 'Goth' (as he always styles himself) of Narbonne can have accumulated so large a store of classical learning. May we believe that, first under Visigothic and then under Saracen rule, the old Provincia which included Narbonne and Marseilles had retained sufficient trace of its old Latin culture to prevent it from being barbarized down to the level of Gregory of Tours?

The longest and best of Theodulfs poems is an address to all Judges, warning them against bribery, partiality, indolence and pride. As has been said, it contains, parenthetically, a long account of the author's journey to the Narbonese Gaul, with Leidrad for his colleague. He says, "I have often perceived that when I inveigh against the bribery of judges the secret thought of my hearers is that I, if I had the opportunity, should do even as they". It is in order to repel this insinuation that he tells the story of his journey down the valley of the Rhone to those 'Hesperian' lands round Narbonne which gave him birth. At every place he was beset by corrupt aspirants to his favour. One man offered a silver vase on which were carved with marvellous skill some of the labours of Hercules. This vase should be Theodulf's if he would only consent to annul the deed of enfranchisement by which the petitioner's parents had given freedom to a multitude of slaves. Another, who had a dispute about the ownership of some cattle, offered as a suitable bribe a robe woven in Saracenic looms, in which a cow with her calf was depicted with marvellous skill. And so on with many other gifts, costly if offered by the rich, of trifling value if offered by the poor, but all distinctly put forward as bribes, and as such rejected by Theodulf. He truly remarks that these things would not have been offered to him unless similar gifts had been accepted by many of his predecessors. It was probably the unfavourable impression which he thus received of the venality of Frankish judges which caused him to write these words of solemn warning against a wide-spread vice.

Interwoven with the practical advice which Theodulf gives to the judges we find some interesting pictures of the forensic life of a Frankish city : "When the dull murmur of the law-suits calls you to the Forum and you have to execute the duties of your office, first resort to some holy place and pray God to direct your actions that you may do nothing displeasing to Him. Then, according to custom, repair to the gates of the resounding Forum, where the band of litigants expects you. When you are on your way, perhaps some poor man will address to you words of entreaty, some man who may afterwards say that he could not have speech of you while you walked surrounded by your people. You go forward, you are received within those proud doors, while the common people are shut out. But let some faithful and compassionate servant walk near to you, to whom you can say, "Bring into our presence that man who uttered his complaint in such a loud voice" : and so having introduced him into the judgment-hall, discuss his cause first, and afterwards attend to every one in his own order.

"If you ask my advice when you should go to the Forum, I should say "Go early," and do not grudge spending the whole day on the judgment-seat. The more a man ploughs, the better harvest he will reap. I have seen judges who were slow to attend to the duties of their office, though prompt enough in taking its rewards. Some arrive at eleven and depart at three. Others, if nine o'clock sees them on the bench, will rise therefrom at noon. Yes, if they have anything to give, you will not find them till three in the afternoon; if anything to receive, they are there before seven. The man who was formerly always late, is now brisk enough in his movements.

"Gluttony is always to be avoided, but especially at the time when the duty awaits you of handling the reins of justice. He who devotes himself to feasting and slumber, comes with dulled senses to the trial of causes, and sits in his court flabby, inactive, mindless. Some difficult case comes on, the rapid play of question and answer demands his keenest attention, but there he sits and sways to and fro, lazy, panting, overcome with nausea and pain, in crass hebetude. Beware therefore of too abundant banquets, and especially of the goblets of Bacchus. If you are a drunkard you will be laughed at in stealth by all your people. One passes on the hint to another, and soon the brand of infamy will be fixed upon you.

"The janitor of the court must control the gaping crowd, and not suffer the lawless mob to rush into the hall and fill the building with their noisy complaints, of which, the louder they shout, the less one can understand. But he too must be a man of clean hands, and must be expressly admonished not to take any douceurs from the people. Alas! this is a vice which every janitor loves. The janitor loves a bribe, and among his masters the judges you will scarce find one in a thousand who hates it".

Before we part from the works of this keen-witted, if not grandly inspired poet, we must listen for a short time to his description of the court of King Charles at Aachen, as contained in his poem 'Ad Carolum regem,' written about the year 796.

After listening to prayers in 'that hall whose fair fabric rises with marvellous domes' (doubtless the great church of St. Mary), the king proceeds to the palace. The common people go and come through the long vestibules; the doors are opened, and of the many who wish to enter a few are admitted. One sees the fair progeny of Charles surrounding their father, Charles the younger in his adolescent beauty and the boyish Louis, both strong, vigorous, with minds keen in study, and able to keep their own counsel. Then the virgin band, Bertha, Hrotrud and Gisila, and their three younger sisters; no one more beautiful than the others. With these is joined the fair Amazon, Liutgarda, 'who shines both by her intellect and her wealth of piety, fair indeed by her outward adornment, but fairer yet by her worthy deeds, beloved both by nobles and people; free-handed, gentle, courteous ; she seeks to benefit all, to injure none.' (One may be allowed here to suspect a veiled allusion to the opposite character of her predecessor, Fastrada.)

The children crowd around their father in friendly rivalry of good offices. Charles takes from him his heavy double pallium and his gloves, Louis takes his sword. The daughters receive the loving kisses of their sire. Bertha brings roses, Hrotrud violets, Gisila lilies, Bothaid apples, Hiltrud bread, Theoderada wine. All these maidens wear beautiful jewels, some red, some green; golden clasps, bracelets and necklaces. One delights her father by her graceful dance, another by her merry jokes.

Then draws near the king's sister, the holy Gisila. She kisses her brother, and her placid face shows as much joy as can co-exist with her joy in the heavenly Bridegroom. She begs Charles to explain to her some dark passage of Scripture, and he teaches her that which he has himself learned of God.

A description of the courtiers follows.

Thyrsis (whose Teutonic name we know not) is the active and able but bald chamberlain whose business it is to regulate the entrance into the presence-chamber, admitting some and courteously excusing himself for preventing the entrance of others.

Flaccus (Alcuin) is 'the glory of our bards, mighty to shout forth his songs, keeping time with his lyric foot, moreover a powerful sophist, able to prove pious doctrines out of Holy Scripture, and in genial jest to propose or solve puzzles of arithmetic'. Sometimes these questions of *Flaccus* are easy, sometimes desperately hard. Charles himself is often one of those who rather desire to find than succeed in finding the answers to these 'Flaccidica.'

Richulf (bishop of Mainz) comes next, strong of voice, yet with polished speech, noble by his art and his fidelity. If he has tarried long in distant regions he has returned thence not empty-handed.

Homer (Angilbert) is absent; else my Muse should sing to him a song of delight.

*Ercambald (*chancellor from 797 to 812) has two tablets in his hand, on which he writes down the king's orders and hums them over to himself with inaudible voice

Lentulus (whose real name we know not) brings in some apples in a basket. He is a faithful fellow with quick perceptions, but very slow in speech and gait.

*Nardulus (*the name is perhaps meant for Einhard) rushes about hither and thither like an ant. His little body is inhabited by a mighty spirit. He is now bringing in big books and now literary arrows to slay the Scot.

At the mention of this Scot—to whose identity we have unfortunately no clue—Theodulf bursts into a storm of fury; fury surely fictitious and merely humorous. "Such kisses will I give thee as the wolf gives to the donkey. Sooner shall the dog cherish hares or the fierce wolf lambs than I, the Goth, will have any friendship with the Scotsman. Take away one little letter, the third in the alphabet, a letter which he cannot himself pronounce, and you have the true description of his character, a sot instead of a Scot".

After the banquet the Theodulfica Musa is called upon to sing. All kings and chieftains love to hear her voice, but a certain Wibod (possibly a count of Perigueux, another enemy or pretended enemy of Theodulf) cannot abide it. He shakes his thick head of hair thrice or four times at the minstrel, and in his absence hurls out dreadful threats. But only let the king summon him to his presence, and in he goes with shambling gait and trembling knee; a very Jove with his awful voice but a Vulcan with his lame foot.

So, with a torrent of pretended indignation against this Wibod and the mysterious Scot the poem concludes, the pious author praying his readers in the name of that Christian charity which beareth all things not to be offended by anything that he has written.

I trust that I have not dwelt too long on the histories of these *littérateurs* in Charles's court. In reading their lives and their poems—small as the literary merit of these latter may be—one feels how broad a chasm divides them from the illiteracy and barbarism of the Merovingian days. True, the intellectual impulse came from abroad, and pre-eminently from our own great Northumbrian scholars. But it was Charles's supreme merit to have attracted it to himself, to have made his court the focus of all the literary light and beat of Western Europe, to have offered the richest prizes in Church and State as the rewards of intellectual eminence. As has been before said, the age of Charles the Great was a veritable literary and architectural Renascence, and even the mimic combats of the wits of the court, their verbal subtleties and classical affectations, remind us not seldom of the literary coteries of Florence in the age of the Medici.

Like that brilliant age, moreover, was the age of Charlemagne in its care for the manuscripts of classical antiquity, only that where the Florentine bought, the Frank superintended the copying of the priceless manuscripts. The very characters bore the impress of the new movement of literary reform. Small but clear uncials took the place of the barbarous scrawl of the two preceding centuries. Monastery vied with monastery in the splendour and the number of its parchment codices. For the fragments of Greek literature which have been preserved we are of course chiefly indebted to Constantinople, but it is difficult to calculate how great would be the void in extant Latin literature had it not been for the revival of letters at the court of Charlemagne.

CHAPTER V

POPE AND EMPEROR.

To a student of the life of Charles the Great the question will sometimes suggest itself whether his connection with the affairs of Italy and the Church of Rome brought him more of gladness or of vexation. Often when his head was already weary and his hands over-full with the care of his long wars against the heathen, there would come some message from over the Alps which seemed to cause his cup of bitterness to overflow. Even such a message came to him in the spring of 799; a rumour of terrible deeds done in Rome, which was followed in July by the actual appearance in his camp at Paderborn of a ghastly figure, the successor of St. Peter, the most venerated person in Western Europe, with bloodshot eyes, with pallid face, with mutilated tongue which could scarce speak the customary words of blessing. What barbarous hands had inflicted such cruel wounds on the holy Pope of Rome? Not the hands of 'unspeakable Lombards,' nor even of tyrannous Byzantine officials, but the hands of his own Romans, of ministers of his Church, brought up in the shadow of the Lateran. To understand what had happened we must go back rather more than three years to the day after the death of Hadrian.

Leo III, who on the 27th of December, 795—only two days after the decease of his predecessor—was raised to the vacant throne, was by birth a Roman His education had been purely ecclesiastical, and through the incense-smoke of the conventional praises of the biographer we may perhaps discern that he was an eloquent man, and eminent as an alms-giver, both from his own funds and from those supplied to him by admiring members of his congregation. He had passed through the grades of deacon and presbyter, and was officiating as *vestatarius* when the unanimous choice—so it is affirmed—of the nobles, clergy and people of Rome raised him to the pontificate.

One of the earliest cares of the new Pope was to write to the Frankish king assuring him of his humble obedience and promising fidelity to his person. Charles replied in a letter brought by the 'Homeric' Angilbert, in which he condoled with the Roman Church on the death of his 'sweetest father' Hadrian, mentioned the fact that he had intended to send some presents (part of the Avar spoil), which, since too late for Hadrian, were now offered for the acceptance of Leo, and desired the new Pope to confer with Angilbert 'on all matters which might seem necessary for the exaltation of the holy Church of God, the stability of your honour, and the consolidation of our patriciate'.

Both to Angilbert and to Leo himself Charles speaks of the necessity that the Pope should obey the canons and show purity in morals, firmness in faith, and honesty in his conversation. Viewed in the light of subsequent events, this anxious care for the Papal morality suggests the thought that Charles or one of his advisers, possibly Alcuin, had heard unfavourable reports as to the stability of character of the eloquent and popular *vestatarius*.

One paragraph in this letter is so important as describing the relation—in itself so hard to define—between Pope and Frankish King, that it will be well to translate it literally : "For as I made a covenant of holy compaternity with your most blessed predecessor, so I desire to conclude an inviolable treaty of the same faith and love with your Blessedness, that by your prayers drawing down upon me the grace of God, I may be everywhere followed by the apostolic benediction, and the most holy seat of the Roman Church may be always protected by our devotion. It is our duty, with the help of God, everywhere externally to defend the Church of Christ with our arms from the inroads of pagans and the devastation of infidels, and internally to fortify it by our recognition of the Catholic faith. It is yours, most holy Father, with hands like the hands of Moses raised in prayer to God, to help our warfare, so that by your intercession, by the gift and guidance of God, the Christian people may everywhere and always win the victory over the enemies of His holy name, and the name of our Lord Jesus Christ may be magnified in all the world".

This conception (which was also the Roman conception) of the duties of the Frankish monarch towards the Church was aptly symbolized by the presents sent him by Leo in announcing his own elevation to the pontificate. They were, the keys of the *confessio* or crypt in which reposed the body of the Apostle Peter, and the banner of the City of Rome. So thoroughly united were now the two ideas of the Galilean fisherman and of the City founded by Romulus. Probably, even to themselves, Hadrian and Leo would have found it hard to explain how much they claimed on behalf of the one and how much on behalf of the other.

At this day the pilgrim who visits the Eternal City may see the graphic embodiment of these ideas in a mosaic the original of which was perhaps affixed to the walls of the Lateran in the very year of Leo III's accession. On an eighteenth-century building adjoining the Lateran church may be seen portrayed, on a brilliant gold background, the gigantic figure of St. Peter, who dispenses gifts to a suppliant on either side of him, men of smaller stature, as is befitting for contemporaries when brought into the presence of the saints of old. On his right hand kneels Pope Leo, to whom he is giving the pallium of hierarchical pre-eminence; on his left, King Charles, wearing a moustache, and with a curious conical cap on his head, to whom he gives the consecrated banner. In the barbarous misspelled Latin of the time the Apostle is implored to give life to the pious pontiff Leo, and victory to King Charles.

For certain reasons which are not very clear to us, the position of the new Pope was a precarious one. Throughout his long papacy he seems always to have been hated by a party among the Roman nobles. Possibly there was something in his moral character which gave an easy handle to slander—it is not denied that his enemies accused him of adultery and perjury—but again it may be fairly argued that the scoundrels who mutilated his body would not hesitate, if the occasion offered, to murder his good name. Certain it is that the most conspicuous of his assailants were two men, nephews of the deceased Pope Hadrian, one *nomenclator* and the other *sacellarius* in the Papal court, Paschalis and Campulus.

Let us look for a moment at the previous career of these two Papal nephews. In a letter of Hadrian to Charles written in May, 778, we find that 'our nephew Paschalis' is sent by the Pope to recall the citizens of Terracina to their obedience. In two letters written a little later, Campulus, bishop of Gaeta, appears as the informer concerning the machinations of the Greeks and Beneventans. The name being not a very common one, it seems probable that this was the same person as Hadrian's nephew. Thus we have two men whose detestable deeds committed against the venerated person of the Pope are about to be related, high in office in the Roman Church and curia, and evidently placed there by the favour of their uncle. Hadrian's own character must suffer somewhat for the ill deeds of his kinsmen. Either he was himself unscrupulous in the promotion of his relatives, or he was grievously deficient in discernment of character.

On the 25th of April, 799, the Pope prepared to ride along the street which is now called the Corso, and forth along the Via Flaminia, in order to celebrate the Greater Litany. This ceremony had taken the place of the old Pagan Robigalia, and, like that festival, was intended to implore the Divine Providence to avert rust and mildew from the springing corn. As the Pope set forth from the Lateran palace, the *primicerius* Paschalis met him, and with hypocritical courtesy apologized for not being robed in his chasuble. "I am in weak health", said he, "and therefore have come without my *planeta*". Doubtless the fact was that the heavy chasuble would have hindered the bloody deed upon which his soul was set. The Pope gave him his pardon, and the two conspirators, as if in lowly attendance upon him, and with words of treacherous sweetness on their lips, followed in his train.

The procession was meant to go forth by the Porta del Popolo, cross over the Ponte Molle, and wind round under Monte Mario to St. Peter's. The chief rendezvous for the citizens was the church of St. Lawrence in Lucina. At the neighbouring monastery of St. Stephen and St. Silvester the main body of the conspirators was assembled. They rushed forth and clustered round their two leaders. The people who had assembled to view the procession, unarmed and prepared only for a religious rite, dispersed in panic terror. Leo was thrown violently to the ground; Paschalis stood at his head and Campulus at his feet; some of the ruffians in the crowd tried to cut out his tongue, others struck him in the eyes, and then they dispersed, leaving the Supreme Pontiff of Rome blinded and speechless in the middle of the Corso

There was evidently a great lack of plan and purpose in the truculent villains who did this cruel deed, and there is also a disposition on the part of the Papal biographer to exaggerate the injuries inflicted on the unhappy pontiff in order to magnify the miracle of his recovery. According to this authority, the impious men, 'like veritable Pagans', returned to their victim, and finding him still alive, dragged him to the '*confessio*' of the monastery of Stephen and Silvester, and there 'again twice more thoroughly pulled out his eyes and tongue, and striking him with divers blows and clubs, mangled him and left him only half alive, rolling in his blood before the very altar'. It is not easy to recover the exact details of this atrocity, but on the whole it seems safe to accept the cautious statement of some of the Frankish annalist that the conspirators mutilated the tongue of their victim and endeavoured to blind him, but did not entirely succeed in the latter operation.

The Pope was at first confined in the monastery of the two saints, Stephen and Silvester, but fearing a rescue his captors conveyed him by night to the monastery of St. Erasmus on the Coelian, a Greek foundation, whose abbot, or (as he was styled) *hegumenos*, appears to have been in league with the malefactors. While he was imprisoned here, a miracle, according to the biographer, was wrought by the intercession of St. Peter, and 'he both recovered his sight, and his tongue was restored to him for speaking'. Moreover, there was still some loyalty left in the servants of the Lateran Court. The chamberlain Albinus, taking counsel with some faithful friends, planned successfully his master's escape from the Greek convent. He was let down the wall by a rope in the night-time, and being received by his friends at the bottom was conveyed by them to St. Peter's. The people, in whose hearts there was doubtless a reaction of pity towards the victim of such a barbarous outrage, gathered round him, and in the familiar words of the Psalter praised 'the Lord God of Israel who alone doeth marvellous things, the Lord who is the light and salvation of His people', for the deliverance granted to His servant. The conspirators, who felt themselves baffled, were well-nigh ready to turn their arms against one another in their rage and terror, but in fact accomplished nothing but the ignoble revenge of sacking the house of the faithful Albinus.

Still Leo's position in the great but unfortified basilica of St. Peter was by no means free from danger. It happened however that Winichis, the brave general who defeated the Greeks in 788, and who had since been made duke of Spoleto in succession to Hildeprand, was now at St. Peter's in the capacity of *missus* from King Charles. He had a band of soldiers with him, and marching at their head he escorted Leo to the safe shelter of the Umbrian stronghold, Spoleto. From thence in the early summer he set forth upon his journey to the Frankish court, accompanied, says the biographer, by delegates—bishops, nobles of Rome and provincial nobles— from all the chief cities of Italy. After meeting first Charles's arch-chaplain Hildebald and then his son Pippin, who were sent to welcome him on to Frankish soil, he arrived, as we have seen, at Charles's camp of Paderborn about the month of July. He was received by the king with all the usual demonstrations of reverent welcome, and he with his large train of attendants had another camp pitched for them near the royal tents. Apparently Charles reserved judgment on the charges brought against Leo (for his opponents also found their way to the camp and persisted in their accusations) until the matter should have been thoroughly sifted by a commission sent for that purpose to Rome. But in the meantime king and courtiers listened to the marvellous story of the miraculous restoration of sight to the ruined eyes and the power of speech to the mutilated tongue, and the Pope's ministrations were invoked for the consecration of the new church which Charles had erected at Paderborn; an evident proof that Leo was still in the eyes of his powerful protector the lawful pontiff. In the act of consecration the Pope deposited in the altar of the church some relics of the protomartyr Stephen which he had brought with him from Rome, assuring the king that their mysterious efficacy would protect the church from a repetition of the destruction which it had before frequently undergone at the hands of the heathen.

Were the summer months of 799 during which Leo abode at the court of Charles occupied by a negotiation between the two heads of Christendom, the result of which was that Leo was restored to the pontificate on imperial condition of raising Charles to the Imperial throne? That is an assertion which has been sometimes made, but it rests on mere conjecture; there is not a shred of contemporary evidence in support of it; and, at any rate in the crude form in which I have here stated it, the assertion lacks probability.

At the same time we may well believe that Leo during these months of his abode at Paderborn perceived, what may have been hidden from him before, that the learned men and the churchmen at Charles's court, with their heads full of the literature and the memories of ancient Rome, true men of the Renaissance as they were, had conceived the idea of reviving the old and genuine dignity of Roman Imperator—something distinct from the spurious imitation of it which passed current at Constantinople—on behalf of their mighty Frankish lord. Four of the capital cities of the old Empire, Milan, Trier, Ravenna, Rome, already recognized Charles as their master, while two only, Constantinople and Nicomedia, remained to the 'Greek' Emperors. The extent of old Imperial territory which owned the sway of the Frank was enormously larger than the dwindled heritage of the East over which Irene ruled, and there were great and fair territories in central Europe which Varus and Drusus had failed to conquer, but which Charles, the enlarger of the Empire had won for civilization. All these arguments were doubtless often urged in the halls of Aachen and by the camp-fires of Paderborn ; and Charles probably listened to them, pleased but not convinced by his courtiers' zeal for his exaltation.

We have seen that Angilbert had already used the epithet 'Augustus' of his royal master; but it is in Alcuin's correspondence that the word Empire first clearly emerges. He had received a somewhat languid invitation from Charles to repair to the court and meet the apostolic exile. But, happily for us, the invitation did not appear to him to be a sufficiently direct command to make it necessary for him in his feeble state of health to undertake the journey from Tours into the troublous regions of Saxon-land. To this feeling of slightly offended dignity we probably owe the fact that at this critical period of Charles's career we are able to trace in Alcuin's correspondence the advice given to the king by his chief counsellors.

In one very important letter written by 'Flaccus Albinus' to 'the peaceful king David' immediately after the receipt of the tidings of the outrage in the streets of Rome, Alcuin says :—

"Hitherto there have been three persons in the world higher than all others. One is the Apostolic Sublimity which is accustomed to rule by delegated power the seat of St. Peter, Prince of Apostles. But what deeds have been done to him who was ruler of that see your worshipful Goodness has deigned to inform me.

"The next is the Imperial Dignity and secular power Emperor, of the Second Rome. How impiously the Governor of that Empire has been deposed, not by strangers, but by his own people and fellow-citizens, universal fame hath abundantly reported.

"The third is the Royal Dignity, in which the providence of our Lord Jesus Christ hath ordained you for the ruler of the Christian people, more excellent in power than the other aforesaid dignities, more illustrious in wisdom, more sublime in the dignity of your kingdom. Lo, now upon you alone reposes the whole salvation of the Churches of Christ. You are the avenger of crime, the guide of the wanderers, the comforter of the mourners, the exaltation of the righteous.

"Have not the most flagrant instances of impiety manifested themselves in that Roman see where formerly religion and piety shone most brightly? These men, blinded in their own hearts, have blinded their own Head. These are the perilous times formerly predicted by the Truth itself, because the love of many is waxing cold.

"On no account must you forego the care of the head. It is a smaller matter that the feet than that the head should be in pain".

Alcuin proceeds to explain and expand this oracular utterance. Charles during this year (799) was intent on one of his great campaigns against the Saxons, sending his son Charles to harry Bardengau, the old home of the Lombards, calling in the aid of Sclavonic tribes beyond the Elbe, planning extensive transportations of Saxons into Rhine-land and repeoplings of their country by Franks. All this work, even when it is necessary—and here he repeats a previous warning against the exaction of tithes from the Saxons—Alcuin considers to be comparatively unimportant. It is at best healing the pain of the feet, while the whole head is sick and the whole heart faint. The City of Home and the Church of Home are the points to which he thinks that his patron's attention should be mainly directed.

It may be said that in all this we have no direct mention of the assumption of the Imperial title. This is true, but it is easy to see how arguments like those employed by Alcuin would lead up to that result. If Charles was already above the Emperor in power and wisdom, let him not be afraid to assume at least an equality of rank with him. If Home was to be firmly governed and the repetition of such outrages as that of the 25th of April was to be prevented, let him take some title of more awful import than that anomalous 'Patriciate of the Romans' with which for the last quarter of a century he had been presiding over, but hardly guiding, the fortunes of Italy. Above all, if he was to realize his great ideal of a foster-father, guide, and protector of the Church, if he was to be the Constantine of this later age, let him be called, as Constantine was called, *Imperator Romanorum*.

All these speculations and suggestions, however, might have remained mere academical exercises but for the two events which had horrified the world, and which had darkened the atmosphere of the New and the Old Rome. These two events, the deposition and cruel punishment of Constantine VI, and the mutilation of Leo III, concurring as they did in the last years of the eighth century, facilitated, nay necessitated that other great event which fixed the fate of Europe for centuries. That a woman—and such a woman—should pretend to occupy the throne of the Caesars, that the Head of Western Christendom should be attacked and half-murdered in the streets of his own capital, these were two portents which shocked the conscience of the world, and which seemed to show that nothing less than a revolution, which should be also a return to the elementary principles of the great World-Empire of Rome, could cure the deep-seated malady of the age.

After a few months' residence at Paderborn, Pope Leo set out on his southward journey. He was escorted by a brilliant company, at once a guard of honour for his person on the journey, and a strong commission to try his case on their arrival in Rome. On this commission rode two archbishops, Hildibald of Cologne and Arno of Salzburg, five bishops, and three counts.

On the 29th of November Leo re-entered Rome, amid vivid manifestations of popular joy. The great ecclesiastics, the nobles, the body (whatever it may have been) which now called itself the Senate of Rome, the little army of the *Ducatus Romae*, the nuns, the deaconesses, all streamed forth to the Ponte Molle, with banners and with psalmody, to meet the returning Shepherd and assure him of the joy of his flock at his reappearance. There too were seen the members of the four great *Scholae* or guilds of foreigners, Franks, Frisians, Saxons (from England), and Lombards, who were now settled in Rome, and had quarters assigned to them between St. Peter's and the castle of S. Angelo. All flocked with the pontiff to the great basilica on the Vatican, where he celebrated mass, and all partook of the holy feast.

Next day, after keeping the festival of St. Andrew, the Pope proceeded in state through the City to the Lateran palace. Here, after an interval the length of which we know not, Charles's ten commissioners took their seats in the great *triclinium*, and for a week or more examined into the charges which Paschalis and Campulus had brought against Leo, declared them to be unfounded, and sent the accusers as criminals into Frank-land, probably in order that the king himself might decide upon their punishment.

About a year was to elapse before the return of Leo was followed by its natural and all-important consequence, Charles's fourth visit to Rome.

In the first place, shortly after Leo's departure there appeared at the Frankish court an ambassador named Daniel, who was sent by Michael, the Patrician of Sicily, and who, having discharged his commission, was dismissed with marks of high honour and favour by the Frankish king. This was in fact the last of three embassies which had come in three successive years from the Byzantine court, or from its representative in Sicily. In 797, a certain Theoctistus had come from Nicetas, governor of Sicily, bringing a letter from Constantine VI, which was perhaps a cry for help from the doomed Emperor. In 798, Michael, Patrician of Phrygia, and Theophilus, a presbyter, brought a letter from Irene, apparently announcing her son's dethronement, on account of the insolence of his manners, and her own possession of the solitary throne. The object of this embassy was evidently to strengthen Irene's position by forming an alliance with the Frank. It appears to have been successful, and a sign of the restored friendship between the two states was the return to Constantinople of Sisinnius, brother of the Patriarch Tarasius, who had apparently been in captivity ever since the war of 788. Lastly came the above-mentioned embassy, probably from this same Michael, now promoted, to the governorship of Sicily. All these indications show that at this time Charles was not unwilling to accept the olive-branch so persistently tendered by the Augusta of Constantinople.

The autumn of this year (799) was saddened for Charles by the tidings of the death of two of his bravest warriors, slain in battle with the barbarians of the Danube. Gerold, duke of Bavaria, brother of the beloved Hildegard, was slain with two of his officers by a troop of insurgent Avars, while he was riding in front of his followers and cheering them on to the encounter; Eric, duke of Friuli, fell at Tersatto, the victim of an ambush laid by the barbarous Croatians. The scene of this disaster, together with other indications, shows that Istria now formed part of the Frankish dominions : an important conquest, to which we are unable to assign a date, save that it must have been before the year 791. The death of Eric was an especially heavy blow for his royal master. It was he who had penetrated (795) into the far-famed and mysterious Avar Hring, and carried off its stored-up treasures. He had been a generous benefactor to the Church, a liberal almoner to the poor, and in all things, as far as we can trace his actions, a type of the Christian hero. His friendship for Paulinus, bishop of Aquileia, who composed for him a manual of the Christian life called 'Liber Exhortationis,' and who lamented him after his death in a dirge which recalls David's lament over Jonathan, is a beautiful incident in an age of violence and bloodshed.

King Charles spent the winter of 799 at Aachen, and the other tidings which were brought to him there were all of a joyful kind. The subjugation—as men fondly hoped the final subjugation—of the turbulent Celts of Brittany, the expulsion of the Moors from Majorca, the surrender of Huesca in Arragon, all these successes were reported to him in the course of that winter. Not less welcome probably was the arrival of a monk from Jerusalem, bringing relics and other offerings 'from the place of the Lord's resurrection', a present from the Patriarch of the Holy City to 'the great King of the West'. It was apparently on Christmas Day itself that the Syrian monk was dismissed in all honour from the palace, escorted by another monk named Zacharias, who was to bear the royal gifts to the Holy Place.

With the approach of spring, Charles left his palace at Aachen, sailed down the Rhine or the Meuse into the German Ocean, coasted along till he came to the mouth of the Somme, and there landed at the monastery of S. Riquier, of which his irregular son-in-law Angilbert was head. The king's business in those regions was to strengthen the defences of the coast, and equip some kind of a fleet to repel the incursions of the Northmen, those terrible incursions which were to stain with blood the pages of the next century and to destroy so much of the infant civilization of the Anglo-Saxon and Frankish lands.

Again putting to sea, he sailed up the Seine to Rouen, and from thence journeyed by land to the shrine of St. Martin at Tours. His avowed object was to perform his devotions at the tomb of Gaul's greatest saint, but it cannot be doubted that he also desired to converse about the affairs of his kingdom with that trusted adviser, Alcuin, who was abbot of St. Martin's monastery. Some months before, Charles had invited him to be his companion in the meditated journey to Rome, but Alcuin had declined, alleging that his feeble body, racked with daily pains, was unfitted for the fatigues of so long and toilsome a journey. "You chide me", he said, "that I prefer the smoke-grimed roofs of Tours to the gilded citadels of the Romans: but I know that your Prudence remembers the saying of Solomon, "It is better to dwell in a corner of the house-top than with a brawling woman in a wide house." And let me say it in all courtesy, iron (the iron of warlike weapons) hurts my eyes more than smoke. Tours, thanks to your bounty, rests in peace, content with her smoky homes. But Rome, which has been once touched by the discord of brethren, still keeps the poison which has been instilled into her veins, and thus compels your venerable Dignity to hasten from your sweet abodes in Germany in order to repress the fury of this pestilence".

Since, then, Alcuin persistently refused to visit Charles, Charles repaired to the monastery of Alcuin. It was indeed time that he should visit the Neustrian portion of his dominions, for he had not seen them for twenty-two years; so persistently Austrasian in his sympathies was this great king, whom Napoleon and his courtiers loved to speak of as a Frenchman.

The king's sojourn at Tours was prolonged by the illness and saddened by the death of his wife, his last wedded wife, the bright and genial Liutgarda. She died on the 4th of June, and was buried near the shrine of the soldier-saint. The widowed husband returned by way of Orleans to Paris and Aachen, held a great *placitum* at Mainz in August, and in the autumn started on his memorable fourth journey to Rome. He went at the head of an army, for the affairs of Benevento wore a threatening aspect, the young prince Grimwald again stirring mutinously against the Frankish yoke. We hear of him first at Ravenna, where he tarried seven days, and then at Ancona, from whence he dispatched his son Pippin on the usual ravaging expedition against the lands of the Beneventans. On the 24th of November he arrived at Rome. On the previous day the Pope had gone to meet him at Mentana, fourteen miles from Rome, and after partaking of supper in his quarters, returned to the City for the night. On the morning of the 24th Charles entered Rome, being received by the citizens, the ecclesiastics, the guilds of foreigners, with the same display of banners, the same chanting of devout hymns which had welcomed the returning Leo. At the foot of the Vatican hill he dismounted and walked slowly up the steps of St. Peter's (we do not hear, as on a former visit, of his kissing the sacred stairs), while Pope and clergy sang loud their praises.

Seven days after Charles's triumphal entry into Rome a synod of all the great Roman ecclesiastics and Frankish nobles was convened in St. Peter's basilica. The Papal biographer, intent on all that redounds to the glory of his order, bids us note that the King and the Pope, who were seated, called on the archbishops, bishops and abbots to resume their seats, but that all the other priests and nobles remained standing. The King then, with that fluent and majestic eloquence of which he was master, set forth to the assembly the Discussion reasons for this, his fourth visit to Rome, and the charges necessity for a close investigation of the crimes urged against Leo by his enemies. At this point there is a slight divergence between our two sets of witnesses. The Frankish annalists say that the great initial difficulty of the investigation was that no one was found willing to formulate the charges against Pope Leo. Of course that might mean either (which is the more probable supposition) that the charges were wicked fabrications, or that in face of the royal favour manifested towards the Pope no one dared to come forward as his accuser. The Papal biographer, on the other hand, tells us that all the archbishops, bishops and abbots with one accord said, "We do not dare to judge the Apostolic See, which is the head of all the Churches of God. For to it and its Vicar all we are answerable, but the See itself is judged of no man. So has the custom been from of old; but as he, the supreme pontiff, shall ordain, we will canonically obey." Then the venerable chief [Leo] said, "I will follow the footsteps of the Popes my predecessors, and am prepared to purge myself from these false charges which wicked men have blazed abroad against me." '

All our authorities agree that this self-vindicating oath was in fact the sole event of the trial, if trial, it may be called. 'On the next day at St. Peter's all the archbishops, bishops and abbots, and all the Franks in the King's service and all the Romans being present together in that church, the Pope in their presence took the four gospels in his hand, ascended the *ambo,* and with a clear voice said, "It hath been heard, dearest brethren, and spread abroad in many places, how evil men have risen up against me and laid grievous crimes to my charge. In order to try this cause, the most clement and most serene lord, King Charles, together with his bishops and nobles, hath come unto this City. Wherefore I, Leo, pontiff of the Holy Roman Church, being judged by no man and constrained by none, of mine own free will do purify and purge myself in your sight and before God and His angels, who knoweth my conscience, and before the blessed Peter, Prince of Apostles, in whose basilica we stand; as thus : These criminal and wicked deeds which they lay unto my charge, I have neither perpetrated nor ordered to be perpetrated; as God is my witness, before whose judgment-seat we shall appear and in whose sight we stand. And this I do of mine own free will, for the removal of all suspicions; not as if any such procedure were found in the canons, nor as if I would impose this custom or decree [as a precedent] on my successors in Holy Church, or on my brothers and colleagues in the episcopate." This solemn oath of innocence having been sworn, the churchmen sang the litany and gave thanks to God, the Virgin, and St. Peter.'

In order to dismiss this mysterious business of the attack on the Pope's character we may slightly anticipate the order of events. It was probably after the lapse of several weeks that Pasehalis and Campulus and their associates, brought back from their exile in Frank-land, were led into Charles's presence, with the chief nobles of the two nations, Frankish and Roman, standing round them, and bitterly upbraiding them for their evil deeds. The ruffians in their disgrace fell out with one another. Campulus said to Pasehalis, 'In an evil hour did I behold thy face. It is thou who hast brought me into this peril'. And so with all the others: their mutual chidings and upbraidings were a clear confession of guilt. They were condemned to death as guilty of treason—an important evidence of the sovereign character which the Pope of Rome had now assumed—but on the intercession of the Pope the sentence was commuted into one of banishment.

On the same day on which Pope Leo performed his solemn act of self-exculpation, the presbyter Zacharias returned from Jerusalem with two monks who were commissioned by the Patriarch to bring to Charles the keys of Calvary and of the Holy Sepulchre, together with the banner of Jerusalem. The precise import of this act was perhaps doubtful. Certainly the Caliph Haroun-al-Raschid would not have allowed that it conferred on the Frankish king any territorial sovereignty over Jerusalem. Still it was in a certain sense a recognition that the holiest place in Christendom was under the protection of the great monarch of the West, and in so far it helped to prepare men's minds for the impending revolution.

An interval of three weeks followed, undescribed by any of our authorities; but which we may fairly conjecture to have been occupied by those deliberations between Frankish nobles and Roman ecclesiastics which are described by the author of the *Chronicon Moissiacense*, and which prepared the way for the next act in the drama.

At length the fullness of time was come, and Charles, attended probably by all his Frankish courtiers and by a multitude of the citizens of Rome, went to pay his devotions on the morning of Christmas Day in the great basilica of St. Peter. That building has been often named in these pages, but I have not hitherto attempted to describe it. If we would imagine its appearance at the close of the eighth century, or indeed at any period before the beginning of the sixteenth century, the chief requisite is absolutely to exclude from our mental vision the vast Renaissance temple which Julius II and Leo X, which Bramante and Raffaele and Michael Angelo have reared upon the Vatican hill. If we must think of some still existing building, let it be S. Ambrogio at Milan or S. Paolo Fuori at Rome rather than the existing St. Peter's. Let us follow Charles and his nobles in imagination to the great basilica on the morning of Friday, the 25th of December, 800. They mount up from the banks of the Tiber by a long colonnade which stretches all the way from the castle of S. Angelo to the threshold of St. Peter's. They reverentially ascend the thirty-five steps to the platform, on which the Pope and all the great officers of his household stand waiting to receive them. Charles himself,

'In shape and gesture proudly eminent,'

with his yellow locks tinged with grey and with some furrows ploughed in his cheeks by the toils of twenty Saxon campaigns, towers above the swarthy, shaven ecclesiastics who surround the Pope. All Roman hearts are gladdened by seeing that he wears the Roman dress, the long tunic with the scarf thrown over it, and the low shoes of a Roman noble instead of the high laced-up boots of a Teutonic chieftain.

After the usual courteous salutations, the blended train of nobles and churchmen follow Hadrian and Charles into the basilica. They traverse first the great *atrium, measuring 320 feet by 225. In the* centre of the *atrium* rises the great fountain called Pinea, the water spouting forth from the top and from every bossy protuberance of an enormous fircone. This fountain was placed there by Pope Symmachus, the contemporary of Theodoric, who, like Leo III himself, was well-nigh

'Done to death by evil tongues.'

Round the fountain have begun to cluster the marble tombs of the Popes of the last four centuries. They pass on : they enter the basilica proper, consisting of five naves; (the central nave much wider than the rest), divided from one another by four rows of monolith columns. These columns are ninety-six in number[2], of different materials, granite, Parian marble, African marble; and they have very different histories ; some, it is said, being brought from the Septizonium of Septimius Severus, and others from the various temples of heathen Rome. They are of unequal height; and not only this inequality, but many signs of rough work, notwithstanding all the splendour of gold and silver plates and the vivid colouring of the mosaics on the walls, give evidence of the haste with which the venerable fabric was originally reared—men say by the order and with the co-operation of Constantine himself—in the days when Christianity could yet scarcely believe in the permanence of its hardly-won victory over heathenism. Between the pillars of the central nave are hung (as it is a feast day) costly veils of purple embroidered with gold, and at the further end of the church the gigantic cross-shaped candelabra, hanging from the silver-plated frame-work of the triumphal arch, with its 1,370 candles, lights up the gloom of the December morning. This triumphal arch, which, with the long colonnade leading up to it, was an essential feature of the early Roman basilica, is doubtless adorned with mosaics of saints and martyrs, and spans the entrance to the apsidal tribune, which is the very Holy of Holies of Rome. For here, before and below the high altar, is the *confessio* or subterranean cave in which the body of St. Peter, rescued from its pagan surroundings, the circus of Nero and the temples of Apollo and Cybele, is believed to repose in the coffin of gilded bronze provided for it by the reverent munificence of the first Christian Emperor. Over the high altar rises a baldacchino supported by four porphyry columns, and by others of white marble twisted into the resemblance of vine- stems. Keeping guard as it were in front of the *confessio* are many statues of saints and angels. Here, as if in bold defiance of all the edicts of iconoclastic Emperors, Gregory III has reared an *iconostasis* covered with silver plates, on which are depicted on one side the likenesses of Christ and His Apostles, on the other those of the Virgin Mary and a train of holy maidens; and following in his footsteps Hadrian has placed near the *iconostasis* six images, made of silver plates covered with gold. At the entrance of the choir stands the image of the Saviour, with the archangels Gabriel and Michael on either side of Him, and behind, in the middle of the choir, is the Virgin Mother, flanked by the Apostles St. Andrew and St. John. All the floor of this part of the basilica is covered with plates of silver. Behind, at the very end of the church, is seen the chair of St. Peter's successor, with seats for the suburbicarian bishops—the cardinal-bishops as they are already beginning to be called—in the curve of the apse on either side of him.

The basilica proper, that is the part within the *atrium*, measured 320 feet by 226. The best idea of its dimensions will be obtained by comparing it with the existing church of S. Paolo fuori le Mura at Home, which is 306 feet long by 222 broad. That church also has its four rows of columns, its triumphal arch adorned with mosaics, its *confessio* with a reputed apostolic tomb surmounted by a baldacchino borne by porphyry columns and guarded by apostolic statues, and behind the triumphal arch it has its round apsidal end. Thus, notwithstanding its own extremely modern date, it may both in size and arrangement be considered as the best representative now available of the basilica of St. Peter at the end of the eighth century.

One thing more we note in passing, that the St. Peter's of Leo III was about a century older than its modern representative, reared by Julius II and Leo X and Paul III, is at the present day.

Such then was the great and venerable building, encrusted with memories of half a thousand Christian years, in which Charles the Frank knelt on the Christmas morning of the year 800 to pay his devotions at the *confessio* of St. Peter. Assuredly if he himself was ignorant of what was about to happen, neither the Roman citizens nor the Frankish courtiers shared his ignorance. Assuredly there was a hush of expectation throughout the dim basilica, and all eyes were directed towards the kneeling figure in Roman garb at the tomb of the Apostle.

Charles rose from his knees. The Pope approached him, and lifting high his hands placed on the head of the giant king a golden crown. Then all the Roman citizens burst into a loud and joyful cry : 'To Carolus Augustus, crowned by God, mighty and pacific Emperor, be life and victory'. Thrice was the fateful acclamation uttered. Then all joined in the 'Laudes,' a long series of choral invocations to Christ, to angels, to apostles, to martyrs, and to virgins, praying each separately to grant the newly-crowned Emperor heavenly aid to conquer all his foes.

Thus the great revolution towards which for three generations the stream of events had been steadily setting was accomplished. Once more an Emperor of the Romans had been acclaimed in Rome, the first of that long line of Teutonic Augusti, the last of whom laid down the true Imperial diadem in the lifetime of our fathers at the bidding of the son of a Corsican attorney.

Thus far all our authorities are agreed. It is important now to notice the points in which, without contradicting, they nevertheless diverge somewhat from one another.

(1) The Frankish annalists both assure us that after Lauds had been sung, Charles 'was adored by the pontiff after the manner of the ancient princes. The Papal biographer conveniently omits this fact, which the Roman *Curia* did not desire to remember, but there is no reason to doubt that it actually occurred, nor that such reverence as the Patriarch of Constantinople would have paid to Justinian or Heraclius, the Bishop of Rome paid to his now acknowledged lord, Carolus Augustus.

(2) Theophanes says that the Pope anointed Charles with oil from his head to his feet, and arrayed him in a royal robe and crown. This thorough anointing, which would have required that Charles should have been stripped naked in the sight of the whole assembly, does not agree with any of the other accounts, and is in itself improbable. It probably arose from some confusion with the next item of information.

(3) The Papal biographer informs us that 'on the same day' (probably at a later hour) 'the Pope anointed with the holy oil his most excellent son Charles (the younger) as king.' This, though not mentioned by the annalists, is quite intelligible. As his predecessor had anointed Pippin king of Italy and Louis king of Aquitaine, so he now anointed their brother Charles as king, probably king of the Franks, that being a title which was perhaps left open for him by his father's promotion to a higher dignity.

(4) His (The same biographer mentions the costly gifts which were presented to the shrine of St. Peter by Charles and his family, after the celebration of Mass which followed the coronation. They were 'a silver table with its feet' (whose weight is not stated), 'a golden crown with jewels to hang over the altar, a golden paten, and three large chalices, one of them set with gems.' The mere gold in these vessels weighed 216 pounds, equivalent in value to more than £10,000 sterling.

(5) A most important statement, and one that has given rise to almost endless discussion, is that made by Einhard in his Life of Charles:— 'At this time he received the name of Imperator and Augustus. Which he at first so much disliked, that he declared that he would never have entered the church on that day, though it was a high festival, if he could have fore-known the pontiff's design. He bore, however, with great patience the odium that attached to him on account of his new title through the indignation of the Roman Emperors'. And he vanquished their stubbornness by his own far-surpassing magnanimity, sending to them frequent embassies, and in his letters addressing them as brothers.'

I reserve my comments on this important statement for a later paragraph.

The remainder of Charles's visit to Italy may be described in a few words.

The winter was occupied in settling the affairs of Charles's the State and the Church in the new relations to one in Italy, another which resulted from the re-establishment of the Empire. One of the most important of these was that henceforward the consent of the Frankish Emperor was necessary for the consecration of a newly elected Pope.

As Grimwald was still unsubdued, a second expedition was sent under Pippin to reduce him to obedience, but it does not appear to have achieved any decided success. Probably malaria, as well as the Lombard sword, defended the independence of the Samnite duchy.

On Easter Day (April 4, 801) Charles was again in Rome. Three weeks afterwards he visited Spoleto, where, in the second hour of the night, he witnessed a tremendous earthquake which shook the whole of Italy and brought down in ruin the roof of *S. Paolo fuori at Rome.*

From Spoleto he went to Ravenna, where he spent some of the early days of May; from Ravenna to Pavia, arriving there about the beginning of June. In the old palace of the Lombard kings he received the tidings of the arrival of an embassy from the Caliph Haroun-al-Raschid. From Pavia he went to Ivrea, and so over the Great St. Bernard to Switzerland, and down the Rhine to his beloved Aquae Grani, where he spent the remainder of the year.

Now that Charles has recrossed the Alps and sits once more in his palace at Aachen, no longer now as mere *Rex Francorum et Langobardorum* and *Patricius Romanorum*, but as Augustus and Imperator, we may suitably consider what were the causes and what was the significance of the peaceful revolution—for such in fact it was—effected in the basilica of St. Peter on Christmas Day, 800.

It is hardly necessary formally to discuss the theory which prevailed a hundred years ago, that there was in this act an intentional revival of the Western Empire which had lain dormant since the deposition of Romulus Augustulus in 476. Doubtless this was something like the practical result of Charles's coronation. After an interval of suspense, uncertainty and mutual suspicion, the two powers of East and West at last settled down into an attitude, not of partnership, hardly of friendship, but of mutual toleration, and accepted the Adriatic as the dividing line between the two Empires. And yet, near two centuries later, a monk of Salerno writing the history of his city, an Italian city, under the influence of strong anti-Frankish feeling, could say, 'The men about the court of Charles the Great called him Emperor, because he wore a precious crown on his head. But in truth no one should be called Emperor save the man who presides over the Roman, *that is the Constantinopolitan* kingdom. The kings of the Gauls have now usurped to themselves that name, but in ancient times they were never so called.'

In truth the epithet 'one and indivisible' which the French Republic used of itself when threatened by the armies of partitioning invaders, might have been applied to the Roman Empire at any time previous to the ninth century. There were jealousies and heart-burnings (as the readers of this history know right well) between the East and the West, between Arcadius and Honorius, between Leo and Ricimer; and sometimes these quarrels were on the point of bursting into the flame of war. Still the wars thus threatened, like the wars which were actually waged between Constantine and Julian or between Theodosius and Eugenius, would have been regarded as civil wars. The great earth-encompassing *Imperium Romanum* remained, at least in theory, one, and no more convincing proof of its unity, of its indestructible feeling of organic and all-pervading life, could be given than was afforded by the marvellous reconquest of Italy by the generals of Justinian.

We must then recognize the fact that the Pope when he placed the crown on the head of Charles, and the Roman people when they shouted 'Long life to the most pious Augustus, great and pacific Emperor of the Romans,' were, in theory at least, assailing the throne of Irene, and claiming for the great Austrasian monarch dominion over all the lands, from the Pillars of Hercules to the river Euphrates, over which the Roman eagle had flapped its wings.

This fact, that the assumption of the Imperial title was of necessity a challenge to the court of Constantinople, the only Christian state which could for a moment pretend to rival the Frankish kingdom in wealth and power, was doubtless one reason (as Einhard implicitly assures us) for Charles's unwillingness to be hailed as Augustus. For that this unwillingness was a mere pretence, that Charles when he expressed his dissatisfaction with the ceremony was merely copying the *Nolo Episcopari* of eminent ecclesiastics, seems to me both unproved and improbable. He was not a spiritual ruler, nor expected to utter any phrases of conventional humility. It may be true, it probably is true, that the subject of the change of his title from *Patricius* to *Imperator* had often been discussed in his presence by such men as Alcuin, Angilbert, and Leo himself; and the proposal had probably found a certain degree of acceptance in a mind such as his, which was always inspired by large and lofty ambitions. But he saw, as perhaps Alcuin did not see, the practical inconveniences of a permanent estrangement from the Byzantine court. He may possibly have already entertained the strange project of acquiring the Imperial crown by a matrimonial alliance with Irene. At all events, he wished to choose his own time and way for the great revolution, and saw with dissatisfaction his hand forced by the officiousness of Leo III and the enthusiasm of the Roman people.

We may perhaps be enabled to understand a little better the state of mind of the Frankish hero if we compare his position with that of Julius Caesar when Marcus Antonius at the festival of the Lupercalia offered him a kingly crown, or with that of Cromwell, when after much deliberation and many swayings of his mind backwards and forwards he finally rejected the title of King offered to him by his Parliament. In both of those cases there was much to be said in favour of the proposed change, and there were strong reasons, quite apart from any motive of mere vanity or ambition, why the foremost man in the state should accept the offered title. In both of those cases the great man's adherents—not in mere flattery and courtiership—were more anxious than he himself for the augmentation of his dignity. There also the statesman felt the obstacles, invisible to the less highly trained perceptions of his followers, which made the change a perilous one. The all-important difference between those cases and this which we are now considering is that in them the negative arguments prevailed, while with Charles the intervention of the sacrosanct chief of Western Christendom, dispelled all doubts, ended all hesitation, and by proclaiming the Teutonic Caesar fixed the form of European polity for centuries to come.

This very intervention of the Pope was, however, in all probability one of those circumstances of the revolution which made it unacceptable to the new Augustus. If the thing had to be done—and probably he had made up his mind to accept its necessity—he would have wished it done in some other way: by the invitation of his Frankish nobles; by a vote of the shadowy body which called itself the Roman Senate (if such a shadow still haunted the north-western corner of the Forum); by the acclamations of the Roman people; or by all these instrumentalities combined, but not by the touch of the Pontiff's fingers. He foresaw, probably with statesman-like instinct, the mischief which would accrue to future generations from the precedent thus furnished of a Pope appearing by virtue of his ecclesiastical office to bestow the Imperial crown. And certainly he did what in him lay to destroy the force of the precedent. No bishop of Rome or of any other see presided over the ceremony when in 813 he promoted his son Louis to the Imperial dignity. The mischief, however, was incurable. It became the deep-rooted conviction of the Middle Ages that the Emperor, if he would be an Emperor of unchallenged legitimacy, must receive his crown in Rome from the hands of the successor of St. Peter. And not only so, but the absolutely erroneous idea that the Pope had by virtue of his plenary power over states and kingdoms transferred the Imperial dignity from Constantinople to Rome, was adopted by one canonist and monkish historian after another, till it at length found full and loud expression in the Decretal published by Innocent III in 1201, in which he upheld the cause of Otho of Brunswick as candidate for the Imperial crown against Philip of Swabia. The story of the Translation thus passed into the collection of the Decretals, and as part of the canon law of Europe reigned supreme for three centuries, till at the time of the Revival of Learning this fiction, along with the Donation of Constantine, the Decretals of the false Isidore, and others like itself, came tumbling to the ground.

Truly is it said by Professor Dahn, 'All the claims which were ever asserted by the great Popes against the Emperors, their theory of the Two Swords, the whole conception according to which the Pope as successor of St. Peter, as representative of God upon earth, was entitled to grant or to refuse to grant the Imperial crown as his *beneficium* to the German king ("Petra dedit Petro, Petrus diadema Rudolfo"); all this theory which makes the king the Pope's vassal in respect of the Imperial crown, rests on that one ceremony in which the first Emperor received the crown from the hand of the Roman Pope.

It is reasonable to infer that so far-seeing a statesman as Charles perceived this cloud on the horizon of the future, and that his perception of it had something to do with that enigmatic saying of his to Einhard, 'Had I known what Leo was about to do, I would never have entered St. Peter's on that Christmas morning.' There is also another consideration, scarcely noticed hitherto, which, as it seems to me, may have rendered Charles averse to the proposed revolution. He had three sons, Charles, Pippin, Louis. He intended Louis to reign after him in Southern Gaul, Pippin in Italy and Bavaria, while Neustria and Austrasia, the proper home of the Franks, with their old and time-honoured capitals, Metz, Soissons, Paris, and the great Rhine-stream itself, dearest of rivers to

Charles's heart, were all to be the portion of his eldest son Charles, likest of all his children to himself, who was undoubtedly to hold the predominant place in the royal partnership. Presumably therefore Charles was to be the future Emperor, but the city from which he was to take his title, the city which as Emperor he was to be pre-eminently bound to cherish and protect, would be included in the dominions of a brother, perhaps of a rival. Here was a danger, patent and obviously to be apprehended, though in the actual course of events the lamentable death of both the two young princes, Charles and Pippin, prevented its actual occurrence. We have, I think, no hint of the way in which Charles himself proposed to deal with it, but it may well have been one of the elements in the case which rendered him less eager than Alcuin and Angilbert to hear the joyful acclamations of the Roman people, 'Long life to Carolus Augustus.'

Of the other chief actors in the scene the motives are not so hard to discover. The Frankish nobles and great churchmen doubtless felt their own dignity exalted by becoming the servants of a Roman Emperor. The Roman people seemed to regain the right, lost for nearly four centuries, of conferring by their acclamations the title which gave to its wearer 'the lordship of the habitable world.' And as for the Pope himself, may we not consider that if he renounced for the present his dream of establishing himself as the absolutely independent sovereign of central and southern Italy, he saw his advantage in the restoration of a strong Imperial rule which would make such outrages as those perpetrated upon him by Paschalis and Campulus thereafter impossible? And still the consolidation of the Papal States would go forward, though in theory he would have to hold them as a *beneficium* from the new Augustus. In practice, who could tell, with that magnificent precedent of a Pope-conferred crown, whether the relation might not one day be inverted, and the Pope become, as Boniface VIII claimed to be, lord paramount of the Emperor.

CHAPTER VI

CHARLES AND IRENE.

THE coronation of Charles the Frank as Emperor of the Romans would perhaps have formed the most fitting conclusion, as it would certainly have been the most dramatic close to this history. It seems, however, more satisfactory to continue the narrative till the death of the new Emperor, as we shall thus have an opportunity of tracing the effect of the revolution of 800 on the statesmen and courtiers of Eastern Europe.

To Charles personally the first fourteen years of the ninth century were a time of comparative rest from the toils of war, of legislative activity for the welfare of his Empire, but also of heavy family affliction through the loss of those upon whom he had reckoned to carry on his glorious work into the next generation.

He spent the year 802 at Aachen, chiefly occupied in revising the national codes and reinvigorating the internal administration of his Empire. We hear now for the first time of his great institution of *missi dominici,* men who were, so to speak, the staff-officers of his administration, sent into every province of his Empire to control the actions of the local courts in the interests of peace and righteousness, pre-eminently to maintain the cause of the stranger, the fatherless and the widow, and also to see that the ecclesiastical government was conducted in accordance with the canons, and that the old anarchy and licentiousness did not creep back into the Frankish Church. For the office of *missi* Charles chose chiefly, but not exclusively, archbishops, abbots, and other high dignitaries of the Church, men whose character he had tested during their residence at his court, and whom he felt that he could trust to uphold his standard of right against a grasping count or turbulent mark-grave.

One of the chief duties imposed upon these new officers in the great capitulary of Aachen (March, 802) was the administration to his subjects of a new oath of fidelity, not now to the Frankish King, but to the most serene and most Christian Emperor. 'I order,' he says, 'that every man in my whole kingdom, whether ecclesiastic or layman, each one according to his prayer and his purpose, who may have before promised fidelity to me in the king's name, shall now repeat that promise to me in my name as Caesar. And those who may not yet have made that promise shall now all do so, from twelve years old and upwards. And let this be done in public, so that all may understand how many and how great things are contained in that oath, not merely, as many have hitherto supposed, that they shall not conspire against the Emperor's life, nor let his enemies into the realm, nor be privy to any treachery against him. Far greater duties than these are involved in this oath'. The capitulary then enforces the obligation of each man to abide in the service of God and to dedicate to Him all his bodily and intellectual powers; to abstain from perjury and fraud of all kinds; not to filch the lands of the Emperor nor conceal his fugitive slaves; neither by force nor fraud to do any injury to the holy churches of God, to orphans, widows or strangers, 'forasmuch as our Lord the Emperor, under God and His saints, has been appointed protector and defender of all such'; not to lay waste the land which a man holds in fief from the king in order to enrich his own adjoining property; always to follow the king's banner to war; not to hinder the execution of his writ, nor to strive to pervert the course of justice in the provincial assembly. All these duties are implicitly contained in the new *sacramentum* which is to be administered to the subjects of the Emperor.

Two years after the issue of this capitulary, in 804, came the final close of the long, dreary, and desolating war for the subjugation of the Saxons. It was accompanied by the transportation of ten thousand Saxons with their wives and children, from those districts which had ever been foremost in rebellion, to distant and widely separated provinces of Germany and Gaul. At last the spirit of that proud people was broken. The bishops of Bremen, Munster, and Paderborn could enjoy their princely revenues and rule their wide provinces in peace. Christianity was triumphant, and the 'ban' of the Most Serene Emperor commanded unquestioning obedience from the Rhine to the Elbe.

In November of this same year the Emperor heard the tidings of an intended visit of Pope Leo III to his court. The occasion of this visit was a remarkable one. Charles had heard in the previous summer a startling rumour that some of the actual blood of the Saviour had been discovered—presumably by a miracle—in the city of Mantua. He asked the Pope for a report on this wonderful discovery; and Leo, probably not sorry to have an excuse for leaving Rome where he had many enemies, visited Mantua to obey his patron's behest, and then for the second time crossed the Alps. He was met by the young king Charles at St. Maurice and escorted with much reverence to Rheims, near to which city he met the Emperor. Soissons and Quierzy were the chief stages in their joint journey to Aachen, at which place they kept their Christmas together. Unfortunately no record is preserved to us of the conversations which Emperor and Pope held with one another, whether about the Mantuan prodigy or the many important affairs of Church and State which were doubtless discussed between them. Soon after Epiphany (January 6, 805) Leo III took his departure for Rome, and Charles saw his face no more.

Wars with Denmark, fitful but not unimportant, occupied the years from 808 to 810. Göttrik (or Godefrid), king of Denmark, an obstinate heathen, seemed likely at one time to hold the same place as chief foe of the Franks and their Christianity which had once been occupied by Widukind the Saxon. But towards the end of the year 810 came tidings that Göttrik had been murdered by one of his own body-guard, and Hemming his nephew gladly concluded a peace, which was unbroken during the remainder of the life of Charles.

This year, 810, is one of great importance in the negotiations between Charles and the Eastern Caesar, and to the earlier stages of these we now turn, after this slight sketch of the events which were occurring in Western Europe.

A general view of the question may be obtained by extracting a few sentences from the chief authorities on either side.

Einhard, the trusted minister of Charles's old age, writes (as we have already seen): 'He bore with great patience the odium that attached to him on account of his new title through the indignation of the Roman Emperors. And he vanquished their stubbornness by his own far-surpassing magnanimity, sending to them frequent embassies, and in his letters addressing them as brothers.'

In an earlier chapter the same author writes : 'The Emperors of Constantinople' ['observe that they are not here spoken of as Roman Emperors], 'Nicephorus, Michael, and Leo, of their own accord seeking his friendship and alliance, sent to him many ambassadors. With whom—notwithstanding the strong suspicion caused by his assumption of the Imperial title, as if he were desirous to wrest the Empire from them—he succeeded in establishing a very durable treaty, so that no occasion for offence remained between the two parties. For to the Romans and Greeks the power of the Franks had always been an object of suspicion; wherefore also this proverb is current among the Greeks, "Have the Frank for a friend, do not have him for a neighbour".'

We now turn to Theophanes, the Byzantine noble-man and monk, the enthusiastic champion of 'the most pious Irene', on account of her zeal for the images of the saints. He says : 'In this year (800-801), on the 25th of December, Carolus, king of the Franks, was crowned by Pope Leo; and having planned to cross over to Sicily with a fleet, he changed his mind and chose rather to be married to Irene, sending ambassadors for this purpose, who arrived in the following year.'

'Next year (801-802) the legates who were sent by Carolus and by Leo the Pope arrived in presence of Irene, praying her to be yoked in marriage with Carolus and so to bring together in one the Eastern and the Western lands. To which proposal she would have agreed had not the Patrician Aetius hindered her, he being at that time the all-powerful minister, and intriguing to obtain the diadem for his own brother'.

This passage of the Byzantine historian gives us some important information.

I. As to Charles's alleged designs on Sicily. As has been already said, we are told that in the year 799 an ambassador named Daniel came from Michael, prefect of Sicily, to Charles's court at Paderborn; that he was there at the same time as the fugitive Pope Leo, and was dismissed with great honour by the king. We have no mention of any commands with which this Sicilian ambassador was entrusted by the Empress. Have we here a cry for help and an offer of transferred allegiance on the part of a prefect of Sicily who is revolting from the rule of Byzantium? Again, in the year 801 or 802 we find a certain Leo, a captain of the guard, a Sicilian by nation, fleeing from Sicily and taking refuge at Charles's court; but as he is also spoken of as an ambassador sent by Irene 'to confirm the peace between the Franks and Greeks', it is possible that we are here only dealing with the case of one of Irene's creatures involved in her downfall (shortly to be described), and fearing to face the anger of her enemies. Still these slight hints, combined with the words of Theophanes, incline us to the belief that the new Emperor may have cherished the very natural ambition to add Sicily to his Italian dominions. The project may have fallen through on account of the insufficiency of his fleet, or may have been laid aside in order not further to embitter his relations with Constantinople. Sicily never formed part of the Frankish Empire, and only a few years after Charles's death began its long servitude to Saracen conquerors.

II. We note that, according to the narrative of Theophanes, the ambassadors of Charles were accompanied by legates from the rope. We can well understand that Leo, if he had not originally suggested the matrimonial scheme, would earnestly desire its success. However plainly we can now see that the current of events was setting towards the separation of the Eastern and Western Churches as its inevitable end, no Pope, who believed in the prerogatives which he claimed, can have accepted such a conclusion without a pang. The iconoclastic schism was at an end.

Irene was nearer to the Pope on the question of image-worship than Charles. Why not unite the chiefs of the Eastern and Western world by the bonds of holy matrimony, and through them rule supreme over an undivided Christendom

III. The cunningly-devised scheme, however, came to an untimely end. Charles's ambassadors were Jesse bishop of Amiens and Helmgaud, apparently one of Jesse and the counts of the palace. Perhaps one of the messengers was not very happily chosen, for Bishop Jesse, though Alcuin praises 'the deep bull-like bellow of his voice, so fitting in one who has to read the scriptures to the people', was considered by Pope Leo (to whom he was sent on an embassy six years later, with Helmgaud again for his companion) to be an unfit person to be employed as the Emperor's representative and an unsafe depositary of state secrets. But success in the mission was not possible whoever had been the messenger. Irene, after she had by a ghastly crime got rid of her son's rivalry, became a puppet-ruler in the hands of the eunuchs of her palace. The two chiefs, Stauracius and Aetius, fought hard for the mastery, but the duel was ended by the sickness and death of Stauracius in the summer of the year 800. Aetius, hereby left in a position like that of Grand Vizier in Irene's cabinet, began to plot for the elevation of his brother Leo to the Imperial throne, and he was not disposed to allow his plans to be thwarted by this wild scheme of the marriage of his mistress to a Western barbarian.

Soon there supervened another and more powerful reason for the failure of the negotiations. While Jesse and Helmgaud were still lingering at Constantinople they witnessed a revolution by which Irene herself was hurled from the throne. Possibly the rumour of the marriage negotiations had alarmed the national pride of the Greeks; more probably the arrogance and ambition of the eunuch Aetius had roused the opposition of some powerful Byzantine nobles. Taking advantage of the Empress's sickness and her consequent absence at the suburban palace of Eleutherium, the grand treasurer Nicephorus, accompanied by Nicetas, chief captain of the guard (whom Aetius supposed to be his friend), and by many other great officers of state, presented himself at the fourth hour of the night before the doors of the Brazen Palace, the innermost sanctuary of Imperial grandeur, and obtained admission from the palace guards, who believed, or pretended to believe, that the intruders came by command of Irene, wearied of the ascendency of Aetius, to proclaim Nicephorus as her colleague. The palace gained, all the rest was easy. Soldiers were sent at dawn to arrest Irene at the Eleutherium, and Nicephorus with his adherents Emperor, went in procession to the 'Great Church' of St. Sophia, where he was crowned by the patriarch Tarasius, once Irene's own supple minister. Theophanes, who abhors Nicephorus and cannot forgive the wrong done to the 'most pious Irene, the lover of God,' declares that the common people cursed both the crowner and the crowned, but that the nobles of Irene's party, who had received so many benefits at her hands, either turned traitors, or were stricken with a sort of numb despair, and felt as if they were dreaming when they saw 'that wise and noble lady, who had striven so gloriously for the faith, pushed off her throne by a swine-herd like Nicephorus'. Even the heavens, he suggests, shared the sullen indignation of the citizens. The face of the sky was dark, and the cold, unusual for an autumn day at Constantinople, foreboded the chill suspiciousness of the new Emperor and the griping penury to which he would reduce his people.

On the next day Nicephorus went alone and unattended, with no Imperial state, to the room in the palace where Irene was imprisoned. He pointed to his sandals, not purple like those of an Emperor, but black like those of an ordinary subject: he assured her that he had been reluctantly compelled to assume the diadem, and cursed the turbulent ambition of his supporters. Then in gentle tones he tried to soothe her fears, he gave a little homily on the evils of avarice, and conjured her to deal frankly with him and tell him where all the Imperial treasure was deposited. With more dignity than might have been expected from a woman who had loved empire so passionately, Irene said that she had recognized the hand of God in her unexpected elevation to the throne, and now recognized the same hand, chastising her for her sins, in her deposition. She had been often warned, she said, of the ambitious designs of Nicephorus, but had rejected what she believed to be the calumnious aspersions on his loyalty, and had preserved his life. Too late she learned that those calumnies were true. However, he was now her Emperor, and she as his subject would pay him reverence. She only asked to be allowed to retire to the palace of Eleutherium which she had herself built, and there spend the rest of her days in privacy. Her request, said Nicephorus, should be granted if she would swear to reveal to him the place of deposit of the Imperial treasure. She swore on the honourable and life-giving wood of the cross that she would show him everything, to the last obol: and straightway fulfilled her promise. He, having obtained what he desired, transported her, not to the palace of Eleutherium, but, first, to a convent on Princes' Island in the Sea of Marmora. Then fearing that the hearts of the people were again turning towards her, he removed her, on a bitterly cold day of November, to the island of Lemnos, where she was kept under strictest guard. She died on the 9th of August in the following year (803), and her body was removed to Princes' Island, and buried in the convent which she had founded there.

Theophanes relates—surely with a slight touch of malice—that the deportation of Irene took place under the very eyes of the legates of 'Carulus' who were still abiding in the city. There does not seem to have been any rumour of an expedition by the Frankish Emperor to deliver or to avenge the lady of his choice. The days of knight-errantry were not yet, and there was no touch of romance in Charles's offer of marriage. It was only a cold-blooded piece of political calculation, and that calculation had failed, as it was assuredly bound to fail in any event. Had Charles succeeded, had he broken up the happiness of his home by introducing into the gay and brilliant circle of his sons and daughters at the waters of Granius, this grim and sanctimonious Medea of Byzantium, he would have found after all that the Eastern diadem was not to be purchased, even by such a sacrifice. It was in the nature of things impossible that the Rhine could be ruled from the Bosphorus or the Bosphorus from the Rhine. The proposed alliance between Constantine VI and Hrotrud, had it taken place before 800, might have changed the face of Europe; but now, after the challenge had been given to Byzantium by Charles's coronation as Emperor at Rome, no makeshift scheme of marriage could heal the fatal schism. East and West must remain divided for evermore

CHAPTER VII

VENICE.

THE new Emperor Nicephorus who had won the diadem from Irene belonged neither to the best nor to the worst class of Byzantine sovereigns. His office before he mounted the throne had been that of Grand Logothete or Arch-treasurer, and a Grand Logothete he remained to the end of his career. He was intent on finding out new sources of taxation, and re-imposed some duties on imports which Irene had perhaps unwisely remitted for the sake of popularity. In pursuance of the same end he deprived the convent and church lands of the exemption from the hearth-tax which they had hitherto enjoyed. At the same time, though not reverting to the iconoclastic policy of the Isaurian Emperors, he showed himself languid in his defence of orthodoxy, and refused to persecute the Paulician dissenters from the Catholic Church. He thus came into collision with that fierce defender of the faith, Theodore of Studium, and his name is therefore loaded with abuse by the bigoted Theophanes. This abuse, as he did not redeem his heresy by military talent, like Leo III and Constantine V, as he fought feebly against the Caliph Haroun-al-Raschid, and as his life and reign ended in a terrible disaster, inflicted by the Bulgarian ravagers, has clung perhaps too persistently to his memory. Clio may always safely scold an unsuccessful sovereign.

On his first assumption of the diadem, Nicephorus, perhaps feeling the need of some strong external support, showed himself willing to enter into diplomatic relations with Charles, though the title of the Frankish Augustus challenged his Imperial claims even more directly than those of a female sovereign like Irene. Overlooking this fact, however, Nicephorus commissioned three ambassadors, a bishop named Michael, an abbot, Peter, and a white-uniformed officer of the guards named Callistus, to accompany Charles's legates, Jesse and Helmgaud, on their return to the Frankish court. They found the Emperor July (?), at Salz on the Franconian Saale, were courteously received by him, and carried back with them what we should call a draft treaty of peace between the two monarchs, bearing Charles's signature. There can be little doubt that this document contained some stipulation for the recognition by the Eastern Caesar of the Frank's imperial dignity: but it is equally plain that this recognition was withheld. The answer from Constantinople, though eagerly expected, did not arrive: there was for eight years a suspension of diplomatic relations between the two courts, and the Empires drifted from a position first of sullen isolation and at last of active and declared hostility.

What may have been the motive of Nicephorus for thus uncourteously closing negotiations which he himself had opened we are not informed. Possibly he saw that his own subjects would not tolerate a recognition which seemed like a dethronement of the New Rome in favour of the Old. The relations between the two Churches also were becoming more and more embittered, and the two disputes, ecclesiastical and political, acted and reacted upon one another. On the one hand, we have (in 809) the piteous complaint of the monks on Mount Olivet to the Pope that the abbot of S. Saba called them heretics and cast them rudely out of the cave of the Nativity at Bethlehem, because they sang the Nicene Creed with the added words concerning the Holy Spirit, which proceedeth from the Father and the Son.' 'Pray inform our Lord Charles the Emperor,' they say, 'that we heard these words, which we are accounted heretics for using, sung in his own chapel'. They evidently hoped that the long arm of the mighty Frank, the rival of Nicephorus and the ally of Caliph Haroun and his son, would be stretched forth to protect them from the arrogant Greeks'. On the other hand, Nicephorus the patriarch of Constantinople (who was raised to that dignity in February, 806, on the death of Tarasius) was, throughout the lifetime of his Imperial namesake, forbidden to hold any communication with the see of Rome, evidently because Leo was supposed to be devoted to the interests of Charles.

The quarrel thus commenced between the two Empires was fought out in the Waters of the Adriatic, and we must therefore turn our attention to the little cities of maritime Venetia which have hitherto (save for one passing allusion in the letters of Hadrian) been unnoticed since the year 740, when they took part in the recapture of Ravenna from Liutprand

At the period of that recapture we found the Venetian islanders trying abortive changes in their constitution, substituting *Magistri Militiae* for Dukes, and then finally settling down again under the rule of their old chief magistrate, the *Dux Venetiarum*.

The title of *Doge*—the form which this Latin word assumed in the Venetian dialect—has been made famous over the wide world by the exploits and the disasters, the virtues and the vices of the statesmen who for 'a thousand years of glory' presided over the fortunes of the Venetian state. But for that very reason I prefer not to use it at the present early period of their history. Too many and too proud associations are connected with that form of the name. In the eighth century the Duke of Venice differed little from the Duke of Naples or any other duke of a city under the Byzantine rule, save that perhaps already the people had a larger share in his election than in most of those other cities. Therefore the first man in the Venetian state shall still be to us a Duke and not a Doge.

After the restoration of the ducal dignity, three dukes, *Deusdedit, Galla,* and *Domenicus* (surnamed *Monegarius),* followed one another in somewhat rapid succession. Each precarious reign came to a violent end. Deusdedit (742-755) was supplanted by the traitor Galla; Galla (755-756) was upset by a popular revolution; Monegarius (756-764) was the victim of a conspiracy; and each duke as he fell from power was subjected to the cruel punishment of the plucking out of his eyes, a punishment which the Venetians had perhaps adopted from their Byzantine overlords.

The only point in the history of these shadowy dukes which seems worthy of notice is the limitation which the Venetians imposed on the power of Monegarius.

Joannes Diaconus informs us that the Venetians when they had raised this duke to power, 'after the fashion of the vulgar herd, who never remain long in one fixed purpose, but with superstitious folly are always looking out for one political nostrum after another, in the first year of Monegarius' duchy set over themselves two tribunes, who were to hold office under the ducal decree; an expedient which they tried' [but apparently tried vainly] 'to repeat, for each successive year of his tenure of the duchy'. We surely behold in this abortive attempt to limit the power of the sovereign the promptings of the same spirit which in the fourteenth century devised the Council of Ten and in the fifteenth gave birth to the awful tribunal of the Invisible Three.

On the deposition of the unpopular Monegarius a citizen oh Heraclea named Mauritius was elected duke, a grave and statesmanlike man, who seems to have governed the islands well for twenty-three years (764-787). It was perhaps a sign of his statesman-like prudence that he accepted the long low island of Malamocco (which had been the seat of government since the accession of Deusdedit) as his residence, and did not attempt to make his native city Heraclea once more the capital. For still the Genius of the Venetian Republic had not found its destined home. It was to be found at Malamocco, on the Lido, at Torcello; anywhere but on the hundred islands of the Deep Stream. However, the day was drawing near. In the eleventh year of Duke Mauritius' reign (775) the little island of Olivolo, the easternmost of the cluster on which Venice now stands, was by Papal authority erected into a new bishopric; an indication that inhabitants were beginning to settle in that neighbourhood.

Party spirit, as we can see from the annals of that stormy time, ran high in the Venetian islands. The old rivalry between Heraclea and Equilium may probably have been still smouldering. It is also clear that there were two parties in the confederacy, one of which looked towards the sea and was in favour of loyal submission to the Byzantine Emperor, while the other looked landward and was ready to accept patronage (not perhaps domination), first from the Lombard and then from the Frankish rulers of the Terra Firma of Italy. It is indeed inherent in the nature of things that this should be so. Venice's only chance of obtaining or preserving freedom or self-government lay in the balanced strength of these two Empires, either of which could crush her if it stood alone. And moreover the course of her trade required that she should be on fairly good terms with both these powers, each of which was a customer, while each supplied her with some part of the staple of her trade. From Charles's dominions she received the Frisian wool which she wove into cloth, and exported in the shape of rugs and mantles to the Saracens of Bagdad. On the other hand, from all the countries of 'the gorgeous East' she was beginning to import the costly fabrics of silk and velvet, the mantles trimmed with peacock and ostrich feathers, the furs of sable and ermine which she was sending over the passes of the Alps for sale to the splendour-loving nobles of Rhineland and Burgundy.

Along with this legitimate trading, however, the Venetian islanders appear to have carried on a traffic in slaves, of a kind which was condemned by the conscience of Christian Europe. In the days of Pope Zacharias, as we learn from the Liber Pontificalis, Venetian merchants were wont to visit Rom, and in the markets of that city (such markets as that wherein Gregory the Great saw the boys from Deira exposed for sale) they bought a multitude of slaves, both male and female, whom they shipped off to Africa to be sold to the subjects of the Abbasside or Aglabite Caliphs. Though slavery was not yet a forbidden institution, this selling of Italian peasants, baptized Christians, into bondage to the Moors, shocked the feelings of Christendom. Zacharias redeemed the captives whom the Venetians had bought, and prohibited that trade for the future in the markets of Rome: but it is not probable that he had the power to prevent it in other cities of Italy. It seems likely that the slave trade for which Charles rebuked the subjects of Hadrian and the shame of which the Pope threw back upon the 'Greek' traders, may have been, in part at least, carried on by the enterprising merchants of Heraclea and Malamocco.

The only blot on the wise administration of Duke Mauritius, so far as it has been recorded, was his attempt to make the ducal dignity hereditary in his family. Nine years before his death he persuaded the Venetians, 'eager to give him pleasure', to associate with him in the duchy his son Joannes, who after his death reigned for some time alone, and in the seventh year (787-804) of, his reign associated with himself his son Mauritius II. Neither son nor grandson seems to have been a worthy ruler of the Venetian state. Of Joannes, the chronicler writes, 'Neither by written document nor by oral tradition can I find that he handled affairs well for the advantage of his country'. He remarks in passing that in the time of the joint government of these two men, Joannes and Mauritius, 'the sea overflowed so much that it unreasonably covered all the islands'.

During all this time, and in fact for nearly seven centuries longer, the ecclesiastical head of the Venetian state was to be found at the little city of Grado, fifty miles away from Venice, wearing the proud title of patriarch, and often disputing with his neighbour and old rival the patriarch of Aquileia. At the beginning of the ninth century, John, patriarch of Grado, had in some way incurred the displeasure of the duke of Venice, who sent his son, the young Mauritius, with a fleet to execute his vengeance. The patriarch was captured and was thrown headlong from the loftiest turret of his palace. 'His death,' says the chronicler, 'caused great grief to his fellow-citizens, for he was slain as an innocent man, and he had governed the Church of Grado for thirty-six years'. He was buried near the tombs of the martyrs, and for generations the stain of his blood upon the stones was shown to wondering visitors.

The successor of the slain patriarch was his kinsman, Fortunatus of Trieste. A restless and intriguing politician rather than a churchman, Fortunatus devoted all his energies to avenging the murder of his relative with perhaps the additional object of wresting the ecclesiastical province of Istria from his rival of Aquileia and subduing it to his own jurisdiction. Some years after the time which we have now reached, Pope Leo, even while pleading for the bestowal of some ecclesiastical preferment on Fortunatus, added a postscript begging the Emperor Charles to care for his soul and admonish him as to the discharge of his spiritual duties. 'For I hear such things concerning him as are not seemly in an archbishop, neither in his own country nor in those districts of Frank-land where you have given him preferment.'

The intrigues of the new patriarch against the dukes of Venetia having been detected, he was compelled to take refuge in Charles's dominions. He crossed the Alps, and at last reached the Emperor's court, which was still being held at Franconian Salz. In order to conciliate Charles's favour, he brought with him as a present two ivory doors carved with marvellous workmanship. These doors perhaps resembled the curious ivory plaques, representing scenes from the life of the Saviour, which still adorn the episcopal throne of Maximian at Ravenna. At the same time two Venetian tribunes, Obelerius of Malamocco and Felix, together with some others of the chief men in the islands, fled to the mainland, but did not go further than the city of Treviso. Whether or not their flight was the result of a discovered plan of rebellion in which Fortunatus was their accomplice we are not clearly informed, but so it was that the Trevisan refugees, in correspondence with their partisans in Venetia, succeeded in effecting a revolution. Obelerius was chosen duke; Joannes and Mauritius, who evidently had lost all hold on the affections of the people, fled to the mainland, Mauritius across the Alps into Frankland, Joannes to Mantua, and neither of them ever returned to the island-duchy.

Obelerius (whom the Frankish annalists call Willeri or Wilharenus) held the ducal office for six years; and with him were associated two of his brothers, first Beatus and then Valentinus. This period is one of the most important but also one of the most obscure in the early history of Venice. There was evidently a sharp struggle for supremacy between the Byzantine and the Frankish parties in Venetia, but on which side the ducal influence was thrown it is not easy to say. Later tradition assigned to Obelerius a Frankish wife (whom one chronicler, in defiance of all known facts, even called a daughter of Charles), and declared that under her influence he played the traitor to the true interests of his country and made himself the pliant instrument of the Frankish court. On the other hand, we find him accepting at the hands of the Greek general Nicetas the dignity of Spatharius, and his brother Beatus going with the same Nicetas to Constantinople and returning decorated with the honour of a consulship. Probably the fact was that the Venetian dukes were in their heart true to neither power, but trimmed their sails adroitly, as the breeze seemed blowing most steadily from the East or from the West, and thus made themselves suspected by both.

However, one fact vouched for by the Frankish annalist stands out clear and incontestable. In the 806, Venetia with the opposite coast of Dalmatia became for the time a recognised part of the Western Empire. In the Christmas of that year, Charles was holding his court at the villa of Theodo on the Moselle, and 'thither came [the so-called] Willeri and Beatus, dukes of Venetia, together with Paulus duke of Zara, and Donatus bishop of the same city, ambassadors of the Dalmatians, with great gifts, into the presence of the Emperor. And there the Emperor made an ordinance concerning the dukes and their subjects, as well of Venetia as of Dalmatia.' This is the first mention that we have had of Dalmatia, the first hint that Charles's empire was extending down the eastern shore of the Adriatic; and it is perhaps accounted for by the fact (recorded by Joannes Diaconus) that the two Venetian dukes soon after their accession had 'sent forth a naval armament to lay waste the province of Dalmatia'. That is to say, that Obelerius and Beatus having decided, for the time, to accept the protection of Charles rather than that of Nicephorus, constrained their Dalmatian neighbours to follow their example.

The subjection of Venetia and Dalmatia to the Frankish power, although but temporary, seems to have been the exciting cause which changed the smouldering ill-will of the Byzantine ruler into active hostility. In the latter part of the year 806 a fleet was sent from Constantinople into the Adriatic under the command of the patrician Nicetas. Dalmatia appears to have been first subdued, and then the fleet came into Venetian waters. Fortunatus the patriarch, that stormy petrel of Venetian politics, who had not long returned to his see of Grado, quitted it in haste when the ships of Nicetas were seen in the distance, and fled again to his Frankish patron. The operations of Nicetas seem to have been completely and speedily successful, and through the greater part of the year 807 he remained with his fleet in the Venetian waters, wielding probably the same kind of authority which an exarch of Ravenna had possessed while exarchs still remained. It was at this time that Obelerius received from Nicetas the dignity of Spatharius, and consented that his brother Beatus should go, virtually as a hostage, to Constantinople. The young Frankish king Pippin had evidently at this time no fleet with which he could pretend to meet the Imperial squadron, and he was fain to consent to a suspension of hostilities till August, 808, which gave Nicetas time to return to Constantinople. He took with him not only the ducal hostage Beatus, but two prisoners, Christopher, bishop of Olivolo (a young Greek who had become a vehement partisan of Fortunatus and had thus probably been drawn into anti-Byzantine courses), and the tribune Felix, who had taken a leading part in the revolution of 804, and had perhaps thus incurred the displeasure of Constantinople. Both these captives appeared in the presence of 'Augustus' (Nicephorus), and were by him sentenced to perpetual banishment.

To this period is referred one of the most mysterious events in the early history of Venetia—the partial destruction of the city which had once been her capital, the proud and turbulent Heraclea. That the destruction was the work of Venetian hands is clear, but the motive which prompted it is not manifest. We have not heard for some time of the old feuds between Heraclea and Equilium, but it is probable that they had broken out afresh. There are some indications that Equilium herself shared the fate of her rival—Dandolo records at great length the names of the families belonging to both cities which were transported thence to Rialto—and it seems possible that the other islanders came to the conclusion that this sempiternal quarrel would only be appeased when the waters of the lagunes flowed over the burnt ruins of both the rivals. Possibly, too, the party which looked seawards and eastwards for the future of Venetian politics, deemed it desirable to destroy such of the cities as were situated on Terra Firma, lest they should be used hereafter as hostages by the Frankish lords of Italy and hinder the free and unshackled growth of the city of the Lagunes.

At the end of the truce the Byzantine fleet returned first to Dalmatia and then to the Venetian waters, where it abode during the winter. Its commander was now not Nicetas but an officer named Paulus, and he early in 809 made an attack on Comacchio, the city which, as we have seen, marked the extreme northern limit of the Papal territory. The attack was successfully repelled by the garrison—we have no indication whether its commander was in the Papal or the Frankish service—and after this failure Paulus opened negotiations for peace with the young king of Italy. It is possible that herein he somewhat exceeded his commission: but, however that may be, the negotiations came to nothing, being frustrated, as the Franks believed, by the tricks and devices of the dukes of Venetia, whose interest required that the two Empires should continue hostile. The Byzantine admiral, discovering their treachery, and having reason to believe that they were even plotting his assassination, weighed anchor and sailed away from the lagunes, leaving the ungrateful islanders to their fate.

Now, in the year 810, followed that great invasion of Venetia by Pippin which is the first conspicuous event in the history of the island-state, an event glorified by painting and by song, but as to the real history of which we are still profoundly ignorant. It is a hopeless task to attempt to combine the various accounts of this campaign into one consistent narrative, and they must therefore be reproduced separately with all their mutual divergences. We have (1) the Frankish account of the affair, (2) the early, and fairly trustworthy, Venetian account of it, (3) the Byzantine version, and (4) the legends which passed current concerning it in the thirteenth century, and which may contain some precious grains of historic truth, or may be absolute romance.

I. The Frankish narrative: 'Meanwhile King Pippin, roused by the perfidy of the Venetian dukes, ordered [his generals] to make war on Venetia both by sea and land, and having subjected that region and received the surrender of its dukes, he sent the same fleet to lay waste the shores of Dalmatia. But when Paulus the prefect of Cephalonia came with the Eastern fleet to the help of the Dalmatians the royal [Frankish] fleet returned to its own quarters'.

II. The early Venetian narrative: 'Meanwhile the treaty which the peoples of the Venetian [islands] had of old with the Italian king was at this time broken by the action of King Pippin. For that king moved forward an immense army of the Lombards in order to capture the province of the Venetians; and when with great difficulty he had passed through the harbours which divide the shores of the islands, he at last came to a certain place which is called Albiola, but he was by no means able to penetrate further in, and there the dukes, begirt by a great array of the Venetians, boldly attacked the same king, and by the grace of God a triumph was given to the Venetians over their enemies, and thus the aforesaid king retired in confusion.'

III. The narrative of the Emperor Constantine Porphyrogenitus: 'Many years after the departure of Attila there came [against Venetia] Pippin the king, who then ruled over Pavia and other kingdoms, for this Pippin had three brothers who ruled over all the Franks and Sclavonians. Now when King Pippin had come against the Venetians with great power and a multitude of people, he encamped on the mainland on the other side of the channel between the Venetian islands, at a place which is called Aeibolae. The Venetians then, seeing King Pippin with his power coming against them and intending to disembark with his cavalry at the island of Madamaucus, for that is the island nearest to the mainland, by throwing masts [across] blocked up the whole of the passage. Pippin's followers being thus defeated in their design, since there was no other available passage, took up their quarters for six months on the mainland, and made war every day on the Venetians. The latter went on board their ships and stationed themselves behind the masts which they had placed there, while King Pippin stood with his people on the shore. The Venetians fought with bows and missile weapons, not suffering them to cross over to the island. Then King Pippin, being at his wits' end, said to the Venetians, 'Come under my hand and sovereignty, since you belong to my country and sphere of rule'. But the Venetians answered, 'We are servants of the Emperor of the Romans, and not of thee'. But [at last] being overcome by the harassment which he caused them, they made a treaty of peace with King Pippin on condition of paying a large tribute. But from that day the tribute has been continually diminished, yet it subsists even till the present time: for the Venetians pay to him who holds the kingdom of Italy or of Pavia every year thirty-six pounds of uncoined silver'.

IV. The legendary story: 'Belenger (Obelerius), duke of Venice, was a traitor, and went to France with the priest Fortunatus and his wife, and persuaded Charles, son of lord Pippin, and Emperor, to invade Venetia. He came to Methamaucus (Malamocco), which was at that time a very fair city of the Venetians, and when the inhabitants saw King Charles approaching with his great array, they all fled, both great and small, into the capital city of the Venetians which is called Rialto, and there remained in Methamaucus only one old lady. Then when Charles was in seizing of that city, he began the siege of the capital, and was there for six months, his men living in tents along the seashore, and making prisoners of the Venetians who passed that way in their ships. But one day when the Venetians came to the melée with the Franks, having great quantity of bread in their ships they hurled some of it against the Franks. This disheartened Charles, who hoped to reduce the enemy by famine. Then he sent to seek for the one old lady who was left behind in Methamaucus. When she was brought into his presence his retainers treated her discourteously, but he said to her, "Tell me, dost thou know of any device by which I may enter yonder city?" The old lady said, "They were bad men who fled away, taking all the city's treasure with them, and left me here to perish miserably. But if you will give me two squires who will conduct me into that city, I know many poor men there who, if you will give them some of your money, will make such a contrivance as shall bring you and your men into the city." The Emperor hearing this believed the old lady, gave her some of his money, and caused her to be rowed across into the city, where she spoke to the duke and revealed to him all that the king had said to her. Hereupon the duke gave her a hundred artisans, with whom she returned to the king, and said, "Sire, give of your substance to these men that they may make a bridge of osier wood across the water by which your horsemen may enter the city." Then King Charles gave of his substance to these artisans, and they bought boats and wood and ropes, and made the bridge over the water and bound it fast to the ropes. And when King Charles saw the bridge he believed right well that his men might mount upon it and go into the city. And the old lady said to him, "Sire, let your men cross over this bridge by night and they will find the Venetians in their beds and you will have the city without fail."

'When the night came, the Franks went with their horses on to the bridge, and the artisans who had made it began to sail towards the city. But when the horses smelt the water they began to fall this way and that, and broke their legs, and knocked their heads against the sides, and thus they broke the bridge, and the riders fell into the water and were drowned therein.

The old lady and the Venetian workmen fled into the city, and the Venetians went on board their ships and surrounded Methamaucus and found there King Charles the Emperor, who was in a great rage and cursed grievously when he saw the loss of so many of his men and horses, and the sea covered with their dead bodies and the wreckage of the bridge scattered hither and thither. And when the Emperor saw the Venetians with their navy all well-armed, he said, "Where is the Duke?". Then they prayed him to come on shore, and my lord duke Beatus met him there, and Charles and all his knights dismounted, and the Emperor asked Beatus for news of his brother, duke Belenger, and said before all the Venetian nobles that Belenger had counselled him to come and take Venice, to which Beatus and the other Venetians said nothing, because they were determined to take vengeance of Belenger. Then they prayed King Charles to come and see the chief city of the Venetians. And the king kissed the duke and all the other noble Venetians who were there, and then he went on board the duke's vessel. And while they were sailing along lord Charles held a mighty great spear in his hand, and when he saw the greenest and deepest water, he threw his spear into the sea with all his force and said, "As surely as that spear which I have thrown into the sea shall never be seen again by me, nor by you, nor by any other creature, so surely shall no man in the world ever have power to hurt the kingdom of Venice, and he who shall desire to hurt her, on him let fall the' wrath and the vengeance of our Lady, as it has fallen on me and on my people." All the clergy and people of Venice were assembled to meet King Charles when he landed, and on his return from the church to which he at first repaired they gave him a great banquet, and then escorted him to Ferrara'. The chronicler then goes on to describe the measures taken with reference to the traitorous duke 'Belenger,' but we need not further follow his untrustworthy recital.

It has seemed better to quote this romance at length in order that the reader may see the whole absurdity of it at once. It cannot be necessary to point out its utterly unhistorical character. Charles the Great probably never visited Venice : he was certainly not south of the Alps in the year 810. Nor is the story made credible by substituting Pippin's name for that of his father. The loaves of bread discharged from the Venetian catapults; the old dame of Malamocco with her hundred working men from Venice; the bridge (more than a mile long) from Malamocco to Rialto made by the Venetian artisans and broken to pieces by the stumbling horses,—all these incidents evidently belong to the domain of mere fiction and are inspired by the wildest spirit of medieval mythology. But the historian of Venice will never be able entirely to disregard even this preposterous legend, since, pruned of some of its more obvious absurdities, it has found a place in the classic pages of Andrea Dandolo, and it is portrayed in two large pictures by Vicentino on the walls of the *Sala dello Scrutinio* in the Ducal Palace. For generations to come, visitors to Venice will no doubt gaze upon those painted romances and believe that they record actual events in the earliest history of the great Republic.

When we come to discuss the small residuum of historic fact at the bottom of all this foam and froth of patriotic imaginings, all that we can safely say is that the young king Pippin instituted a strict blockade of the Venetian islands, which may have lasted for half a year; that he possibly made an unsuccessful attempt to penetrate to the inner group of islands, which was, however, of the less importance because Malamocco not Rialto was still the chief seat of the Venetian state; but that the injury which his blockade did to the commerce of the islanders was so considerable that in the end, seeing themselves abandoned by their Byzantine protectors, they consented to accept Charles as their overlord, and to pay him a certain yearly tribute.

That this was in fact the result of Pippin's expedition, that it was not a failure in the end, whatever partial reverses he may have met with, is sufficiently shown by the words of the Emperor Constantine Porphyrogenitus, whose account of Pippin's Venetian campaign seems on the whole the most worthy of credence. He had no motive to magnify, but rather strong motives to minimize, the degree of the Venetian subjugation to the Western ruler: yet he evidently implies that Pippin's operations, though by no means brilliant, were on the whole successful.

We shall find, however, that Frankish domination over Venetia was short-lived. The real world-historical importance of Pippin's invasion lay in the fact that it opened the eyes of the Venetians to the insecurity of their position at Malamocco and the other islands of the outer barrier of the lagunes. One of their first acts after the restoration of peace was formally to remove the capital of their state to the place named the Deep Channel (Rivus Altus). There, in that little cluster of islands, sheltered from attack by land or sea, in a spot whose narrow and winding channels were accessible to commerce but inaccessible to war, they reared that wonderful city which has made the name of Rialto for ever memorable in the literature of the world.

This was the true foundation of Venice, the true beginning of her proud history. All that had gone before was but a prologue, spoken on some one or other of the outlying islands, to the mighty drama of the Bride of the Sea. It interests us Englishmen to remember that only eight years before the foundation of the new Venice, Egbert the West-Saxon, having been long an exile at the court of Charles the Great, returned to his own country, and assumed, first of all his race, the title of King of England. The two ocean queens were born, as it were, on the same day.

After receiving the submission of Venice, Pippin sailed to the coast of Dalmatia, but here he was met by a Byzantine navy under the command of Paulus, Prefect of Cephalonia, and was compelled to retire without having achieved any conquest. Very soon after his return he died, on the 8th of July, 810, and was buried at Milan, where his tombstone, a slab of white marble, was discovered not many years ago in the church of St. Ambrose. What was the nature of the disease which carried off the young, brave, and 'beautiful king of Italy in the 33rd year of his age', we are not informed. It is an obvious conjecture that it was connected in some way with his Venetian and Dalmatian campaign, and that either chagrin at his partial failure or a fever caught during his encampment by the lagunes winged the arrow of death: but this is only a conjecture unsupported by any sentence in our authorities.

Pippin left five daughters, who after his death were educated at their grandfather's court, and a son, Bernard, whose story is one of the saddest pages in the family history of the Carolingians. Two years after his father's death he was proclaimed king of Italy (or perhaps rather in official style, king of the Lombards), and was sent to govern his father's realm, which had during the interval been ruled by *missi dominici*, chief among them Charles's cousin Adalhard, abbot of Corbie, the generous defender of the divorced Desiderata[2]. Bernard was probably at this time about fifteen years of age. His revolt sis. against his uncle Louis the Pious, his cruel death, and the depressing influence of remorse for that crime on his uncle's character, all lie outside the range of this history.

Before the news of the death of Pippin had reached the Byzantine court, Nicephorus had despatched to Italy a messenger, Arsafius the *Spatharius,* to see if he could arrange terms of peace between the two great Adriatic powers. There was this advantage in directing the embassy to Pippin, king of the Lombards, that the difficult question of the recognition of Charles as Emperor of the Romans was thereby evaded, but that advantage was of course lost when the ambassador, arriving at Milan or Pavia, found the palace empty and Pippin in his grave. However the old Emperor, who had long been waiting for some such tender of the olive-branch from Constantinople, succeeded in inducing Arsafius to cross the Alps and take up with himself at Aachen the web of diplomacy which was to have been woven with his son. A few sentences from Charles's letter to Nicephorus, written in the early part of 811, will best explain the then existing posture of affairs :—

'We have received with all honour the ambassador Arsafius, whom you sent with a verbal message and with letters to our son Pippin, of blessed memory. And though he was not accredited directly to us, yet perceiving him to be a prudent man, we have held discourse with him and given diligent heed to the things which he had to relate. And with good reason, for his messages, both written and verbal, were so full of the desire for peace and mutual charity that only a fool would have found them uninteresting. Wherefore, as soon as we heard that he had come to the borders of our realm, a happy instinct moved us to desire that he should be brought into our presence; and now since he to whom he was sent, our dear son, by God's providence has been removed from human affairs, we resolved that he should not return empty-handed nor with the disappointment of a mission unperformed.

'And not only so: but looking back to the time when, in the first year of your reign, you sent the metropolitan Michael, and the abbot Peter, and the life-guardsman Callistus to settle the terms of peace with us and to federate and unite these two realms in the love of Christ, we remained like one standing on a watch-tower, waiting for the appearance of the messenger or the letter which should bring back to us the reply of your amiable Brotherhood. But now—such is the natural weakness of the human mind—hope in this matter had well-nigh given place to despair. Still we trusted in Him who never deserts those who put their confidence in Him, and believed that, as the

Apostle says, He would not suffer our labour to be in vain in the Lord. Therefore we greatly rejoiced when we heard of the arrival of your messenger the glorious Spatharius Arsafius, believing that we should arrive at the much desired certainty concerning the things which were left uncertain, and that we should receive your answer to the letters which we gave to your aforesaid messengers. And so in fact it has proved, for we look upon the words and letters which have thus been addressed to our son as substantially containing the desired reply. Wherefore with thanks to Almighty God who has thus breathed into your heart the desire for peace, we at once without doubt or delay have prepared our embassy to your amiable Brotherhood'.

This letter is important as a comment on Einhard's words, 'Charles bore with patience the indignation of the Roman emperors and vanquished their stubbornness by his frequent embassies and fraternal letters'. It explains the strained relations which undoubtedly for eight years (803-811) existed between the two empires. And it entirely disposes of the erroneous statement made by Dandolo, and on his authority largely adopted even by accurate historians, that the arrangement for fixing the boundaries of the two empires, which I am now about to describe, was concluded in 803 instead of eight years later.

It was a striking illustration of the wide-reaching character of Charles's statesmanship that the ambassadors from Constantinople met at Aachen the ambassadors from Cordova who had come to negotiate a peace on behalf of the Emir El Hakem, the tyrannical sovereign of Moorish Spain.

The ambassadors whom Charles now despatched to Constantinople were three, Haido bishop of Basle, Hugo count of Tours, and Aio a Lombard of Friuli. The terms of the treaty of peace which they were authorized to conclude were on Charles's part the surrender of the Venetian islands and of the maritime cities of Dalmatia, that is practically of the whole coast-line of the Northern and Eastern Adriatic. On the part of Nicephorus there can be no doubt, though it is nowhere distinctly stated in our authorities, that the essential condition was the recognition of Charles as Emperor, that is virtually the admission that the Empire was now no longer one, but two.

Charles's abandonment of Venice involved the abandonment of the duke Obelerius, who had certainly been disloyal to the Byzantine, if not too faithful to the Frank. The ambassadors who were sent to Constantinople took him with them in their train and handed him over to the Eastern Caesar, along with the Sicilian Leo who, as we have seen, ten years before had fled for refuge to Charles's court. Obelerius was probably condemned to perpetual exile, certainly not put to death, since twenty years later he returned to Venice and attempted a counter-revolution which cost him his life.

As the claim of the Eastern Emperor to the overlordship of Venice was now undisputed, the election of a successor to Obelerius and his brothers—all now deposed—was held under the presidency of Arsafius, and the choice fell upon Agnellus who, according to the lately introduced expedient, had two tribunes assigned to him yearly as his assessors. Agnellus, who figures in the later histories of Venice as Angelo Participazio or Badoer, seems to have been a wise and prudent ruler. His son Joannes was for a time associated with him in the sovereignty, and men of the lineage of Agnellus were generally to be found on the list of the dukes of Venice for nearly a century and a half from his elevation.

This duke is a figure of especial interest for all lovers of art, as he was the first founder of the great Ducal Palace. The building raised by him was still standing at the end of the tenth century when Joannes Diaconus, chaplain of the Doge of Venice, wrote his history.

As we are here leaving the story of the Venetian to commonwealth it should be mentioned that the fortunes of the patriarch Fortunatus appear not to have been neglected by his Frankish patron. As a result of the negotiations at Aachen this refugee bishop seems to have been permitted to return to his see of Grado, to which by Charles's permission he was probably allowed to subject the dioceses of Istria.

The fact that in this severance between the Eastern and Western Empires, Venice was allotted to the former, was of transcendent importance in the history of the Queen of the Adriatic. It is true that her subjection to the Augustus at Constantinople was of the gentlest kind and transformed itself with little difficulty, in the course of the ninth and tenth centuries, from subjection to alliance. Still that subjection, or connection, did exist and always enabled Venetian statesmen to plead that they were de jure as well as de facto independent of the Western Empire, thus preventing them from being swallowed up in that morass of feudal anarchy into which the Carolingian Empire sank so soon after the death of its founder. Had it not been for the treaty of Aachen it is possible that instead of the gorgeous city of the Rialto the world would have seen a petty town with insignificant commerce, taxed and tolled, and judged or misjudged without mercy at the caprice of some turbulent little baron, her feudal superior.

CHAPTER VIII.

THE FINAL RECOGNITION.

THOUGH the treaty of Aachen was virtually concluded with Nicephorus, its final ratification did not fall within that Emperor's reign. When Charles's ambassadors arrived in Constantinople, they probably heard the terrible tidings of the overthrow of Nicephorus by the Bulgarians. The Logothete-Emperor had collected a fine army and had led it, confident of success, against his turbulent neighbour Crum, king of the Bulgarians. The campaign opened brightly: he took and plundered Crum's palace, and received an embassy from that barbarian suing almost abjectly for peace. Puffed up with success, Nicephorus refused to grant it and thereupon the Bulgarian king, driven to despair, drew a line of circumvallation round the camp of the invaders, harassed and terrified them by 'alarums and excursions,' and finally at nightfall stormed their camp and slew Nicephorus himself, nearly all his officers, and private soldiers more than could be numbered. The disaster must have been as signal as the defeat of Valens by the Visigoths, and like that defeat, it was the result of a combination of arrogance and bad generalship. The head of Nicephorus, severed from his body and fixed on a pole, was for days exhibited by the victor in savage scorn to the officers of the barbarous tribes who served under his banner. After this he caused the flesh to be removed, mounted the skull in silver, and was wont to invite the Sclavic chiefs who visited his palace to drink to him out of the skull of a Roman Emperor.

The son of Nicephorus severely wounded in the great battle, reigned but for a few months, and was then removed into a monastery to die. On the second of October (811), Michael the grand chamberlain, son-in-law of Nicephorus, was acclaimed as Emperor. The new Emperor, who reigned but for two years, was one of the most insignificant monarchs who ever received the homage of the servile courtiers of Constantinople.

Chosen apparently for no other reason than his reputation for orthodoxy, he reversed in all things the policy of Nicephorus, scattered in lavish gifts to the Church and to the populace the treasures which his father-in-law had accumulated, persecuted some of the heretics whom his father-in-law had protected, and ruled during his brief span of royalty as the passive instrument of the monkish fraternity. Being obliged at last to go forth to battle with the Bulgarians, and being ignominiously defeated, he resigned the throne without a struggle to a popular general, Leo the Armenian, and retired to a monastery, where he droned away thirty-two years of life unfeared and therefore unmolested.

To this insignificant ruler, however, before his deposition fell the duty of ratifying the treaty with the Frankish prince, and thus establishing that duality of Empire in the Christian world which endured for six centuries and a half, till the fall of Constantinople. He despatched an embassy to Charles, consisting of Michael, Metropolitan of Philadelphia the life-guards-man Arsafius and his comrade Theognostus, to ratify the peace which had been all but concluded with his predecessor. Michael and Arsafius had made the journey before, the former in 803, the latter in 810. Theognostus, as far as we know, was strange to diplomacy. The new Emperor, trembling on his uneasy throne and possibly thinking of the possibility of enlisting Charles as his helper against the terrible Bulgarians, eagerly consented to an alliance on the terms previously arranged, and begged that it might be made to include his son Theophylact whom he was about to associate with him as a colleague, and whom he vainly hoped that the people would hail as his successor. The same ambassadors were charged to renew the friendly relations with the Pope, interrupted during the reign of Nicephorus. The Metropolitan and the two *Spatharii*, accompanied by the returning ambassadors of Charles, made their appearance at Aachen in the early days of January, 812. Having displayed the rich gifts which they brought from the lavish Michael, they were admitted to a public audience in the great church of the Virgin Mary. Written instruments setting forth the terms of the peace—doubtless as settled by the embassy of 811—were exchanged between the Emperor and the Eastern ambassadors in the presence of the great nobles of the Frankish realm, and this transaction being ended, the ambassadors, who had probably brought a trained choir along with them, burst forth into sacred song praising God for His mercy vouchsafed to the great Basileus, Charles. Basileus in the official language of the Empire was now the technical word expressive of the sublime Imperial dignity, while Rex was reserved for the lesser herd of barbarian potentates. The recognition was thus complete. The accredited representatives of the Augustus of Constantinople had greeted the Frankish chieftain as Emperor.

This fact was in itself irreversible. Henceforth no one could deny that there was both an Eastern and a Western Empire, and Charles could with confidence thus describe the two realms in a letter which he addressed a year later to his beloved and honourable brother, the glorious Emperor Michael.

After they had fulfilled their commission at Aachen, the Eastern ambassadors journeyed to Rome, and there, while bringing the Patriarch's greetings to the Pope, and thus resuming the interrupted communication between the Churches, they at the same time solemnly handed to the Pope in St. Peter's the treaty of peace between the two Emperors, and received it back from him stamped in some unexplained way with the seal of his approval.

How far the Emperor's relations with the still unsubdued portions of Italy may have been affected by these changing relations with the Eastern Empire we are not informed. We hear nothing of help previously given by Constantinople to Benevento, but the state of affairs between the Frankish king and the Samnite duchy had been for some years about as bad as it could possibly be. Partly, this was due to the personal antagonism between the two rulers. On the one side (I am speaking of a time previous to 810) stood Pippin, young, brave, and headstrong, eager to distinguish himself in war and indignant that there should be any power in Italy independent of him and his father. On the other stood Grimwald, last hope of Lombard rule in Italy, some years older than Pippin, but still young, mindful of his father's wrongs and his own captivity, determined to escape from the odious necessity of professing himself Charles's 'man,' and of proclaiming—by the date of his charters, by the effigy on his coins, by his very garb and the manner of trimming his hair, that the Lombard was subject to the Frank.

The mutual attitude of the two princes is well expressed by a tradition which is embalmed in the pages of Erchempert. 'Pippin spoke thus by his ambassadors to Grimwald, "I wish, and am determined with the strong hand to enforce my wish, that like as his father Arichis was subject to Desiderius, king of Italy, so Grimwald shall be subject to me". To whom Grimwald thus replied :—

"Free was I born and noble my forbears on either side,
So by the help of my God, free will I ever abide."

Gladly would we know whether the Lombard prince uttered his defiance in the correct Latin elegiacs in which the chronicler has couched it, or whether he could still speak in the Lombard tongue words not quite unintelligible to the men of the Rhineland.

The war between the two states resolved itself into a long duel between Spoleto and Benevento, in which, though with some vicissitudes, the fortune of war was on the whole favourable to the Franks. In 801 Teate (Chieti) was taken and burnt by them and its governor Roselm was made prisoner. In 802 Ortona on the Adriatic surrendered, and the Spoletan border was thus pushed forward from the Pescara to the Sangro.

In the same year a more important capture was made. Lucera, that upland city looking towards Mount Garganus which seems destined by nature for a fortress, and where long after in Hohenstaufen days Frederick II stationed his military colony of Saracens, was taken after repeated sieges and a Frankish garrison was placed therein. In a few months, however, the fortune of war turned. Grimwald marched to the attack. Winichis, the Frankish duke of Spoleto, victor many years before in the battle with the Greeks, now lay sick (probably of malarial fever) within the walls of Lucera. The defence languished, and at last Winichis was obliged to surrender the city and his own person into the hands of the besiegers. He was honourably treated by the knightly Grimwald, and the next year was set at liberty, apparently unransomed.

The long duel, in the course of which Benevento had suffered much from the ravages of the Frankish troops, was at last brought to an end by the death of the two chief combatants. In 806 Grimwald died and was succeeded by another prince of the same name, who is said to have previously distinguished himself by his personal bravery in the first great war with Pippin. The new prince, who is called sometimes Grimwald II and sometimes Grimwald IV, was perhaps himself more peaceably inclined than his predecessor, and Pippin may have had enough in Venetian affairs to occupy his attention. In 810, as we have seen, Pippin himself died, and two years later, immediately after the dismissal of the Byzantine ambassadors, his son, the young Bernard, at a general assembly held at Aachen was, as has been said, solemnly declared king of Italy, and sent to govern his new kingdom with the help of the counsels of his cousins, older by two generations than himself, Wala and Adalhard. The influence of the latter counsellor seems to have been especially exerted in the cause of peace, and in the same year (812) an arrangement was concluded whereby the prince of Benevento agreed to pay a sum of 25,000 solidi down, and a further sum of 7,000 solidi annually.

The payment was distinctly spoken of as tribute, and there seems to be no doubt that the prince of Benevento, though keeping the reins of government in his hands, fully acknowledged his dependence on the Frankish king and his Imperial grandfather. So ended the last glimmer of Lombard independence in Italy.

The connection with the Eastern Empire, chiefly maintained by two cities, Naples and Otranto, may some perhaps have died out in some other parts of Italy more slowly than we suppose. There is a curious entry in Annales Einhardi for the year 809, that 'Populonia in Tuscany, a maritime city, was plundered by the Greeks who are called Orobiotae' (Mountain dwellers). Who are these highlanders, so wedded to the Byzantine sovereignty that their very name is Greek, who plunder 'the sea-girt Populonia' on its promontory just opposite the isle of Elba? Possibly they may have been corsairs from the other side of the Adriatic, like the Dalmatian pirates who were so long the plague of Venice, but if they were highlanders of the Apennines or of the mountains of Massa or Carrara, we have here a hint of a strange unwritten chapter of Italian history.

During all this early part of the ninth century the thundercloud of Saracen piracy and conquest, which was to break so terribly over its central years, was growing darker and darker. The chronicler mentions six invasions of Corsica by the Moors of Spain between 806 and 813, repelled with various fortune by the Frankish admirals. The great peace with Cordova, concluded in 810, does not seem to have had any effect in staying these piratical raids. One of the invasions is described immediately after the mention of that peace, and in 813 we find the Moors not only attacking Corsica and Sardinia, but, in order to revenge a defeat which they had sustained from a Frankish general, invading Nice in the Narbonese Gaul and Civita Vecchia in Tuscany. The Saracen had thus indeed drawn very near to Rome. Even in Charles's lifetime the City which gave him his Imperial title was obviously in danger from the Islamite rovers of the sea.

CHAPTER IX

CAROLUS MORTUUS.

The last years of the great Emperor were in the main years of peace. Rivals and enemies, Eastern Caesars, Saracen Caliphs, Italian dukes, were all courting the friendship of the triumphant Frank : but as has been already said, they were years of heavy family affliction and years also of increasing sickness and infirmity. In 806 he summoned a general assembly at the Villa of Theodo, and there declared to the chief nobles and ecclesiastics of his realm his scheme for the partition of his Empire after, his death. Only the three sons of Hildegarde were to inherit his power, the unhappy rebel, Pippin the Hunchback, though still alive, being of course excluded from the succession. The details of this intended division are preserved for us in a Capitulary issued from Nimwegen on the 6th of February, 806.

According to its provisions, Louis was to have Aquitaine, nearly the whole of Burgundy, Septimania, Provence, and the Frankish conquests in Spain. Pippin was to have Italy, the greater part of Bavaria, Alamannia south of the Danube, and the lands conquered from the Avars and Croatians. All the rest of Charles's dominions, that is the kernel of the old Frankish monarchy, Neustria and Austrasia, parts of Burgundy, Alamannia and Bavaria, Frisia and the newly conquered Saxonia with Thuringia, in fact the whole of Northern Gaul and Northern Germany, was to fall to the lot of Charles, who, as the eldest son, was certainly thus to receive the lion's share of the inheritance. It was provided that each of the two other brothers was to have access to the dominions of Pippin, Charles by way of Aosta and Louis by way of Susa, in order that they might go to his help in case of his being attacked, probably by the Byzantines. Elaborate arrangements were made for the division of any lapsed share between the two surviving brothers in case the brother who died first left no children of his own. As none of these provisions ever took effect it is not necessary here to describe them in detail, except to observe that in the event of Pippin's dominions having to be divided between Charles and Louis it was arranged that Charles should receive certain regions 'up to the limits of Saint Peter.' This provision seems to show that in 806 the Pope was recognized as temporal ruler at least of the Exarchate and Pentapolis. In this important document Charles earnestly exhorted his sons to dwell in peace and harmony with one another, and he did his utmost to prevent the up-springing of any such roots of bitterness as the attempt to seduce a brother's vassals from their allegiance, the refusal to keep in safe custody a brother's hostages, and other similar evidences of ill-will. He doubtless was aware of the feud which had for some time existed between Charles and Pippin, and which, allayed for the time by the inspiring influence of the tomb of St. Goar, might possibly break out afresh when his own controlling presence should have vanished from their midst.

But all these schemes and all these fears dissolved into nothingness at the breath of the universal Conqueror. In July, 810, as we have already seen, Pippin, king of Italy, breathed his last. On the 4th of December, 811, the younger Charles himself, the son who most faithfully reproduced the lineaments of his father's character—brave, strong, devout—died in the flower of his age. He died unmarried, the project once entertained of marrying him to the daughter of the English king, Offa of Mercia, having failed of fulfillment. It was in the same year (811) that Pippin the Hunchback ended his life of melancholy failure; and the year before (810) the princess Hrotrud, who was to have sat upon the throne of Byzantium, died also, she too only on the threshold of middle life. Of the friends who stood round Charles's throne, and who had once lightened the cares of state by their wise counsels or made bright the hours of leisure by their jokes and their repartees, how many had now left him for the silent land! The faithful Fulrad had died long ago; Angilram of Metz, who succeeded him as virtual prime minister, was dead also. His successor, Hildibald of Cologne, still lived : hut Alcuin had died amid the smoke-begrimed dwellings of Tours six years before the death of Pippin; and Paulus Diaconus, who had never returned from his retreat on Monte Cassino, he too had died at the close of the old century. So many of the lesser trees of the forest had fallen, but of the one goodliest tree of all it might still be said—

'With singed top its stately growth, though bare,
Stands on the blasted heath.'

The terrible bereavements which Charles had endured left him but one son to inherit his vast dominions, and that son not only the least efficient of all the three, but the least efficient whom the strong Arnulfing stem had yet produced : a man who might have passed through life creditably as abbot of an Aquitanian convent, but who was doomed to disastrous failure when the time should come for him to try to bend the bow of Ulysses. Louis the Pious, Louis the Debonnair, Louis the Monk or Louis the Gentle, by whatever name he might be called, though 'most zealous of all the Emperors on behalf of the Christian religion', was, by the confession of one of his admirers, 'apt to give undue heed to the advice of his counsellors, while he gave himself up to psalmody and diligent reading.' Not such was the man to keep in their appointed orbits all those mighty planets that now revolved round the re-erected throne of the Emperor of Rome.

In the late summer of 813 Louis, who had just conducted a successful campaign against his father's old enemies the Basques, was summoned to Aachen, where, in accordance apparently with the decision of a select council held at the same city in the spring he was to be associated with his father in the Imperial dignity. It is a noteworthy fact that in Charles's scheme for the division of his dominions, previously described, no mention was made of this, the most splendid jewel in the whole treasury of his titles.

Doubtless in his secret heart Carolus Augustus in the year 806 hoped that his eldest son, the heir of his name, would also be the heir of his proud surname, but partly perhaps from fear of arousing the jealousy of Pippin (sovereign of the land in which Rome lay) and partly from some remembrance of the old tradition that the dignity of Roman Imperator was elective, not hereditary, Charles, while partitioning all his other sovereignties, left this his Imperial title undisposed of. But though an Emperor could not directly bequeath the diadem, he could share with one of his sons in his own lifetime the right to wear it; and this was what Charles, 'by divine inspiration' (as was said by his biographer), now resolved to accomplish. After the arrival of Louis a great assembly of the nobles of the realm, 'bishops, abbots, dukes, counts and lieutenant-governors was held in the palace on Saturday the 10th of September (813). Here the aged Emperor asked each man, from the highest to the lowest, if it was his pleasure that the title of Emperor should be handed on by him to his son Louis. All with exultation answered, 'Yes : it is God's counsel in this thing'. On the next day, therefore (Sunday, 11 September), the old Emperor, dressed in splendid regal attire, with the crown on his head and accompanied by his son, proceeded to the great church which he had built and decorated after the manner of S. Vitale at Ravenna. On a high altar dedicated to the Saviour lay a golden crown. Father and son prayed long before it, and then Charles, addressing Louis, admonished him first of all to love and fear Almighty God, to keep His precepts, to govern His Church, and guard it from evil men. Then he bade him show unfailing kindness to his sisters, to his younger brothers, his nephews and his other kinsmen. Then, to reverence the bishops as his fathers, to love the people as his sons, to repress the proud, to be a comforter of the monks, and a father to the poor; to choose for his ministers faithful and God-fearing men who would abhor unjust gains; to eject no man from his office except for good and sufficient cause, and to show himself devoid of blame before God and all the people. In the presence of the multitude Charles said, 'Wilt thou obey all these my precepts?'. Louis answered, "Most willingly, with the help of God'. Charles then lifted the crown from the altar and placed it on the head of his son. Mass having been sung, they all returned together to the palace, the father, both in going and returning, leaning on the arm of his son. After many days Louis, having received magnificent gifts, was dismissed, to return to his own kingdom of Aquitaine. Father and son embraced and kissed each other at parting, till they began to weep, but for joy, not for sorrow.

In the narrative of this great ceremony we observe one notable omission. The rite was solemnized in a church and was connected with the worship of the Most High, but the central act, the placing of the crown on the young Emperor's head, was not performed by the Pope of Rome or by any other ecclesiastic. There was surely a meaning in this exclusion of the priestly element. Pippin had been crowned by Boniface and anointed by Stephen II; Charles as Emperor by Leo III, and even Louis himself as king of Aquitaine had been crowned by Hadrian. But Charles by his own solemn coronation of his son in sight of all the spiritual and temporal lords of Francia, seemed emphatically to indicate to future generations that no intervention either of the Roman Pontiff or of any archbishop or bishop in his dominions was necessary in order to create a Roman Imperator. Much trouble and many bewildering debates would have been spared to his successors had this principle been clearly comprehended by them and their subjects.

At the same *generalis conventus* at Aachen, the young Bernard, who possibly had previously held but a delegated authority over Italy, was formally proclaimed king of that land.

The coronation of Louis was the last of a series of acts by which the great Emperor showed that he knew he was near the end of his career. The abortive partition of 806 of course pointed in that direction. Since then his health had more visibly failed, and for four years, from 810 onwards, he had suffered grievously from gout. In 811 he drew up an instrument, solemnly attested in the presence of certain of his friends, by which he directed the manner in which the money, jewels, fine raiment, and other chattels in his treasury were to be disposed of after his death. The whole treasure was to be divided into three parts, and two of these thirds were to be distributed among the churches of the twenty-one metropolitan cities of his Empire. The remaining third was to be divided between (1) his children and grandchildren, (2) the poor, and (3) his household servants.

To the anxious hearts of his counsellors and his people many signs seemed to indicate the impending calamity. Eclipses were frequent in the last three years of his life, and men remembered that in 807 the planet Mercury had appeared like a little black spot on the surface of the sun, and had remained there for eight days. Then in 810, when he went forth to his last campaign against his stubborn foe Göttrik of Denmark, rising one day before dawn, and riding forth from his camp, he beheld a brilliant meteor fall from right to left across the cloudless sky. The bright light startled his horse, which threw the Emperor to the ground. His sword-belt and the clasp of his mantle were both broken; the spear which he always carried in his right hand flew forth and fell twenty feet beyond him. When the attendants came to raise him therefore, they found him unarmed and without his regal mantle—an evident sign that he would soon be unclothed of his dignity by death. In addition to these portents, there were earthquakes at Aachen which shook down the stately portico erected between his palace and the church. In the inscription which ran round the interior of the church separating the upper from the lower arcades, the word PRINCEPS disappeared from its proper place after the name KAROLUS. To the excited and alarmed minds of men even the catastrophe that befell the great bridge over the Rhine at Mainz which had been built by Charles's command, a catastrophe in which the labour of ten years was destroyed by three hours' conflagration, was reckoned as another omen of impending doom.

In January, 814, all these gloomy portents found their fulfillment. Charles was attacked by fever, which he hoped, as on previous occasions, to vanquish by abstinence from solid food. But to the fever was added pleurisy, with which his weakened body was unable to cope. On the seventh day of his sickness he received the sacrament from the hands of his friend and counsellor Hildibald, Archbishop of Cologne. He lay in great weakness all that day and the following night. On the morrow at dawn, still fully conscious, he raised his right hand and marked the sign of the Cross on his head and breast. Then gathering up his feet into the bed, crossing his arms over his chest, and closing his eyes, he gently chanted the words, 'Lord, into Thy hands I commend my spirit,' and soon after expired'.

The great Emperor had left no orders as to his place of burial, and to wait for the funeral ceremony till his son should arrive from Aquitaine seemed undesirable. Long ago, in 779, he had expressed a wish to be buried by the side of his father in the abbey of S. Denis, but that charge seems to have been forgotten by the new generation of courtiers that had since grown up, perhaps even by Charles himself. Since then had arisen the lordly pleasure-house which he had reared at Aquae Grani, and in the holy fane beside it, dedicated to the Virgin Mary, men deemed that it was most fitting that his body should await the general resurrection. Having been washed and reverently tended, the corpse was carried amidst the lamentations of the people to the great basilica, and there interred on the very day of his death. A gilded arch was raised over the tomb bearing his image and this inscription :

'Under this tombstone is laid the body of Charles, the great and orthodox Emperor, who gloriously enlarged the kingdom of the Franks, and prosperously governed it for forty-seven years. He died a septuagenarian in the year of our Lord 814, the seventh Indiction, 28th of January'.

The lamentations of the people of Aachen over the dead hero were assuredly no mere conventional tribute dispeople, to his kingly state. His great personality had filled the minds of all his subjects in Central Europe, and already, even during his lifetime, Poetry, which was to be so busy with his name in after-ages, had begun to throw her glamour over his career. But as the Trojan women round the grave of Hector, so the subjects of Charles mourned their own coming misfortunes in mourning him. The horizon was growing dark around them; the war-ships of the Northmen and the Saracens were beginning those piratical raids which were to make the ninth and tenth centuries one long agony, and men's hearts failed them for fear when they thought of monastic Louis standing in the breach instead of his heroic father. The grief and forebodings of the people probably found utterance in many mournful effusions similar to one which has been preserved to us, written by a monk of Bobbio, and which is called

Planctus de Obitu Karoli.

From the sun-rising to the sea-girt West
Is nought but tears and beatings of the breast.
    Woe's me! my misery!
Romans and Franks, and all of Christ's belief,
Pale with dismay, declare their mighty grief.

Infants and old men, chiefs of glorious state,
Maidens and matrons, mourn our Caesar's fate.

Father he was of all the fatherless:
Widows and aliens his name did bless.

O Christ! who rulest from on high the blest!
Give, in Thy realm, to Carolus thy rest.

This prayer do all the faithful urge today:
For this the widows and the virgins pray.

Now the calm Emperor, ended all his toil,
Lies underneath the cross-surmounted soil.

Woe to thee, Rome! and to thy people woe!
Thy greatest and most glorious one lies low.

Woe to thee, Italy! fair land and wide,
And woe to all the cities of thy pride!

Land of the Franks! in all thy bygone days
Such grief did never thy free soul amaze,

As when King Charles, august and eloquent,
'Neath Aachen's sods his stately stature bent.

O Columbanus, let thy tears be poured,
And with thy prayers for him entreat the Lord.

Father of all! omnipotent in grace,
Grant him on high a radiant resting-place.

Yea, in Thine inmost holiest oracle,
Let him, 0 Christ, with Thine Apostles dwell.
    Woe's me! my misery!

As might be expected from a monk, the author of this complaint dwells more on the religious than on the political or military side of Charles's great life-work. This view obtained general assent as the centuries rolled on. While medieval dukes and barons delighted to trace up their lineage even to illegitimate descendants of the great Emperor, while minstrels and troubadours found their best inspiration in the luxuriant growth of romance which sprang up around his tomb, the Church remembered with gratitude the great victories which he had won for her against the Lombard, the Saxon, and the Saracen, and at last in solemn council placed the stalwart and free-living hero on Charles, high amid her list of saints. It is true that the canonization, having been decreed by the anti-pope Paschal III, did not meet with universal acceptance, and in Italy especially seems never to have found willing worshippers, but in Germany and in France the office composed in honour of St. Charles was widely popular, and to this day the exhibition of his relics, which is made every seven years in the great cathedral at Aachen, attracts a multitude of votaries, and is not a mere antiquarian spectacle, but a religious function reverently witnessed by thousands of the devout peasants of Westphalia.

CHAPTER X

THE LIFE OF THE PEOPLE.

THE story has now been told of the external events in the history of Italy during the seventy years which followed the death of Liutprand. We have read the letters of Popes, and witnessed the coronation of an Emperor, but have we drawn any nearer to the beating heart of the nation? Can we at the end of the story form any clearer idea than we possessed at the beginning as to the manner of life which men led in Italy during those dim chaotic years? Can we with any persuasion of its truth paint the picture of a Roman, a Lombard, or a Frankish home in the Italy of the eighth century? Do we know what men were thinking as they dressed their olives and their vines, or can we catch even a syllable of the gossip of the market-place, during those two generations while Italy was cutting the cables which bound her to Constantinople and accepting the dominion of the Frankish Augustus?

I fear it must be confessed that we have not the requisite materials for conducting any such enquiry into the social state of Italy in the eighth century. Literature altogether fails us. We have no Sidonius and no Claudian to disclose to us by letters or poems what was passing in the minds of men. The fountain of Paulus's story-telling has run dry, and even the Lives of the Saints, which often give such quaintly interesting anecdotes of social life, seem to fail us here. Our only resource must be to reap such scanty harvest as we may from the laws of the latest Lombard kings and the Capitularies of their mighty successor.

Speaking generally, we may say that in the laws of Later Ratchis and Aistulf (no laws of Desiderius have come laws, down to us) we see something of that tendency towards gentler manners and more liberal views which we found in the laws of Liutprand when compared with those of Rothari In the prologue to the laws of Ratchis a claim is expressly made on behalf of progress in the art of legislation. 'The lofty Rothari,' says the king, 'drew up his code under Divine inspiration, for the benefit of the God-preserved nation of the Lombards. His successor Grimwald, that most excellent king, after careful consideration of the hard cases which were brought before him, relaxed some rules and tightened others. Then by God's mercy our own foster-father, that most wise prince Liutprand, adorned as he was with all modesty and sobriety, after long and anxious vigils, expressed his desires in an edict which, with the consent of his faithful Lombards and their magistrates (*Judices*), received his solemn confirmation. Now, by the help of the same Divine Redeemer, I Ratchis, after taking counsel with the magistrates of the Lombards, that is of those who dwell within the borders of Austria, Neustria, and Tuscia, find some things to be just and right in the statutes of my predecessors, and other things to have need of amendment,'—which amendments are accordingly made in the pages that follow.

We observe in these laws, and also in those of the next king, Aistulf, a tendency to exact fewer oaths of compurgation and attestation, 'which', as Ratchis remarks, 'through love of gain often lead men into perjury', and to rely more on the written deed, which, we may presume, more of the Lombard warriors could now decipher than in the first century after their great migration.

There is also a disposition to look more favourably on the claims of women to a share in the inheritance of a deceased ancestor. Thus in the case of a Lombard dying intestate and without male issue his maiden aunts are let in to a share of his estate, from which, before, they were excluded. Thus also a Lombard's widow was no longer strictly limited to the *meta* and *morgincap*, which alone she might inherit under the laws of Liutprand. Her husband might now leave her a life-interest in the half of his other property, a power which was, however, subject to certain limitations if she were a second wife, in order to guard the interests of the step-children.

The emancipation of slaves seems to have been going steadily forward, and was, on the whole, favoured by the legislator. Probably the cause of freedom was helped even by an apparently restrictive law of Aistulf's (dated March 1, 754), which recited that 'some perverse men, when they had received their freedom, slighted their benefactors, and many masters, fearing to be thus treated, shrank from enfranchising their slaves.' It was therefore enacted that if a Lombard chose to emancipate his slave by the most solemn process, but at the same time to insert in the deed of enfranchisement a clause retaining the right to the freedman's services during his own lifetime, he might do so, thus virtually turning the gift of freedom into a bequest.

Sometimes a Lombard would for the good of his soul leave a certain part of his property to 'venerable places' (churches or convents), and would direct that the slaves who cultivated it should receive their freedom and a small allotment of land for their support. It often happened, however, that the dead man's heirs disregarded his will, removed the landmarks which protected the allotment, and brought back the cultivators into slavery. This injustice was repressed by another law of Aistulf's, and the 'venerable places' were charged with the duty of seeing that the testator's intentions were not disregarded. Even if the testator were too near his end to comply with the regular form of manumission 'round the altar' and if he only indicated to the priest who ministered at his deathbed the name of the slave whom he desired to enfranchise, such dying request was to be held valid and the man was to receive his freedom, 'for it seems to us,' said Aistulf, 'the greatest possible benefit that slaves should he brought out of bondage into freedom, seeing that our Redeemer condescended to become a slave that He might set us free.' Noble words surely, even though uttered by the 'quite unspeakable' Aistulf.

In the case of a deed of emancipation a question might be raised, 'What consideration should be stated in the deed?' The king answers without hesitation, 'The slave's past services: they are the consideration for his freedom, for you cannot expect a slave to have anything else to offer.'

But notwithstanding all these indications of lessened weakness barbarism, the laws of these two Lombard king's show how chaotic was still the social condition of their subjects. First and foremost among the causes of unrest was that besetting sin of barbarous monarchies of barbarous republics, a corrupt and cowardly judicature. King Ratchis, who had a soul above the savagery of his nation and who evidently had some real yearnings after righteousness, says in one of his laws, 'I call God to witness that I cannot go anywhere to listen to a sermon, nor ride abroad (with any comfort), because of the cries for justice of so many of the poor'.

In order to redress these wrongs King Ratchis directs that every judge shall sit daily on the judgment-seat in his city, and not intrigue for his own advancement, nor give his mind to the vanities of the world, but dwell by himself, keeping open and unbribed justice for all. 'If at any time he shall neglect to do justice to his *ariman* [free Lombard neighbour], whether the man be rich or poor, he shall lose his judgeship and pay his guidrigild, half to the king and half to the man to whom he has denied justice'. And the judge was moreover to exact from his own subordinate magistrates the same oath of incorrupt judgment and the same observance of that oath which he was ordered to render to the king.

When the courts of law fail, for any cause, to give forth such decisions as correspond with men's natural sense of justice, a semi-civilised people is apt to take the law into its own hands and to substitute the 'wild justice of revenge' for the halting logic of the law-courts. Such seems to have been the case in Lombard Italy. 'In every city,' Ratchis complains, 'evil men are forming *zabae* or combinations against the magistrates.' The slight hints which the law gives us as to the nature of these 'zabae' remind us sometimes of an Irish land-league, sometimes of a Neapolitan 'camorra' or a Sicilian 'mafia.' If any man unites himself with only as many as four or five others in order to defy the authority of a judge, to prevent people resorting to him for justice, or to oppose the execution of his decree after trial of a cause, he is to undergo the penalty imposed on the crime of sedition. But the same law repeats and enforces the penalties against idle and unjust judges, evidently showing that, in the king's opinion, combinations against the law were the result of unrighteous judgments.

A curious illustration of the lawless character of the times is afforded us by a law of King Aistulf's. 'It has come to our ears that when certain men were going with a bridegroom, to escort the bride to his house and were making their procession with paranymph and bridesmaids, some perverse men threw over them dung and filthy water. As we have heard that this outrage has been perpetrated in other places, and as we foresee that tumults and even murders are likely to be the result, we order that every free man who is guilty of such an offence shall pay 900 *solidi*, half to the king and half to the bride's legal representative'. If the deed has been done by slaves, their master must purge himself of all complicity in their guilt, or else pay the appointed fine of 900 *solidi*. In any case the slaves shall be handed over to the bride's representative, to be dealt with according to his pleasure'.

It seems probable that we have in this incident something more than the unmannerly horse-play of Lombard villagers. The successful bridegroom has probably won his bride from an envious neighbour, whose disappointment and rage are expressed in this filthy outrage, which as the king perceives, unless promptly and severely punished, may easily blossom into an interminable blood-feud. Even so from Buondelmonte's marriage with the daughter of the Donati sprang the long agony of the civil wars of Florence.

Jealousy of all foreigners, including the dwellers in Roman Italy, and suspicions born of the Lombard's precarious tenure of dominion, are clearly shown in the laws of both the kings. Thus Ratchis says, 'We have been informed that certain evil men creep into our palace, desiring to find out our secrets from our favourites, or to worm out from our porters or other servants what we are doing, that they may then go and trade upon their knowledge in alien provinces. Now it appears to us that he who presumes to pry into such matters as these is not true in his faith towards us, but incurs grave suspicion [of treason]; wherefore we decide that whenever any one is discovered thus offending, both he who reveals the secret and he to whom it is revealed shall incur the risk of a capital sentence, and shall suffer the confiscation of his goods. For, as the Scripture saith, "It is a good thing to hide the secret of the king, but to reveal the works of God is honourable".

It is in accordance with this suspicious—shall we say Chinese—policy of self-seclusion that we read in another law of King Ratchis, 'If any magistrate or any other person shall presume to direct his envoy to Rome, Ravenna, Spoleto, Benevento, Frankland, Bavaria, Alamannia, Greece, or Avar-land without the king's order, he shall run the risk of his life, and his property shall be confiscated'.

So too Aistulf orders the passes to be guarded, 'that our men may not pass over nor foreigners enter into our country without the king's command.' 'Concerning navigation or commerce by land. No one ought to undertake a journey on business or for any other cause without a letter from the king or the consent of his magistrate: and if he transgresses he must pay his *guidrigild*'. Another even more interesting law makes direct mention of 'Romans' (that is no doubt the dwellers of the *Ducatus Romae* and other fragments of Imperial Italy), as the persons with whom intercourse was forbidden. 'This also we wish concerning those men who without the king's permission trade with Roman men. If he be a magistrate who presumes to do this, he shall pay his guidrigild and lose his rank. But if he be a simple freeman (*arimannus*), he shall lose all his property and go with shorn head [through the streets], crying aloud, 'So let all men suffer who, contrary to the will of their lord the king, engage in trade with Roman men, when we have a controversy with them'

The close-cropped head of the unpatriotic trader was probably a satire on the 'Roman style' of wearing the hair of which we have so often heard. The royal legislator in the pride of his national conservatism says to his rebellious subject, 'Since you are ashamed of the flowing locks of your forefathers and will trade with those well-trimmed, dainty citizens of Rome, we will shear away all the hair that Nature has given you, and send you bald-pated, a derision to all men, to cry aloud your ignominy through the city.'

Evidently whatever possibilities of advancement and culture slumbered in the Lombard's soul he had still in him much of the stolid barbarism of his forefathers. He was not yet nearly so ready to amalgamate with his Latin neighbours as the Visigoth and Ostrogoth had been three centuries before him. And he too must therefore in all fairness bear his share of the blame for having delayed the unification of Italy.

We have now to consider what effect the Frankish conquest produced on the social condition of Italy. The conjecture may be hazarded that at any rate for some time no very obvious change resulted from that conquest. As has been already pointed out, the policy of Charles the Great was to put himself at the head of the Lombard nation, and we have no sign that his rule was generally felt as an insult or humiliation by the people of Alboin. Something of the old Teutonic kinship may still have bound the two nations together. Their languages—in so far as either nation still used the old German speech and had not changed it for the Latin *volgare*—may have been not wholly unintelligible to one another. We have not, moreover, any evidence of a design on Charles's part to reverse the conditions which had prevailed in Italy for two centuries or to put the descendant of the Lombard conqueror under the heel of his Roman serf.

One great change Charles certainly seems to have made, though probably not on the very morrow of the conquest. The Lombard dukes, with their undefined and dangerous power, were replaced by Frankish counts—one probably to every considerable city—directly responsible to their Frankish sovereign. It is suggested with some likelihood that this change was brought about during Charles's long visit to Italy in 781, after the revolt of Hrodgaud of Friuli had shown him the danger of leaving too much power in the hands of the old dukes of the Lombards.

Doubtless one result of the conquest was to make of the all the inhabitants feel that the power of the Catholic Church, and pre-eminently of the See of Rome, was more firmly rooted than before, though even under the Lombards the long list of grants of land, of slaves, and of houses to ecclesiastical persons gives us a vivid idea of the hold which the Church, notwithstanding her quarrels with the kings, had upon the minds of the people. One change doubtless took place, to the material enrichment of the Church, namely the more uniform arid systematic collection of tithes, the punctual payment of which is frequently insisted upon in Charles's edicts. In each city also the power and prestige of the bishop were greatly augmented. In many important matters he had virtually a concurrent jurisdiction with the count. These two great functionaries were exhorted to act in harmony with each other, but probably the bishop would be encouraged to report to his sovereign if he deemed that there was anything in the proceedings of the count deserving of censure.

Our best information as to the social condition not only of Italy but of all other portions of the Frankish Empire is to be derived from a study of the Capitularies, those marvellous monuments of the energy and far-reaching, all-embracing statesmanship of the great Emperor. Doubtless any one who expects to find in these documents a scientific system of legislation will rise from their perusal disappointed. The Capitularies are not and do not pretend to be a code. They are far more concerned with administration than with legislation properly so called, and if they must be compared at all, it should rather be with the minutes or memoranda of the English Privy Council than with the codes of Justinian or Napoleon.

To the mind of a modern legislator, probably a disproportionate part of these edicts will seem to be devoted to the affairs of the Church; but Charles truly perceived that in the Church lay the one best hope of civilizing and humanizing the chaotic populations of his Empire, and that with a corrupt, a profligate, and an ignorant clergy the task would be hopeless. Therefore, though not himself a stern moralist, he insisted with almost passionate earnestness on a reformation of the manners of the clergy: though not himself a man of high literary culture, he pressed upon the churchmen, his subjects, the duty of acquiring for themselves and imparting to others at least an elementary knowledge of science and literature.

'Diligently enquire' he says to his commissioners, 'how every priest has behaved himself in his office after his ordination: because some, who were poor before they took orders, have grown rich out of the property wherewith they ought to have served the Church, and have bought themselves allodia and slaves and other property, and have neither made any advance in their own reading, nor collected books, nor increased the vessels belonging to the Divine service, but have lived in luxury, oppression, and rapine.'

'Let the priests', according to the Apostle's advice, withdraw themselves from revellings and drunkenness : for some of them are accustomed to sit up till midnight or later, boozing with their neighbours : and then these men, who ought to be of a religious and holy deportment, return to their churches drunken and gorged with food, and unable to perform the daily and nightly office of praise to God, while others sink down in a drunken sleep in the place of their revels.'

'Let there be schools in which boys may learn to Schools read. In every monastery and bishop's palace let there be copies of the Psalms, arithmetic-books and grammars, with Catholic books well-edited: since often when men desire to pray aright to God they ask amiss owing to the bad editing of their books. Do not allow your boys to corrupt the text either in writing or reading. And if you need to have a Gospel or Psalter or Missal copied, let it be done by men of full age, with all diligence'.

'Enquire how the priests are wont to instruct catechumens in the Christian faith, and whether, when they are saying special masses either for the dead or the living, they know how to make the required grammatical changes, in order to turn the singular into the plural number or the masculine into the feminine gender'

'Let the churches and altars be better built. Let no priest presume to store provisions or hay in the church'

'Let all the people, in a reverent, prayerful and humble manner, without the adornment of costly raiment, or enticing song, or worldly games, go forward with their litanies, and let them learn to cry aloud the Kyrie Eleison, not in such a rustic manner as hitherto, but in better style'

'Let not the scribes write badly: and let every bishop, abbot, and count keep his own notary'

Some of the passages which have been here quoted do not apply specially to Italy, but there can be no doubt from the general tenour of Charles's administration that he strove to raise the standard of literary cultivation in Italy as well as in other parts of his dominions. The need was at least as great in Rome as in the cities by the Rhine: it was probably greater. In reading through the Capitularies one is struck by the extremely barbarous character of the Latin in the 'Lombard Capitularies' as compared with those published at Aachen. The fault is probably that of the Italian secretaries by whom they have been transcribed, and we thus reach a similar conclusion to that which is forced upon us by a perusal of the Liber Pontificalis and the papal letters. At the close of the eighth century Rome was the last place in which to look for correct Latinity, or even a moderate acquaintance with the classical authors. Scholarship, which had died out on the banks of the Tiber, was born anew by the Ouse and the Tyne, in the archiepiscopal school at York, and the monastery of Jarrow.

But important as was Charles's work in guarding the morality of the Church and raising the standard of literary culture, he himself would doubtless have declared that the most important of his duties as supreme ruler of the state was the defence of the rights of the weak and helpless, and the repression of tyranny and corruption on the part of the rich and the powerful. Over and over again, Charles repeats that it is his sacred duty to protect the widow and the orphan. For this he pledges his 'ban', that mysterious word which was in after years to bear so awful a meaning when offenders were put to the ban of the Empire.

The eight-fold 'ban', the eight crimes which were considered to be especially against the peace of 'our' lord the king ' and which were punishable with a fine of 60 *solidi*, were :—

1. Dishonouring holy Church.
2. Injustice towards widows.
3. The like towards orphans.
4. The like towards the poor man who cannot defend himself.
5. Rape or abduction of a freeborn woman.
6. Fire-raising ; the burning of another man's house or stables.
7. *Harizhut*, the forcible breaking down of another man's hedge or cottage.
8. Refusal to go forth with the host

Two important administrative changes were made by Charles in order to guard the poorer class of his subjects at one end of the social system and his own sovereign authority at the other from the injustices and encroachments of the functionaries whom he was compelled to employ, yet who were in a certain sense the common enemies of both.

I. The first of these changes was the introduction of *scabini*, or, as we should call them, jurymen, into the courts of justice. It is admitted that in the earlier stages of Frankish and probably also of Lombard society the free men had been in a certain way associated with the king's officer in the courts of justice, but the procedure was apparently fitful and irregular: the frequent attendance of a large body of free men at the courts became a burden to themselves, and the whole custom of popular cooperation in the administration of the law was in danger of falling into disuse. Charles accordingly directed that out of the body of free men in each district there should be chosen seven men, untainted by crime, whose duty it should be to decide, not only as our jurors do, on questions of fact, but also on questions of law, in the presence of the count, *centenarius*, or other judicial officers. To these men was given the name *scabini*; they were chosen sometimes by the count and people jointly, sometimes by the king's commissioners (*missi*), but once chosen they probably held their office for life. That office was evidently an honourable one, and, at least during the ninth century, they probably acted as an important check on the lawless proceedings of a corrupt or arrogant governor. One interesting passage in a late capitulary, issued from Charles's court at Aachen, shows that their duty consisted quite as much in courageous condemnation of the guilty as in protection of the innocent. 'Let not the *vicarii* suffer to be brought before them those robbers who have been previously condemned to death by the count. If they dare to do this, let them suffer the same punishment as the robber himself, because after the *scabini* have judged and condemned a man it is not permitted to either count or *vicarius* to give him back his life'. It is important to observe that in this and other passages the actual decision is recognized as being the work of the *scabini* alone. The count has to give effect to the verdict (as we call it), but he has nothing to do with pronouncing it, nor is he allowed to set it aside. In the law itself we seem to have an indication of a state of things like that which has sometimes existed in the back- settlements of America and has led to the 'wild justice' of lynch-law; cases in which the moral sense of the community calls for the execution of a criminal, who through fear or favour is shielded by the governor of the State. An especial interest for us in this institution of the *scabini* is furnished by the fact that, though it came into Italy from over the Alps, the most numerous proofs of its existence, at least throughout the ninth century, are furnished by Italian documents.

II. The second expedient to which Charles resorted in order to secure justice for the humblest of his subjects and keep his provincial governors in order, was that of *missi dominici*, or, as we might translate the words, 'royal commissioners'.

We have in the recent course of this history made acquaintance with many *missi* or envoys of Pippin and Charles speeding southwards with messages from their master, sometimes to the king of the Lombards, sometimes to the Emperor at Constantinople, most frequently of all to the Pope. But the *missi* whom we are now considering, and who are generally known by the addition *dominici*, have a different office from these. They are not ambassadors, but are more like the staff-officers of an army, sent from head-quarters in order to see that every regiment is in a state of efficiency. They were generally sent forth two and two, a layman being joined with a distinguished ecclesiastic in each commission. Their duties were so manifold that it is hard to give a succinct description of them; but they were undoubtedly ordered to watch with jealous vigilance the proceedings of all functionaries acting in the king's name, and to see that neither the rights of the crown nor the liberties of the subject suffered either through their lethargy or their rapacity. In the province to which they were accredited they had to review the *heriban*, or national militia, and exact the fines payable by all liable to military service who failed to attend the levy. They were to see to the exaction of tithes and the due observance of the Lord's Day; to defend the rights of churches, widows, orphans, and all who had special need of their protection; to see that the landowners who held *beneficia* from the king or the church were not impoverishing the *beneficium* in order to enrich their own adjoining properties; to choose *scabini*, advocates, and notaries in the several places visited by them, and to hand in, on their return to head-quarters, a list of the persons so nominated. Finally—and this seems to have been one of their most important functions—they were to conduct enquiries as to the legal status of such alleged slaves as claimed to be free men. We know from a certain capitulary of Charles, which describes in pessimistic tone the disorders of the land, that great ecclesiastics as well as secular nobles were at this time forcibly reducing the poorer free men to beggary and slavery. So keen in some cases was the slave's desire for freedom that he was believed to have actually murdered a relative, father, mother or uncle, who being incontestably a slave might have disproved his claim to be born free and so have dragged him back into servitude.

There can be little doubt that the control exercised by the *missi dominici* in the king's name was cordially detested by the counts and other permanent officers of the state. Even where the governor was not actively rapacious and unjust, he was apt to procrastinate in the performance of his duties. For a day's hunting or some similar diversion he was too ready to shorten or altogether omit the holding of his *placitum*. Now came the two Imperial *missi*, the very note of whose character was strenuousness, who held their office only for a year, and were intent on showing to their master at the year's end a good report of work done in his name. These men listened to the complaints of disappointed suitors for justice, tore to shreds the official excuses for procrastination and delay, tested the venal evidence of the great man's dependants, and in short made the corrupt or lethargic count feel that life was not worth living till the backs of the *missi* were turned and they were once more safely on their road. In a capitulary which three of the Imperial *missi* put forth on their own account (probably about the year 806), at the commencement of their tour, they hint a consciousness of their own unpopularity. 'Moreover,' say they, 'take good heed lest you or any one in your service (as far as you can prevent it) be found guilty of any such trickery as to say, "Be quiet! be quiet! till these *missi* have passed this way; and after that we can settle these cases comfortably with one another"; and so either avoid or at any rate postpone the giving of justice. Strive rather that all may have been duly settled before we come to you.'

It has been well said by a German commentator on the functions assigned to the *missi dominici*, that in order to form a right estimate of the value of this institution we must ask ourselves what would have been the state of the Empire without it. 'We have abundant evidence of the grasping character of the Frankish [and probably also of the Lombard] grandees. We see their unceasing attempts to aggrandize themselves at the expense either of the Emperor or of the still existing remains of the free commonalty. We observe how these selfish endeavours, if not strenuously resisted, must have injured trade and commerce and the general well-being of the people. It was the *missi* who alone could battle against these tendencies, armed as they were with yet greater and more wide-reaching powers than those of the counts, but with powers which, on account of the shortness of their duration (generally not more than a year or two) and the peculiar way in which they were entrusted to them, were less liable to selfish abuse. Thus we have perhaps to thank the institution of the *missi* for the fact that the poor independent freeholder did not disappear even sooner than was actually the case, that the Emperors, Charles's successors, were not earlier stripped of their power for the benefit of those who had once been only the Emperor's officers.' Still even in Charles's time, notwithstanding all his efforts for the protection of his people, the residuum of official tyranny which he could not succeed in suppressing was working great evil in the land. We seem to be reading over again the well-known lines in Goldsmith's Deserted Village when we read the *Capitulare Langobardicum* issued by Pippin (of course with his father's approval) from his palace at Pavia, probably in the spring of 803 :—

'We hear that the officers of the counts and some of their more powerful vassals are collecting rents and insisting on forced labours, harvesting, ploughing, sowing, stubbing up trees, loading waggons and the like, not only from the Church's servants [probably on *beneficia* granted by the Church], but from the rest of the people; all which practices must, if you please, be put a stop to by us and by all the people, because in some places the people have been in these ways so grievously oppressed, that many, unable to bear their lot, have escaped by flight from their masters or patrons, and the lands are relapsing into wilderness.'

Some years later, in the *Capitulare de Expeditione Exercitali*, published at Aachen in 811, the old Emperor utters a doleful lamentation over the general reign of violence and lawlessness throughout his dominions, an anarchic tyranny which prevents him from getting a proper supply of free and well-fed soldiers for the national militia.

' 1. The bishops and abbots,' he says', 'have no proper control over their tonsured clergy and the rest of their "men"; nor have the counts over their retainers.

' 2. The poor complain that they are being thrust out from their property, and that, quite as much by the bishops and abbots and their *advocati*, as by the counts and their *centenarii*.

' 3. They say that if a poor man will not give up his property to the bishop, abbot, or count, these great men make some excuse for getting him into trouble with the courts, or else are continually ordering him on military service till the wretched man, quite ruined, *volens nolens* has to surrender or sell his property. At the same time his neighbour who has surrendered his property [and thus become a serf instead of a free man] is allowed to remain at home unmolested.

' 4. They say that bishops and abbots as well as counts are sending their free men home [instead of causing them to serve in the army] under the name of household servants. The like is done also by abbesses. These are falconers, huntsmen, tax-gatherers, overseers, *tithing-men*, and others who entertain the *missi* and their followers.

' 5. At the same time they constrain poorer men to go against the enemy, while they allow men of means to return to their homes.'

The rest of the complaints deal chiefly with the diminished authority of the counts over their own *pagenses*, and with cases of flat refusal to answer to the ban of the Emperor summoning them to the field. The whole Capitulary gives an idea of tendencies towards disorganization and disruption, hardly kept in check even during the lifetime of the mighty Emperor himself, strong set For this was in truth the question which presented current itself for solution at the beginning of the ninth century, feudalism. Was Western Europe to escape from feudalism or to undergo it? Was she to be welded together by the strong hands of a series of monarchs like Charles into a well-compacted Empire, such as the old Roman Empire had been at its best estate, governed by a highly trained, well-organized class of administrators, going forth from the seat of empire to enforce the will of their sovereign in distant provinces and returning thereto at regular periods, with rhythmic movement like the pulsation of the heart? Or was the right to govern, with all its privileges and all its temptations, to be grasped by those representatives of the sovereign as their own private property, used for their own aggrandizement in wealth and power, and transmitted from father to son like a hereditary estate? The Roman proconsul or the feudal baron which was it to be for the next seven centuries? The answer is well known. Whatever may have been the wise and noble designs of the great Austrasian king, his assumption of the title of Augustus did not lead up to the formation of a state like that which was ruled by Hadrian or Antoninus, but led instead to the Feudal Anarchy, which history has called, with unintended irony, the Feudal System.

The reader may perhaps have noticed that I have refrained from using the technical terms of feudalism in describing the political relations of Charles and his subjects; that 'suzerain,' 'vassal,' 'homage' have been generally avoided in these pages. This has been done because the feudal relation had not yet in the time of Charles the Great acquired that definiteness and precision which it possessed in later centuries. Yet the potent germs of feudalism were undoubtedly working in the body politic. There was the practice of 'commendation'; *beneficia* were held of the Church or the king on the condition of performing certain services; the lord (senior) had his dependent followers (*homines*); even the word *vassus* is of frequent appearance in the Capitularies. The political solution was already crystallising into feudalism, and possibly no king or emperor could have arrested the development of the process. Charles himself in his Capitularies recognises and defends the feudal obligation. 'Let no man,' he says, 'renounce his lord after he has received from him so much as the value of one solidus, with these exceptions; if the lord desires to kill him, or to beat him with a stick, or to defile his wife or daughter, or to take from him his inheritance. . . . And if any lord summon his retainers to assist him in doing battle with an adversary, and one of the compeers shall refuse to obey the summons and shall remain negligently at home, let that *beneficium* which he possessed be taken away from him and given to the man who abides true to his fealty.'

Here we have not only a full recognition of the right of the lord to his vassal's military service, but also (which is more extraordinary in so great a statesman as Charles) we have imperial sanction given to that most anti-social of all feudal practices, the levying of private war. Herein we see how different after all was the Roman Empire remodelled by Charles the Great, from the Roman Empire of the Caesars. Imagine the astonishment of Augustus or Hadrian at finding such a sentence among the edicts of a successor.

In this brief and imperfect sketch of the internal organization of Charles's Empire I have necessarily hinted at some of the causes which were to frustrate many of his noble and far-reaching plans. We all know that, as a matter of fact, the disruptive agencies that were at work throughout his vast dominions were too mighty for his feeble successors to contend against; that the diverse races which had seemed to be welded together into one commonwealth by the labours of himself and his ancestors, sprang apart in one generation after his death, and that the treaty of Verdun signed by his grandsons practically constituted France, Germany, and Italy into three separate countries with something like their present boundaries. We know too that feudalism triumphed over all the attempts of the central power to check its progress, that duke and marquis and count and baron made their titles hereditary, and became virtually, each one, sovereign in his own domain ; that thus ten thousand disintegrating influences destroyed the unity not only of the Empire, but even of each of the three kingdoms into which it was divided.

But all this belongs to another chapter of history from that which is closing before us. In the course of my now completed work I have attempted to follow the fortunes of Italy and the successive races of her conquerors during nearly five hundred years. The story opened by the death-bed of Julian in a tent on the Assyrian plain; it closes by the tomb of Austrasian Charles, with the notes of the *Planctus de Obitu Karoli* ringing in our ears. In that space of half a millennium, kingdoms have risen and fallen; the one great universal Empire has crumbled into hopeless ruin; the Teuton, the Slave and the Hun have seated themselves in the cities of the old Latin civilization; the religions of Jupiter and of Woden have faded away before the spreading light of Christianity, and the religion of Mohammed has overspread three continents; the whole outlook of the world has been changed. Now in 814 the Debateable Land is traversed. It is true that the waters of Chaos will still for centuries continue to roll over Europe, but the old classical world has finally passed away, and we see fully installed before us those two great figures, the German Emperor and the sovereign Roman Pope, whose noisy quarrels and precarious reconciliations will be the central events of European history during the Middle Ages.

The end

PART ONE

BOOK I
THE VISIGOTHIC INVASION
INTRODUCTION.
SUMMARY OF ROMAN IMPERIAL HISTORY.

CHAPTERS
I. EARLY HISTORY OF THE GOTHS
II. JOVIAN, PROCOPIUS, ATHANARIC.
III. VALENTINIAN THE FIRST
IV. THE LAST YEARS OF VALENS
V. THEODOSIUS
VI. THE VICTORY OF NICAEA
VII. THE FALL OF GRATIAN
VIII. MAXIMUS AND AMBROSE
IX. THE INSURRECTION OF ANTIOCH
X. THEODOSIUS IN ITALY AND THE MASSACRE OF THESSALONICA
XI. EUGENIUS AND ARBOGAST
XII. INTERNAL ORGANISATION OF THE EMPIRE
XIII. HONORIUS, STILICHO, ALARIC
XIV. ALARIC'S FIRST INVASION OF ITALY
XV. THE FALL OF STILICHO
XVII. ALARIC'S THREE SIEGES OF ROME.
XVIII. THE LOVERS OF PLACIDIA
XIX. PLACIDIA AUGUSTA
XX. SALVIAN ON THE DIVINE GOVERNMENT

PART TWO

BOOK II
THE HUNNISH INVASION

I. EARLY HISTORY OF THE HUNS.
II. ATTILA AND THE COURT OF CONSTANTINOPLE.
III. ATTILA IN GAUL.
IV. ATTILA IN ITALY.

BOOK III
THE VANDAL INVASION AND THE HERULIAN MUTINY

I. EXTINCTION OF THE HUNNISH EMPIRE AND THE THEODOSIAN DYNASTY.
II. THE VANDALS FROM GERMANY TO ROME.
III. THE LETTERS AND POEMS OF APOLLINARIS SIDONIUS.
IV. AVITUS, THE CLIENT OF THE VISIGOTHS.
V. SUPREMACY OF RICIMER. MAJORIAN.
VI. SEVERUS II, THE LUCANIAN. ANTHEMIUS, THE CLIENT OF BYZANTIUM.
VII. OLYBRIUS, THE CLIENT OF THE VANDAL. GLYCERIUS, THE CLIENT OF THE BURGUNDIAN. JULIUS NEPOS, THE CLIENT OF BYZANTIUM. ROMULUS AUGUSTULUS, SON OF ORESTES.
VIII. ODOVACAR, THE SOLDIER OF FORTUNE.
IX. CAUSES OF THE FALL OF THE WESTERN EMPIRE.

PART THREE

BOOK IV
THE OSTROGOTHIC INVASION.

I. A CENTURY OF OSTROGOTHIC HISTORY.
II. THE REIGN OF ZENO.
III THE TWO THEODORICS IN THRACE
V. FLAVIUS ODOVACAR.
V. THE FRIGIAN WAR
VI. THE DEATH-GRAPPLE.
VII. KING AND PEOPLE.
VIII. THEODORIC AND HIS COURT
IX. THEODORIC'S RELATIONS WITH GAUL.
X. THEODORIC'S RELATIONS WITH THE EAST.
XI. THEODORIC'S RELATIONS WITH THE CHURCH.
XII. BOETHIUS AND SYMMACHUS.
XIII. THE ACCESSION OF ATHALARIC.
XIV. JUSTINIAN.
XV. BELISARIUS.
XVI. THE LOVERS OF AMALASUNTHA.

BOOK V
THE IMPERIAL RESTORATION
535—553

I. THE FIRST YEAR OF THE WAR
II. BELISARIUS AT CARTHAGE AND AT NAPLES.

III. THE ELEVATION OF WITIGIS.
IV. BELISARIUS IN ROME
V. THE LONG SIEGE BEGUN.
VI. THE CUTTING OF THE AQUEDUCTS.
VII. THE GOTHIC ASSAULT.
VIII. ROMAN SORTIES.
IX. THE BLOCKADE
X. THE RELIEF OF RIMINI.
XI. DISSENSIONS IN THE IMPERIAL CAMP.
XII. SIEGES OF FIESOLI AND OSIMO.
XIII. THE FALL OF RAVENNA.
XIV. AFFAIRS AT CONSTANTINOPLE
XV. THE ELEVATION OF TOTILA.
XVI. SAINT BENEDICT (480 – 547)
XVII. THE RETURN OF BELISARIUS.
XVIII. THE SECOND SIEGE OF ROME.
CHAPTER XIX. ROMA CAPTA.
XX. THE RE-OCCUPATION OF ROME.
XXI. THE THIRD SIEGE OF ROME.
XXII. THE EXPEDITION OF GERMANUS.
XXIII. THE SORROWS OF VIGILIUS.
XXIV. NARSES AND TOTILA.
XXV FINIS GOTHORUM. THE LAST OF THE GOTHS

PART FOUR

BOOK VI.
THE LOMBARD INVASION.

I. THE ALAMANNIC BRETHREN.
II. THE RULE OF NARSES.
III. THE LANGOBARDIC FOREWORLD
1. Early Notices of the Langobardi by Greek and Roman Writers.
2. The Saga of the Langobardi
3. War with the Heruli
4. War with the Gepidae.
IV. ALBOIN IN ITALY.
V. THE INTERREGNUM.
VI. FLAVIUS AUTHARI.
VII. GREGORY THE GREAT.
VIII. GREGORY AND THE LOMBARDS.
IX. THE PAPAL PEACE.
X. THE LAST YEARS OF GREGORY
XI. THE ISTRIAN SCHISM.

BOOK VII
THE LOMBARD KINGDOM
A.D. 600-744

I. THE SEVENTH CENTURY.

II. THE FOUR GREAT DUCHIES.
I. The Duchy of Trient (Tridentum).
II. The Duchy of Friuli (Forum Julii).
III. The Duchy of Benevento (Beneventum).
IV. The Duchy of Spoleto (Spoletium).
Note A. Ecclesiastical notices of the Lombards of Spoleto in the Dialogues of Gregory the Great. Life of St. Cetheus.
III. SAINT COLUMBANUS.
IV. THEUDELINDA AND HER CHILDREN.
V. THE LEGISLATION OF ROTHARI.
VI. GRIMWALD AND CONSTANS.
The Story of St. Barbatus.
VII. THE BAVARIAN LINE RESTORED.
VIII. STORY OF THE DUCHIES, CONTINUED.
IX. THE PAPACY AND THE EMPIRE.
X. THE LAWS OF LIUTPRAND.
XI. ICONOCLASM.
XII. KING LIUTPRAND.
XIII. POLITICAL STATE OF IMPERIAL ITALY.
XIV. POLITICAL STATE OF LOMBARD ITALY.

PART FIVE

BOOK VIII.
FRANKISH INVASIONS.

I. INTRODUCTION. THE MEROVINGIAN KINGS. EARLY FRANKISH HISTORY.
II. THE EARLY ARNULFINGS
III. PIPPIN OF HERISTAL AND CHARLES MARTEL
IV. DUKES OF BAVARIA
V. THE GREAT RENUNCIATION
VI. THE ANOINTING OF PIPPIN
VII. THE DONATION OF CONSTANTINE
VIII. THE STRUGGLE FOR THE EXARCHATE
IX. THE PONTIFICATE OP PAUL I (757-767).
X. A PAPAL CHAOS.
XI. THE PONTIFICATE OF STEPHEN III.
XII. RAVENNA AND ROME.
XIII. THE ACCESSION OF POPE HADRIAN.
XIV. END OF THE LOMBARD MONARCHY.

BOOK IX
THE FRANKISH EMPIRE
774-814

I. THE PONTIFICATE OF HADRIAN I.
Frankish and Byzantine Affairs,
II. THE PONTIFICATE OF HADRIAN I.
Italian Affairs.
III. TASSILO OF BAVARIA.
IV. TWO COURTS : CONSTANTINOPLE AND AACHEN
V. POPE AND EMPEROR.
VI. CHARLES AND IRENE.

VII. VENICE.
VIII. THE FINAL RECOGNITION.
IX. CAROLUS MORTUUS.
X. THE LIFE OF THE PEOPLE

Printed in Great Britain
by Amazon